INTERNET WORLD™ GUIDE
TO ONE-TO-ONE
WEB MARKETING

INTERNET WORLD™ GUIDE TO ONE-TO-ONE WEB MARKETING

CLIFF ALLEN

DEBORAH KANIA

BETH YAECKEL

WILEY COMPUTER PUBLISHING

JOHN WILEY & SONS, INC.

New York • Chichester • Weinheim • Brisbane • Singapore • Toronto

Publisher: Robert Ipsen
Editor: Cary Sullivan
Assistant Editor: Pam Sobotka
Managing Editor: Erin Singletary
Electronic Products, Associate Editor: Mike Sosa
Text Design & Composition: Pronto Design and Production, Inc.

Designations used by companies to distinguish their products are often claimed as trademarks. In all instances where John Wiley & Sons, Inc., is aware of a claim, the product names appear in initial capital or all capital letters. Readers, however, should contact the appropriate companies for more complete information regarding trademarks and registration.

This book is printed on acid-free paper. ∞

This publication is designed to provide accurate and authoritative information in regard to the subject matter covered. It is sold with the understanding that the publisher is not engaged in rendering professional services. If professional advice or other expert assistance is required, the services of a competent professional person should be sought.

Internet World, Web Week, Web Developer, Internet Shopper, and Mecklermedia are the exclusive trademarks of Mecklermedia Corporation and are used with permission.

Library of Congress Cataloging-in-Publication Data:

Allen, Cliff, 1948-
        Internet world guide to one-to-one Web marketing/Cliff Allen,
Deborah Kania, Beth Yaeckel.
        p. cm.
        Includes index.
ISBN 0-471-25166-6 (pbk. : alk. paper)
1. Internet marketing. 2. Web sites--Design. 3. Internet advertising.
4. Internet (Computer network) 5. World Wide Web (Information retrieval system)
I. Kania, Deborah, 1963-   .
II. Yaeckel, Beth.   III. Title
HF5415.1265.A418 1998
658.8'00285'4676--dc21   97-48813
                                                          CIP

Printed in the United States of America.

10 9 8 7 6 5 4 3 2

CONTENTS

ACKNOWLEDGEMENTS

- Our families and friends, especially Carolyn Allen, Chris Allen, Mike Kania, Dan Snider and whose love, support, encouragement and patience made this book possible.

- Kara Russelo, who held down the fort while we disappeared.

- David and Sherry Rogelberg, our first-class partners at Studio B and the Computer Book Cafe.

- The wonderful folks at John Wiley and Sons especially one of their great assets, our editor, Pam Sobotka whose words of wisdom and enthusiastic praises were invaluable to us throughout this process.

- Regis McKenna, Don Peppers, Martha Rogers and other marketing experts whose thought-provoking ideas were the inspiration for this book.

- Jupiter Communications, an influential force in Internet research, for their generous assistance with research and statistics.

- Mecklermedia, an exceptional organization who made this book possible.

- All of the innovative organizations represented in this book and those who spent time answering our pestering e-mails, especially John Funk, founder of InfoBeat; Ann Meyers and Kathleen Campbell with Keystone Financial; Mike Adams, president of Arial Software; Mary Meeker, managing director at Morgan Stanley; DoubleClick's Wenda Harris Millard; Kathleen Bagely of Accipiter; Cathy Laird of Quote.com; Thomas Parkinson of Peapod; David Shumate of Lakeville Engineering; Darrell Ticehurst of InsWeb; Sylvia Lacock of Well Engaged; Lisa Lopuck co-founder and the Creative Director of electravision; Melissa Joulwan, Editor of Go, girl! Magazine; Jill Davidson of Edmunds; Jennifer Penunuri of Netscape; Dave Fester, Group Product Manager, IE4 team at Microsoft; Deborah Lacy, Director of Marketing Communications of BackWeb; and Wendy McCarthy of Pointcast.

INTRODUCTION

"In the Information Age, all businesses will become service businesses."

Regis McKenna, Real Time.

Our book was created to help you sort through all of the Web technologies that are available to build relationships with users. You will learn from folks just like you who want to create a loyal user base or create a competitive advantage. Regis McKenna introduced marketers to the idea of customer-centered marketing in his book *Relationship Marketing*. Then, Don Peppers and Martha Rogers, authors of *The One to One Future: Building Relationships One Customer at a Time* and recently, *Enterprise One to One: Tools for Competing Interactive Age*, established a paradigm shift with their research and writings about the benefits of building relationships with each customer. Our book will build on these important marketing methods as it relates to the doing business and servicing customers via the Web.

Who Will Find This Book Useful

If your Web site is an integral part of your overall strategy, then it must be treated strategically. Web sites that are *pet projects*, will return less than desired results accordingly. Some of these technologies can be expensive to build and maintain, so will want to have a clear objective of what you want to accomplish with them. Our book will help you identify how one-to-one Web marketing can work for different Web business models: marketing communications, commerce, advertiser-supported services and community.

Our book will be a useful resource if you are a marketing executive, marketing manager, business manager, direct marketer, Webmaster, new media manager, interactive technology manager, or someone who has similar responsibilities—basically, anyone focusing on the *marketing side* of Web management. You will benefit from our book's combination of marketing strategy and Web technologies. Our book will provide you with tangible guidance using real examples and experiences.

Chapter 1: One-to-One Web Marketing Overview

In Chapter 1 we set the stage for one-to-one Web marketing. We discuss the principals forged by well-respected relationship marketing experts. Once you have absorbed these principals, then the rest of the book will show you how to apply these principles to your Web site creation, enhancing and marketing. One-to-one marketing is the future of marketing, and the Web is one of the best mediums to leverage all of the benefits including fostering customer loyalty and staving off competition. One-to-one Web marketing will enable you to build relationships with your customers—one at a time, over time.

Chapter 2: One-to-One Web Interactivity

It is easy to become enamored with interactivity technologies such as animation, 3-D, video and audio. However, one-to-one Web marketing is most successful when these technologies are used in a way that allows users to have a dialogue with you. In Chapter 2, we discuss true interactivity vs. interactivity for interactivity's sake. When implemented in a way that allows personalized interaction, interactivity can be an entertaining, engaging and useful way to build relationships on your Web site.

Chapter 3: One-to-One E-mail

E-mail is the most prevalent activity on the Internet. More people spend time with using e-mail that the Web. In this chapter we show you how to use e-mail to pull people back to your organization and your Web site on a regular basis. There are emerging technologies that allow you to send each customer their own personalized e-mail so you can build a relationship with all of your users and customers on at a time. Chapter 3 shows you how to write effective e-mail messages and subject lines so that the e-mail will be useful instead of being mistaken for spam and deleted before being read by the recipient.

Chapter 4: One-to-One Web Site Personalization

As the number of Web site grow, and the size of the average Web site becomes larger you will want to consider enlisting one of the Web site personalization technologies. Early in the history of the Web surfers visited sites and saw the same information every other Web surfer saw. Now there are many sites that create a different Web site experience for each user. With the integration of databases and the use of user tracking and profile information, Web sites can now provide personalized content. Chapter 4 will show you how personalized Web sites can make it easier for your customers to do business with you.

Chapter 5: One-to-One Push

Push is considered one of the Internet's *killer apps*. Push can provide an active way to get information to customers, business partners, employees, etc. The chapter will discuss how push works and how to apply it to your one-to-one Web marketing efforts. According to Eric Schmidt, CEO of Novell, Internet bandwidth will triple every year. This will certainly help push become more acceptable for Internet, intranet and extranet communications. The chapter will provide numerous examples and tips to apply to your push initiative.

Chapter 6: One-to-One Web Community

In Chapter 6, we will discuss how online communities can provide a one-to-one experience for users. The chapter will explore the history, emergence and popularity of this Web phenomenon. Online communities were first used as a way for people to interact socially with others in the Internet. Now many companies are establishing online communities to allow customers to interact with other customers, and for customers to interact with company representatives. Users of Web sites with chat and discussion forums typically spend more time on these sites versus sites without these features. The chapter will explore a few different online community models.

Chapter 7: One-to-One Web Presentation and Conferencing

Chapter 7 provides an in-depth look into how to conduct presentations and conferencing over the Web. You will become familiar with the multimedia communication and application standards and technologies as well as how to select the best Web conferencing technology for your marketing needs. It will also discuss what types of presentations you can make to enhance your one-to-one Web marketing efforts. The chapter will show you how to create the optimum blend of graphics, audio and video to make maximum use of the bandwidth limitations of today's Internet.

Chapter 8: One-to-One Web Advertising and Promotion

Online advertising has moved from simple Web banners to full-motion video. Web advertising and promotion can now be targeted to specific people, or even block advertising from being viewed by people who don't fit the target market. The online advertising future will allow TV commercial-like advertising. There is even advertising that doesn't require users to click to another site to perform a transaction—they bring the transaction to the user right in the Web banner. Chapter 8 will discuss the many types of advertising and promotion that can be implemented on the Web. The chapter will also discuss the role of advertising networks and advertising management software in enabling targeted and one-to-one advertising.

Chapter 9: One-to-One with Web Site Tracking

Most Web managers have the ability to track user interaction with their Web site. There are many products and services available that help capture and report Web site activity. Chapter 9 will explain all of the nuts and bolts of Web site traffic analysis. The chapter will explain how the use of online guest books can enhance your ability to learn more about your users. The chapter will also discuss how to capture and track online sales leads and information inquiries.

Chapter 10: Integrating One-to-One Web with Other Marketing Systems and Processes

The key to providing one-to-one Web marketing is the integration of the Web and databases. Chapter 10 will explain how databases are being tied to Web sites to enhance marketing and service. The chapter will discuss the two-way nature of Web-to-database integration and how you can bring other databases such as customer databases and purchasing history in to the one-to-one Web marketing process. The chapter will also discuss related concepts such as data mining and data warehousing and how they can be used to enhance your efforts to satisfy each customer according to their individual profile and interactions with your organization.

Chapter 11: One-to-One Web Privacy

What makes one-to-one Web marketing possible, also has caused a lot of uproar in the Web community. Chapter 11 will discuss the controversy surrounding online privacy from both the users' and marketers' perspectives. In order to overcome this very real hurdle, the chapter will provide you with ways to allay your users fears regarding the privacy invasion.

Chapter 12: The One-to-One Web Marketing Future

In this chapter we mix a little serious business with a little fun. We discuss what is in store for one-to-one Web marketing and show you a sneak peek into some really leading-edge, Star Trek-like, one-to-one communications.

ONE-TO-ONE WEB MARKETING OVERVIEW

> "...because in an economy driven by information and dependent upon appealing to ever more particalized marketplaces, it is individual information that has the greatest worth."
>
> Jim Taylor and Watts Wacker, The 500 Year Delta

In 1991, marketers we were inspired by the introduction of Regis McKenna's book, *Relationship Marketing* (1991, Addison-Wesley). In his book, McKenna discussed the age of customer-centered and knowledge-based marketing. Then the marketing floodgates opened in 1993 with the best-selling book, *The One to One Future* written by Don Peppers and Martha Rogers (1993, Doubleday). At that time, Peppers and Rogers discussed the combined future of marketing and technology and described one-to-one technologies of the future. They discussed the characteristics of one-to-one marketing using individually addressable technologies and mass customization. Even though their book was written before the existence of the Web, they described technologies that sounded very much like what we now know as the Web.

In this chapter, we provide an overview of relationship and one-to-one marketing concepts. We set the stage for putting these concepts into action in your Web development and marketing efforts. The most important thing to remember when thinking about and implementing these technologies is that technology by itself will not make you successful on the Web. It is the balance of your company's best practices and the creative implementation of the technologies that will make your site a success.

2001: A Web Odyssey

The Web is changing the way we communicate and conduct business; however, it is still a relatively small market. For many companies, it is considered one market segment, for others it is their entire marketing effort. The Web is still primarily used as a marketing communications vehicle by most corporations. In September 1997, RHI Consulting released the results of a survey of chief information officers (CIOs). In this survey, CIOs were asked, "Does your company have a Web site?" The respondents who indicated they had a Web site (50 percent) were asked how they use the Web site. Here are the results:

Advertising/marketing/public relations: 66%

Customer service/tech support: 9%

Research: 7%

E-mail: 5%

Electronic commerce: 4%

Employee recruitment: 2%

Education: 2%

Other/don't know: 5%

We Web site managers and marketers have many opportunities to explore and implement what the Web can offer. There have been many predictions of what the Web will look like and how it will behave by the year 2001. Here is a sampling of soothsaying:

IDC Research predicts the Web population will grow to 174.5 million in 2001, up from 50.2 million in 1997.

Cowles/Simba Information projects that Web user sessions will hit 15.79 billion in 2000, yielding 94.76 billion page views.

IDC Research predicts that in December 2001, 39 percent of online users will buy goods and services on the Web as compared to 25 percent in December 1996.

IDC Research forecasts the amount of commerce conducted over the Web is expected to grow from $2.6 billion in 1996 to more than $220 billion during 2001.

The Web has grown from a novelty exploited by computer technologists to a useful communications, marketing, and commerce platform. We've seen it expand from simple text-based search engines to the creation of *navigation engines*. Search engines such as Excite have become content sites with search capabilities, and The Mining Company was created to help users gain more value from the Web with the assistance of real live human Web guides. One navigation engine that is changing how we experience the Web is the Alexa Web navigation service (www.alexa.com). It is a free service where users download a navigation tool and the toolbar follows users as they navigate the Web.

Alexa gives users detailed information about the current site they are visiting, recommends other sites based on path analysis of other users, allows users to vote whether they like the site or not, and allows users to communicate with others via Alexa's Instant Messaging Service. As you can see, Alexa's goal is to enhance the user's experience in a one-to-one fashion. The service is free because it uses advertising to fund the service.

History of Web Marketing

It is hard to associate the word *history* with the World Wide Web since it is still such a new phenomenon. The Web is still about possibilities where we have only begun to leverage all of the power of the interconnections between computers, peoples, nations, and cultures. But it is certainly fun to look back in amazement at what has already been accomplished with and on the Web.

Full Circle: The History of Marketing

In the many years before the Industrial Age, marketing was done by the local merchant—the butcher, the baker, and the candlestick maker. The local merchant knew everything about his or her customers, by memory or by recording information on accounts. This interaction between customer and merchant was one-to-one marketing. Even today, where there are still local neighborhood butcher shops, the butcher will remember his or her best customers by making personal recommendations based on the knowledge he or she has of all prior transactions. The butcher remembers that you prefer sirloin and lets you know about a special price on your next shopping trip.

The turn of the nineteenth century was the dawn of mass marketing. This era was typified by mass production of goods and mass advertising. There was little recognition of market segments. Everyone had the same ad in *Life* magazine for cigarettes, soap, and other mass-produced products.

With the emergence of the Information Age, computing became more cost-efficient, and databases became a useful tool for marketing. In the 1970s, we saw the practice of using demographics in marketing come into full bloom. In the 1980s, the use of lifestyle data, psychographics, became the next big trend in marketing, and in 1991, well-known marketing guru Regis McKenna introduced marketing managers to the concept of relationship marketing. Another marketing revolution, the one-to-one marketing mantra, closely followed.

With one-to-one marketing, we can be merchants of the high-tech kind. We can provide similar services as the local merchant using databases and interactive software and systems such as Web site personalization and one-to-one Web conferencing.

Circa 1993—Age of WOW! (We're On the Web!)

"World Wide What?" In 1993 the Web was relatively unknown. In 1991, Tim Berners-Lee created a graphical way to share data among scientists. It spread like wildfire and became a useful communications vehicle by 1993. In 1993 NCSA Mosaic, the first graphics-based Web browser (and precursor to the Netscape's Navigator and Microsoft's Internet Explorer browsers) was introduced. However, even with the explosion of mind-boggling press coverage of the Internet and the thousands of applications on the Internet, the Web had had relatively insignificant penetration among the mass population in 1993—and even today. Morgan Stanley's technology research report, *Advertising Report* (1997, HarperBusiness), showed how long it would take for the Internet to reach 50 million users relative to other communications media.

Radio: 38 years

TV: 13 years

Cable: 10 years

Internet: 5 years (est.)

The Internet's adoption growth is impressive, but it still does not have the audience of the other media. In 1993, individuals and companies began to stake their claims in cyberspace with simple static Web pages in hopes of bringing their thoughts and wares to the entire world. Most of the Web marketing centered around marketers joyfully exclaiming, "We're on the Web!" to each other and anyone else who cared to listen.

Circa 1995—Age of "I Really Think There Is a Future in This Web Thing!"

A feverish rush for many to open up the electronic representation of their physical entities, 1995 was marked by new Web sites popping up every day. According to a Network Wizards statistical count, in July 1995 there were more than 6.6 million hosts on the Internet with 120,000 domains, growing from more than 1.7 million hosts and 26,000 domains in July 1993. Early in 1995 the first batch of companies on the Web were computer and software organizations, followed by corporations building marketing communications sites and a few daring Web entrepreneurs such as Hot! Hot! Hot! (www.hothothot.com), the famous online hot sauce store. It was a time when the Web moved from being a novelty to an actual money-making endeavor. The year was also marked by the start of the scrappy Web browser war with Microsoft's debut of its browser. Web marketing at this time consisted of publishing product and service information on a site, creating and placing banner ads, and alerting newsgroups of company events and product happenings.

Circa 1998—Age of Consensual Marketing

From 1995 to now, Web marketing has become serious business. The Web now totals over 1 million domains and is growing daily. Development budgets have mushroomed, and the Web's audience is now big enough for advertisers and marketers to make it a mainstay in their marketing plans and budgets. The interesting phenomenon Web marketing professionals now have to consider is the concept of *consensual marketing*. This means the online audience has the leverage to determine from whom they will receive marketing messages. It goes well beyond the television remote control phenomenon where the viewing audience can change channels when they do not want to view a TV advertisement. For people to have control over what direct mail they receive, they have to take the initiative to get their name removed from the mailing list. They do not have the ultimate choice of who is using their name and address. The traditional media is characterized by *opt-out* and the Web is fast becoming a place where users can *opt-in* to receive marketing messages.

On the Web, the user has complete control over what, when, and how he or she will receive online advertisements. Then there is the added dimension of the demand for online marketers to protect the user's privacy. The Web population is demanding that marketers tell them what they are going to do with the personal, tracking and transaction information they collect. Users also want to have the choice of what data is collected, if any at all. Consensual marketing will be practiced by all good Web marketers if they want to build loyal and ongoing relationships with their users, prospects, customers, business partners, and other constituents. The adoption of consensual marketing methods is crucial to practicing and taking advantage of the one-to-one marketing the Web allows. This book will deal with all of the issues, opportunities, and practices of one-to-one Web marketers with the key undercurrent of gaining the user's consent in the one-to-one Web marketing interaction.

One-to-One Marketing—The "Reader's Digest" Version

One-to-one marketing and service is not a new concept in the physical world. Nordstrom's, an upscale department store, has a personal shopping service that helps customers buy clothing that best suits their lifestyles, jobs, and personal tastes. Web sites, online stores, and online information services are taking cues from these types of services and are leveraging information technology to bring one-to-one services to the online masses.

To see what the future holds for marketing on the Web, let's review how one-to-one marketing is different from other types of marketing.

Mass marketing. One-to-all or one-to-many communications without specialization of message or medium.

Target marketing. One-to-many or one-to-few communications with specialization of message and medium for each identified segment of the whole market.

One-to-one marketing. One-to-few or one-to-one communications with individualized message and medium for each highly targeted market or individual customer.

There are many good marketing experts with significant ideas about marketing on the Web. For our book, we focused on relationship, one-to-one, and loyalty marketing ideas. We selected notable experts in each of their fields. We hope that we do justice applying their great ideas to the Web. But first we will provide you with a condensed version of key concepts.

Relationship Marketing

Regis McKenna wrote a definitive book, *Relationship Marketing* (1991, Addison-Wesley), about the changes marketers needed to make to become more customer centered with their marketing efforts. Instead of simply producing and distributing goods and services in mass quantities with no choices in features, he discussed how marketers could find a segment of a market and dominate it through relationship marketing. This mindset could enable a company to create products that closely fit the needs of a particular customer set. In order to leverage relationship marketing, marketers needed to move from monologue to dialog with customers. Here is the condensed version of some of the important principles from his book:

- Owning the market
  - Define which whole pie (market segment) is yours and dominate it.
  - Develop products and services to serve that market specifically.
  - Define the standards in that market.
  - Deepen relationships with customers.
- Knowledge-based marketing
  - Integrate the customer into the product and service design process to guarantee the product is tailored to the customer's needs, desires, and strategies.
  - Generate niche thinking—use the company's knowledge of channels and markets to identify market segments that you can own.
  - Develop an infrastructure of suppliers, vendors, partners, and users that help sustain and support your edge in the market segment.
- Experience-based marketing
  - Spend time with customers.
  - Monitor competitors.
  - Develop feedback analysis that turns information about markets and competition into product intelligence.

- Adaptive marketing
  - Sensitivity—communications and feedback channels.
  - Flexibility—organizational structure and operational style that takes advantage of the new opportunities feedback brings about.
  - Resiliency—learn from mistakes.

One-to-One Marketing

Don Peppers and Martha Rogers have written two books on the subject of one-to-one marketing. The books are full of thought-provoking concepts that can be applied to Web site creation and promotion programs. Following are some of the highlights from each book.

The One-to-One Future

The One to One Future was published in 1993, which was well into the high time of database marketing. It presented groundbreaking and earth-shattering concepts to marketers. Here are just a few of the book's key concepts that can be applied using the Web:

Share of the customer. Peppers and Rogers presented the idea of switching the marketer's mindset from share of the *market* to share of the *customer*. Instead of focusing solely on the higher investment of marketing to your entire marketplace in order to increase revenue, you want to also focus on increasing the revenue of each customer—also known as increasing the share of each customer on a one-to-one basis. This idea has the benefit of increased profitability since it is cheaper to increase sales to existing customers than to acquire new customers. Another benefit is that during the process of increasing the share of each customer, you are building longer-term and loyal relationships with customers. In order to maximize the share of each customer, you will need to know what that customer thinks, which can only be done with one-to-one communication mechanisms.

Customer retention versus acquisition. Typically it costs five times more to acquire a new customer than it costs to retain a customer. Most businesses experience a customer-churn rate of about 25 percent annually. According to Peppers and Rogers, if you are able to reduce this by 5 percent, you could add as much as 100 percent to your bottom line. The idea is basic: Higher revenue at the same expense falls directly to the bottom line as higher profit.

Law of repeat purchases. The more successful you are in getting each customer to buy from you, the more you can increase your long-term profits. The more units you sell to a particular and valuable customer, the higher each unit's margin will be over time. The overhead associated with each purchase decreases when the cost of marketing to a loyal customer declines.

Customer dialog. "In the 1:1 future, it won't be how much you know about *all* of your customers that's important, but how much you know about *each* of your customers." The way to apply this concept is to use interactive communications with your customers. Dialog is two way, not one way. It is an exhange of ideas between two parties. Using two-way communications vehicles and feedback mechanisms enables you to learn more than you would through market research. Make it easy for customers to communicate with your organization. Act on what they say in order to build trusting and loyal relationships, which will translate into more sales and better profit margins.

Enterprise One to One

In 1997 Peppers and Rogers dealt the second blow to the marketing community with *Enterprise One to One*. This book revisited the one-to-one mantra with added excitement surrounding the limitless technological possibilities of the Web, interactivity, and the use of customer data. Here are the pertinent concepts from this book:

The new competitive rules. Customer-driven competition is synonymous with one-to-one marketing. With traditional marketing methods, this type of competition was cost prohibitive. Information technology, including Web technology, can raise the competitive playing field because it can track customers, enable interactive dialog, and allow mass customzation where products and services can be created to the specifications of an individual customer.

The learning relationship. The way to build the strongest link between you and your customers is to establish a learning relationship. To do this, follow these four steps:

1. Find out what your customer needs through interaction and feedback.
2. Meet these needs by customizing your product or service, and remember the specifications.
3. Continue interaction and feedback to learn more about the customer's individual needs.
4. Keep your customers satisfied so you do not lose them to your competition.

Convenience and incentive. If you make it convenient for customers to give information about themselves, the better the opportunity you have to learn more about them, and the more they will do repeat business with you. In addition to important personal communications between your customers and company representatives in sales, marketing, and support, the Web and other interactive media can make it convenient for customers to share their thoughts with you. You can also provide an incentive to customers to enter into a learning relationship with your organization—free add-ons, free service, discounts, special memberships, and so forth.

Some rules for the (information) road. Now that you have the powerful one-to-one marketing tool of the Web, you will want to consider how to approach customers for their personal information. First, you don't want to ask for all of the information at once. A learning relationship should be conducted in the long term, especially since markets and customers rapidly change. Second, give the customer the choice in what information he or she wants to provide. This establishes a relationship based on trust, which will widen the communications channel between you and your customer. Third, you want to make the customer's life better with the information you are collecting. You will want to create an equitable value exchange between the information you are collecting and the service you provide in return. Finally, you will want to establish a *Privacy Bill of Rights*. See Chapter 11, "One-to-One Privacy," on how to create privacy policies to increase your customers' confidence in the learning relationship.

One of the profound quotes to remember from the book: "If a firm is not in direct touch with its customers, then every single interaction is a priceless opportunity to learn more."

Building Loyalty Through Marketing

Frederick Reichheld is a leader of Bain & Company's (www.bain.com) Loyalty Practice and author of *The Loyalty Effect* (1996, Harvard Business School Press). He has conducted extensive research to uncover the effect of increasing customer loyalty in various industries. In 1989 he published a study that showed that raising customer retention rates by 5 percentage points could increase the value of an average customer by 25 to 100 percent. Customer loyalty has two important effects on a company.

The first is the customer volume effect. If you can reduce customer attrition, you gain a larger growth in volume of existing customer revenue versus trying to make up lost volume from customer attrition with new customers. The second effect is the profit-per-customer effect. In many industries, companies actually lose money when they acquire new customers, and it takes several transactions over time to see profit materialize from these customers. If you lose mature customers, you actually lose the ability to recoup acquisition investment, break even, or receive profit. Loyal customer spending tends to accelerate over time. The more a single customer orders over time, the more profit a company receives because each interaction generally requires less investment by the company than initial transactions. The goal is to increase repeat purchases by focusing on loyalty-building efforts to increase customer profitability.

The Web: A Relationship-Building Platform

Jim McCann, the founder and president of 1-800-Flowers (www.1800flowers.com), wrote an article for *Upside* magazine in November 1997 entitled "Interactive Customer Service." In this article, he warned that computers are just tools that allow companies to provide interactivity, and they cannot motivate customers or nurture the bond that results in repeat business by themselves. In his words:

> *"Despite our name, 1-800-Flowers, we're in the 'social expression' business, like the people who sell greeting cards and chocolates. Flowers are symbolic, timeless, not high tech. And yet we conduct 10 percent of our business online. We're using this new channel to reach a growing market segment that is embracing new technology and is motivated by convenience. But we've never lost sight of customer satisfaction, which we handle the old-fashion way: one-to-one."*

Jim McCann and his company were pioneers on the Web and their Web site is held as one of the standards among online retailers. His point is important to consider. The Web and one-to-one marketing technologies are only vehicles for building one-to-one relationships with your online customers. The magic of one-to-one marketing happens during the interaction with the customer. Your site should interact with the customer in a nurturing, two-way manner. In fact, there are some interactions that should never be left to the Web to handle such as complex customer support issues. This is where human interaction will succeed. Your Web site should interact with customers in a very human-like way. Put your thinking caps on before you implement what can be very expensive technology. Think about why and how the system will be designed to facilitate relationship building. Be careful not to let the excitement of cool technology drive your one-to-one marketing strategy.

An example of one technology being used to build relationships with online users is LikeMinds (www.likeminds.com). To showcase their patented collaborative filtering technology the company created the MovieCritic Web site (www.moviecritic.com). The site makes recommendations about movies based on an individual user preference profile and the preferences of other like-minded users of the site. A user is asked to rate 12 movies he or she has seen based on a 13-point scale from "Loved It" to "Hated It." MovieCritic then makes on-the-fly movie recommendations, even ones the systems predicts the user will hate. Even though the site's purpose is to simply showcase the technology, over 100,000 users have built profiles and received recommendations and the site receives 15,000 visits per month. Cinemax and HBO use the LikeMinds technology to make movie recommendations and gather user preference information in order to learn more about their viewers. The MovieCritic service is driven by technology but requires human interaction in order to provide value to its users.

Even more personal, LikeMinds solution is Scott Kurnit's Web-based search service, The Mining Company (www.miningco.com). The Mining Company is a guide to what is on the Web. Its unique service is in the hundreds of human Web *guides* that research Web content and publish their findings on the site's 500+ topic areas. Users can also exchange e-mail messages with the topic area guides.

Marketers now have a tool they have been envisioning for many years—a tool that allows them to know their customer more intimately than before. Marketers no longer have to make uninformed decisions about their customers because of the two-way interaction and communication capabilities that the Web allows.

One-to-One Web Marketing Matrix

The purpose of this book is to show you technologies and techniques to increase the return on your Web site and marketing investments. In each chapter we present in-depth discussions on each of the one-to-one marketing applications that can be used on the Web. Depending on your budgets and objectives, you many use one technique, a combination of techniques, or all of them. Table 1.1 outlines the Web marketing technologies and how to apply each of them.

Table 1.1 One-to-One Web Marketing Matrix

One-to-One Web Technology	Uses
Web site interactivity	• Enables users to learn more about your organization, products, or services by allowing them to interact with your Web site or functions on your Web site.
	• Conducts personalized dialog with each user.
	• Provides entertaining and useful Web experience that promotes rememberance and loyalty among users.
E-mail	• Maintains ongoing organization and marketing communications via e-mail announcements and newsletters.
	• Reaches people without requiring a visit to your Web site.
	• Targets e-mail advertising on other organizations' e-mail announcements and newsletters.

Table 1.1 *Continued*

One-to-One Web Technology	Uses
Web site personalization	• Learns more about each user or target markets.
	• Presents personalized recommendations, especially if you serve a wide variety of target markets or provide a wide range of products or services.
	• Automates many processes such as recommendation, cross-selling, and account management.
	• Targets advertising to individuals based on their user profiles; presents a unique Web experience to each customer.
	• Conducts membership and loyalty programs; some can be premium services that customers pay for.
Push	• Maintains ongoing organization and marketing communications.
	• Reaches people without requiring a visit to your Web site.
	• Creates a different channel to each target market for both Internet and intranet applications.
	• Targets advertising to individuals based on their user profiles; presents unique information or marketing messages to each customer.
Community	• Creates online discussion forums among users and with organization representatives (management, sales, customer service, etc.).
	• Increases site traffic and site visit longevity.
	• Promotes site and brand loyalty.
Web presentation and conferencing	• Conducts seminars, sales meetings, and training via the Web.

Table 1.1 *Continued*

One-to-One Web Technology	Uses
	• Decreases the cost of many face-to-face meetings.
Advertising	• Increases awareness and response from the Internet audience.
	• Conducts targeted and one-to-one advertising to optimize ad budget.
	• Conducts response- and transaction-oriented Web ads.
Web site tracking/traffic analysis	• Assesses the performance of your Web site or specific sections of your site.
	• Learns more about your Web visitors and customers.
	• Integrates your user profile and other databases with tracking data (what users are viewing/clicking on) on your Web site.
Database integration	• Makes other back-end, historical, or live data available to your Web site such as product/service information, customer information, purchase transactions, shipping, and account management.
	• Performs database marketing on your Web site or on the Internet.
	• Performs data mining to segment customers (by profitability, site usage, etc.) and form predictive models about future site or transaction activity.

Embracing the One-to-One Web Marketing Challenges

We have a long, one-to-one Web marketing future ahead of us. Now is the time to consider leveraging the potential of the Web to build relationships with customers and users. On the other hand, there are a couple of important obstacles that need to be removed before both you and your customer can truly benefit from one-to-one relationships. The three main hurdles are *expense*, *technology*, and *privacy*.

Expense

Historically, one-to-one sales, marketing, and service came at a premium. Personal shoppers and other personalized services were limited to people willing to pay for the additional value this type of service provides. Some industry pundits believe that the incremental expense to provide personalized marketing and service does not bring the required results to justify the investment. While it is true that personalized Web marketing costs more, one-to-one marketing can pay significant dividends over time in terms of Web site and company loyalty, the ability to stretch your limited marketing budgets by focusing on targeted marketing, higher response rates from targeted advertising, and so on. Each chapter in this book presents some implementation costs associated with each one-to-one Web marketing technology. As we marketers know, there are two variables in the marketing equation: expense and resulting revenue or response. One-to-one marketing, like all marketing efforts, is an investment over the long term.

Technology

Media hype abounds. Artificial intelligence, intelligent agents, personal bots, personalization, collaborative filtering, data mining, and other sci-fi sounding technologies are all the rage in technology magazines and even in more general magazines. These technologies are being applied to the Web at a feverish pace by still relatively few Web sites. Some of the technology is expensive and takes a long time to implement since almost every site needs a custom solution. The integration of databases to the Web is still in progress. Each of this book's chapters provides an in-depth look at a one-to-one Web marketing technology, including any relevant obstacles. For a discussion about Web-to-database integration, see Chapter 10, "Integrating One-to-One Web with Other Marketing Systems and Processes."

Privacy

The privacy issue is an emotional one that raised the discussion about protecting users' personal data to new heights when Web marketers began to use technology and encourage users to register with their Web sites. In order for both the user and the marketer to benefit from one-to-one Web marketing, the marketer must protect users' privacy, give users control over their own personal information, and practice self-regulation in order to prevent governments from stepping in to solve problems. Since this issue is so important to the future of relationship building on the Internet, we dedicated Chapter 11, "One-to-One Web Privacy," to the subject.

Up Next

Chapter 2, "One-to-One Web Interactivity," begins our discussion about one-to-one Web technologies and techniques beginning with Web site interactivity. The chapter outlines the characteristics of good interactivity, including engaging the user, providing give-and-take, gathering data, and building relationships. The chapter also discusses the difference between true and effective interactivity, versus interactivity without purpose. You will also see examples of interactivity that builds relationships with online users.

ONE-TO-ONE WEB INTERACTIVITY

"A great interactive experience is like a great dance, you don't know who is leading."

Charlie Scuba, Northern Lights Interactive

We started creating Web sites at the dawn of the Web revolution. Back then, everyone said, "Please put us up on the Web!" In the infancy years of the Web, companies were in a frantic state to be on the Web because *everyone* was on the Web.

With these companies, we would play (and still do play) a game of 20 questions, such as:

- Who is on the Web?
- Who are your three main competitors?
- Are they on the Web?
- What do you feel are the strengths and weaknesses of their Web sites?
- Are your customers on the Web?
- What kinds of customers are you targeting?
- What kind of information would be useful to your customers or sales force?

Our next question was, "Why? Why do you want to be on the Web? What are you trying to accomplish?"

Silence. "Why are you asking us these questions? You are a Web development firm, don't you just want to take our money?" Some clients would think this to themselves and some would actually say it.

Some had never really thought about the question, "Why?" All they knew was what they had heard or read, that it was what they were supposed to do. So we thought about it for them.

Most Web sites fall into three categories:

1. Sell product.

2. Educate prospective customers about the product (to shorten sales cycle).

3. Entertain. Some sites like www.eat.com use light-hearted interactivity to build a one-to-one relationship between the user and the company or product brand. Their main goal is to get lots of traffic, possibly sell Web ads, and give the customer a good feeling about the company and its products without overtly hitting them over the head with a sales pitch.

"What is the purpose of your Web site?" we'd ask.

We started asking people these questions because they weren't asking these questions of themselves. Marketers have been throwing money at the Web expecting it to be this miracle medium without considering return on investment. The age of "Get on the Web" was from 1993 to 1997. From 1998 on will be the age of "Justify Why You Are on the Web."

In this chapter, we discuss how to use one-to-one Web interactivity to help you create a meaningful Web presence that is *useful* and *necessary*. We discuss true interactivity versus interactivity for interactivity's sake, and many of the benefits and issues regarding Web interactivity. Finally, we explore some interesting applications and products that can help the one-to-one Web marketer implement interactivity to enhance the performance of their Web site.

What Is Web Interactivity?

In order to define what interactivity is, we need to define what it is not. Interactivity on the Web is not simply animation, video, and audio. Too often, Web marketers mistake moving images (i.e., animation), blinking things, and auditory messages with interactivity. With these elements, all you can do is watch. These are passive experiences. They are not interactive. Much like radio and TV, it is a one-way use of this medium that is sending your content.

But why stick to the limitations of past mediums when the Web has the ability to have two-way interaction? Why are so few taking advantage of this and using this medium to its full capability? For some it is fear, ignorance, or bandwidth issues (we'll address this more fully in the section, "Issues"), but mainly it is because this medium is still very new. Just as early TV programs were basically radio programs put on the screen, so have developers and marketers tried to fit this one-to-one round medium peg into the square hole of broadcast media. With the Web's one-to-one marketing and communications capabilities, interactivity technologies can be leveraged to give users a one-on-one interaction.

In their book, *The One to One Future* (1993, Doubleday), Don Peppers and Martha Rogers discuss how critical is it is to engage your customers in dialog. They state that four criteria must be met before it can be considered a true dialog:

1. *All parties to a dialog must be* able *to participate.* Mass media cannot allow for dialog, but the Web can.

2. *All parties to the dialog must* want *to participate in it.* In one to one, that means the subject of the dialog must be of interest to both you and your customer. Most companies try too hard to talk about themselves. The customer only has one interest, "What can you do for me?" Try taking the stance of getting the customers to talk about themselves so that you can better serve them.

3. *Dialogs can be controlled by anyone in the exchange.* Mass media has been doing monologues for years. Enjoy the experience of a free exchange of ideas that can go in any direction. You may be surprised at what you learn.

4. *Your dialog with an individual customer will change your behavior toward that single individual, and change that individual's behavior toward you.* By engaging in dialogs with your clients, you can actually have an effect on their actions.

True interactivity is a one-to-one dialog. It is give and take between the user and you via your Web site. The user provides some information or a request and you, through your Web site, respond by providing information back to the user that pertains to his or her request. It is that simple. If you can remember this simple formula for interactivity, you will always be embracing one-to-one Web marketing.

Some of the technologies that are frequently used for Web interactivity are Shockwave and Flash, Java, database forms, and streaming audio and video. But remember, it is not *what* you use, but *how* you use it.

One-to-one Web interactivity is true interactivity for the purpose of strengthening relationships, creating affinity, sharing moments of connection, and building rapport with your customers.

Benefits of One-to-One Web Interactivity

Some of the benefits of one-to-one interactivity are that it engages the users, has the give and take of true one-to-one marketing, allows you to gather data, and has strong relationship-building implications.

Engage the User

As of the second quarter of 1997, there were 51 million users on the Internet. This number is growing daily. These people need something to do! The biggest complaint that we hear about the Internet is that there is plenty of information but people need direction and guidance to get to it.

There is a lot of aimless wandering going on. So, if someone happens to stumble upon your Web site (which happens a lot on the Web), then you have an obligation as a good one-to-one Web marketer to try to engage that person and make it worth the trip.

As the expression goes, you have one chance to make a good first impression—on the Web, you have a fraction of a chance because escape is just a click away. Imagine if you were at a cocktail party and got pulled into a boring conversation. Wouldn't it be great if you could just click away? The Web affords us that luxury. No one wants to have his or her time wasted, and surfers are basically saying, "Buddy, if I'm on your Web site you better be giving me something of value or I'm out of here!"

We're talking about engaging the user, either through entertainment, information, or amazement. When you engage the user, you are also creating brand awareness and retention. A good example of this is the Snapple Web site (www.snapple.com). To introduce their new diet flavor, the people at Snapple created a scavenger hunt. They scattered six Diet Snapple bottles throughout their site. A bottle can pop up on any given page. Each time the user finds a bottle, he or she automatically comes back to a tracking page, showing how many bottles have been found and which bottles are still out there to search for. This is a great example of one-to-one Web marketing for two basic reasons:

It is engaging and fun. Some of the games on the Web these days are rather simple and some can be annoying or frustrating to the user.

It is an excellent way of introducing a new product by having the player learn the new flavors. When you are playing, you aren't just looking for any Diet Snapple; you are looking for specific flavors.

Give and Take

Because the Web allows for input and output, a Web site can pick up where TV, radio, and print media leave off. The Web is a different medium and has unique interactivity capabilities. It can reinforce and build on the messages presented in the other mediums. For example, if a new TV series is launched, there will usually be radio commercials and newspaper ads. But how about a Web site that introduces the actors who will star on the show and lets visitors guess which character is played by which actor? Then, when the TV show airs, a prize can be awarded to the Web participants who correctly predicted the correct casting of the show. Site participants can even contribute story ideas and try to predict the next episode. The possibilities are endless. The bottom line is that now there is a medium in which the creators and the viewers can interact in an unprecedented away. We, as one-to-one Web marketers, just need to have the creativity to take advantage of this access to our audiences.

Gathering Data

Web marketers have the ability to gather data directly from their viewers in real time, not having to wait for users to mail back some survey. People are receptive to providing data about themselves if they can see the benefit that it will bring them.

We are rapidly approaching the age of customized *information retrieval agents*. These agents allow customers access to their own personalized information. Allen Interactive is working with one client, a large imaging house, to develop a searchable archiving system that will let their clients retrieve their own images for their use. Quite often, a client may need to access one of the print catalog images. It is a long and tedious process for the imaging house to have to search and retrieve archived images for each of their clients—over 100 of them. By creating this "self-service" library, the imaging house is freeing up its staff to continue work while their clients have the freedom and convenience of accessing their photos whenever needed. There are plans to build a Web interface to this imaging house's job-tracking software. This will allow their clients to submit electronic job tickets, check the status of their job, and check on estimated time of completion. Again, this is a valuable service for the client for its speed and convenience. At the same time, it allows the customer service representative to deal with more critical issues than conveying standard status quotes to the client. Clients can get up-to-the-minute, accurate information at their fingertips 24 hours a day and 7 days a week.

Building Relationships

Once you get participants to participate in give-and-take conversations with you and provide you with data, you are in the position of forging and fostering a relationship with them. You have the opportunity to use this information to provide them with items of interest. The key is to be a *champion* for your customers, to always be looking to make their lives easier through the use of your products or services. This approach makes it easy for customers to do business with you, and this makes it easier to increase their loyalty.

Recently, we were researching computers on line and were visiting a Web site of a top PC manufacturer. We were dismayed to find that they had all of their computers listed by their model number—you could select one and then go to a subpage with more details about that model. Here's the catch: How do we know what model we need? They have over 30 listed with no intuitive grouping. As a customer, it would be useful to interact with a recommendation program that asks questions about the intended use of the computer and then recommends which model to consider.

This ties into another pertinent issue: As a one-to-one Web marketer, you must test your Web sites with select customers and vendors to make sure it is truly useful, helpful, and easy to use. It's hard to build relationships with your customers if the process of doing business with you takes too much time or is frustrating. This may sound obvious, but a number of companies get so caught up in Web site design and HyperText Markup Language (HTML) that they forget the marketing aspect of their Web site. It is a tool, use it.

Issues for One-to-One Web Interactivity

Some of the issues of one-to-one interactivity are distraction, expense, and bandwidth. Anyone can become easily enamored with all of the cool Web technologies, but without clear forethought, these technologies can actually be a distracting hurdle to enabling users to have a relationship with you. Interactivity can be expensive, so you will want to consider the opportunity the interactivity (i.e., brand building) brings to you and your customers, or the problem you are solving (i.e., making it easier for customers to find solutions) by using interactivity. Bandwidth will continue to be a technological hurdle for the foreseeable future, so test your interactivity on browsers and computers that your customers have access to.

"Fake Interactivity" Can Be Distracting to Users

What we are defining as *real* interactivity is that in which the participant interacts with your site and, based on his or her actions, the site responds accordingly. Many still consider basic animation, video, and audio to be interactivity, but by themselves they are not. Here are some examples of distracting interactivity that we have seen:

Blinking or spinning logos. Now, what purpose are these serving? Early Web designers learned how to do this when it was the latest thing and put it on their companies' sites because they thought it was cool and fun. Is anyone really benefiting from this? Is any information garnered, transferred, or received? Now, if it was a bouncing logo that could be used as a navigation device to guide someone through a complex Web page, that would be one to one, but just blinking, spinning, flickering? Nah.

Flashing copy. This feature started showing up as a style in HTML 2.0. The companies that have implemented it are probably the same ones who send the gauche direct-mail campaigns and have TV commercials where Crazy Harry is hopping up and down yelling for you to buy his latest product for $19.99. Bottom line, don't use it.

Animation just for animation's sake. Similar to the blinking logo, if it is of no value to your audience, then you will want to give this some additional thought before implementing this on your site. There is still too much "Why? Because we can!" Web designing going on. IBM has a great TV commercial with two guys developing a Web site with a flaming logo just because they can, and IBM pointed out this absurdity.

It Can Be Expensive to Do Well

One-to-one Web interactivity can be expensive to implement, being that much of it requires advanced programming talent (Java, C++, relational database integration) and advanced design talent (Director, Shockwave, VRML 3-D). These resources can be costly and often difficult to find. Interactivity that includes animation, multimedia, and personalization can add significantly to a Web site budget. But again, with a little creativity and ingenuity, simple interactivity can create a powerful, one-to-one experience. Think of interactivity as a good investment when applied in a manner that forges relationships with users and encourages users to spend time with your site and with your company. There are a number of personalization tools to implement impressive one-to-one experiences (see Chapter 4, "One-to-One Web Site Personalization," for more information).

Interactivity Can Require Lots of Bandwidth and Special Plug-Ins

The Web is not a CD-ROM. Too often, when people view something on a computer screen, they expect it all to be equal; which is a reasonable assumption, since TV is all that we see on a TV screen. On a computer screen, however, we can see Web, interactive CD-ROMs, or even multimedia kiosks—and there is a wide range of applications that fall in between. Many Web marketers have been quite disappointed in what the Web can and cannot do. Expectations are set either consciously or unconsciously, and people want to be *wowed*. The truth is that until browsers become more standardized and bandwidths become bigger, there will be some limitations in implementing interactive Web designs. Users will not be impressed with interactivity if it takes too long to gain satisfaction from it.

Applications of One-to-One Web Interactivity

In this section we explore many of the ways that you can implement one-to-one Web interactivity through chat groups, games, problem solving, transactions, surveys, education and business applications, customer service, Webisodes, and intermercials.

Chat and Web Conferencing

In Chapter 6, "One-to-One Community," we talk a lot about the benefits of the one-to-one Web community. But community-building technologies can also be useful for creating one-to-one Web interactivity. By promoting interaction between members and the site organizers through the use of chat or Web conferencing, marketers can have direct access to customer feedback.

Figure 2.1 ShareCentral's interactivity builds relationships.

Purple Moon

This site is a marketing and companion site for the CD-ROM series. Purple Moon's Web site (www.purple-moon.com) is central to the company's three-pronged "transmedia" business strategy designed to make Purple Moon a fun and meaningful part of girls' lives in many different ways.

This approach is based on Purple Moon's four years of research on gender, play behaviors, and technology usage that revealed girls' desire to develop in-depth relationships with life-like characters and indicated their fascination with characters that simultaneously appear in multiple media formats. This site encourages girls to be interactive using their brains and creativity. In Rockett's World, participants are encouraged to write and send in a story line that goes along with the photos.

The site also serves as a communications channel for the girls to be able to exchange thoughts and ideas with each other. In ShareCentral, girls can collect and trade online treasures, send and receive online postcards, and meet other girls with similar interests. This model could be followed for numerous other software product launches—integrally tying in the CD-ROM with the Web. Figure 2.1 shows the ShareCentral Web page.

Games

The one-to-one purpose of gaming is that it is an affinity-building method and also creates a sense of community. Players come back to check their scores and play again.

These sites are for pure entertainment. They hope that you like their site so much that you will come back and bring your friends. High-traffic sites can command huge advertising rates. So, the more fun you are having, the better.

Tater Man! (lark.cc.ukans.edu/~asumner/shock/potato/) allows you to build a face on a potato. People just come to play. There is no advertising on this site and the interactivity has no other purpose than fun. Aaron Sumner, the Webmaster, decided it was something that he wanted to do. The interesting thing is that 19,844 people have vis-

Figure 2.2 Build your own potato character on the Tater Man! Web site.

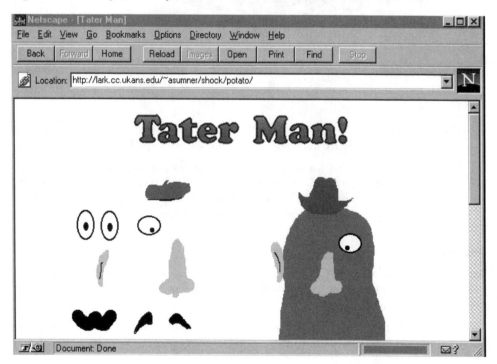

Figure 2.3 Cereal City's Nutrition Camp.

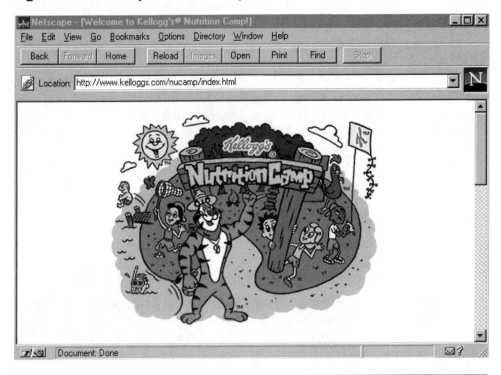

ited this site since May 25, 1996, because the interactivity doesn't have much purpose other than simple fun. Figure 2.2 shows one of the author's spud creations.

Riddler (www.riddler.com) and Happy Puppy (www.happypuppy.com) are very popular content sites—they are fun, entertaining, and highly interactive. These sites exist to create good content, which translates into a lot of traffic. The high traffic results in the sites' ability to generate revenue by selling ads and sponsorships.

Edutainment

Just like the popularity of CD-ROMs, edutainment is popular on the Web. Since everyone wants value from their Web experiences, what is more valuable than learning something?

At Seussville (www.randomhouse.com/seussville/), kids can play all kinds of interactive games. In The Lorax's Save the Trees Game, you catch seeds in a bucket and then plant the seeds wherever you want and a tree will grow. There is also The Cat's Concentration Game, Green Eggs and Ham Picture Scramble, Horton's Who Hunt, and check out the instructions for Elephant Ball.

At Planet K (www.kelloggs.com), kids can go to a nutrition camp where they can play interactive educational games about nutrition. This site allows Kellogg's to build brand awareness and loyalty through interactivity (see Figure 2.3).

When Discovery Network's Animal Planet debuted its new TV series, it also launched the show's *episodic* Web site, meaning the site changes daily based on the episode that is showing on Animal Planet.

The TV series, Once Upon a Tree (www.onceuponatree.com), is about a talking tree, some puppet animals, and some humans who learn to get along by following cues from nature. The site is highly interactive. Kids can e-mail their favorite puppet character and get a response back within 24 hours. On the activities page, kids can take quizzes and get instant feedback on their answers.

Figure 2.4 Invention games.

Figure 2.5 Auto-by-Tel provides interactive online auto buying.

In National Geographic World (www.nationalgeographic.com/features/96/inventions/), kids can play the inventions game with Professor Lou Knee (get it?). See Figure 2.4 for a sample of the site's invention games.

Problem Solving

Another application of one-to-one Web interactivity is problem solving. These types of applications help to fulfill a consumer's need. Need to buy a car? Visit Auto-by-Tel (www.autobytel.com) and try out their new car purchase request system (see Figure 2.5).

Quicken (www.insuremarket.com) will help you with a needs analysis or the risk evaluator, which ask questions like, "How likely are you to be injured by an uninsured motorist?" and then show you the risk based on your zip code and car model. (The answer we got was, "In North Carolina, 7.7 percent of all accidents resulting in injury involved an uninsured motorist," just in case you were curious.) See Figure 2.6 for an example.

Figure 2.6 Online risk evaluator from Quicken.

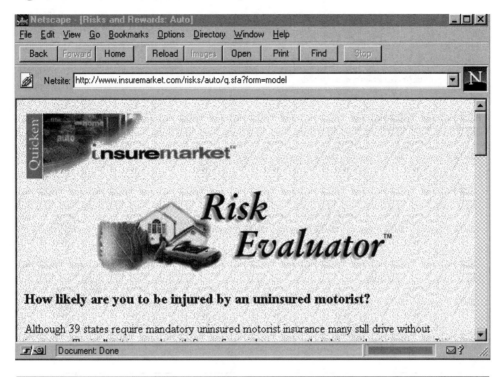

The Interactive Nutritionist (woman.com/body) is a personalized database and guide to healthy eating. If you enter in your height, weight, and age, it tells you the exact amount of vitamins, fats, and fiber you need. Figure 2.7 shows a sample outcome on the site.

The Gap (www.gap.com) has a great interactive Web site. In their "Get Dressed" section, you can try on different Gap clothes on the model and see how they work together. Dockers (www.dockers.com) provides an interactive style/outfit finder based on your personal style (laid-back, tuned-in, dressed-up) and the occasion (everything from a first date to a Sunday brunch or a class reunion).

There are tons of online calculators, estimators, and even this useful currency converter (www.cyberstation.net/~jweesner/ccc/ccc.shtml). Figure 2.8 shows an online currency converter.

There are a lot of uses for this problem-solving model for one-to-one interactivity. Try to help customers to see how you or your products can help them. Try to anticipate some of their problems and offer them solutions on line.

Figure 2.7 Interactive Nutritionist.

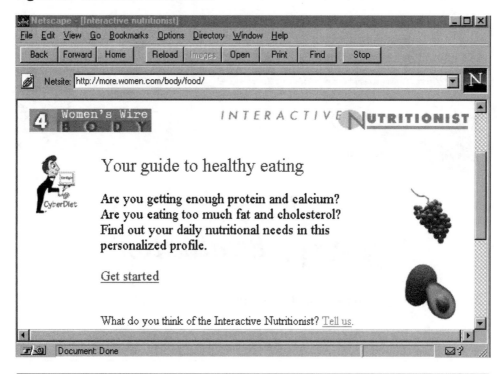

Transaction

Transaction is taking problem solving one step further, but do not misunderstand transactions. Most people think of transactions as e-commerce where something has to be purchased; however, transactions can be gathering information or making a purchase.

Web marketers can use their systems to allow people to transact with ease. You do not want to make it difficult for them to transact on line—that is defeating the primary time-saving purpose of the Web. By offering quality navigation and ease of use, customers will appreciate the new freedom of online transactions. A good example of this is Ticketmaster. Ticketmaster is working with Intel to develop an advanced ticketing service that will deliver rich, interactive content to subscribers' desktops using Intel-based computing and push. This service is scheduled to launch in the second quarter of 1998 as a companion to Ticketmaster Online, which presently sells $3 million worth of tickets per month. The success of Ticketmaster Online is what led to the creation of this new service. This new fully transactional ticketing system will feature customized event listings, 3-D virtual reality, and panoramic viewing of seating charts. This will allow fans to "see" the view from any vantage point and "tour" their favorite facilities.

Figure 2.8 Useful interactivity: currency conversion.

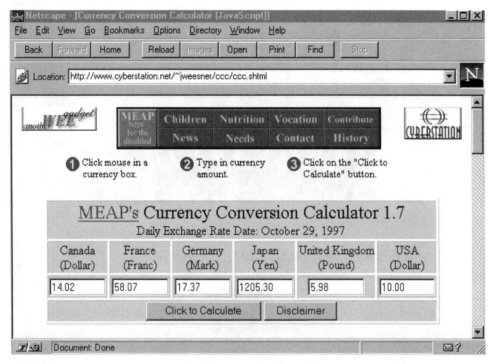

1997 Cybercitizen Report

This study categorized the ways in which cybercitizens use the Internet in the purchasing process, identified a jump in the number of people accessing the Web, and revealed a desire for "true interactivity." "Cybercitizens are no longer just testing the waters," says Thomas F. Hill, vice chairman of Yankelovich Partners and author of the study. "They are coming of age as online buyers." The study examined the online purchasing process, dividing it into three categories:

Shopping: Gathering information about products or services.

Ordering: Requesting a product whether or not the product is paid for on line.

Transacting: Ordering and actually paying for the product. The results

Figure 2.9 Interactive surveys on the Innovation Insights Web site.

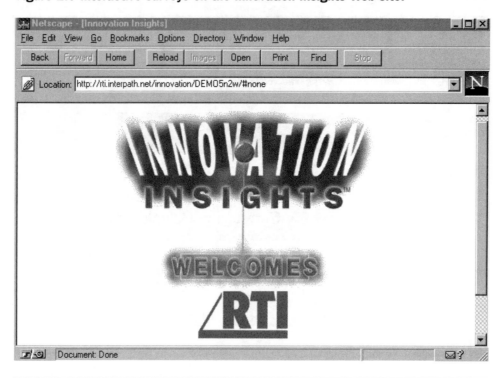

indicate that 63 percent of cybercitizens have shopped on line, 39 percent have ordered, and 23 percent have transacted. "This reveals a side to online retailing previously obscured from view," explains Hill. "By not defining the purchasing steps, previous research has equated the total online retailing opportunity to the 23 percent of online 'transactors.' Beyond this is a vast number of interested shoppers."

Online Surveys

Allen Interactive (www.allen.com) developed an online survey for its client, Research Triangle Institute (RTI). Research Triangle Institute (www.rti.org) is an independent, nonprofit research organization that conducts innovative research in electronics, chemistry, engineering, medical and pharmaceutical technology, environmental protection, public policy, and applied statistics.

RTI's newest project is Innovation Insights, an Internet-based assessment tool to help companies improve how they practice technology innovation. It reveals how well the technical staff and managers at companies

- Listen to customers.

- Share ideas and know-how within the company.

- Use outside technology to leverage R&D.

- Establish a company's culture that encourages innovation.

After asking thought-provoking questions and presenting some intriguing scenarios, Innovation Insights provides Web links to company personnel to help them learn more about innovation. RTI then provides reports for companies, revealing areas for improvement and roadblocks to innovation to help them identify ways to solve technical problems and take advantage of ideas for new products and processes.

The interactivity of Innovation Insights is powered by GuestTrack (www.guesttrack.com), a Web personalization software tool that can "branch" questions dynamically based on a user's response to the previous question. GuestTrack assigns individuals an encrypted identification number and creates a unique database to "catch" a user's responses. Based on those responses, GuestTrack can display pages on-the-fly and unique to that user. GuestTrack's database can then be downloaded and manipulated for individual, company, and cross-company long-range analysis. Figure 2.9 shows the Innovation Insights Web-based survey.

Education

Many top business schools across the country already have global programs where students participate in online conferences and lectures, do chat-based study groups with fellow students across the country and the globe, and jointly work on projects in private server areas accessed through ftp. This will be the wave of the future for the education community. In fact, academia has been using the Web for years to share thoughts and ideas.

Big business can learn a lesson or two from academia by thinking of one-to-one ways of demonstrating their products and services available on their Web sites.

Tutorials

Dr. Robert S. Stephenson, an associate professor in the department of Biological Sciences at Wayne State University, uses Java applets to create simulations of biophysical phenomena for his students. This allows the students to master abstract and difficult concepts by experiencing them instead of just reading about them. One example is *Electrical Interaction of Ions in Solution and the Principle of Electroneutrality* (www.sci-

Figure 2.10 Electroneutrality demo.

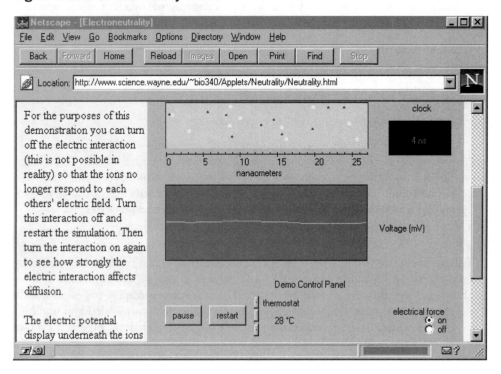

ence.wayne.edu/~bio340/Applets/Neutrality/Neutrality.html), in which students can control the thermostat and turn the electrical force on and off to witness the different results (see Figure 2.10).

Dr. Stephenson feels this is an area of strategic importance because in five years much of the instruction in higher education will be delivered over the Internet.

Distance Learning

Knowledge Ability Ltd. is a British company that provides international consulting and training services on online communication, collaboration, and learning. Dr. John Gundry, director, illustrates their model for the interactivity of distance learning in Figure 2.11.

Distance learning is based on the concept that a tutor leads an online lecture or online seminar, and learners discuss, query, restate, and interpret what they are learning via the Internet. This leads to deep-level, fully embedded learning. Used together with multimedia, learners have both the seminar room and the library on their com-

Figure 2.11 Interactivity of distance learning.

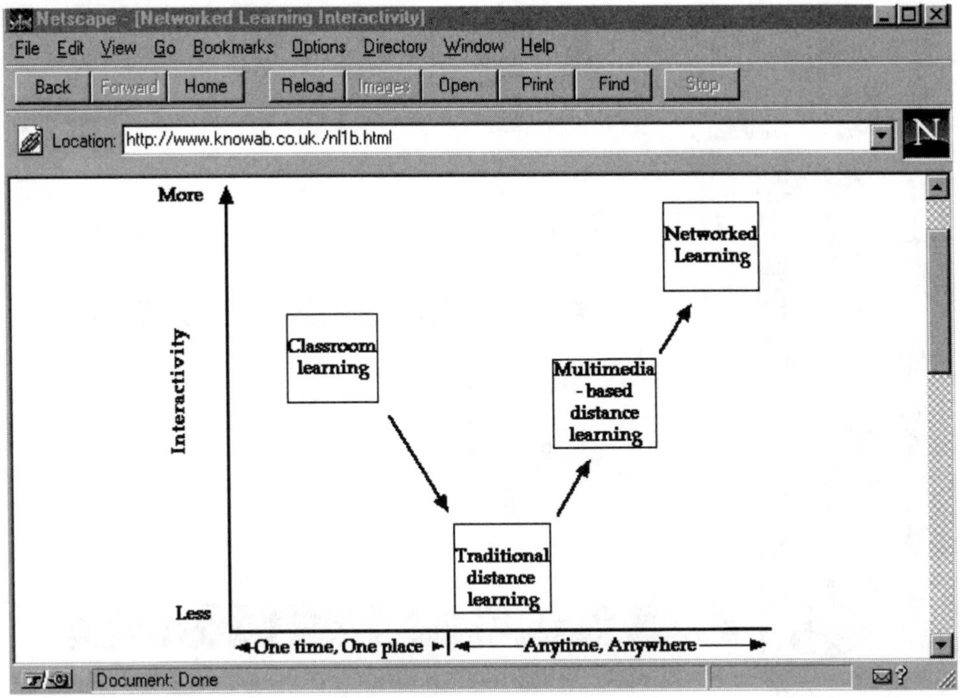

puters. Distance learning is sure to become a necessity for training programs, especially within large corporations with employees throughout the country. Instead of sending employees to regional training sites and paying for hotels and expenses, companies can "subscribe" to different distance learning training programs that are offered throughout the year and sign up their employees.

Retail Course

Reel.com (www.reel.com), an online movie rental store, has a great service for their customers. They have created Cinema U., the Web's virtual film school; it's both an online film club and a learning resource for movie lovers. Its film classes, which center on a group of movies chosen by the instructors, explore specific themes, genres, bodies of work, theories, or moments in history. Classes consist of lectures divided into "before and after customers watch a movie" sections, and online discussion boards, where customers can meet and have dialogs with others who share their cinematic passions.

Figure 2.12 Reel.com's Cinema U.

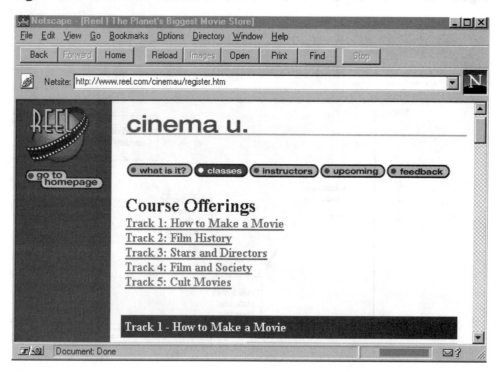

All movies included in the classes are available for rental and, in most cases, purchase from Reel.com, though customers don't need to rent or buy the movies from Reel.com to take a class. They charge $9.95–$14.95 for each course. This model illustrates both one-to-one Web community and one-to-one Web interactivity. Reel.com plans to offer 150 courses next year. Figure 2.12 shows course offerings at Cinema U.

Talk City Launches New Interactive Ads

"'More like TV' is the online advertising mantra," was the pronouncement of Jupiter Communications' Evan Neufeld at Jupiter's Online Advertising conference in New York City. A series of recent announcements, capped off by Talk City's unveiling of a new "time-based" format for complex streamed banner ads, underscores that the advertising industry may be getting exactly what it wants.

Talk City, a major online chat network, unveiled a new form of "time-based" banner ads that use streaming audio and graphics, interact with users, and run up to 4 minutes long in files from 16K to 64K. Toshiba, Toyota, and International Data Group's magazine, *The Web*, showed off "pilots" of their "Intermercials," with Diamond Multimedia Support and Sears slated to produce ads in the format.

Talk City's announcement followed the decision by Netscape and Microsoft to include in the next versions of their browsers support for Virtual Reality Modeling Language, or VRML, a standard that offers a similar potential for creating visually dazzling, interactive multimedia experiences with small files. For the user, Neufeld said it all adds up to a lot of advertising in a lot of different formats. "At this point, you'll see all types of ads on all types of environments, be they chat, push, et cetera."

Chat City's Intermercial format is not based on any one piece of technology. It uses a variety of cross-platform techniques—for example, animated GIFs, Java applets, and dynamic HTML—to achieve similar effects. The 30-second to 2-minute ads that were demonstrated used an applet called Enliven that automatically downloads with the advertisement. The ad then cycles on the screen, describing its product and, in some cases, inviting the user to interact with it— all without threatening to take the user away to a distant corporate Web site.

Talk City CEO Peter Friedman said the ads take advantage of the Web user's ability to focus on several things at a time on the screen. "We find our audience is very loyal and attentive, but also has free cycles," he said. "They will pay attention to an ad that streams through the chat and even talk about it." For example, a Toshiba ad invited the user to press buttons on the banner, which then demonstrated different features of a Toshiba computer.

VRML, which leapt to greater prominence with the Mars Pathfinder mission when it enabled users to explore data sent back from the Red Planet in an easily accessible 3-D format, also opens up possibilities for new forms of advertising. A Pepsi ad, shown at SIGGRAPH, demonstrated some of the language's potential: In the banner-format ad, a Pathfinder-like robot rolls across the Martian surface until it bumps into a monolithic Pepsi can. Using television-style animation and camera moves, the ad is less than 12K. Linda Hahner, founder and president of Out of the Blue, the company that produced the ad, said the Mars mission, in one stroke, made VRML "a done deal." "For the first time ... we don't have to ask, 'Do people want 3D? Do they want streaming animation and sound?' Of course they do."

For now, browsers require a plug-in or a separate VRML application to view VRML ads, but with Netscape and Microsoft pledging their support, that will soon cease to be an issue. Echoing the sentiments of Jupiter's Neufeld, Hahner said she sees streaming and VRML technologies making for a massive shift in how advertising is employed on the Internet. "If you provide Web users with a cool experience, with sound and 3D animation, they'll go and find it. The Mars mission proved that," she said. Hahner says advertising is moving toward trying to draw users in by creating an exciting experience. "Instead of confrontational ads, like we're seeing today ... people will choose to go to ads." The advertisements, she said, will promise the user an interesting, interactive, multimedia experience, and "that is not an artificial promise."

Business Applications and Online Customer Service

A critical reason for one-to-one Web interactivity is return on investment (ROI). Companies need to be doing more with their Web sites in order to justify the cost and acquire more and better customers. Web sites are being integrated into actual business processes, such as customer service and additional services offered only via the Web. While sites have always been considered a marketing function, we will see even more targeted use of the Web for promotions and launches.

Promotion

Now that statistics are becoming available and Web traffic is being analyzed for type and quality of visitor, marketers are more able to target their promotions, ads, and content to fit the needs of the exact "visitor" who is coming to their site. Instead of randomly introducing your message via television to whomever is watching the program, flipping channels, or passing by the TV, on the Web you have a captive audience that comes to visit you at your site. Bingo! They already have an interest in your products. What a perfect opportunity to introduce a new product or service to your audience.

Gap E-nails

The Gap (www.gap.com/gap/gapnews/enailsintro.html) is using its Web site to introduce its newest product, Gap Colors—a new line of nail polish inspired by the colors of the company's fall clothing line. Not only is The Gap deviating from its main bread and butter by getting into a type of product that it doesn't normally carry—cosmetics versus clothing—it is launching it with an interactive fun approach. Customers can select a polish color and paint the fingernails of the model's hand, mix and match colors, and wear different colors on different nails. We are also impressed by The Gap's multicultural foresight that lets the customer change the skin tone of the hand to match those of different nationalities. And, of course, the model's hand starts out wearing this season's hottest color of nail polish, blue.

Kodak Picture Network

The Kodak Picture Network (www.kodak.com/daiHome/kpn/demo/demo.html) is an Internet service that allows members to use the access and distribution power of the Internet to view and share their favorite pictures with family and friends.

Users simply request this service at their nearest participating Kodak Premium Processing retailer. To have the pictures placed on line, customers simply check off the box for Kodak Picture Network on the photo-finishing bag when they drop off their film for processing. When they pick up their prints, they'll also receive a claim number to access their photos on the Internet.

The Kodak Picture Network provides easy access to members' pictures in a password-protected account. When they're on line, members can view them whenever and wherever it's most convenient. They can also add captions to pictures and delete the photos they no longer want to keep.

This is a great value-added service that encourages people to use Kodak film. Plus, it is a really innovative and fun way to use the Web. These days, when many people have family across the country, this is a terrific way to share photos without having the expense of having to get and mail duplicates (that will probably get tossed in a drawer once they've been seen).

One-to-one Web marketers can be inspired by this model to extend themselves to offer more to their customers. Kodak could have easily stayed "within the box" of conventional thinking and said "We make and sell film. Period." But instead, it courageously looked beyond its product to see how it could impact and improve the lives of its customers. Kudos, Kodak! See Figure 2.13 for a look at the Kodak Picture Network demo.

Customer Service

By offering customer service expertise via their corporate Web sites, companies are able to drastically reduce their call volume. At Allen Interactive, we often interview

Figure 2.13 The Kodak Picture Network demo.

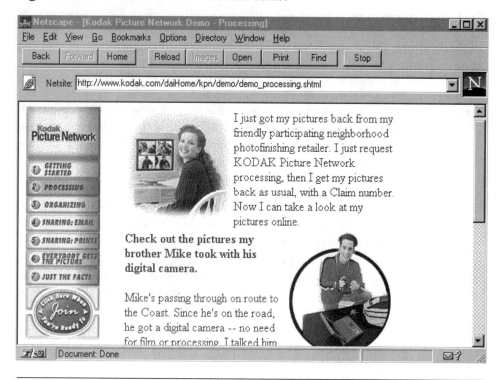

customer service representatives to find out the top 10 most frequently asked questions and then make the recommendation to our clients that they include these FAQs on their sites.

Taking this concept one step further, companies can have online e-mail customer service that guarantees a response within four hours. We think that many people would utilize this service if it were guaranteed that they would get a response. Too often, companies take the turnaround time of e-mails too lightly—requests often get ignored for days. A good rule of thumb is that all e-mails should be responded to with 24 hours. Even if it is just to say, "We've receive your e-mail, we are working on your problem, and one of our representatives will follow up with you today before 5:00 P.M." We have found that customers are willing to wait for days for a solution as long as they know that someone is *working* on it.

Some customers may have a problem but may not have the time to call customer service. Through the use of interactive forms, customers can select questions and enter in scenarios that will then generate a solution and recommendation for them. Companies can offer "chat" areas where clients can enter questions and perhaps get a solution from another customer. These can be monitored by customer service representatives who can post the solution for all to see. These are just a few techniques that can extend the power of phone-based customer service into Internet-based customer service.

Several telephone companies and GTE Corporation are planning Web site redesigns that will add interactivity to their sites. They plan to introduce new database tools, search engines, and back-office systems that will allow customers to seek suggestions on services, find out what is available in their area, check and pay their bills, and order products and services.

"Our paradigm for providing information to customers in the past has been for them to contact us, and then we would have an employee get the information from a database, which meant involving multiple employees," says Sam Taylor, Web presence consultant for BellSouth Corporation (www.bellsouth.com). "We are changing the paradigm so the customer directly—and the employees as well—will be able to access information in many databases with an interface that's intuitive."

GTE is expanding on its ISDN search and purchase feature. Site visitors will be able to enter their zip code to find wireless service availability in their area and receive a listing of the GTE retail locations closest to them. GTE's embellished site will also use intelligent e-mail routing so visitors can send inquiries and get a response from the appropriate source more quickly. GTE expects the new feature to save 24 to 74 hours in processing such inquiries. This new feature of the site is akin to a service GTE's Internet business (www.gte.net) recently put on its site that allows visitors to type in questions and get answers from an existing database of frequently asked questions.

Productivity

The more convenient you, as the one-to-one Web marketer, make it for customers to use your Web site, the better. If customers can order, learn, ask, do, see, hear, and research from the comfort of their homes or offices versus having to drive to a another location, they will.

One-to-one Web marketers should investigate ways to help their clients make their jobs easier. Whether it is ordering a product or conducting a transaction, see how much of the process you can put on the Web—if and only if that is comfortable for your clients. If your customers are not on line yet, offer something so revolutionary that they will want to get on line. We can see grandparents across the world learning how to get on line just to see the latest pictures of their grandchildren on the Kodak Picture Network.

At Web Street Securities (www.webstreetsecurities.com) in the Trading Pit, a stockbroker or home user can buy and sell stocks. This application's uniqueness involves the capability of dynamically showing quote updates from the PC Quote interface. It also can display NASDAQ bids and offers, which are delayed about 30 seconds (see Figure 2.14).

Figure 2.14 Web Street Securities.

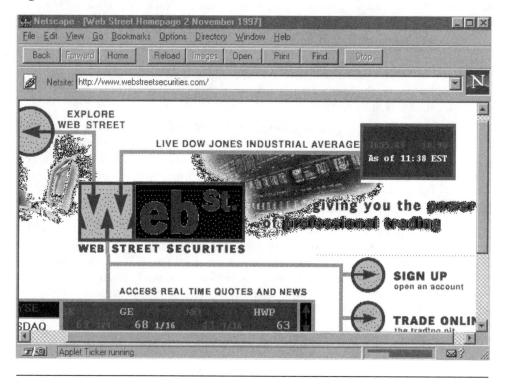

Webisodes

The Webisode. This is one of our favorites and we feel it will be the next wave in Web-based entertainment. A Webisode is an episodic story told via the Web. The content changes on a daily, weekly, or monthly basis. Some Webisodes simply tell a story; however, for the purpose of one-to-one Web interactivity, we are interested in the Webisode in which the users can actually participate and alter the story. This is one-to-one interactivity.

NBC's Thrilogy Profiler Companion Site

"Jack of All Trades" (www.jackotrades.com) is the infamous, fictional serial killer being tracked on the popular NBC series, *Profiler*. Viewers can participate with the lead character from the show to help investigate these crimes. By accessing information on Violent Crimes Task Force personnel, case files, and evidence in an ongoing criminal investigation, the viewer can become a part of the team and help to solve these crimes and apprehend the infamous Jack of All Trades (see Figure 2.15).

Figure 2.15 NBC's *Profiler* TV Show companion site.

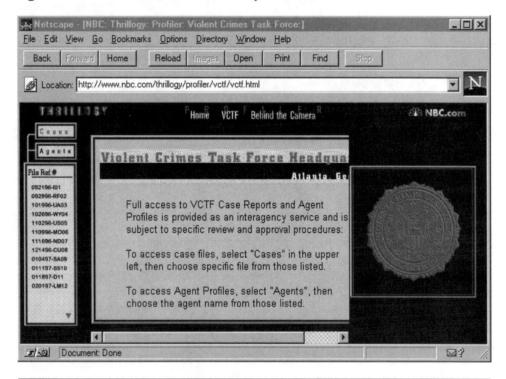

Spangler and Associates

This isn't really a Webisode, but we wanted to mention it in this section because the user is definitely led down a path of discovery. Spangler and Associates (www.spangler.com) is a strategic design and marketing firm. This site is intriguing because the company created an *experience* for its visitors. This experience is simply uncovering information for the user to learn more about the company. By its engaging Shockwave navigations, Spangler allows the user to truly explore its site. The best part of this site is the "Cut to the chase" link of the homepage—for either the bandwidth impaired or those who don't have the time or the patience to explore; users can get everything they need here. Figure 2.16 shows the site's interactive navigation.

Intermercials

You may ask, "What is an intermercial?" We've all heard of infomercials, but intermercial? An *intermercial* is an interactive commercial and on the Web that is an inter-

Figure 2.16 Spangler and Associates' interactive navigation.

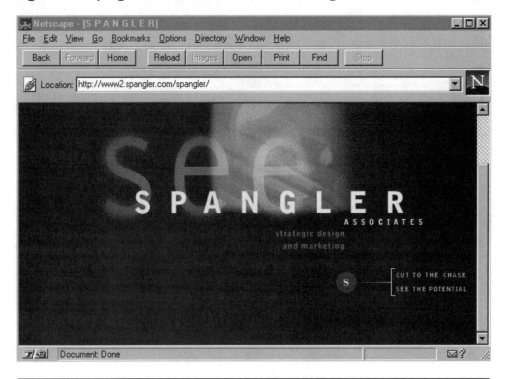

active banner ad. These are banner ads with pulldown menus where users can make selections on the banner and change the path of their click-through.

On AltaVista's homepage, there is a banner ad with the headline, "Is your domain name still available?" Then it has a graphic with *www. your-name.com* (in what looks like a data field box, but is fake) and a Submit button that says, "Secure it instantly online!" This ad is for Webcow.com, and it has the right idea but fails to execute it correctly. Wouldn't it be cool if you could fill in your-name.com and hit the Submit button and have it really go check in InterNIC and see if it is available? Then, if it were, Webcow could say, "Would you like us to register your-name.com for you? It will only cost you $39."

One of the first companies to implement the intermercial was AT&T. AT&T implemented an interactive advertising strategy for its Olympic Games Web site (www.olympic.att.com) for the 1996 games in Atlanta. These intermercials, via Java, Shockwave, QTVR, and HTML forms, provided online users with 20- to 30-second bursts of interactivity. The ads enabled Web users to access AT&T's Online Games, view live video feeds of AT&T's Global Olympic Village in Atlanta, and take a virtual tour of the Olympic Museum—all without having to leave their existing session. This nearly tripled traffic to the AT&T Web site.

Transparent access to fully interactive animated ads without a plug-in? The Enliven Client is the first cross-platform solution for robust ad delivery. You automatically download the Enliven Client (about 20K) as a Java applet the first time you play an Enliven ad. After that, you reuse the Enliven Client every time you play Enliven—no need to download again.

A Macromedia Director Xtra is available to qualified developers for converting Director 5.0 ad content to Enliven format for streaming over the Internet. Creating Enliven ads is as simple as "Save as Enliven" from the Director 5.0 menu.

Jupiter Predicts the Future of Intermercials

According to a new report from research firm Jupiter Communications, by the year 2001, advertisers will dedicate, on average, one-quarter of their budgets to each of these two emerging models. One-quarter will go to banners, which currently represent 80 percent of online ad spending. "Banners—mainly interactive ones—will remain a big part of the media mix," said Peter Storck, director of Jupiter's Online Advertising Group. "But as sponsorship and interstitial opportunities emerge, advertisers are going to take to these models; they'll spend more freely, and that will be welcome relief for leading publishers."

Jupiter predicts that 5- to 10-second animated interstitials (what Jupiter calls "intermercials")—limited mainly to push platforms so far—will be commonplace on the Web by 1999. Advertisers will be drawn to the intrusive nature and high branding potential of intermercials.

The report predicts that the media buys of savvy advertisers will also increasingly center on deals to cobrand content with well-matched publishers, mainly in the form of sponsorships. Jupiter names three factors that will drive advertisers toward this model: return-on-investment (ROI) pressure, the unprecedented accountability of online media buys, and the desire to connect more deeply with consumers than unclicked banners allow.

As for ad content—ad material a consumer clicks to—Jupiter predicts that shrewd advertisers will increasingly "nest" it on publishers' sites, in microsites, and in banners themselves. As advertisers find that nested ad content can result in more, and deeper, user engagement than content on their own Web sites, they will increasingly turn toward it.

Additional Web Interactivity Resources

The Shockzone   www.macromedia.com/shockzone

The DHTML Zone   www.dhtmlzone.com/

The Future of One-to-One Web Interactivity

The future of one-to-one Web interactivity is going to be very exciting. More bandwidth will allow for more complex and advanced interactivity. More tracking and analysis breadth will allow us to tabulate the results of these activities, causing more big businesses to invest in research and development and making willing to be the early adopters of these methods and to "step up to the plate."

Web users will have active participation with serious content. Marketers will be able to make predictive versus assumptive recommendations based on previous knowledge they have on their clients. There will be intelligent shopping carts that help users choose what to buy. The carts will make predictions and recommendations based on the information in the user's profile.

Students will be across the globe but still sitting beside each other in their electronic classrooms. Ad agencies will be well versed in intermercials. Big businesses will be investing heavily in online advertising.

 See Jupiter's predictions in the case study, "One-to-One Web Interactivity," on this book's companion Web site.

Chapter 3 discusses the one-to-one marketing capabilities of e-mail. E-mail can be an effective tool to pull users back to your Web site and remind customers to do business with you. E-mail products are evolving to incorporate personalization and database technologies in order to send a different e-mail to each customer. The chapter also provides information on the benefits of advertising in other organization's e-mail newsletters or services.

ONE-TO-ONE E-MAIL

"The marketer's mindset should always be to evaluate the value proposition from the perspective of the user."

John Funk, Founder of Mercury Mail and InfoBeat

E-mail is the most popular Internet activity. There are more people with access to e-mail than with access to the World Wide Web. E-mail marketing can go out and grab the users' and customers' attention and interest without requiring them to even start their Web browser. In fact, most of the newer e-mail systems support hyperlinks within the e-mail message that launch the browser and connect the user directly to the relevant site or page. Even more exciting is the new support for HTML that makes e-mail messages look a lot like what would be seen in the browser, with hyperlinks, graphics, and even multimedia.

Of course, like many Internet-related technologies, there is some controversy, which, in this case, can be summed up in one word: *spam* (and we're not talking about lunch). Spam is unsolicited e-mail broadcasts that are indiscriminate, untargeted, bandwidth-unfriendly, and almost 100 percent of the time unwelcome.

Here are a few e-mail statistics, courtesy of Michael Tchong's *ICONOCAST E-Mail Newsletter*, that will whet any e-marketers appetite:

- There are over 60 million people worldwide sending over 1 billion e-mail messages per month.

- Forrester Research (www.forrester.com) predicts that there will be more than 135 million people in the United States who will communicate via e-mail by the year 2001—almost half of the country's population.

- The 1997 *Computer Industry Almanac* predicts the number of people with Internet access will grow to 450 million users at the turn of the century.

Interesting e-mail factoids:

- Telephone directory companies now offer services that let people include their e-mail addresses alongside their standard telephone listing.

  On the flip side:

- According to the seventh GVU survey (www.cc.gatech.edu/gvu/user_surveys/), 61 percent of respondents delete spam without reading the message, 19 percent ask to be removed from the list, 11 percent actually read the e-mail, and 5 percent retaliate against the spammer.

- There is a healthy debate among industry, users, and government organizations on setting guidelines for e-mail broadcasting.

- There are many organizations forming to heighten awareness about spam, such as Junkmail and The Coalition Against Unsolicited Commercial E-Mail, and some cyberactivists have resorted to more drastic measures, such as blocking newsgroup postings. Take a look at the plethora of anti-spam organizations and resources at this location on Yahoo!: www.yahoo.com/Computers_and_Internet/Communications_and_Networking /Electronic_Mail/Junk_Email/.

- Software products are being created to filter messages from known e-mail solicitors, such as Softwiz's SPAM Attack Pro (www.softwiz.com). There are also services that help people remove their names from e-mail marketing lists.

The controversy over spam has made e-mail marketing an uphill battle for Web marketers. It will be interesting to see what happens over the next couple of years. Many people are advocating that the Internet industry self-regulate before the government does. E-mail can be a great tool for one-to-one Web marketers to use to form lasting relationships with customers. E-mail can also play a useful role in customer service. In order to make sure this tool becomes an accepted medium, marketers should listen to their users and customers when it comes to their opinions and preferences regarding e-mail. This chapter covers the fine and delicate art of using e-mail, which can be a very effective and efficient electronic marketing tool.

Benefits of One-to-One E-Mail

In their book, *The One to One Future* (1993, Doubleday), Don Peppers and Martha Rogers stated that one-to-one media is "individually addressable." Internet technology, such as e-mail, has evolved to become individually addressable via personalization and customization. E-mail makes it easier and cheaper to communicate with users, prospects, and customers. The primary benefits of one-to-one e-mail include its ability to form a lasting relationship with a customer, increase repeat purchases or visits, and provide an inexpensive "push" mechanism where the information is pushed out to the user, rather than requiring the user to remember to come visit your Web site.

Forming Relationships with Customers

E-mail broadcasts and one-to-one personalized e-mails enhance a Web marketer's ability to form loyal, long-lasting relationships with customers through personalized dialog. The more you know about your customers, the easier it is to provide them with the things they value.

The Electronic Newsstand (www.enews.com) is the ultimate resource for magazine information and subscriptions on the Web. The site's personalized e-mail news service, Ny newsstand, uses cutting-edge push technology to provide users with customized, value-added content. Electronic Newsstand customers may choose to monitor as many of the 25 channels as they wish. Each channel is delivered on the same day each week for example, Business every Monday, Sports every Friday, and so forth.

In addition to servicing Newsstand users, the e-mail service benefits advertising sponsors more than traditional banner advertising for the following reasons:

- Sponsors can target ads to users that match specific demographic profiles.

- E-mail dispatches are delivered only to users who request them.

- Dispatches are delivered directly to a user's in-box as a distinct message. In contrast, a banner ad is easily lost among the many items compete for a user's attention on a Web page.

- Most e-mail platforms now let users click on a URL in an e-mail message and link directly to a corresponding Web page.

My Newsstand also helps the Electronic Newsstand attract and retain customers and reminds users to visit the site regularly. In addition, the service is a powerful user-relations tool. For example, the marketing staff at the Electronic Newsstand used the service to recontact users and reestablish interest in the service. Those who replied via e-mail were sent all news services, Newsstand Notes (a weekly update telling "What's New") and a free promotional Electronic Newstand mug. The promotion had a 40-percent response rate and the Electronic Newsstand increased their e-mail delivery by nearly 50 percent. Figure 3.1 shows an Enews by Email message.

In addition to building customer relations, e-mail marketing can also help you compete more effectively. Since we are all feeling the pinch of time, we only have enough capacity to spend time on Web sites that provide us with the most value. Therefore, if a customer highly values your e-mail service, he or she will spend more time with you and less with your competitor. If you are a practicing one-to-one Web marketer, then you have a powerful tool to enhance your competitive position. In their second best-selling book, *Enterprise One to One* (1997), Don Peppers and Martha Rogers

Figure 3.1 Electronic Newsstand's Enews by E-Mail service.

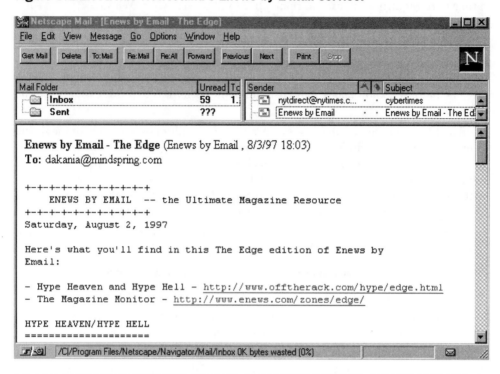

postulate "Give your customer the opportunity to teach you what he wants. Remember it, give it back to him, and keep his business forever."

Peppers and Rogers believe that when customers invest time in customizing your offering to their liking, they will continue to invest additional time. One-to-one e-mail can mimic a personalized sales call, which is the most effective one-to-one communication. A sales visit to a customer is the most expensive way to acquire or maintain a customer. E-mail is a highly effective alternative and is relatively low in cost.

Increasing Repeat Customer Visits or Purchases

As the familiar saying goes, "If you build it, they will come." As we Web site owners know, however, this is simply not true. Now, with e-mail: If you tell them to come, they will come. If your site provides a valued experience or service for customers, and you send them periodic e-mails, you will increase repeat visits by these customers—especially with hyperlinks embedded in the e-mail message. Of course, the e-mails must provide value

Figure 3.2 Quote.com's QNews e-mail service.

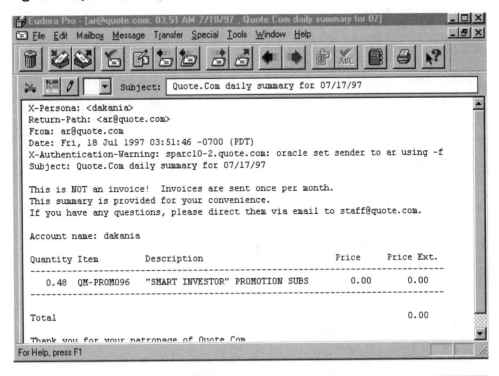

```
Eudora Pro - [ar@quote.com, 03:51 AM 7/18/97 , Quote.Com daily summary for 07]     _ |□| ×
File  Edit  Mailbox  Message  Transfer  Special  Tools  Window  Help                _ |&| ×

Subject:  Quote.Com daily summary for 07/17/97

X-Persona: <dakania>
Return-Path: <ar@quote.com>
From: ar@quote.com
Date: Fri, 18 Jul 1997 03:51:46 -0700 (PDT)
X-Authentication-Warning: sparc10-2.quote.com: oracle set sender to ar using -f
Subject: Quote.Com daily summary for 07/17/97

This is NOT an invoice!  Invoices are sent once per month.
This summary is provided for your convenience.
If you have any questions, please direct them via email to staff@quote.com.

Account name: dakania

Quantity Item        Description                           Price    Price Ext.
-----------------------------------------------------------------------------
   0.48  QM-PROMO96   "SMART INVESTOR" PROMOTION SUBS        0.00      0.00
-----------------------------------------------------------------------------

Total                                                                 0.00

Thank you for your patronage of Quote.Com

For Help, press F1
```

as well, or customers will not sign up to receive it or will remove themselves from the list. With the increasing number of Web sites still vying for the small, albeit quickly growing, universe of online users and customers, experienced Web marketers know they need to provide a value-added service like e-mail to get people to continue to visit their site.

In 1994, Quote.com (www.quote.com) began as the first online financial information service, and now has 1.5 million visitors per day. It offers QNews to its users, a subscription-based personalized news service that delivers news from more than 500 sources based on a customer's financial portfolio. Users can also select how often to receive the e-mail reports in real time: on the hour, or at the beginning or end of the trading day. Chris Cooper, Quote.com's founder, believes that many of their customers would cancel their service if the e-mail service was no longer provided. Quote.com also sends e-mails to all registered users, in addition to those who have signed up for QNews, once every two months with information about promotions. Figure 3.2 shows an e-mail from the QNews e-mail news service.

Figure 3.3 Dummies Daily HTML-based e-mail loaded with computer tips, hyperlinks, and advertisements.

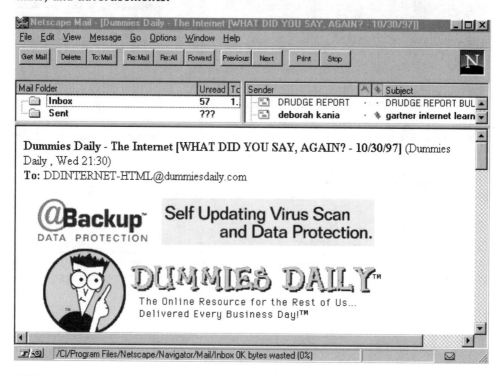

Providing an Effective "Push" Mechanism

E-mail can be used as a cost-effective alternative to implementing a push technology. Push technologies allow you to *push* information, advertising, and other content out to a customer without requiring the user to visit your site to get the content. The benefit of push is that it can *pull* customers to your site and company. E-mail can be used as a push mechanism to serve as a reminder and build relationships with customers. (See Chapter 5, "One-to-One Push," for an in-depth discussion of push technology.)

TipWorld (www.tipworld.com) is one of the most popular Web sites on the Internet. The *TipWorld* newsletter comes in text- or HTML-based e-mails that serve over 1.2 million subscribers. TipWorld is part of PC World Online Services, which also created the Dummies Daily e-mail news service based on the best-selling "Dummies" book series. Users have several to choose from: Dummies Daily Microsoft Word 97, Dummies Daily Microsoft Excel 97, Dummies Daily The Internet, Dummies Daily Computing Basics, Dummies Daily Quicken, and Dummies Daily Web After Five. The

Dummies Daily e-mails "push" information to computer users who want to learn more about almost any computing topic. A sample of Dummies Daily's HTML-based e-mail is shown in Figure 3.3.

In the article, "Casting Your Fate with E-Mail," in *PC Week* (April 1997), Jesse Berst promoted e-mail as the best push method for the time being for these reasons:

Broadest reach. At least 70 million people already have e-mail. PointCast (the most successful push channel) has just over 1 million users.

Nothing new required. Most push services require the installation of a special client on every single desktop machine.

Bandwidth forgiving. Most e-mail downloads happen in the background, so even large messages can be delivered without penalty to the end user.

Nonintrusive. Studies show the average white-collar worker gets interrupted six dozen times per day by calls and co-workers. Most push services add to this burden by interrupting the user every time something new arrives. By contrast, e-mail sits in an in-box until someone is ready to read it.

At the same time, Rob Enderle, an analyst for Giga Information Group (www.gigaweb.com), says that e-mail and push each provide their own "value metaphor." E-mail has the ability to be more widely accepted by advertisers as a push mechanism because it can provide a better ability to target specific users, even to the point of one-to-one marketing, whereas push is best for a more mass-marketing model.

The Spam Controversy

Spam. It could be the undoing of e-mail. E-mail marketing could be a short-lived marketing method if the Internet industry doesn't take steps toward self-regulating. Spam is unsolicited commercial e-mail that is broadcast to many people without their consent. Why is it called spam? The term reportedly comes from a Monty Python skit in which the word "spam," referring to the canned-meat product, was repeated continually. The word was used within the Usenet newsgroups when one posting was sent to many people.

Bulk e-mailers like Cyber Promotions (www.cyberpromotions.com) and Quantum (www.quantumcomm.com) were sued by Internet Service Providers (ISPs) for sending unsolicited commercial e-mail. Much of the controversy comes from these companies "harvesting" e-mail addresses from newsgroups, Web pages, and other sources, and reselling the names to marketers. This is all done without the knowledge of the e-mail address owner. The other issue is that ISPs have to deal with disgruntled customers who receive the e-mail, as well as network traffic problems when the mass e-mailings are broadcast. E-mail list brokers, ISPs, trade organizations, consumer groups, and the Federal Trade Commission (www.ftc.gov) are working together to form guidelines that will protect users from receiving unwanted spam yet allow e-mail to become a legitimate online marketing tool.

A survey by World Research (www.survey.com) confirmed the concern users have about unsolicited commercial e-mail. Two-thirds of the respondents were in favor of regulation of spam. Only 7 percent said they "loved" junk e-mails or found them useful. If this survey reflects public opinion, then it is a strong indication that e-mail marketing should be conducted with guidelines set by the e-mail marketing industry. If e-mail marketing is to be accepted, Web marketers should consider practicing these guidelines suggested by industry advocates and organizations:

- Put the word "advertisement" in the subject line of the e-mail.

- Disclose the sender of the e-mail.

- Allow users to get off the e-mail marketing list easily. Include a hyperlink or instructions on how users can remove themselves from the list or "opt-out" from future mailings.

- Do not sell the e-mail list to another marketer without the user's consent.

Organizations and companies have now put services into place to help online users filter out spam and remove themselves from bulk e-mail lists. Mindspring (www.mindspring.com), an ISP, offers a free e-mail filtering to its subscribers called the "Spaminator." This filter checks against a database of known spammers and blocks the e-mail before it gets to the user's e-mailbox.

Some Trade and Anti-Spam Organizations Dedicated to the Spam and E-Mail Marketing Issues

- Direct Marketing Association (www.the-dma.org) is known for setting consumer-friendly guidelines for physical direct mail and is now participating in efforts to set standards for e-mail marketing, including a preference service, the e-Mail Preference Service (e-MPS), for people to put themselves on a list of users who prefer not to receive e-mail solicitations.

- Internet E-Mail Marketing Council (www.iemmc.org) was formed by well-known, bulk e-mail service companies Cyber Promo, CyberTize EMail Inc., Integrated Media Promotion Corp., Internet Savings Group, and Quantum. The association is "dedicated to promoting the responsible and ethical use of direct e-mail as a marketing tool on the Internet."

- Junkmail.org (www.junkmail.org) was created and is maintained by the

---

Center for Democracy and Technology (www.cdt.org) and the Voters
Telecommunications Watch (www.vtw.org/uce).

- The Coalition Against Unsolicited Commercial E-Mail (www.cauce.org) was
formed by a group of Internet users whose purpose is to promote legislation that amends 47 USC 227, the section of U.S. law that bans junk fax-
ing, to also include junk e-mail.

- Spam Media Tracker (www-fofa.concordia.ca/spam/news.shtml) is a collection of news stories and articles written about spam.

Opt-In or Opt-Out?

Rosalind Resnick is president of NetCreations, Inc. (www.netcreations.com) and also a
leading advocate for allowing users to "opt-in" or choose to receive e-mail advertisements. Her company provides the PostMaster Direct Response service that allows marketers to send messages to targeted e-mail lists that are "100 percent opt-in." Opt-in
is different from opt-out in that opt-out sends e-mails without the consent of the user
and puts the burden on the user to remove him- or herself from the list, which can
sometimes be a very arduous task. Opt-out is a good practice, but opt-in may turn out
to be more rewarding for you and your customers. Here is an adaptation of a story in
one of Ms. Resnick's *Digital Direct Marketing* letters regarding key techniques for successful e-mail campaigns:

Let recipients "opt-in" before they "opt-out." The most "politically correct" way to build an Internet marketing list is to allow users to come to
your Web site and sign up voluntarily to receive e-mail about particular topics, and then give them a chance to get off the list every time you send them
a message.

Send recipients only information that they signed up to receive. Marketers
have the responsibility to send only the information requested by the user.

Give your recipients value. No matter how politically correct your system,
commercial e-mail takes up recipients' time and bandwidth. Also provide
incentives to join the list, such as a coupon or a giveaway.

> **TIP** For the benefit of both you and the user, recipients of e-mail should be
> given the ability to get off your e-mailing list. This will save you the cost
> of e-mailing messages to people who will never visit your Web site or buy
> products from your company.

How to Conduct Your Own E-Mail Marketing

"...the reality is that millions of us willingly accept advertisements when they serve our purposes."

Robert Seidman, Editor-at-Large, from "E-mail, the Ugly Duckling of E-Commerce," *NetGuide Magazine*

E-mails can be a powerful way to strengthen the bond between you and your users or customers. In order to accomplish this you will want to provide e-mail notifications or newsletters that have the primary objective of informing rather than selling. Building relationships with your audience or customers is not a short-term objective, so the horizon for payoff on this endeavor should be a long one. Here is a step-by-step approach for creating and broadcasting e-mail messages:

1. **Determine goals for the mailing**. Do you want to increase brand awareness, encourage sales transactions, provide an information service, conduct a loyalty program, provide another outlet for your advertisers, and so forth?

2. **Develop key information topics**. These can be editorial or editorial plus advertising or sponsorship.

3. **Develop a plan**. Determine period, process, and people.

4. **Promote a new service**. Offer something new and unique on your site and on the Web.

5. **Include "calls to action" in e-mail text**. These could be promotions, feedback, surveys, and so forth.

6. **Reinvent your e-mail service as necessary**. Do not forget to provide customers with a way to give you feedback.

> **TIP** "You have to make the messages interesting and informative, not just sales pitches. You can't send them too often (once a week is too often, every 2–3 weeks is probably about right). Links within the e-mail that take people to relevant pages work well and encourage people to get more information."
>
> Cyndy Ainsworth, Virual Vineyards (www.virtualvin.com)

In a June 1997 *Marketing Tools* magazine article (www.marketingtools.com), it was reported that IDG List services (www.idglist.com) created successful e-mail marketing campaigns based on four components:

Opt-out. New subscribers are given an opportunity to exclude themselves from the e-mail rental list as part of the registration process.

Source notification. A header appears in each e-mail transmission that identifies who is sending the message. At the end of the message, recipients are told how to get off the mailing list.

Relevancy. Only material relevant to the audience is sent. All messages are approved by the list owner.

E-mail provider. All list renters are required to use IDG's e-mail service provider, ensuring list security and minimizing the risk to the advertiser.

How to Write Direct E-Mail

As you are already aware, the Internet is a whole new marketing medium that requires a special way to communicate in order to be effective. If you do not want your e-mail to be discarded before it is even read, some care needs to be taken when writing e-mail messages or newsletters.

There are two main components to e-mails: the subject line and the body. Each component requires a particular style of writing. The subject line is much like an advertising headline or the first line in a letter. The body of the message is where you convey information and entice readers to take action. The body of the message will not be read if the subject line doesn't motivate the recipient to open the message.

Writing Effective Subject Lines

With the controversy over spam, one idea e-mail marketers have is to put the word "advertisement" in all unsolicited commercial e-mail. Insight Direct (www.insight.com), a pioneering online computer superstore, sends out e-mail notices that identify themselves as advertisements. Here is a sample:

```
**AD** Do these prices make you go "Hummmm"?
**AD** Can you find a better deal?
```

There is a fear among marketers that putting the word "ad" or "advertisement" in the subject line of an e-mail will ensure that no one will read your message. If you provide a valued service to your customers, then they will read nearly all the e-mail messages you send to them. If the message is not an unsolicited commercial e-mail (i.e., customers have signed up for or elected to receive the e-mails), then you do not need to identify the e-mail as an advertisement. However, you will still need to provide the recipient with an intriguing and/or informational subject line. In his book, *Cyberwriting* (1997, Amacom), Joe Vitale offers these suggestions:

*   The subject line needs to serve as a powerful headline. Think of what would interest readers.

- Don't come across as too sales-oriented.

- The safest bet is to use a benefit headline.

- Use your "Unique Selling Proposition." How does your product or service differ from your competition's?

- If something is new, put "New" in the subject line.

- Be specific and don't tease people with empty phrases.

- Use emotional words.

- Be relevant.

Here are examples of some effective subject lines:

Earn $50,000 in 5 hours.	PostMaster Direct teaser to promote a service.
Dummies Daily The Internet	Dummies Daily E-Mail Service, identifying who sent the message.
[THE KEY TO A SAFER WORLD—7/31/97]	The e-mail and a lead for a feature story. This works well when the user signs up to receive the e-mails.
Win a $20,000 Trip	The New York Times Direct. Who wouldn't open this e-mail?
New Product Gossip of the Day	TipWorld, an e-mail service for computer enthusiasts.

Writing Effective E-Mail Messages

The body of the e-mail message should be concise. If you are providing news on several topics, then dedicate a paragraph for each. If the message has a single purpose, then make the message brief, using several paragraphs. Here are some things to consider when writing e-mail:

Write according to your marketing communications objective. Is it a direct-response promotion? Informational news and tips? Teaser? Survey? Each type of communication requires a different "voice." For example, a teaser would have text that is vague and intriguing, whereas informational tips would be very factual and short. In all cases, your objective should be to get users to act on the e-mail, and the e-mail should be worth every minute of your audience's very valuable time.

Be sensitive to your audience. Is the e-mail targeted to consumers? Business professionals? Men? Women? Youths? Remember that your audience is now from all corners of the world. Be careful when using humor; it doesn't translate well in the writing, especially when used in our global marketplace.

People read in a different way on the computer than when they read a book or newspaper. Users typically scan when they read on line, versus taking the time to read an article in a magazine from start to finish. E-mail text should be short in length and narrow in width.

Figure 3.4 shows an excerpt from C|Net's *Digital Dispatch* (www.cnet.com), a weekly newsletter that is sent to more than 850,000 recipients. C|Net is an experienced distributor of e-mail newsletters. Since their e-mails are longer, they provide a useful table of contents.

Here are some helpful writing resources from the Internet:

Style Guide for E-mail	www.dse.vic.gov.au/style.htm
The Copywriting Profit Center	www.mrfire.com/Knowledge/Copywriting/index.html
Electric Pages	www.electric-pages.com

Four Steps to E-Mail That Gets Read

Mike Adams, President

Arial Software

www.arialsoftware.com

1. Don't let your e-mail be mistaken for spam. Imply or state why the recipient is getting the e-mail.

2. Include personal information. Personalized e-mails provide a unique message to each user, which gives recipients a feeling that they are receiving personal attention.

3. Make it easy for recipients to remove themselves from your mailing list. Do not waste precious time and marketing dollars on people who are no longer part of your target market.

4. Provide an easy course of action. Include a "mailto:" and Web site URL address to increase response rates.

*Warning: Excessive E-Mail Can Be Hazardous to Your Customer's Health and to Your
Marketing Budget*

With the information overload most of us are experiencing, one-to-one Web marketers
should help to alleviate this problem rather than add to it. A study by the Electronic
Messaging Association (www.ema.org) found that more than 70 percent of workers felt
overwhelmed by the amount of e-mail received each day—office workers send and
receive an average of 178 e-mails per day. A study by the Institute for the Future
(www.iftf.org) predicts that more than 7 trillion e-mail messages will be sent annually
by the year 2000.

In David Shenk's book, *Data Smog* (1997, HarperCollins), he states that we all benefit from the increasing availability and accessibility of information, but we can also
suffer from having too much. As human beings, we have a limit to our capacity of
receiving and processing information. Mr. Shenk believes:

> *"At a certain level of input, the law of diminishing returns takes effect;
> the glut of information no longer adds to our quality of life, but instead
> begins to cultivate stress, confusion, and even ignorance."*

In order to avoid creating messages that will get tossed out—much like the junk
mail that arrives in all of our mailboxes—you should be sensitive to your customers'
or users' capacity for information. You want to make sure that your information or
marketing messages are providing value to your customers. By doing this, you will
enhance your communications with customers, which in turn will help you meet your
marketing, sales, or other goals associated with your e-mail marketing endeavors.

Although e-mail marketing can be conducted at a very reasonable cost, continuing
to send e-mail to users who do not value them is a waste of time and marketing
budget.

One-to-One E-Mail Applications

E-mail marketing is a new field, gaining rapid acceptance. E-mail can range from one-
to-many applications to one-to-one applications that are integrated with customer
databases. Following is a discussion of ways to create your own e-mail marketing system for your Web site, and what e-mail advertising options are available to promote
your site, your company, and your products.

Managing Your Own Mailing List Server

Although not precisely a one-to-one Web marketing method, a mailing list server is a
relatively inexpensive tool that enables you to build ongoing relationships with your
online constituents. Even with its one-to-many orientation, a mailing list server can be
an effective marketing tool. Some mailing list server software products are free and

Figure 3.4 A sample of ClNet's Digital Dispatch.

```
X-Persona: <dakania>
Return-Path: <owner-dispatch@DISPATCH.CNET.COM>
Approved-By: dispatch@CNET.COM
Approved-By:  CNET Digital Dispatch <dispatch@CNET.COM>
Date:         Thu, 7 Aug 1997 15:27:29 -0700
Reply-To: dispatch-faq@CNET.com
Sender: CNET Digital Dispatch <DISPATCH@DISPATCH.CNET.COM>
From: CNET Digital Dispatch <dispatch@CNET.com>
Subject:      CNET Digital Dispatch, August 7, 1997: email, e-com-
merce,
              and Apple
To: Multiple recipients of list DISPATCH <DISPATCH@DISPATCH.CNET.COM>


CNET Digital Dispatch: email, e-commerce, and Apple
August 7, 1997
more than 850,000 subscribers


This week on CNET:
1.   Email clients
2.   What is e-commerce?
3.   As the Macworld turns
4.   New product reviews
5.   Glaser: fun with you-know-who
6.   BUILDER.COM: designing for differences
7.   GAMECENTER.COM: 3D games
8.   CNET TV: cyberstalking; U2 on tour; and the Free Tibet Webcast
9.   EVENTS.COM: Lollapalooza; San Jose Jazz Festival
10.  DOWNLOAD.COM: learn how to chat
11.  "Your turn": does Microsoft compete unfairly?
12.  Top ten reasons Microsoft invested $150 million in Apple
13.  Jobs!
14.  Subscribe and unsubscribe
15.  Coming soon: Snap! Online


Copyright 1997 CNET, Inc. All rights reserved.
```

the rest are very reasonably priced, especially considering their enhanced features and ease of use.

Figure 3.5 iVillage's AboutWork Web site.

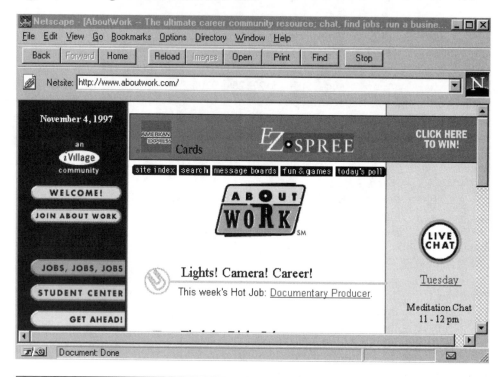

A mailing list server allows you to keep a regular dialog with your Web site visitors or customers. By sending out periodic e-mail notices or e-mail newsletters, your customers will be reminded that your Web site is still out there in cyberspace. Periodic mailings can help "pull" customers to your Web site on a regular basis. Since customers must choose to sign up to receive the electronic mailings, they are less likely to look at these messages as unsolicited e-mail or spam—especially if the information provided is of value to the recipient.

AboutWork (www.aboutwork.com), one of iVillage's (www.ivillage.com) advertiser-supported online communities, is a collection of popular Web communities. AboutWork is a meeting place for people who want to find and share information about jobs, career planning, working at home, starting a business, and other related subjects. AboutWork uses the Majordomo list server (a discussion about Majordomo list servers is covered later in this chapter) to allow online participants to sign up for AboutWork News, a weekly e-mail newsletter. The e-mail newsletter contains information, advertising, and polls, and is attached to the discussion groups.

Figure 3.6 Typical mailing list server system.

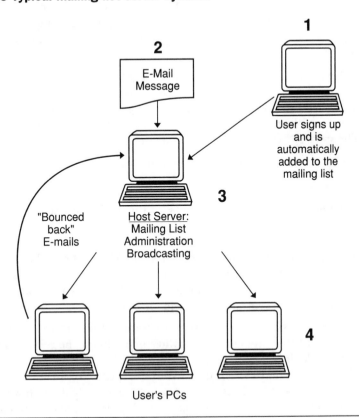

The marketers at AboutWork ask for personal information from users as they sign up such as personal interests, income, Web habits, and so forth. Although AboutWork News does not use the information to personalize the e-mails (this functionality is coming), this practice of collecting information is useful in order to learn more about the users of the site and provide advertisers with meaningful information. They determine programming and content for the audience, as well as the types of customers they should promote and attract to the Web site. Figure 3.5 shows the AboutWork homepage.

Technology Overview

Mailing list server programs automate the management of Internet mailing lists. If you have hundreds or thousands of customers, a list server will save you a lot of time. The mailing list software allows you to broadcast one e-mail message to many people simultaneously. There are several mailing list software applications available that support Unix, Windows NT, Windows 95, and Macintosh server platforms. If you want to implement and manage the system yourself, some programming skills may be required, as well as some knowledge of operating systems, Web servers, and programming languages.

Once you have selected a mailing list server program, you will need to determine if you will host it on your server, with your ISP, or with a mailing list hosting service. If you do not have a dedicated server to host the mailing list yourself, contact your ISP to host the list for you. When the system is set up, it will typically function as shown in Figure 3.6. The steps associated with the mailing list process are

1. Users sign up for the e-mail notifications or newsletters.

2. You construct the e-mail message.

3. The e-mail message is sent to the address for the mailing list server.

4. The e-mail message is broadcast to all users.

When the user signs up to receive e-mails from a Web site, he or she submits an e-mail address to the site via an e-mail message or online form. The list server automatically adds the user to the mailing list database and sends a confirmation e-mail to the user. Figure 3.7 shows a typical confirmation notice.

When an e-mail message or newsletter is created, it is sent to the list address and is broadcast to all Web site customers who signed up for the service. Figure 3.8 is an excerpt from iVillage's *AboutWork News* e-mail message that is sent weekly to subscribers. You will see that hyperlinks to Web site URLs are included in the message. This is a useful way to pull users to your site, especially if you have a promotion where you would like a high rate of response. Hyperlinks and e-mail addresses that are embedded inside e-mails make it easy for the user and increase the likelihood of response. Not all e-mail programs support embedded hyperlinks, so you will need to instruct users to copy and paste, or enter, the link into their Web browsers. You will also notice that the e-mail contains several small "sound bites" of information. This approach is user friendly in that it doesn't require a lot of download time, which can be frustrating to users and to information system or network administrators.

AboutWork News is broadcast to more than 175,000 users on a weekly basis via e-mail through Hotmail (www.hotmail.com), Netscape's Inbox Direct (www.netscape.com), and America Online. According to Michael Rose, iVillage's director of marketing, the e-mail newsletter is a customer retention tool that provides them with significant click-through results from users linking directly from the e-mail to the Web site.

Figure 3.7 iVillage's AboutWork News mailing list subscription confirmation.

```
X-Persona: <dakania>
Return-Path: <owner-aboutworknews@xanadu.ivillage.com>
Date: Sun, 27 Jul 1997 16:39:56 -0400 (EDT)
To: dakania@mindspring.com
From: Majordomo@ivillage.com
Subject: Welcome to aboutworknews
Reply-To: Majordomo@ivillage.com
```

Welcome to the aboutworknews mailing list! Please save this message for future reference. Thank you. If you ever want to remove yourself from this mailing list, you can send mail to Majordomo@xanadu.ivillage.com with the following command in the body of your email message:

unsubscribe aboutworknews dakania@mindspring.com

Here's the general information for the list you've subscribed to, in case you don't already have it: Thank you for taking the first steps to joining the About Work Community. Expect to receive a weekly newsletter containing information on what's new at About Work. www.aboutwork.com

Costs and Benefits of a Mailing List Server

Mailing list software costs can range from free to a few thousand dollars. The additional Web server usage and traffic will also add to the cost of your site operations. Add to that the human resources required to manage the system and write the editorial and marketing copy. Virtual Vineyards (www.virtualvin.com), a pioneering and leading online merchant that specializes in wine, food, and gifts, provides an e-mail notification service. They state that the cost to implement was minimal and they have achieved their goal of building community, reminding customers of offerings and building confidence among patrons regarding recommendations from Peter Granoff, Virtual Vineyards' wine expert, proprietor, cofounder and general manager. Mr. Granoff personally writes the e-mail notifications that are sent using an automated mailing list server.

If your goal is to form lasting relationships with your Web audience or customers, a mailing list will enhance your ability to achieve this goal, at a reasonable expense. What is particularly nice about mailing lists is that you can measure its success very easily. A successful list keeps growing, one user at a time. If people do not find your e-mailings

Figure 3.8 iVillage's AboutWork News weekly e-mailing.

```
X-Persona: <dakania>
Return-Path: <owner-aboutworknews@ivillage.com>
Date: Mon, 06 Oct 1997 14:56:20 -0500
From: AboutWork <awmail@ivillage.com>
Reply-To: awmail@ivillage.com
Organization: iVillage, Inc.
To: aboutworknews@ivillage.com
Subject: AboutWork News
Sender: owner-aboutworknews@ivillage.com
Reply-To: awmail@ivillage.com
AboutWork News-October 6, 1997
<TO UNSUBSCRIBE SEE END OF MAIL>
*-*-*-*-*-*-*-*-*-*-*-*-*-*-*-*-*-*-*-*-*-*-*-*-*-*-*-
AboutWork Poll
(Where Your Vote Counts)
In order to work well with others, what quality is it most important
to possess?
Go Vote!
www.aboutwork.com/newspoll
*-*-*-*-*-*-*-*-*-*-*-*-*-*-*-*-*-*-*-*-*-*-*-*-*-*-*-
Job Tip of the Week
"Working on a team that's spread out over several locations? Make
sure to meet in person at least once. Yes, I know all about how well
videoconferencing can work (not that it's ever worked perfectly in
any meeting I've been in), but nothing substitutes for sitting next
to a person for an hour or two. After a few hours, you'll be walking
the same walk and talking the same talk. You'll know the same jokes.
You'll know the weird mannerisms. And you'll be ready for some
distance."
- AboutWork Shift Coach Hope Dlugozima
www.aboutwork.com/experts/hopeqanda.html
Love About Work but hate email? To be removed from our list,
send email to:
        mailto:majordomo@ivillage.com
Then put this in the message body:
        unsubscribe aboutworknews
```

valuable, they will unsubscribe. It is perfectly normal to have some turnover or "churn" in your list since experienced marketers know they cannot be all things to all people.

Another way to determine whether or not your e-mailings are valued is to ask for feedback. An interesting phenomenon about the Internet is that people tend to be more open with their opinions than they would be if they were in a face-to-face meeting or on the telephone. By providing an e-mail address—or a dedicated Web site URL that links a feedback form—in the e-mail message, your customers can readily provide comments, suggestions, and ideas about your service.

Products/Services

There are a few products or services you can use to create and manage a mailing list server. You can choose between an automated or moderated mailing list server based on your marketing objectives or resources. In the next section, we have included a list of resources to give you more information about implementing your own mailing list server.

Automated, Receive-Only Mailing Lists

One of the simplest ways to send e-mails to a large group of users—without a lot of human interaction or resources—is to use a broadcast or automated, receive-only method. This allows you to provide useful information to all of your users or subsets of users. The following mailing list server applications and services will handle much of the administration and management associated with maintaining a list server, including handling "bounced back" e-mails that were undeliverable.

Free Mailing List Software

Majordomo	www.greatcircle.com/majordomo/
Majordomo FAQ	www.cis.ohio-state.edu/~barr/majordomo-faq.html
Majordomo (Macintosh only)	leuca.med.cornell.edu/Macjordomo
Pegasus Mail	www.pegasus.usa.com/

Mailing List Software

AltaVista Mail Server '97	www.altavista.digital.software.com from AltaVista Internet Software
GroupMaster from Revnet Systems	www.revnet.com (also hosts mailing lists)
ListProc from Corporation for Research and Educational Networking (CREN)	www.cren.net
ListServ from L-Soft International Inc. (also hosts mailing lists)	www.lsoft.com

---

| ListStar (Macintosh only) from Quarterdeck Corporation | www.starnine.com |
| Lyris from Shelby Group Ltd | www.lyris.com |

Mailing List Hosting

| SparkNET's Majordomo Hosting Service | www.majordomo.com |

Moderated Discussion Lists

Another way to use a mailing list server program (like the ones just mentioned) is to create a discussion list that acts like a forum, similar to Usenet newsgroups. This is a great way to move further down the path to one-to-one e-mail marketing. A discussion list basically allows you to exchange ideas with your users or customers. Typically these e-mail discussion groups allow users to exchange ideas between one another, while you moderate the discussion. The discussion list moderator receives and reviews all incoming e-mail messages before they are posted. This process takes time, but it also ensures that the messages are "fit to print" and do not include bad language, irrelevant information, or unsolicited advertising.

Discussion groups are typically administered via e-mail, but more of them are now being conducted using the Web interface. Although a discussion list does not have the "real time" benefits of chat, it can be a way to form a sense of community with your audience. If you would like to see discussion groups in action, visit these sites:

| Liszt, the mailing list directory | www.liszt.com |
| Online Advertising Discussion List | www.o-a.com |

One alternative to moderated discussion lists are "open" lists. The benefit of having an open list is that it doesn't require the time it takes to moderate the list. However, the list owner (you) has little control over what is being posted to the discussion lists. Finally, another alternative is to have a "closed" list that restricts the use of the list. One example of this is on *The Wall Street Journal* Interactive Edition Web site (www.wsj.com), which has several discussions at any given time, but are restricted to customers who have signed up and paid for the online edition of the business newspaper (see Figure 3.9)

Mailing List Resources

If you are interested in setting up and managing an electronic mailing list, here are a few useful resources:

C|Net: "How to set up and run your own Internet mailing list" (www.cnet.com/Conent/Features/Howto/Mailing/)

Figure 3.9 *The Wall Street Journal* **Interactive Edition Web-based discussion forum.**

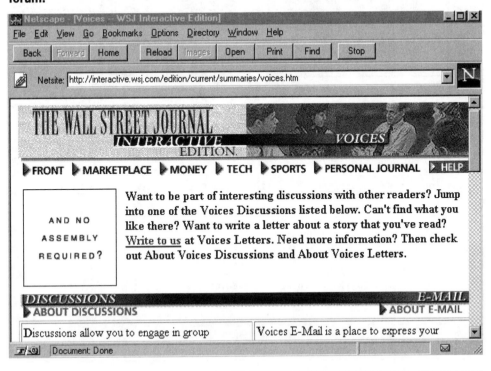

Mailing List Management Software FAQs (a little outdated, but still useful) (www.yahoo.com/Computers_and_Internet/Software/Internet/Electronic_Mail /Mailing_Lists/)

SparkNet Corporation (www.sparknet.net), a full-service Internet services company that provides a specialized Majordomo mailing list hosting service has several useful mailing list articles (www.majordomo.com/infocenter/articles/index.html)

Managing a Personalized E-Mail Service

With the integration of databases with the Web and e-mail, personalizing content to a user's or customer's profile is a relatively new and rapidly growing electronic marketing application. The popular city Web site directory, CitySearch (www.citysearch.com), has created Scout, which is a very impressive personalized Web and e-mail service. The

Figure 3.10 Sample e-mail from Travelocity's Fare Watcher service.

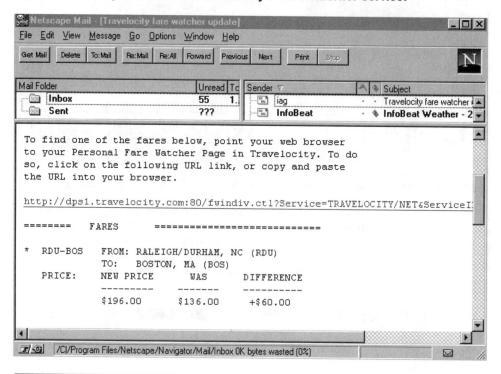

To find one of the fares below, point your web browser
to your Personal Fare Watcher Page in Travelocity. To do
so, click on the following URL link, or copy and paste
the URL into your browser.

http://dps1.travelocity.com:80/fwindiv.ctl?Service=TRAVELOCITY/NET&ServiceI

======== FARES   =============================

* RDU-BOS   FROM: RALEIGH/DURHAM, NC (RDU)
              TO: BOSTON, MA (BOS)
   PRICE: NEW PRICE   WAS   DIFFERENCE
              ---------   -------   ----------
              $196.00 $136.00   +$60.00

service allows users to create customized Web searches from several categories such as art, history, movies, sports, and theater. There are numerous subjects that users can select within each category. Scout allows users to receive weekly e-mail newsletters in several subjects. It also provides users with the ability to receive postcards from his or her favorite store or organization via e-mail. Scout is highly customizable by subject and by the neighborhood in which the user lives.

Travelocity (www.travelocity.com) is a leading "one-stop" consumer-direct travel service Web site and is integrated with the well-known SABRE online travel reservation services. Travelocity was launched in March of 1996 and now has over 1 million registered users. Travelocity is a combination of travel-related content, electronic commerce, and community. The site offers a wealth of travel tips, fun and informative travel editorials, discussion and chat forums, interactive maps, travel merchandise, and an online travel booking service for air, car, and hotel reservations. Users can also build a personal travel profile, including the location of their travel agency where they can pick up the tickets that are ordered online.

Travelocity offers the free, customizable, and automated Fare Watcher e-mail service to its registered members. The Fare Watcher e-mail service monitors airfares in up to five markets for daily price fluctuations (plus or minus at least $25). A sample personalized e-mail shown in Figure 3.10 shows the fares and also includes travel tips, links to travel information, and reservation pages on the Travelocity Web site.

By customizing or personalizing the e-mail the recipient receives, it becomes a one-to-one marketing communication with the customer. Just as mailing list servers are useful to enhance communications with customers, personalized e-mail services can further enhance a Web marketer's ability to build loyalty or increase sales. According to Bill Binnings, the director of sales and advertising at Travelocity, "The fare special e-mail notification has proven to be a powerful marketing tool. Fare Watcher was a natural fit between technology and customer needs. E-mail messages are sent to Travelocity members to announce the end of a fare special or airline fare war. While SABRE Interactive and Travelocity are very sensitive to the spam issue, we have found, through market research, that the vast majority of members appreciate notifications and reminders that can save them money."

The Fare Watcher e-mail service is tied directly to Travelocity's goal of bringing value to its customers so they will choose Travelocity as their primary source of travel information and transactions. Travelocity also broadcasts a monthly e-mail newsletter that contains useful information about navigating the site, shortcuts, and new online features. The newsletter also contains valuable information about travel in general and tips on how to make trips more pleasant. Travelocity plans to move more toward one-to-one Web marketing by further integrating travel content with the reservation process incorporating each customer's personal information and preferences.

Technology Overview

Personalized e-mail systems are a combination of an e-mail server and a database. To date, most systems have been developed by each site owner, but software products and services are emerging to allow Web marketers to add this functionality to their site without having to build it from scratch. InfoBeat (www.infobeat.com) provides personalized e-mail news and information including finance, sports, entertainment, news, weather, and reminder services. Figure 3.11 shows how the InfoBeat system works.

There are three databases used to create an InfoBeat e-mail message: subscriber information and profile (e.g., which service the user prefers to receive and any personalization specifications), outside information (e.g., weather conditions for the user's specific geographic location), and advertising data. The e-mail engine creates and sends e-mail according to a schedule. There is another system that logs activity such as successful and unsuccessful e-mail transmissions. A subscription management system handles incoming e-mail messages; for example, people signing up for the service, modifying their profile, or canceling services.

Figure 3.11 InfoBeat.

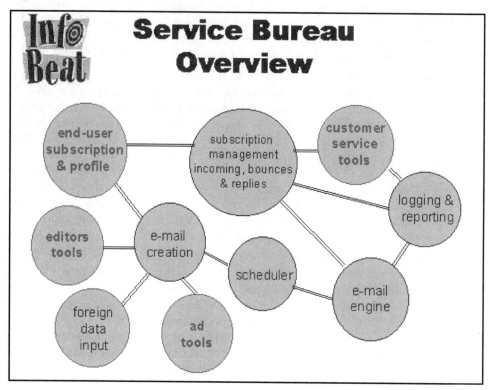

Costs and Benefits of Personalized E-Mail

The cost for a personalized e-mail system is higher than the cost associated with setting up a mailing list server. The personalized e-mail system also takes more time to implement. If you are already practicing database marketing, you have a head start with the systems, databases, and processes. A personalized e-mail system could take several months to implement, depending on the complexity of the desired system and level of expertise of the people building it.

The added benefit may outweigh the incremental cost over implementing a simple mailing list server. Personalized e-mail systems can deliver one-to-one communications, which can build strong loyalty among users, especially with the prevalence of info glut. Users can choose to receive just the information that is of the *most* value to them. Recipients look forward to receiving their personal information, and are more likely to read the e-mails. Bill Binnings from Travelocity estimated "that the cost would be higher if we 'forced' each interested member to search the system themselves rather

Figure 3.12 How personalization enhances an e-mail message.

BEFORE PERSONALIZATION:

"Dear customer, Just wanted to let you know that we
now have a new software product you may be
interested in: Super Marketing Wizard. Come check
it out at our web site: www.smw.com."

AFTER PERSONALIZATION:

"Dear James, You've been a customer with us for two
years now, and because we like to keep our most
valuable customers informed of our newest
technologies, we thought you would appreciate this
personal note about our new software, Super
Marketing Wizard. Come check it out at our web
site: www.smw.com."

Courtesy of Mike Adams, president of Arial Software

than serve the information to them." Figure 3.12 shows an example of what an e-mail system can do to use databases to personalize e-mail.

Products/Services

The market for e-mail marketing products and services is still relatively new, with new solutions becoming available. Each system offers different features that enable you to create and manage your own personalized e-mail service.

Campaign—Arial Software

Campaign is an e-mail software program developed by Arial Software (www.arialsoftware.com) that allows Web marketers to create and broadcast targeted e-mail campaigns themselves. Campaign uses Arial Software's ActiveMail engine to provide the ability to create personalized e-mail messages, database integration and filters, message scheduling, and campaign building. Other Arial Software products include

SignUp. Collects Web page form data and puts it into a database.

Respond. Automatically replies to e-mail with information requested by the user.

Director. A package bundle containing three software applications: Campaign, SignUp, and Respond.

InfoPress Email-On-Demand—Castelle/Ibex

InfoPress Email-On-Demand (www.ibex.com) is not a personalized e-mail system from the standpoint of the ability to broadcast custom e-mails. It is an automated and personalized e-mail fulfillment system. Marketers can use it to enable users to request and receive specific information via e-mail. When the user sends an e-mail to the InfoPress Email-On-Demand system, the system sends an e-mail back that contains a catalog of documents. This "catalog" acts like a document order form, and items on the e-mail order form are determined by the marketer. After the user places an X next to the information of interest and sends back the reply, InfoPress Email-On-Demand retrieves the documents and e-mails them to the user in formats such as Adobe Acrobat, MS-Word, and text.

UnityMail—Revnet Systems

UnityMail from Revnet Systems (www.revnet.com or www.unitymail.com) is a database-driven e-mail system that allows you to create a database of recipients based on user profile information. UnityMail provides database filtering capabilities so you can target specific user segments within a database with e-mail messages that are tailored to each segment. The system also provides tools that allow you to build Web-based forms that capture user data directly into a database from a Web site.

"Directronic" Mail

The terms directronic mail, direct e-mail, mailcasting, e-mail push, bulk e-mail, spam and even electronic trash have all been used to describe using e-mail for direct marketing purposes. There are many e-mail lists available to buy. Many lists are not targeted at all, some lists are targeted, and then there are lists that are very targeted and only contain users who have elected, or opted-in, to receive relevant e-mail. The highly targeted e-mail lists move the marketer closer to the one-to-one Web marketing model. For example, if you have a new Web site that provides useful resources for home decorating then, as a one-to-one Web marketer, you will want to locate an e-mail list that matches your target audience. You will most likely be interested in e-mailing lists that contain women who are ages 25–50, have a certain level of income, subscribe to books and magazines related to decorating, have bought home furnishings, and other characteristics.

Demographic and psychographic (e.g., lifestyle) information should be supplied by e-mail list brokers to ensure that you are receiving the best and most targeted e-mail list. It will be up to you to investigate each type of list and list owner to determine which one is the most appropriate for your message. Alternatively, nontargeted, bulk lists are usually much larger and less expensive than targeted ones. These types of lists are appropriate for more "mass marketing" type campaigns where your product has broad appeal among many types of users.

You should expect a lower percentage of responses from nontargeted e-mail lists than from highly targeted lists. In general, a 2- to 3-percent response is the average response rate for all types of online direct marketing. Targeted lists plus a good promotion can pull a response that is many times larger. For example, the typical mailing from PostMaster Direct's NetCreations (www.netcreations.com) targeted, opt-in e-mail lists yields a 7- to 9-percent response rate, and some campaigns have yielded their customers as much as 30- to 40-percent response. NetCreations provides more than 2 million e-mail addresses in 1,500 categories.

Direct e-mail campaigns can be conducted at a fraction of the cost of sending out physical direct mail and have the added benefit of immediate response. Users receive the e-mail, click on a hyperlink at that moment, and increase the likelihood of further transactions such as buying something, filling out a survey, reading an article, clicking on other ads, taking time within your Web site, or becoming a repeat visitor. On the other hand, other traditional direct marketing methods should not be discontinued. Many marketers advocate that an integrated marketing campaign is the most effective approach for gaining and retaining customers. Direct e-mailings are sent by the list owner in much the same way as you would broadcast a message using a mailing list server system. Since they broker lists, the list owners conduct the e-mail broadcasts.

TIP — Even with the attractive low cost of conducting e-mail campaigns, you should continue to use other marketing vehicles to gain and retain customers. The Web and e-mail have their unique benefits, just as television, radio, print advertising, direct mail, seminars, trade shows, and other marketing programs have their own value within an integrated marketing campaign.

Costs and Benefits of Using Direct E-Mail Lists

The cost of buying a list for an e-mailing varies. The model is similar to traditional list brokering for physical mailings: Highly targeted lists are more expensive than nontargeted, bulk e-mail lists. For PostMaster Direct's e-mail lists you will pay between 10 and 20 cents per name. This price includes the list rental, e-mail distribution, and merge/purge. The postage for sending a physical mailing can range from about 8 cents to almost 30 cents per piece. Add to this the cost of creating and printing a direct-mail piece, which can range from a few cents to a few dollars each. It is easy to see how cost-effective direct e-mail can be; however, your message will only reach these prospects or customers who have e-mail or Internet access. The overall benefits of direct e-mail lists include:

• A cost-effective way to reach online users.

- E-mail campaigns can take a few days or weeks to prepare and send versus the number of weeks or months it may take to complete a physical mailing.

- Direct e-mail lists are highly targeted and are a one-to-one method for reaching prospects.

- They provide you with the ability to easily motivate immediate response by recipients with embedded hyperlinks.

- They allow you to conduct test mailings as you would for traditional direct mail. The log creation capability of hyperlinks can produce highly granular test data. You can measure right down to the individual recipient.

Products/Services

The e-mail list industry is new, but it is growing at a rapid pace. There are a few types of e-mail list services available to the Web marketer: highly targeted opt-in mailing lists, bulk e-mail lists, discussion groups/lists that can be sponsored or mailed to, and e-mail-based loyalty and promotional programs. Also, many e-mail marketers have been capturing the physical mailing addresses of their e-mail users, and are now making these lists available for rental.

Opt-In E-Mail Lists

Email Exchange (business-to-business)	www.emailex.com
PostMaster Direct from NetCreations	www.netcreations.com

Direct/Bulk E-Mail Lists

21st Century Marketing	www.21stcm.com
CyberPromotions	www.cyberpromo.com
Electronic Direct Marketing	www.edmarketing.com
Internet Marketing Group	www.emailmedia.com
Internet Media Group	www.internetmedia.com
Worldata	www.worldata.com

Discussion Groups/Mailing Lists

Liszt, the mailing list directory	www.liszt.com
Direct E-mail List Source	www.copywriter.com/lists/index.htm

E-Mail Related Promotions/Loyalty Programs

There is a segment of electronic promotions that uses e-mail as the engine to facilitate loyalty programs for Web marketers. One-to-one Web marketers can take advantage of the personalization capabilities of these services. Here is a sample:

BonusMail (www.bonusmail.com, www.intellipost.com) rewards users by giving them points when they receive and view advertisements, and additional points if they take advantage of the advertising offer. Marketers pay approximately 10 to 15 cents per advertisement delivered to the user.

Yoyodyne (www.yoyodyne.com) runs e-mail-based Internet games. Participants play the games for prizes and marketers can sponsor the games.

Buying Advertising Space on Free E-Mail Services

There are several e-mail services that are free for users. The only "cost" is that the user has to read advertising sent by the services. Hotmail is the leading provider of free Web-based e-mail with over 5 million users. A Hotmail e-mail user registers for his or her free e-mail account by filling out a questionnaire that captures demographic information. Hotmail delivers about 5 million ad banners per day. Marketers can buy non-targeted and highly targeted ad banners on the Hotmail site.

Juno.com is another of the larger Web-based free e-mail services, with more than 2.5 million users. It has the capability of targeting advertisements based on demographics such as geographic location, age and gender, household income, occupation, level of education, purchasing habits and plans, patterns of computer use, hobbies and interests, marital status, and number of children in the household.

GeoCities is an online community where users can receive free e-mail and personal Web pages. The site receives over 60 million visits per month and it has over 750,000 e-mail subscribers. Just a few of the advertisers include American Airlines, Auto-by-Tel, Honda, IBM, L.L. Bean, Polaroid, Sears, and *The Wall Street Journal*. In addition to online banner ads, GeoCities provides advertising opportunities within each of its communities, e-mail advertising opportunities, and the designing of special e-mail newsletters marketers can sponsor.

Costs and Benefits of Advertising on Free E-Mail Services

Hotmail Web advertising rates range from about $9,000 per 500,000 advertising impressions (the number of times the ad appears in one month) to about $16,000 for targeted ads. Discounts are given when the advertiser signs an ad contract for multiple months. The overall benefit of placing banner or e-mail advertising with free e-mail services is their ability to provide a targeted audience for your marketing messages. A Forrester Research (www.forrester.com) report states that "Having information like this [demographics] allows free e-mail services to offer advertisers true, demographically targeted delivery of ads...Targeted delivery based on hard demographics remains somewhat rare on the Web, and therefore a real draw for advertisers."

Although these services offer the ability to target certain users with advertising, they still provide service to people with particular demographics who sign up for free e-mail or elect to be part of an online community. Therefore, a marketer can target within this highly consumer-oriented segment of online users.

It won't be long before these target ad delivery mechanisms, such as e-mail, become one-to-one ad delivery vehicles. There are software and services being introduced that allow this kind of razor-sharp *narrowcasting*, where one-to-one Web marketers will cost-effectively deliver a single, individual marketing message to one person.

Products/Services

There are several services on which you can place advertising. You will want to request demographic information from the services to ensure they are reaching your target audience(s).

Free E-Mail Services

CommTouch	www.commtouch.com
Excite Mail	www.mailexcite.com
GeoCities	www.geocities.com
Hot Mail	www.hotmail.com
Juno Online	www.juno.com
NetAddress	www.netaddress.com
Rocket Mail	www.rocketmail.com

Buying Advertising Space in an E-Mail News or Newsletter Service

E-mail news and newsletters provide added value over e-mail advertising and can be even more effective in pulling higher response rates for Web marketers. The premise behind this ability is that if the e-mail recipient takes time to read the message, the more likely it is he or she will act on the advertising, sponsorship, or promotion included in the e-mail. Since the recipient has elected to receive the news or newsletter and he or she values the information, the organization is more credible in the user's or customer's mind. Thus the advertising has added credibility by association.

Costs and Benefits of Advertising Within E-Mail News/Newsletters

InfoBeat (www.infobeat.com), formerly known as Mercury Mail, is a free e-mail news service where the editorial can be customized by the user. InfoBeat serves over 1.5 million subscribers with electronic information in several categories such as news, weather, stocks, sports, entertainment, and reminders. An advertiser will pay approximately $40 per thousand messages for text-based e-mail and $60 per thousand messages for HTML-based e-mail.

As stated earlier, the main benefit of advertising in e-mail news or newsletters is the editorial content. There are many Web sites that provide an e-mail service to their customers and also offer advertising opportunities for Web marketers. For example, *Wired* magazine (www.wired.com) has a couple of e-mail news services such as *Wired News Delivery*, *HotWired's HotFlash*, and *Webmonkey Newsletter. Wired* provides sponsorship opportunities for these weekly newsletters. Web marketers whose target prospects meet the same demographic criteria as *Wired's* audience will benefit from higher advertising response rates.

 With an advanced e-mail advertising delivery system, users go through profiling steps to get the content delivered, and therefore might represent a more responsive audience. Advertising can be targeted based on demographic profile, geography, or content of interest. These e-mail publishers have the capability of customizing frequency levels to advertisers: high frequency for branding programs and low frequency for response programs.

Kris Pederson, President of KPMedia

Products/Services

There are several services on which you can place advertising. You will want to request demographic information from the services to ensure they are reaching your target audience(s).

E-Mail News and Newsletters Samples

GolfWeb Insider	www.golfweb.com
HotWired Hot Flash	www.hotwired.com

E-Mail News and Newsletters Samples *Continued*

InfoBeat	www.infobeat.com
Netscape's InBox Direct	www.netscape.com
New York Times Direct	www.nytimes.com
Quote.com	www.quote.com
TipWorld	www.tipworld.com
Webmonkey	www.hotwired.com/webmonkey/

HTML-Enabled E-Mail

Many Internet e-mail programs now support HTML, which is used to format Web pages. Supporting HTML tags enables marketers to send e-mails that contain hyperlinks, tables, fonts, and graphics. These elements enhance the e-mail message and make the message look much like a Web page. The *New York Times* online edition (www.nytimes.com) has an e-mail service called "New York Times Direct" that deliv-

Figure 3.13 HTML-based e-mail from *The New York Times*.

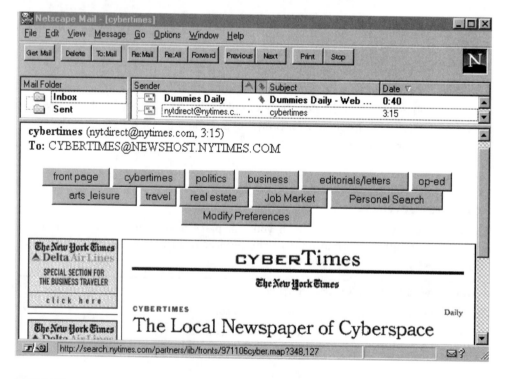

ers e-mail news to a user's e-mailbox. The e-mail message supports HTML and sends a graphical message, including advertising, as shown in Figure 3.13.

HTML-based e-mail can be a very appealing alternative to push technology in that it provides the appeal of graphics without requiring the user to download desktop software—the messages are delivered via the e-mail software already installed on the user's computer.

The Future of One-to-One E-Mail

With the industry becoming more sensitive to online users and their feelings about unsolicited commercial e-mail, e-mail will become a standard and accepted way to provide advertising messages to prospects and customers. E-mail technology will continue to evolve to become easier to implement and administer, as well as easier to integrate with company databases. This will enable Web marketers to benefit from the power of one-to-one marketing. Multimedia e-mail that includes audio and video will also become more prevalent, which will provide marketers with a cost-effective push method. Push technology will not replace e-mail. E-mail and push will coexist and be applied according to each technology's particular strengths. In addition to multimedia, e-mail will become more customizable and interactive. Customers will be able to conduct transactions via e-mail and not have to go to a Web site to place orders for products or services.

E-mail will continue to grow and be the most prevalent activity on the Internet. We have already seen the merger of e-mail and voice technology—people can now call in and listen to their e-mails! There are also products and services available that let people check their e-mail from anywhere—someone else's computer, an airport Internet kiosk—through the Web browser. We may continue see a morphing of technologies to enhance marketers' ability to communicate with each customer no matter where he or she is located.

Web Site   Go to the companion Web site for the InfoBeat case study, "One-to-One E-Mail."

Chapter 4, "One-to-One Web Site Personalization," discusses the benefits and costs of Web site personalization. If you have a site that has many content choices or you do business with more than one target market, then Web site personalization can help you save your users' time in seeking information about what your organization has to offer. Web site personalization systems and e-mail marketing systems can be integrated using the same user profile database.

ONE-TO-ONE WEB SITE PERSONALIZATION

4

"Information technology is the quintessential 'engine' of fractious, late 20th century democracy, in which individuality is prized and people won't tolerate being pawns of big institutions or a mass marketplace."

Regis McKenna, "Stalking The Information Society," *Upside* magazine, January 1995.

The ever-fragmenting society has provided more choices for people, who prefer having choices versus not. However, the incredible number of choices has also caused anxiety and confusion. Although the World Wide Web provides a world of information with access to any type of information possible, the Web is beginning to become segmented. The first phase of the Web was centered on anonymity and unprecedented access to information. We are now in the second phase, which is characterized by the *clustering* of information and the need for users to identify themselves in order to receive enhanced value from the Web in the form of time savings and personalized communications.

The second phase of the Web will be a place where online users gravitate to specialized online communities, super sites, channels, and Web sites that *narrowcast* specific information to a segment of the online user population. For example, if you visit Excite (www.excite.com), you can find many online communities that are focused on several areas, including books, business, financial, computers, film, games, hobbies, health, learning, lifestyle, music, politics, news, shopping, sports, television, and travel. All of the major search engines now provide users with a personalized news and information service. As of October 1997, all of the top five sites ranked by 100hot Web Sites (www.100hot.com) provide personalization capabilities:

1. Netscape provides Netcenter.
2. Yahoo! provides My Yahoo!
3. Microsoft provides Microsoft Personal Information Center.
4. AltaVista provides personalization of search functions.
5. Pathfinder provides a Personal Edition.

In order to save people time and build relationships, the Web will become a venue for targeted dialog between user and Web site owner. Jupiter Communications (www.jup.com) defines this next phase as one that "will be marked by services that enable a more proactive, ongoing dialog between content provider and consumer."

According to a 1996 Intelliquest (www.intelliquest.com) survey, almost half of the respondents stated that information that was tailored to their needs was a reason why they revisited a Web site. Here is how the respondents ranked reasons for repeat visits:

Very entertaining: 56%

Grabs my attention: 54%

Extremely useful content: 53%

Information tailored to my needs: 45%

Thought provoking: 39%

Visually appealing: 39%

Highly interactive: 36%

Loads quickly: 1%

According to the 1997 Cybercitizen Report by Yankelovich Partners (www.yankelovich.com), the key to the success of online commerce in the future is the user's ability to personally interact with a Web site. The study revealed that more than two-thirds of respondents prefer more human-like transactions when they shop online. Users want timely answers, product recommendations based on their tastes and preferences, and personalized interaction.

The increasing availability of technology and the decreasing cost of technology have spawned a producer-consumer dynamic that centers on increased choice and competition, which leads to a decline in brand loyalty. The emergence of a clustering of the Web added to the technological capabilities of the Web to provide an individualized experience will present a new opportunity and challenge for all Web site owners and marketers. This chapter discusses how a Web marketer can provide personalized information to their online constituents and takes a peek into the future of one-to-one Web site personalization.

The Benefits of One-to-One Web Site Personalization

One-to-one Web site personalization will work if you follow the basic idea of *value exchange*. This means that you will get something of value from your customers and users (e.g., loyal and profitable relationships) if you provide them with something of equivalent value (e.g., personalized attention).

Benefits to Web Marketers

One-to-one Web marketers will receive several benefits from providing personalization on their sites, including customer loyalty, competitive advantage, lower marketing costs, ability to identify the most profitable customer relationships, additional revenue from premium services, and the ability to adapt and improve their sites, products, and services.

Loyalty

There is a war going on among online bookstores. The scrappy, upstart stores like Amazon.com (www.amazon.com) and Powells (www.powells.com) are going up against firmly established, cash-wealthy stores like Barnes & Noble (www.barnesandnoble.com). Early on in the competition for online customers, price became an important differentiating factor. Competing solely on price presents increased risk of failure, especially in a new industry. Now services are the key to a competitive edge. To compete with the established brand awareness of Barnes & Noble, Amazon.com took a technological and service approach to acquiring and retaining customers. Amazon.com gives users the ability to locate and purchase more than 2.5 million books. It offers several personalized services, including cross-selling, recommendations, and easy online ordering. Barnes & Noble now offers book recommendations and an online community. Web marketers need to become one-to-one Web marketers in order to increase their customers' loyalty to their Web site or company.

Every organization exists in a competitive industry arena. The benefits of loyalty flow straight to the bottom line. When a customer takes time to invest in teaching your organization more about his or her wants, needs, and purchases, he or she now has ownership in the relationship with you. The cost to the customer to switch to your competitor continues to increase as he or she does more business with you. In his book, *The Loyalty Effect* (1996, Harvard Business School Press) Frederick Reichheld describes the challenge of loyalty as a *leaky bucket*. The water in your bucket is your existing customer base. The water filling up the bucket is the new customers you are acquiring. The size of the leak in the bottom of the bucket is the rate of customer attrition. The bigger the leak in the bottom of the bucket (customer attrition), the harder you have to work to fill up the bucket (customer acquisition). Getting new customers is more expensive than selling to existing customers. Thus, it is less expensive to decrease the size of the hole in the bucket than it is to increase the amount of water needed to fill up the bucket. Here are the main benefits of customer loyalty:

Profitability. The revenue growth and cost savings associated with loyal customers lead to increases in profitability over the long term.

Referrals. Loyal customers can be your best and most cost-efficient advertisers. It has been shown that customer referrals produce a better quality of customer versus customers that come to your Web site or business from advertising or other forms of lead-generating communications. These referrals can also translate into profitable and loyal customers much faster.

Second chances. Loyal customers will give you a second chance if you mess up once in a while.

Tailoring your Web site to your customers' needs is the first step in the loyalty process. The next step is to integrate your Web site into other processes, such as sales, marketing, purchasing, account management, customer services, and so forth.

Competitive Advantage

The speed of microprocessors has increased dramatically. In 1965 Gordon Moore predicted the exponential growth in the speed of a computer chip. Known as Moore's Law, it predicted that the advance in the logic density of a transistor would result in a doubling of processor power every 18 months. The increasing speed and decreasing cost of the microprocessor has allowed the rapid adoption of personal computers on corporate desktops and in homes. The computer has aided a significant decrease in production cycle times and a significant increase in the number of products being introduced into the marketplace. The increasing number of products and services has caused the marketplace to become more fragmented and segmented.

According to Regis McKenna, author of *Relationship Marketing* (1991, Addison-Wesley), computer technology has turned uninformed customers into informed customers. He believes that uninformed customers are easily satisfied. In general, people have much more access to information—especially with the Web—and they can comparison shop more easily. He states:

> "Customer technology literacy presents a challenge to manufacturers. Customers are no longer pushovers. They want to understand more about the products they buy. They are skeptical and critical, and more often dissatisfied...As more customers become more knowledgeable—and more critical—about technological products, companies must become more sensitive to customer needs."

The accessibility of information and companies on the Web is a mixed blessing. For online users, the Web gives them unprecedented access to products and companies, which enables users to gather comparative data much easier than ever before. For online marketers, this has added fuel to competitive fires. The access and immediacy of the Internet presents Web marketers with a new challenge of acquiring and keeping online customers for the long run. Building brand loyalty takes time, but the Web requires marketers to grab the users' loyalties as soon as they visit their Web sites, and to continue the process in a very determined and relentless manner.

Web technology itself will not give you a competitive advantage. Making it convenient for your online customers or users to gain a substantial benefit from what your organization offers will be key to your competitive advantage. One-to-one Web site personalization will help you serve each customer to his or her individual satisfaction, over and over again. When an online customer takes the time to tell you what he or she needs and wants, he or she now has an investment in your service. As long as this personalized service provides your customer with value, he or she will do business with you more often, and will think long and hard about switching to your competitor—especially if it means having to go through this investment process all over again with your competitor. If you are in a highly competitive market, where services and products are perceived as equal, then individualized service will help you compete effectively.

In their second book, *Enterprise One to One*, Don Peppers and Martha Rogers presented their "new competitive rules". They believe that the Interactive Age will require customer-driven competition, also known as one-to-one marketing. Customer-driven competition will become critical to success in a competitive marketscape. The good news is that information technology can help because it can provide

Customer tracking. The combination of databases and Web tracking allow Web marketers to keep track of all interactions with customers on an individual basis.

Interactive dialog. The Web allows Web marketers to engage in interactive dialog with customers using online feedback forms and e-mail. With the ability to incorporate video and voice on the Web, communications will become more interactive and will happen in real time.

Mass customization. Web site personalization will enable Web marketers to customize the user's interactions with the site. The Web can also enable companies to deliver information, services, and products more efficiently.

The online search engine business has become extremely competitive. Most of the top search engines such as AltaVista, Excite, InfoSeek, WebCrawler, and Yahoo! receive most of their revenue from advertising. These top search engines provide a customized service to users, from search preferences to a highly customized news page. Coincidence? No. Since the online advertising market is still relatively young and small, search engines need to attract and keep users in order to attract and keep online advertisers. Advertisers are requiring better demographic information from the search engines' users. The customization services on the search engines assist them in making this kind of data available to advertising because they capture user profile information, select their customization preferences, and collect information from user interaction with content and advertising.

Lower Marketing Costs

One-to-one Web marketing is now possible because information technology is cheaper and more prevalent now. The Web has the potential of minimizing the cost per thousand (CPM) customers that you reach with your marketing messages. By fostering loyalty you also will decrease the costs associated with marketing to each customer over time because customers will not need the same level of marketing investment as they did when you first acquired them as customers.

Cost of Information Technology

Information technology has enabled companies to shift dollars that are typically spent on onsite customer visits as well as other more expensive sales, marketing, and service activities. Face-to-face sales meetings are more expensive than telephone or videoconferences, especially if you want people from more than one remote office involved. Mailing documentation to a customer is more expensive than directing the customer to your Web site, or sending the documentation via e-mail, FTP, or PDF. The cost of a telephone salesperson is greater than an intelligent system that suggests the appropriate item using the same product and customer database the telephone salesperson would use. Order processing by customer service personnel is more expensive than order processing by an electronic commerce system. The Internet is already providing companies with ways to decrease communication, transaction, and account management costs.

Web site personalization will require sites to collect and store user data and interact with other back-end databases and systems. There will be an additional technology and marketing investment to design a personalized site; however, Web sites that are database driven will reduce the time and costs associated with the continuous process of updating and revising.

| TIP | Did you know that a Web personalization system that is being used by online customers can also be used by your company's representatives who provide service to potential customers, or existing customers, by telephone? If you have built a Web personalization system that assists online users in finding personalized information and solutions or accesses their account information, you will streamline the customer marketing and service process to allow sales, marketing, and service

departments to use the same system. (See this chapter's Case Study on the companion Web site for information on how Keystone Financial built a system that is used by customers and by their own customer service representatives.)

Acquisition Versus Retention

It has been said that it costs five times more to acquire a new customer than it does to get business from an existing customer. Since the Web is still a relatively new medium, all organizations on the Web will need to invest marketing dollars and resources in acquiring new customers. However, if you start the process of encouraging customer retention by using Web site personalization or other loyalty-building systems, you can move down the path to profitability much faster. A customer retention strategy must be mapped out early in your Web plans and should be as important as attracting customers.

Many Web sites are available to customers, and the amount of time customers have for browsing is limited. Therefore, you want them to become regular patrons of your site. Your goal should be to make your site an indispensable resource for customers. Web site personalization technology will not accomplish this alone. You should think of the value and benefit behind the reason why you personalize the Web site. This will lead to customer retention. Personalized Web site information is just the first step. What does a customer then do with this personalized information?

Can they view it and store it on your system, and their system?

Can they modify it?

Can they use it to purchase?

Can their dedicated sales account manager view it?

Can they interact with other customers who have similar profiles to exchange ideas?

Can this information remind them of their next purchase in terms of what to order and when so they don't run out of inventory?

Can they be informed of a special offer that is associated with their preferences in the future?

Can this information be incorporated into the distribution channel or shared with divisions or related companies?

These are just a few of the things that can be done with Web personalization that can help you retain customers beyond the first interaction. The Electronic Newsstand (www.enews.com) provides information about print magazines and enables Web users

Figure 4.1 My Newsstand on The Electronic Newsstand.

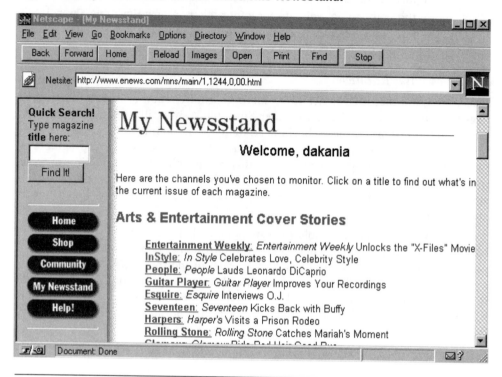

to subscribe to magazines while online. With its My Newsstand feature, users can customize which magazine *channels* they would like to monitor. There are about 25 channels to choose from such as Arts & Entertainment, Music, Travel and so on. Once a user has registered they can access My Newsstand to view his or her own customized magazine list and excerpts from current issues. Figure 4.1 shows a sample configuration of My Newsstand.

Just remember these thoughts about customer retention from Frederick Reichheld in his book, *The Loyalty Effect* (1996, Harvard Business School Press):

> *"...we discovered some years ago that raising customer retention rates by 5 percentage points could increase the value of an average customer by 25 to 100 percent."*

Law of Repeat Purchases

In order to increase the return on investment on your Web site, you will want more customers visiting your site more often. The more you interact with or sell to a single customer, the more you will reduce your marketing and technology expenditures on that customer over time. This translates into a higher profit margin per customer in the long term. Don Peppers and Martha Rogers call this concept the *law of repeat purchases*. This is in contrast to the mass-marketing approach, which requires discounted prices or higher promotional expenses to increase volume. One-to-one Web marketers can take advantage of this concept if they have the ability to interact with and track customers site visits, requests for information, or online purchases. This enables you to learn more about your customers and return to them the best value for their investment to ensure they will be back to your site often.

Identifying the Most Profitable Relationships

Not all customers provide the same value to your organization. Web and information technologies can be combined to serve each customer according to his or her individuality. These technologies can also be used to evaluate each customer's value. This allows you to segment your customers into categories as suggested by Peppers and Rogers in their book, *Enterprise One to One*:

MVCs. Most valuable customers (MVCs) are those who have the highest lifetime value (LTV). Your objective with this customer group is to center your marketing activities around customer retention.

SVCs. Second-Tier Valuable Customers (SVCs) are those who have the highest unrealized potential. Your objective with this group is to center your marketing activities around customer growth.

BZs. Below-zero (BZ) customers are those who will most likely not produce enough profit to justify the costs associated with serving and marketing to them.

LTV is a calculation of your customers' value according to their duration of their relationship with you and the amount of money they spend with you or their number of interactions with you. Once LTVs are determined for your customer base, you can tailor your marketing programs and Web site to each customer's needs and his or her potential worth to your company.

The only way to identify the most profitable relationships with customers or users is through interactive dialog and interaction tracking. The Web has the unique ability to track customers. Your site can also be tied to databases and other systems such as sales, marketing, purchasing, shipping, and support. Customer data is required to determine which customers are your most profitable ones. This data can be used for all Web site models—with or without electronic transactions. If your site is mostly informational or community oriented, then profitability will not be measured in purely economic terms. If your Web site is advertiser supported, you will have two sets of customers to evaluate: your users and your advertisers. Each customer type will be measured with different factors.

For example, if your site is informational, then you can use technology and services to segment your user population. You can provide a special membership program based on frequency or user profile. Advertiser-supported sites can give discounting or special services based on volume and types of advertising (e.g., banners, sponsorships, editorial features). Transactions, interactions, user profiles, and other data that is useful to identify profitable customer relationships will be stored in databases that can be manipulated using report writing or data mining to discover patterns and make predictions about your customers. (See Chapter 10, "Integrating One-to-One Web with Other Marketing Systems and Processes," for a discussion on data mining).

Additional Revenue from Premium Personalization Services

Web site personalization technology can be used to tie into premium services such as frequent flyer or buyer and other membership clubs. Premium services are those types of services for which you can charge the customer to participate. Ticketmaster (www.ticketmaster.com) has a special online club called TMO Plus. The one-year charter membership costs $10. TMO Plus members receive a private ID for secure online ordering, special offers on merchandise, and a special discount on a subscription to its monthly entertainment magazine, *Live! Magazine*. This special service gives interested users special advantages and gives Web marketers an easy way to identify, monitor, manage, and reward loyal customers.

Another example of premium online service is the GolfWeb Players Club (www.golfweb.com). For $2.50 per month, members receive special interactivity and promotions. There is the Scorer's Tent, which calculates a member's golf handicap; the Pro Shop, which offers coupons and discounts on merchandise such as golf clubs and apparel; and the Member's Lounge, where members can chat and track their friends' golf games. Other membership features include the Performance Lab, Teaching Pro, Course Competition, and Leader Board. If there is enough value, you can enhance loyalty among your members. These services also help you segment your customers and identify and reward highly loyal customers.

Adaptation and Continual Improvement of Products and Services

Customer dialog is a way to help you continually improve your Web sites and services. Enabling online discussions with some of your organization's representatives and providing online feedback forms can assist the improvement process. Using Web site personalization, one-to-one Web marketers can also tailor enhancements according to different segments of their user population, down to a single customer. Never before has it been easier to get customers and users to provide you feedback. Technology has decreased the cost and minimized the time it takes to receive and respond to feedback.

Benefits to Customers and Users

Web site personalization provides your online customers with benefits that include choice, significant time savings, and personalized service.

Choice

In his 1995 article, "Stalking the Information Society," in *Upside* magazine, Regis McKenna states, "Choice in itself has become a paramount value, as important as the goods and services offered. The number of products, services, and options in today's marketplace is mind-numbing. This much choice is overwhelming, but most people would rather have many options available to them. For example, Toyota (www.toyota.com) has 13 models in its 1998 inventory: 4Runner, Avalon, Camry, Celica, Corolla, Land Cruiser, Paseo, RAV4, Sienna, Supra, T100, Tacoma, and Tercel. Each model offers a multitude of features and styles—if each of the 13 models has about three options, this equates to 104 combinations of models to choose from, and this is before choosing style, handling, and other individual options. For example, there are three options for the Toyota Camry: CE, LE, and LXE. Customers can also make choices in car color, upholstery, stereo, wheels, power locks, power windows, sunroof, side-view mirrors, and more. This is a far cry from the introduction of the Ford Model T automobile, when there was one choice of car color, black.

Choice is a two-sided coin on the Web. On the one hand, people want it and the Web offers it. On the other hand, it presents a challenge to Web marketers. Choice is one of the basic tenets of the Web. With all of the options and choices the Web has to offer, how do you engender loyalty? Ironically, let customers have choices on your Web site. Let them choose how they want information presented and how to communicate their needs and desires with you. If they choose to change their mind, give them the option of changing their preferences. Customers want to find information and services that match their personal preferences, and they want options.

Web site personalization allows people to build profiles based on their own choices. The registration process itself gives people a sense that they are in control of choosing their preferences. However, let your customers opt-in and opt-out of the personalization process. Nothing frustrates an online user more than being forced to provide information to a Web site in order to participate in personalization. If the frustrated user still wants to participate, he or she will give you false information. In fact, you can be guaranteed to lock out many users if you use this practice. If you provide a paid service, then customers know that they must give a certain amount of personal information. You will want to determine what information is necessary for your marketing objectives and what is optional. Optional information should be presented as an option to the user.

Time Savings

Even though people are spending increasingly more time on the Internet, they want the Internet to save them time over alternative ways of gathering information, interacting with others that are geographically distant, and buying products and services. Since the Web is available 24 hours a day, 7 days a week, customers have the expectation of being able to interact and transact with a Web site at *any* time. In his most

Figure 4.2 Customized product research on Compare Net.

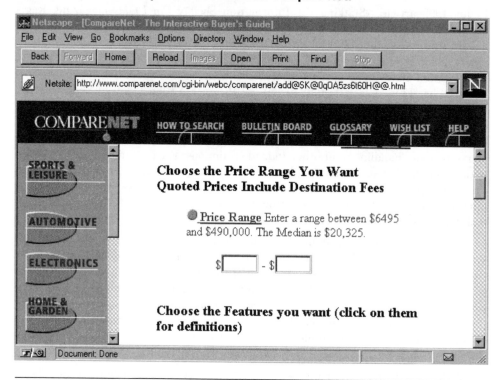

recent book, *Real Time*, Regis McKenna says that the increasing availability of technology has increased the speed of business and the expectation of the consumer to receive instantaneous satisfaction from the organizations he or she does business with. McKenna opens the book's second chapter with a statement that is evident of the new principle for marketing in the Interactive Age:

> *"Right here. Right now. Served up just the way I like it. If the new consumers' expectations were spelled out on a billboard, that is what they would read."*

According to a report from a May 1997 Forrester Research (www.forrester.com) report, the size of Web sites, measured in megabytes of storage, will triple through 1998. This study also concluded that companies will be generating more dynamic content in the future. Web site personalization will help ease the user's burden of finding the information that is most pertinent to him or her, without requiring a lot of needless surfing on your ever-growing Web site (i.e., wasting time). If a user is spending the same amount of time doing needful surfing on your site, he or she will perceive it as a good use of time, and thus a time savings. It has been said that if you can get users to visit your site for more than a couple of minutes, then you have a better chance of encouraging users to become a regular site visitor.

There is a delicate balance where the online audience has a need for immediate gratification and the Web marketer has a need to keep visitors on their site for several minutes in order to have a chance to build a relationship. Web site personalization provides the user with immediate gratification. This personalization model appears to be at odds with marketers' needs to have users spend more time on their site. The key here is to provide an interactive, personal experience that gives the users value. If this is done, then you will no longer have to worry about the time people spend on your site; rather, you will focus on the number of times particular users visit your site over time.

One example of instant gratification and usefulness using Web personalization is Compare Net (www.comparenet.com). Compare Net is a free, Web-based service that allows consumers to do customized searches on products. Users can research a variety of topics such as automobiles, electronics, computers, home appliances, home office equipment, and sports equipment. The service is personalized when users make selections from menus and enter data into fields. Users can select categories, products, features, models, and desired price ranges. The system scours the database for products that fit the users' criteria. Once the system provides users with a list of products, they can then do a side-by-side comparison of products. One personalized feature is Compare Net's Wish List, which allows registered users to store a list of products for future reference. Compare Net also has a bulletin board system (BBS) where users can read and post messages, including classified advertisements, shared experiences, and advice. Figure 4.2 shows the results of a Compare Net search.

Personalized Service

It seems like a luxury to go into a retail store and have one of the salespeople remember you, your name, your last purchase, and your favorite products. People want personalized service as long as it isn't intrusive or pushy. This type of personalized service was typical of how customers interacted with merchants before the Industrial Age and mass marketing. During this time, you would go to your local butcher, baker, and candlestick maker. These merchants would remember you and the aggregation of your past purchases. Of course, this wasn't too difficult for the merchant since there were significantly fewer choices in products. The merchants would keep this profile information in their head or on an account ledger. Now, this level of personalized service comes from upscale merchants or extremely technologically advanced companies. The increasing use of computer technology in the sales and marketing process along with the Web will make what was once considered a luxury the norm.

If you are a customer of the leading online bookstore, Amazon.com (www.amazon.com), then you will experience personalized service. When you go to its homepage,

Figure 4.3 Amazon.com's Instant Recommendations feature.

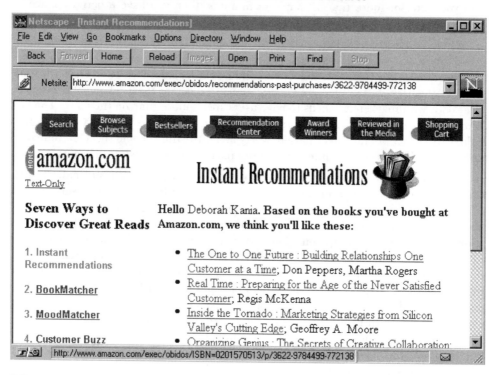

you will receive Instant Recommendations, which are personalized book recommendations ready for your review. The system makes recommendations based on past book purchases. Amazon.com also has these other personalized services:

BookMatcher. The service provides book recommendations based on your preferences in books, both likes and dislikes, as well as the preferences of other Amazon.com customers who like the same books.

MoodMatcher. This a point-and-click recommendation service that isn't based on user profiles, but is a convenient, on-the-fly book selector. You can select a Mood & Occasion from several categories, such as "How do I...bake scones or train my pet," or "A gift for...a computer geek or father." The system will make several recommendations based on the criteria you select.

Recommendations via e-mail. You can sign up to receive monthly e-mails for as many book categories as you like. The recommendations are based on book reviews by Amazon.com editors. There are several book categories spanning from American history to young adult books.

1-Click. This service provides easy ordering based on stored user information, including shipping address, preferred shipping method, and payment information. Customers can store this information, revise the information, and activate the service each time they visit the site.

As you see, Amazon.com doesn't provide personalization for its own sake, they provide specific benefits to the customer. These types of personalized services can build loyal relationships with customers, especially in competitive markets. Figure 4.3 shows the Instant Recommendations feature on Amazon.com.

Technology Overview

Personalization is the combination of Web server software that provides the "engine" which drives the personalization and databases that provide the information that is delivered to the user in a customized way. Figure 4.4 shows a basic Web personalization diagram.

Users can interact with a Web personalization system using their browser, such as Netscape Navigator or Microsoft Internet Explorer; a proprietary software interface; or, in the case of push systems, a special browser. When the user builds his or her user profile to be used in customizing his or her view of the Web, it is stored in a database. Each time a user visits the site, he or she receives a Web page that is tailored to his or her profile. The page is built using page templates instead of static HTML pages. The templates contain special HTML tags that instruct the personalization application server to retrieve data that is tailored to the user. This data can be text, graphics,

Figure 4.4 Web site personalization diagram.

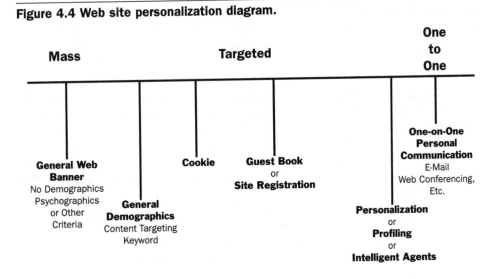

Figure 4.5 Example of an HTML page template.

```
<BODY>
<H1>Hobby Links for #user[name]#</H1>

#user[like-golf|equals|block|yes]#

<H2>Golf Links</H@>

<A HREF="/cgi-bin/guesttrack#user_id#&golf-courses.html>
Links to Golf cources around the country.
</A><P>

<A HREF="/cgi-bin/guesttrack#user_id#&golf-products.html>
Links to catalogs of Golf products.
</A><P>


#end_block#

</BODY>
```

video, audio, and so forth. The page does not *exist* until the page template is populated with the user-specific content. More than one database can be used and integrated with the personalization process (see Chapter 10, "Integrating One-to-One Web with Other Marketing Systems and Processes," for more information about data integration). Figure 4.5 shows an example of what an HTML page template looks like behind the scenes using GuestTrack tags to display a set of golf-related links if the user likes golf.

Peapod (www.peapod.com) is a pioneer in online grocery shopping. Peapod allows people, who live in certain cities in the United States, to sign up to order groceries on line and have them delivered to their door. They have built a special system called the Universal Event Processor (UEP) that creates and manages its customers' personal account files. The UEP records user preferences such as shipping method and the sorting criteria for their personal shopping list. The UEP serves targeted content, called *events*, to its customers. An event can be an online coupon, product recommendations, advertising, promotions, sampling, and more. These events are determined by the targeting methodology which incorporates demographics, data warehousing, and real-time behavior. Peapod created its own system to enable one-to-one online grocery shopping and service. There are companies that provide products and services to help you enhance your site with personalization. Most Web site personalization products also log user interaction. Web sites can be personalized using a few different technology approaches:

Database driven. This is the simplest approach and can work very well for small to medium size sites. This approach is reflected in Figure 4.5. You basically add special HTML-type tags to your Web pages and build logic into the system that tells the Web server which data to pull and deliver to the user based on the logic that developed within the Web server personalization application.

Intelligent agents. This approach is more sophisticated than simple, database-driven Web site personalization. Intelligent agents are software programs that help the user find information. They can be used to filter through large volumes of information and provide the user with only the information that matches his or her interests. Intelligent agents can work on behalf of the user by observing user preferences and site interaction habits.

Collaborative filtering. This approach combines the preferences and interactions of similar users. Users build their own profiles, then the system makes recommendations by sifting through the rest of the user profile database to find users that have similar likes, dislikes, and other criteria. These systems are best for online communities and Web sites that provide products and services based on sensory, emotional, psychological, sociological, or cultural criteria. Some examples include movies, music, art, literature, food, hobbies, and leisure activities.

Expert/rules-based. Expert or rules-based systems are highly sophisticated and make deductions based on built-in experiences and knowledge. These systems can also produce new rules, or learn, or modify existing rules. These types of systems are already employed in manufacturing, finance, and other industries and will become the engines behind sophisticated Web personalization systems.

Hybrid. Some of the Web personalization systems use a combination of technologies to personalize Web content. For example, PersonaLogic's decision guide technology is an *optimization* system that finds results based on the system's underlying data, working statistical models, and user profiles. The user profile creates a *vector*, which helps the system whittle the choices down and present ranked results based on how close these items fit the user profile.

The Cost to Add Personalization to Your Web Site

Business Marketing and *Advertising Age* magazines have a collaborative Web site, NetMarketing (net2b.com), which has conducted surveys that provide Web site creators with the costs associated with implementing certain Web technologies. In September 1997 the magazine conducted a survey of Web development service companies to gauge the costs of adding personalization to Web sites. Table 4.1 shows the results from this cost study.

Table 4.1 The Cost to Add Personalization to a Web Site

	Median price	High	Low
Small site	$10,000	$100,000	$500
Medium site	$16,000	$175,000	$5,000
Large site	$26,125	$250,000	$1,000

Business Marketing magazine, September 1997

The survey asked the participating Web services firms to set a price for personalization based on specifications given using fictitious companies and requirements. The investment required to personalize your Web site will pay off in two ways. First, as we discussed earlier, you will be able to build loyalty to your service by presenting your customers with personalized content. Second, you will receive cost savings in the long term because database-driven sites are simpler and less expensive to manage than managing hundreds and even thousands of static HTML-based Web pages. These two benefits make Web site personalization a compelling undertaking.

Applications of One-to-One Web Site Personalization

Most Web sites can be personalized. If your business model fits into the following categories, then adding personalization will help you serve your online customers more efficiently and effectively:

- One product/service geared to more than one target market
- One target market and several products/services
- More than one target market and several products/services

Web site personalization can act as a matchmaker between users and your offerings. It can provide users with rapid solutions to their information-gathering needs. There are several online models that can benefit from one-to-one Web site personalization.

Web Site Personalization and Online Models

Some of the first types of sites to personalize content to a user's preferences were news sources such as Pathfinder (www.pathfinder.com) and PointCast (www.pointcast.com).

Now there are many different types of Web site models that provide personalized content and services:

- Advertiser-supported Web sites
    - —Free or fee-based news, information, and research services
    - —Search engines
    - —Directories and super sites
    - —Content networks and channels
- Online commerce/catalogs
    - —Consumer
    - —Business-to-business
- Online communities
    - —Consumer
    - —Business-to-business
- Online information centers for "offline" businesses
    - —Store/dealer locators
    - —Product/service information
- Customer service
    - —Account management
    - —Problem tracking
    - —Shipment tracking
    - —Service updates/notifications
- Intranet/extranet
    - —Employee benefits and travel administration
    - —Manufacturer-supplier process integration
    - —Reseller information and account management

What Can Be Personalized?

There are many possibilities for using Web site personalization on your site. You could provide something as simple as a personalized homepage that gives your users the information they had previously selected each time they visit your site. Web site personalization can become as sophisticated as a recommendation system that uses user preferences, user interaction tracking, user purchase history, and the likes/dislikes of

Figure 4.6 Family Success! gives each user his or her own Web site view and experience.

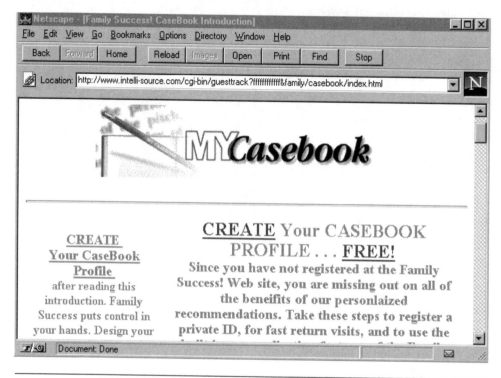

other users based on a similar profile. See the list of Web sites later in the chapter for a sample of one-to-one Web site personalization.

Personalized Web Experience

The user's Web experience itself can be personalized. From a simple targeted message with the user's name to a full-blown personalized *consolidation* of articles, graphics, information, and online discussion groups can make each user's view of your Web site totally unique. For example, the Family Success! Web site (www.intellisource.com/family) provides highly personalized interactivity and information. The site features a *Personal Casebook*. It uses the personalization software to activate password-protected accounts and enable highly interactive activities, exercises, and a private journal that is developed during the Casebook profile-building process and throughout the articles. The Casebook retains coded information of non-intimidating preferences, goals, and family profile information that will continually provide personalized content that is tailored to the user's interests. For instance, if the user prefers outdoor exercise to indoor exercise, the articles recommended in the Health section will be ones about outdoor activities and exercises (see Figure 4.6).

Personalized Information

PointCast (www.pointcast.com) was one of the first news and information services that was customized by users. It allows users to select news topics and sources, and then pushes that information out to the user's computer via a special proprietary browser. Personalized information and news services have exploded on the Web—CNN, the *New York Times*, *The Wall Street Journal*, and other popular news organizations offer personalized Web news.

Personalized information can be a simple and effective one-to-one Web marketing feature you can use to enhance your relationship with online users. Personalization doesn't just have to be informational; it can be fun and interactive also. For example, Gist TV (www.gist.com) provides personalized online television listings. In addition to being able to create your own TV schedules based on your local viewing area, you can interact with the site using a popup window that emulates a remote control! Figure 4.7 shows the remote control.

Figure 4.7 Gist TV's online remote control.

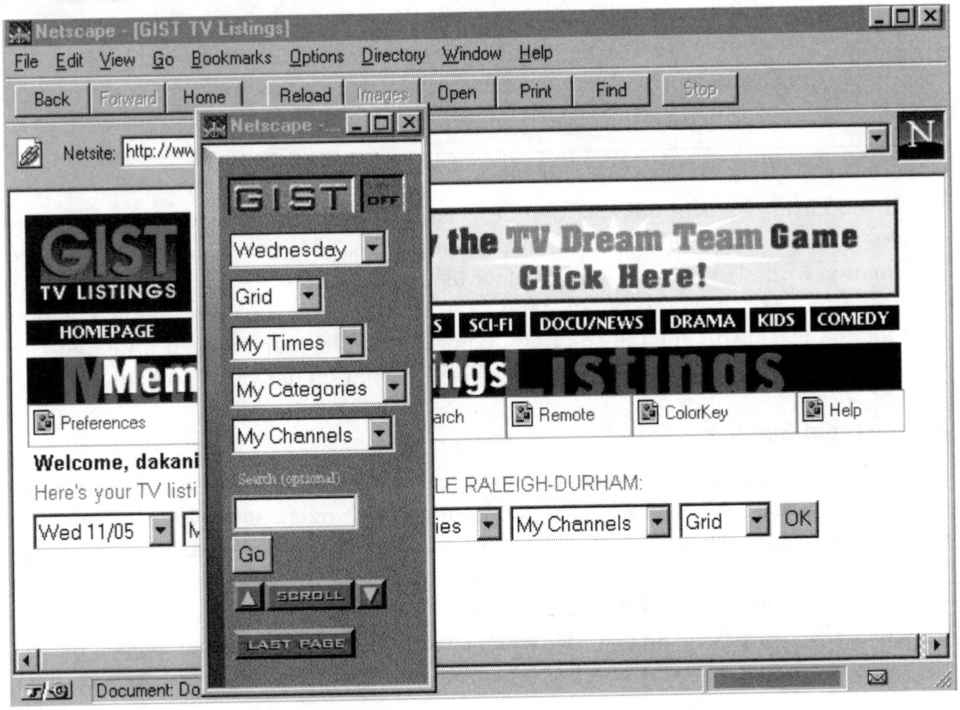

Figure 4.8 The Mining Company puts the "person" in personalization.

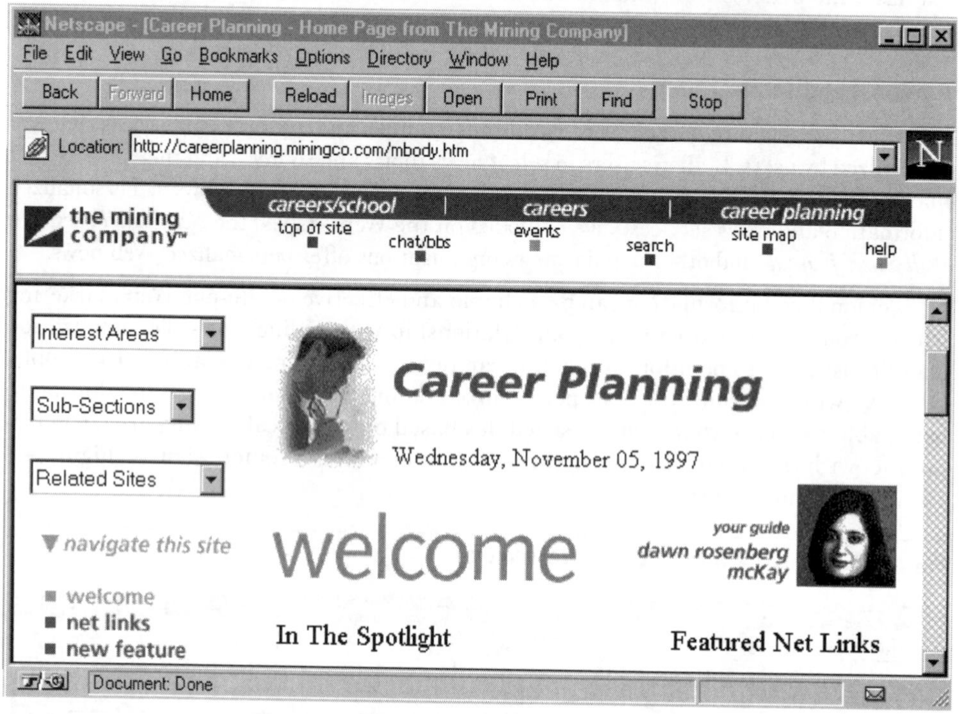

If you have a lot of products, then personalization can make it easy for your customers to sift through information and specifications. You can provide personalized information within a Web site, via e-mail, or using a push vehicle served from your Web site (see Chapter 3, "One-to-One E-Mail," for information about e-mail, and Chapter 5, "One-to-One Push," for information about push). The same user profile and customer databases can be used with these other information delivery mechanisms.

Personalized Service

NewMedia magazine (www.newmedia.com) created a unique twist on the traditional reader service magazines provided to its readers. Print magazines typically provide a reader service card where the reader can make requests for information from advertisers by making selections on a card and then mailing it to the publisher. This process can take many weeks. *NewMedia* magazine provides an online reader service, called i-Serv, on its Web site that can provide readers with instant information from companies they are specifically interested in. Users can download information or fill out a request, called the Request Builder, to receive information via their preferred method—by e-mail, fax, phone, or mail. NewMedia saw its Web site traffic increase by 50 percent when it introduced this personalized service.

American Airlines (www.americanair.com) allows online users to access and administer their AAdvantage frequent traveler account. Customers can redeem their rewards while they are on line. They can book travel as well as access the Web sites of other companies that participate in the program, including rental cars, hotels, and gifts.

The Mining Company (www.miningco.com) is a great example of an additional level of personal service. Instead of simple database-driven personalization, The Mining Company has enlisted hundreds of people, *guides*, to mine the Web for the best content associated with topic areas. The Mining Company has about 500 topic areas with plans to have at least 4000 topic areas. The live human guides behind each topic area are accessible by e-mail for one-to-one communications related to the topic area. Figure 4.8 shows a topic area on The Mining Company Web site.

Personalized Community

Having online communities that users can participate in based on their own needs can be a powerful marketing and services tool. An online community that provides a place for its customers to chat with company representatives, or one another, is one of the most effective one-to-one Web vehicles (see Chapter 6, "One-to-One Community," for a discussion about online communities). You can build communities that are dedicated to certain product lines, subjects, customer segments, and other criteria. iVillage (www.ivillage.com) is a pioneer in the online community concept. iVillage has specialized online communities such as Life Soup, Parent Soup, About Work, and Better Health & Medical Network. For example, the About Work community has message boards, surveys, a weekly newsletter, and an extensive chat room for people who are seeking employment and career information and advice. Within the job search area, users can take an interactive quiz to help them find the career best suited to their own criteria. Users can also submit questions to the Job Guru for one-on-one advice about finding a job.

PlanetAll (www.planetall.com) is an online community of over 200,000 that has taken personalization one step further with interactive and personalized features. PlanetAll allows users to keep in touch with friends, family, and colleagues. It allows users to build a personal profile of their own network of friends and affinity groups (e.g., schools, company affiliations). Users can receive e-mail updates when things change within their groups. The community also enables users to build customized reminders. The site has a Virtual Address Book feature to allow users to create and manage a personalized contact database.

These examples are primarily focused on building online communities—you can translate many of the interactive community features to most any online model to

Figure 4.9 Insight Direct's Tip Wizard cross-selling system.

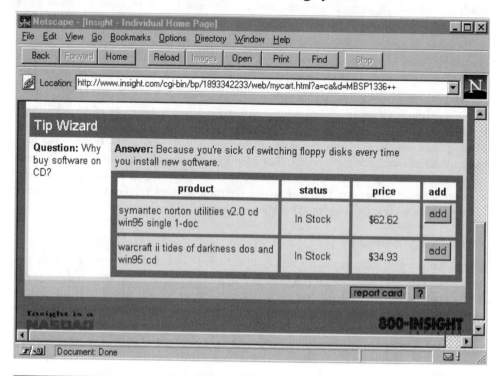

form a one-to-one personalized Web community. For example, if you are a service company that sells water filtration systems, then you could form a community that allows users to share experiences regarding the installation of your systems. You can also host chat systems that can discuss topics such as how to determine which filtration system is best for a user's particular needs. The possibilities are limitless.

Personalized Cross-Selling/Upselling

What has been a successful method of personalized selling for mail-order catalogs can now be achieved using a personalized Web site. When a person requests particular information or purchases a product, a personalized Web site should scour its associated databases to come up with other recommendations to the user. Web sites can pull from user profiles, tracking data, and purchasing data to inform the user of related information, products, and services. This is personalized service at its best and it saves the user lots of time.

For example, if you were ordering a laptop computer, would you find it extremely convenient to also receive information on related products such as a special offer on a leather case, an extra battery, and extended warranty? Amazon.com provides cross-selling each time a customer performs a search on a book. The search results contain additional information such as book subject categories that are related to the book that you are currently searching for. Another example of cross-selling is on Insight Direct's (www.insight.com) Web site. Insight has a special cross-selling system called the Tip Wizard. For example, when you select a laptop computer, the Tip Wizard will bring add-on products to your attention. The Tip Wizard will suggest modem cards, utilities, software, and other related products. The Tip Wizard provides some useful information, or tips, on why these products may be helpful to you. Figure 4.9 shows Insight Direct's Tip Wizard in action.

When the Human Touch Is Required

There are many customer interactions that cannot be replaced by automated Web site personalization systems. There are times when marketing, sales, and service interactions with customers require a *real live* human involved in the dialog with customers. Customer information that has been collected on the Web site can enhance the human interaction. Web sites that use personalization typically will assign a user a unique ID through the use of cookies or by asking the user to provide the Web site with a username and ID. This information can be added to customer databases so when a salesperson or customer service representative is helping the customer, he or she will know much more about that customer. There are some highly customized sales that cannot be conducted via a Web site, but the Web site and data collected by the site can be involved in the sales process.

How Much Information Should You Capture?

Just enough. Early Web sites enabled cookies and provided guest book registrations only because they were able to do so. This provoked privacy concerns among online users. Users gave information and received little or no value in return. Many Web sites are now providing value in exchange for users' information, but users are still tentative about giving personal information (see Chapter 11, "One-to-One Web Privacy," for a discussion on privacy).

The amount of information you request from a user should be directly related to the value you provide to the user in return for his or her information. You should not ask for every bit of information from the beginning. Dialog and loyalty is a long-term process. As your relationship with your customer evolves, there will be a need to continue the information exchange process. If your site allows users to personalize information based on the types of products you offer, you should ask for just enough information to help users customize their preferences. You should only ask for a user's e-mail address if you are going to provide him or her with a periodic e-mail notification or newsletter service. You should only ask for a user's address if he or she wants to be on your mailing list, or the information is needed for shipping and billing. The bottom line is, asking for information that is not directly tied to personalization will only add to your database resources and cost, and neither you or your customer is going to receive added value for the incremental information. You can always ask for necessary information, give users the choice to provide optional information or sign up for optional services such as being added to your or third-party mailing lists.

Sources of Information for Personalization

There are several sources of data to use to create personalized communications. User profile information can be captured anonymously, or in a more candid manner where the user provides more information in order to receive one-to-one communications from the site. Sources of information to enable Web site personalization include:

Cookies. Cookies are pieces of information stored in a text file on a user's computer. Cookies are used to customize Web pages based on the information stored in the cookie file. Cookies are an anonymous method in that they are associated with the computer that is being used to access a Web site instead of the people visiting a site. Cookies can be used to store a unique ID as well as password that will identify the user (the computer) each time the site is visited.

Interaction tracking. Web servers log user site activity. There are also products (such as GuestTrack) that allow Web marketers to track activity according to a particular user. The site can present personalized information based on stored user-tracking information from previous site visits in a real-time manner where information is personalized on- the-fly as the user inter-acts with the site.

Online profile/registration. Guestbooks and other online registration devices allow users to build unique profiles that the Web site can use to pro-vide personalized content. You will want to use a password-oriented online registration when a customer needs to access account or highly personalized (or personal) content.

Customer databases. Customer databases can be used to store and access information that is specific to each customer. Customer data such as addresses, phone numbers, e-mail, inquiries, and purchases can be used to personalize Web information. Online user profile and preference informa-tion can be used in conjunction with customer data to provide one-to-one Web marketing or service. See Chapter 10, "Integrating One-to-One Web with Other Marketing Systems and Processes," for a discussion on how to integrate existing customer databases with your site.

Customer feedback. In addition to customer satisfaction and feedback, online forms and surveys can be a source of information for personalized

Web services and information. You can design your site to associate feedback with a particular user.

You can use one or a combination of the aforementioned sources to enable personalization on your site. The best approach for deciding which methods to use to capture user information will be based on the objective of your Web site. If your site is primarily one where users place orders, track deliveries, and perform account management, then you may need a password-protected user registration that ties into one or more back-end databases or systems such as purchasing, inventory, or shipping. If your site is primarily one that provides personalized information and advertising, then you may want to use a combination of cookies, user tracking, and user profile information.

How to Capture Information Online

The key to receiving good, accurate information from a user is to make it an easy and painless process. Users will become quickly exasperated if

- You ask for a lot of information.
- You provide a registration form that has too many pages (you want to stick to just a few).
- You require the users to provide what they consider to be optional information (i.e., information that has no apparent relevance to personalization).

There are two main formats for collecting information from a user: an online registration form or guestbook, and questions/selections embedded in the Web site.

Online Registration Forms or Guestbooks

Registration forms and guestbooks are popular ways to acquire user profile information in order to personalize the Web site according to the information collected. Online forms and guestbooks allow users to enter information into fields, make selections using check buttons or radio buttons, and submit the information to the site database. Web sites should enable users to access and modify user profile information at any time. See Chapter 9, "One-to-One with Web Site Tracking," for a discussion on the use of guestbooks. Figure 4.10 shows an example registration form.

Embedded Within Web Site Content

In addition to online registration forms, you can build user profiles with questions that are embedded within Web site content. Having questions that are associated with particular content allows you to acquire even more individualized information. Since Web sites are becoming larger and more complex, embedded profile questions can make it easier for users to build their profile on an ongoing basis. Many of your customers have

Figure 4.10 Sample online registration form from Gist TV.

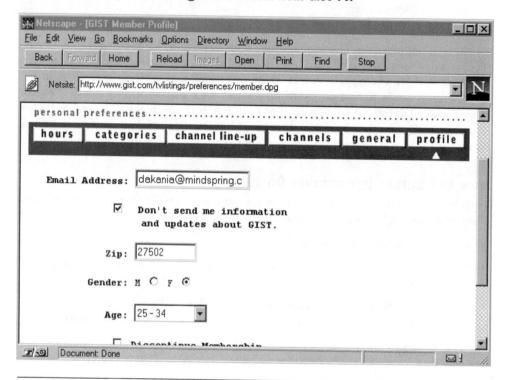

needs that may span multiple product or service categories, so asking for information that is relevant to the part of the site that the user is currently in will increase the impact of your Web site personalization efforts. Once you know several attributes or interests of a user, a Web page can decide what combination of text, graphics, and links to display.

> **TIP** Only ask for user information that is relevant to the Web site personalization you are providing to your users. Do not ask for all of the information up front—one-to-one relationships are built over the long term.

Integration of Tracking and Profile Information

One of the more advanced uses of personalization systems is in relating actual Web page viewing to actual user profile information. Many database programs can be used to join the profile data with the Web server log data so you can perform queries like

How many people who say they like golf saw a particular golf page versus people who didn't say they like golf?

Rank the length of time spent on a particular Web page by the age group of the user?

How is the length of time spent on certain pages related to the education level of the user?

Do people who want weather reports for cities with airline hubs spend time on the travel page?

In addition to learning about the Web usage patterns of people according to their demographic characteristics and interests, the profile data can be integrated into your traditional direct-marketing activities. By using traditional merge/purge mailing list management software, you can add new names to your mailing list and update existing names with new data. This means that traditional direct-mail packages can be targeted much more precisely by using information gathered directly from your audience.

For customers who purchase from your Web site on a regular basis, such as in a business-to-business setting, the profile database can store all of the preferences for products, shipping, and special situations. This information can automatically be used each time the customers return to purchase additional products. The system can even store purchase history information and decide to display specials for frequent buyers or especially good customers.

See Chapter 10, "Integrating One-to-One Web with Other Marketing Systems and Processes," for a discussion on database integration.

Products and Services

There are several products that allow you to add personalization to your site without building the system yourself from scratch. Table 4.2 contains a list of available products and services. Each product or service varies in approach, complexity, and price. You will want to do a careful evaluation of each product you are considering to make sure it fits your specific personalization objectives. Please visit our companion Web site at www.1to1web.com for in-depth information and updates.

Table 4.2 Web Site Personalization Products and Services

Company	Products/Services	URL
Art Technology	GroupDynamo Profile Station Dynamo Retail Station	www.atg.com

Table 4.2 *Continued*

Company	Products/Services	URL
Apple Computer	Web Objects	www.apple.com
Autonomy	Agentware i3	www.autonomy.co.uk
Broadvision	One-to-One Application System	www.broadvision.com
	One-to-One Commerce	
	One-to-One Financial	
	One-to-One Knowledge	
Cyber Dialogue	Dialogue Telescope	www.cyberdialogue.com
FireFly	FireFly Passport Office	www.firefly.net
	FireFly Catalog Navigator	
GuestTrack	GuestTrack	www.guesttrack.com
InTEXT	WebInterests!	www.intext.com
LikeMinds	LikeMinds Preference Server	www.likeminds.com
MicroMass	IntelliWeb	www.micromass.com
NetPerceptions	GroupLens	www.netperceptions.com
Open Sesame	Learn Sesame	www.opensesame.com
Personalogic	Personalogic (service)	www.personalogic.com
Perspecta	Perspecta SmartContent System	www.perspecta.com
W3.com	Personal Web Site	www.w3.com

Hurdles to Implementing One-to-One Web Site Personalization

In order to take advantage of the relationship-building capabilities of one-to-one Web site personalization, the industry will have to overcome some social and technological hurdles. The future for personalization will hinge on privacy and Web-to-database integration.

Privacy

The privacy issue will be the more significant hurdle to jump. Personal information will enable the most one-to-one communication between users and your company. What makes personalization useful also makes it scary to users. Web sites can be personalized while maintaining a user's anonymity. According to Stephen Tomlin, president of PersonaLogic, "Anonymous is the only, most appropriate way to protect users' privacy." The answer to the privacy question lies somewhere in between anonymity and disclosure. Users are willing to provide a certain level of information if they get value and they have the choice in what happens to their information. This point has been proven with the free e-mail services such as Hotmail, where users give personal information and participate in advertising in exchange for their own e-mail. The bottom line is to be up-front with users about how you will be using their information. Just remember these two words: choice and consent. See Chapter 11, "One-to-One Web Privacy," for more information about privacy.

Database Integration

Since Web site personalization is a still a relatively new concept, the integration of legacy or back-end databases is not prevalent on the Web. Many of the major players in the database industry, such as Oracle, Sybase, and IBM, already have solutions that integrate existing databases with Web servers. Most Web personalization systems also provide support for popular databases. See Chapter 10, "Integrating One-to-One Web with Other Marketing Systems and Processes," for a discussion of database integration.

One-to-One Web Site Personalization Resources

Web site personalization is still a relatively new concept, so there are currently only a few resources that are dedicated to it. Please visit this book's companion site, One-to-One Web Marketing Online (www.1to1web.com), for new and updated information and resources on this subject.

Online Resources

Marketing 1:1	www.marketing1to1.com
Marketing Competence	www.argo-navis.com/competence/index.htm
One-to-One Web Marketing Online	www.1to1web.com

Sampling of Personalized Web Sites/Services

In the future the majority of Web sites will have some level of personalization. Here is a list of sites that provide personalization—some provide a little personalization and others are highly personalized.

Company	Products/Services	URL
Amazon.com	Book recommendation services	www.amazon.com
American Airlines	Travel reservations and frequent flyer member services	www.americanair.com
CNN News	Custom news page and clipping service	www.cnn.com
Cisco	Presentation of products by customer type	www.cisco.com
CitySearch	Local business directories and personal Scout	www.citysearch.com
Crutchfield	Matching products with particular vehicle	www.crutchfield.com
CyberMeals	Order take-out and delivery meals from local restaurants	www.cybermeals.com
Disney Vacation Club	Customized vacation planning at Disney resorts	www.disneyvacationclub.com
eToys	Gift registry, occasion reminders, ToySearch	www.etoys.com
Farmer's Almanac	Personalized weather	www.almanac.com
Fedex	Package shipping and tracking	www.fedex.com
FTD	Online flower ordering from local florists, order tracking, and reminder service	www.ftd.com
GM BuyPower	Personalized auto research and purchasing	www.gmbuypower.com
Goodyear	Tire recommendation services	www.goodyear.com
H.O.T. Coupons	Personalized local merchant coupons	www.hotcoupons.com
InsWeb	Customized insurance quoting	www.insweb.com
Jango	Personalized shopping agent	www.jango.com

Company	Products/Services	URL
LookSmart	Personalized Web sources by customer type	www.looksmart.com
MapQuest	Personalized maps	www.mapquest.com
Moviecritic	Movie recommendations	www.moviecritic.com
NetRadio Network	Online music by category	www.netradio.net
NewsBot	Personalized search service for 200 news sources	www.newsbot.com
Overnite	EDGE electronic data services	www.overnite.com
Pacific Bell	Telecommunications solution finder	www.pacbell.com
Quote.com	Personalized financial information	www.quote.com
Quicken	Financial network, personalized portfolio to monitor investments	www.qfn.com
Union Pacific	Railroad invoice and equipment tracing	www.uprr.com
Virtual Emporium	Personal shopper (human) and LiveHelp chat	www.virtualemporium.com
WiseWire	Intelligent Web surfing service	www.wisewire.com

The Future of One-to-One Web Site Personalization

One-to-one Web site personalization is still relatively new so technologies will continue to advance for the foreseeable future. What we will see in the near future is the convergence of real-time and previously collected tracking data. Users who return to a site will receive information based on past visits. This is what Jupiter Communications calls the *active pull* method. Web site personalization will become more sophisticated and will become more integrated with offline sales, marketing, and customer service processes and systems.

 Go to the companion Web site for the case study, "One-to-One Web Site Personalization," Keystone Financial's KeyBuy Online Car Finance Shopping service.

Chapter 5, "One-to-One Push," is dedicated to push technology and its role in one-to-one Web marketing. Push enables Internet and intranet sites to establish a special channel that users can tune into and receive information from without even firing up their Web browser. Push allows one-to-one Web marketers go out and pull users back to their organization because it pushes content to the user. Push can be implemented to provide targeted and one-to-one communications.

ONE-TO-ONE PUSH

> **"Push is interactivity on demand. It's active content for passive viewers, and interactive content for an involved audience. Push is just as much about positioning and marketing as it is about content: It's about providing both content AND context. It's not about producing media, but about delivering an experience."**
>
> Carl Steadman of *Wired*, from "Publishers on Push," a two-week series on Stating the Obvious (www.theobvious.com), a site that provides weekly commentary on Internet technology, business, and culture.

What's all this shoving going on? For months, that's all we've heard about is push. It has been called the Internet's "killer app," but what is it really? There has been so much excitement surrounding this technology—some even say it's all hype. What is this *great deliverer* and how can we as Web marketers get in on the action?

Jim Sterne said in his book, *World Wide Web Marketing* (1995, John Wiley and Sons), "The World Wide Web is a pull medium, not a push medium." At that particular time in the Web's evolution, he was right. It seems like yesterday, and yet it seems like so long ago; hence, the phenomenon we know as "Internet Years," in which technological advances happen in days or hours versus weeks, months, or years in other industries. In just a few years, even the delivery methodology of the Internet has changed. Welcome to the latest darling of the technology and marketing media: push.

Everybody Is Pushing Around

Just to whet your appetite, *Information Week* (August, 1997) took a peek at who's been pushing:

- Lufthansa Airlines (www.lufthansa.com) uses push to alert consumers to fare discounts. Their launch of a pushed airfare-discount alert service is the first phase of what the airline hopes will be an extensive push strategy. "It turns traditional marketing upside down," says Roland Conrady, vice president of new media at Lufthansa in Cologne, Germany. "A customer subscribing to our channel will receive exactly the information he is looking for. There's no better way of marketing."

- Fruit of the Loom Inc. (www.fruitactivewear.com) built its own push application for its Activewear Online extranet for distributors and T-shirt screen-printers. When printers log on from a Web browser, they are alerted to changes in inventory of prespecified shirt sizes, styles, and colors at distributors located closest to them.

- Montgomery Securities in San Francisco (which was acquired by NationsBank in 10/97) plans to use push to distribute reports internally and to outsiders. The technology will distribute transaction summaries, market data, and account information to customers and partners.

- Onsale Inc., (www.onsale.com) an Internet auction house, uses push to broadcast auction bids in real time to a Java applet called BidWatch on users' desktops.

Leading industry analysts have some interesting predictions and statistics concerning push:

- "As the first broadly deployed embodiment of Internet Computing, push will drive the use of the Net well beyond today's manual fetch-it-from-the-Web-site interaction." *The Forrester Report: Push Beyond the Hysteria*

- "Push technology is forecast to account for $6.4 billion of Internet-delivered advertising, transactions, and subscriptions in 2000, according to The Yankee Group. This is one-third of the forecast total of $19.1 billion." *6/9/97 The Nando Times*

In this chapter we take a look at the power of push as a tool for the one-to-one Web marketer, starting with a brief overview. We examine the evolution of push, from e-mail to application distribution to complete desktop integration. We explore how push has been used in the past and about today's new Webcasting options for enterprises. We briefly look at how the technology of push works and also at some of the marketing benefits as well as the controversies. Finally, we examine some products and applications, the future directions for push, and a case study of a successful push campaign. You'll gain some creative insights as to how successful a push campaign can be when you Webcast using the right tools and the right messages to the right customers.

What Is Push?

Push is a method of pushing content over the Web to your targeted audience. Another word for push is "Webcasting," which literally means broadcasting over the Web rather than the more traditional broadcast mediums of radio or TV. Webcasting is, more specifically, *narrowcasting* your message over a channel to a highly targeted audience.

How does it work, you ask? Quite simply, users download the receiver software or use a browser that has it built in and then they personalize their receipt of pushed content by determining the frequency with which they want to receive updates. Before push, marketers had to constantly devise ways to try and *pull* customers to their Web site to view their content. Now they can *push* their content to users who have requested it.

Why would push be of interest to the one-to-one Web marketer? Because it is highly personalized. Viewers specify what topics, types of content, categories, and even Web sites they are interested in. They are willing to give marketers a certain amount of information so that they only receive messages that would be of interest to them. Can you image your mailbox at home only being filled with "junk mail" for things that you actually might buy?

Push is the equivalent of that junkless mailbox in this new interactive age. Messages can be targeted to individuals like never before because we now have the medium to communicate with them directly and interactively. When customers sign up to receive a "channel," they fill out a preference profile. They can change this profile at any time and are in control of what kind of information they will receive. And *you* get to send the right message to the right audience at the right time. A marketer's dream come true!

There are numerous push vendors Webcasting information. The main competitors in push appear to be merging into more full-solution applications and customization to meet many corporations' needs. Many smart marketers are using these push tools to send customers current price lists, update tech notes, send out FAQs on new products, send out software updates, and more.

There is so much push content out there that directories are popping up to help you locate the content you need. The Phlip.net Channel Guide is a search engine and directory for push channels. You can even submit your own channel to be included in its directory or search for online events as shown in Figure 5.1.

Benefits of One-to-One Push

In their book, *The One to One Future* (1993), Peppers and Rogers discussed how companies, by establishing a "learning relationship" with their customers, can increase cus-

Figure 5.1 Phlip.net helps surfers locate online content.

tomer retention simply by making loyalty more convenient for the customer. Push can be used by marketers to establish and maintain these relationships.

The primary benefit of one-to-one push is it's ability to be a targeted and focused advertising medium, allowing you to establish a learning relationship with your customers, become a valuable resource for them, and save them time and money.

Establish a "Learning Relationship"

Push is a great loyalty-building resource in that users must subscribe or *ask* to be pushed to. No more force-feeding our advertising messages down the throats of leery consumers. These users have entered into a one-to-one learned relationship with preferred vendors. By specifying the types of information that they are interested in, users are disclosing valuable information to you that may not be available to your competition.

Since most push applications have the ability to be what Peppers and Rogers call *customerized* based on user preferences, marketers have access to this learned information. Those marketers, who have established this channel of communication with their customers, are privy to their customers' wants and needs.

This information changes over time. Users may alter their profile whenever they choose, and since the marketer has this channel established, they can react to these changing needs in real time. For example, say you are a tennis enthusiast and you like to receive information concerning tennis, be it from tennis racket manufacturers, ball vendors, pro shops, and so forth. What if you twisted your ankle and the doctor said no more lateral sports, so now you have taken up golf. By simply changing your preferences in a push channel, you can now receive information about golf, directly to your desktop.

If push were a traditional medium like direct mail, you would still be receiving information about tennis, which is no longer of interest to you. But with push, the right golf-related companies and organizations are getting the right information to you, at the right time, by simply clicking on a preference to receive golf information instead of tennis.

Become a Resource for Your Customers

By having a constant and reliable "channel" of information continuously flowing between you and your customers, you can become a valuable resource to them. They will become dependent on the information that you provide on a daily or weekly basis. Whether you're Webcasting news and weather or updating a client on price changes, they will appreciate your taking a proactive position in your relationship with them. Rather than waiting for your customers to request information, you should predict their requests and respond to them.

Many push channels are coming on line that are very targeted. Many focus solely on financial information or entertainment. It wouldn't surprise us if soon there were so many specialized channels such as one solely for iguana owners. If you have a friend who owns an iguana and has a difficult time finding a good information source to help her, she would be thrilled if there were an "Iguana Central" channel that would give her all the information she needs about the care and feeding of her iguana.

"Don't Waste My Time"

The original model of the Web was the pull model in which users would have to search the Web for information that interests them and then pull it from the provider's server down to their machine. This can be a time-consuming, tedious, and sometimes frustrating endeavor (even with the use of search engines).

Now, users can subscribe to a personalized agent that will push only the content they want at their convenience. Push frees up time, alleviates the frustration in searching, and always keeps the user up to date.

Great Targeted Advertising Vehicle

Browsers providing push content may lead to a different model for advertisers. Pat Connolly is the founder of Stockpoint (www.stockpoint.com), formerly Investors Edge, a financial service that is one of Microsoft's premier channels. Connolly believes that advertisers may prefer to sponsor certain content providers as a way of creating brand awareness rather than the traditional online model of click-throughs.

Since many subscribers to push channels will view them daily, advertisers have the opportunity to create relationships with these subscribers. Much in the way that Smucker's jams and jelly's sponsors Willard Scott's weather on NBC's *Today* show, these sponsors can touch these people every day. The original online advertising model or click-throughs is based on banner advertising. Marketers track how many visitors "click" on a banner to go to another Web site via the advertising sponsor. Click-through rate can be deceiving—if you have a good content site, do you really want your visitors to leave to go to your advertiser's site? Through sponsorship of channels, advertisers can unobtrusively have a presence in the daily dealings of visitors' lives.

Some Pushy Controversies

According to a January 1996 executive briefing by the research firm Strategic Telemedia, it is a supply sider's dream whose biggest barrier could be customer indifference," meaning this is a user-controlled, vendor-supplied marketing tool and much depends on the tolerance levels of the individual users. Just as we have a choice to watch TV (commercials and all) or tape our favorite program and edit out the commercials, so do subscribers to these many push channels. Some channels are based on an advertising model and the users are willing to tolerate the ads for valuable, free content, others are a fee- or subscription-based model in which subscribers pay for the content in order to be free of advertising. Which model will prevail? Who's to say? It is still early, but many believe there is room for both. Just as there are commercial channels and pay movie channels, we predict the same in the future of push channels.

CDF versus Java: Will the Industry Adopt a Standard?

Microsoft teamed up with PointCast and created a proposed new standard for push creation called "channel definition format" (CDF). This format describes which pages on a site can be subscribed to as channels. It provides Web publishers with the ability to separate channel definition from content, allowing developers to change the definitions without making edits to the actual Web pages of a site. This has been submitted to the World Wide Web Consortium (W3C) to be approved as a standard.

Netscape uses HTML, Java, and JavaScript in its Netscape Communicator 4.0 and contends that HTML tags, Java, and JavaScript are better tools for standardizing channel delivery. After hearing Netscape's issues, Microsoft modified CDF so it would work with Netcaster channels.

Which will prevail? No one knows for sure, yet everyone definitely has an opinion on the subject. So the saga continues. Tune in tomorrow for the next episode of our daytime Web soap: "As the Browser Turns." For more information on these standards, visit Netscape at www.netscape.com and Microsoft at www.microsoft.com.

Bandwidth Load

A NETMarketing study done in the Fall of 1996 stated that 18 percent of all Internet traffic is generated by PointCast users downloading big chunks of preordered data (May 1997). That raised some concern about push's affect on corporate traffic flow for many managers.

Products are even coming out to deal specifically with this bandwidth issue. Packeteer Inc. (www.packeteer.com) has created the PacketShaper IP manager. By assigning priority to network traffic based on either its origination or application type, Information Systems can control some of the drag that these popular channels are putting on corporate systems. IS can even use policy modules that are available for most of the major push players.

PointCast has also offered a solution. PointCast's I-Server 1.2 downloads the information from PointCast Central only once through the Internet Gateway and then distributes it out to the users, thus reducing heavy Internet traffic. Another possible solution to the bandwidth issue is Internet Protocol (IP) multicasting. Paul Boutin of HotWired (www.hotwired.com) explains:

> " This enables Internet protocol (IP) packets to be addressed to all computers on the network rather than to a specific IP address, which designates just one computer. The data are passed around the network the same way a subscription magazine makes its way around an office— rather than republishing another copy for each computer or each end user, all computers read the same copy. IP multicasting was originally developed to enable one copy of a fat digital video transmission to be shared by all users on the network, but the protocol could, in theory, work for other types of content."

Unfortunately, the nature of multicasting makes it not quite Net-ready. Multicasting was designed for video and audio transmission and it assumes that a certain percentage of packets can be lost or dropped between sender and receiver. This won't work over the Internet, where dropping bits of content could prove disastrous. Multicasting cannot become mainstream on the Internet until enough ISPs adopt a common protocol that works for critical information distribution. You can be sure it's coming.

Productivity Issue

Another controversy that is surrounding push is the true value of the content being pushed from a business perspective. Since most subscribers are getting pushed to on company time, many managers are concerned that it is distracting workers from doing productive work. It's the new equivalent of playing solitaire or online games when the boss isn't looking. Many companies are even banning push channels for both bandwidth and productivity issues.

The Evolution of Push

Push was being implemented even before people knew what push was. E-mail, then PointCast, paved the way for what now is commonly called push.

The Original Push: E-Mail

Before there was push, there was e-mail. Savvy Internet marketers have been using e-mail as a push vehicle for years. But now smart one-to-one marketers may want to consider using e-mail as an affordable and reliable method of push.

Although e-mail is not as technologically sophisticated as push, e-mail is the most prevalent Internet application. Push has very tempting features for the marketer, including the ability to incorporate full-blown multimedia, video, audio, and so forth. However, push has many features that may limit its applicability for most Web marketers: the bandwidth requirements of push are substantial, the end user must download desktop client software, and it can take much more time, money, and resources to implement.

Several companies have emerged that can package graphical content to be delivered via e-mail, including Netscape's In-Box Direct, Mercury Mail, and Digital Bindery. As with all Web marketing technologies, each one has its strengths, and your decision to use a particular technology should be based on your marketing objective, the needs of the user, and, of course, your budget. Michael Tchong, the creator of the popular Cyberatlas (www.cyberatlas.com), provides an e-mail notification service to his users on his ICONOCAST Web site (www.inconocast.com). Although he has a Web site, he prefers to do most of the communication with his users via e-mail. He has chosen to use e-mail for these reasons:

It's fast. E-mail possesses none of the excess baggage that makes surfing such an unpleasant experience (huge GIF files, slow connections, dead links, poor navigation, etc.).

It's universal. No special software is required.

It's intrusive. No need to make mental notes to visit a URL.

There are many ways to use e-mail for marketing and communicating with your customers one-to-one or one-to-many. See Chapter 3, "One-to-One E-Mail," for a discussion on e-mail marketing and advertising.

The First Push: PointCast

In February 1996, PointCast(www.PointCast.com) introduced most of the world to the concept of push. By registering and choosing their preferences, users received PointCast specific news on topics of interest to them, such as CNN, CNNfn, *Time*, *People* and *Money* magazines, Reuters, PR Newswire, BusinessWire, Sportsticker, and Accuweather. PointCast supplied national and international news, stock information, industry updates, sports scores, and weather from around the world—all via the Web, directly to our desktops.

The original "active desktop" (Microsoft has now trademarked this phrase), PointCast's SmartScreen technology automatically begins running headline news and advertisements as a screensaver when a viewer's computer is idle. Right now, PointCast is the most popular consumer-oriented push delivery system for news. It has more than 1 million active users and 250,000 new registrations each month.

Interestingly, PointCast does not consider itself a "push" company. It is a news and information service that happens to use push as its delivery vehicle. Its main focus is on content. This is an important assertion and something that we as marketers should take note of.

 Marketers should not push for push's sake. We could easily become a culture that is so enamored by the technology that we forget that it is the content that is critical, not the vehicle.

The New Push

The new push revolution is centered around more practical business applications versus the more traditional push model of Webcasting news and sports. The main players in this arena of deploying business applications and solutions are BackWeb, Intermind, NETdelivery, and Marimba (see the section, "Mediated Delivery," later in this chapter). Our fifth product category, intranet, deals with this extensively. We're highlighting these unique applications, and one-to-one Web marketers will quickly see how push can be a powerful vehicle to conduct relationship marketing.

As seen in Figure 5.2, Children's Television Workshop, the creators of Sesame Street (www.sesamestreet.com), uses push to deploy an interactive coloring book in which the picture changes daily.

Figure 5.2 Kids can color in this interactive coloring book.

The Mars Pathfinder Web site allowed users worldwide to virtually navigate NASA's Sojourner Rover over Mars' surface via Marimba's Castanet technology. Using a standard browser, users were able to access NASA's Pathfinder Web site (mars.graham.com/wits/) and subscribe to a Marimba Castanet channel (see Figure 5.3). This Pathfinder channel then continually sent news, information, and images from Mars throughout the Rover's journey.

"This project demonstrates Marimba's commitment to showing how our advanced Internet technologies, typically provided to businesses, can be applied to social and scientific projects," said David Cope, Marimba's vice president of marketing. "Marimba's technology allows users to go way beyond having static information pushed in people's faces. Castanet allows users around the world—literally hundreds to millions of users—to easily receive and interact with rich applications over the Internet. It's this interactivity of applications that is enabling the Internet to become a true utility, ultimately leading to real information transfer—learning."

Figure 5.3 Witness the Web Interface for Telescience (WITS) rover simulation system.

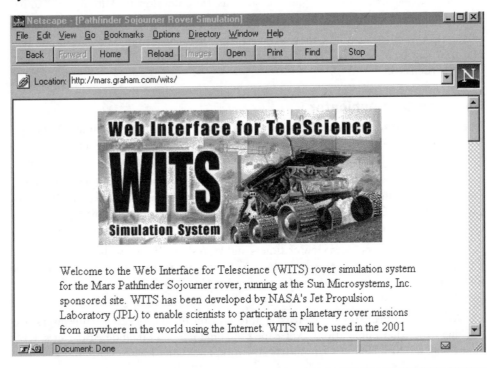

The Browser Push for Dominance: Microsoft's Internet Explorer Versus Netscape Communicator

The battle of the browsers is on once again, but this time, the battle is centered around push.

Microsoft's Internet Explorer 4.0

Internet Explorer 4.0 is very different than 3.0 in that it is integrated directly into the browser with preconfigured buttons of premier channels. More than 30 content providers have agreed to create "Active Channel" push content for Microsoft. Some of these providers include CNN, Disney Online, Discovery Online, Dow Jones, ESPN, *People*, the *New York Times*, and Warner Brothers Online, as well as some well-known online-only-providers like C|Net and iVillage.

Users also have the option to subscribe to more than 200 other content providers by searching in the "Channel Guide" on Microsoft's Web site. Almost any content provider can be listed in the guide as long as they develop in Microsoft's "Active Channel" format and provide a description of the content.

Users can customize how they receive these channels, either as a full-screen format that can be saved as a "desktop item" for later reading or as tickers, e-mail, or even a screensaver.

Netscape Communicator

Netscape's newest browser, Netscape Communicator (which includes Netscape Navigator 4.0), is centered around its latest push product, Netcaster. Companies and individuals can use Netcaster to subscribe and receive pushed dynamic Web content.

While Microsoft's solution is based on CDF, Netscape uses HTML, Java, JavaScript, and Marimba's Castanet to deliver content via its Netcaster module. Users can use Netscape Channel Finder to locate the best channels on the Net and can even access Marimba's Castanet channels with Netcaster's built-in Castanet Tuner.

Netcaster also lets users view channels and Web sites off line at their convenience. Other elements of Communicator include Netscape Navigator 4.0, Netscape Collabra for group collaboration, Netscape Composer for HTML editing and publishing, and Netscape Conference for real-time audio conferencing.

A *webtop* feature displays Netcaster information on the desktop while users are working with other applications. Netscape's channel partners include ABC News, CBS Sportsline, CNNfn, Hearst's HomeArts Network, and Time Inc. New Media.

Applications of Push Products

Rosalind Resnick, a veteran online publisher and marketer, defined these four types of push delivery models (*NetGuide* 5/97):

Self-service delivery. This model is primarily intelligent agents that update prespecified sites for you for offline viewing.

Aggregated delivery. Similar to a TV network or commercial online service in that it provides users with a wide variety of content and advertising choices packaged in a single offering.

Mediated delivery. This model lets Internet users control what information they receive from participating marketers and publishers by selecting from a menu of choices on the mediator's Web site.

Direct delivery. This model delivers content directly to your desktop.

To these models we'd like to add a fifth category

Intranet delivery. This model provides document distribution and access internally, but many have started to use this model for distribution via corporate extranets.

Self-Service Delivery

"Self-service delivery" gives the user the tools to download Web pages for later viewing. The tools can also be configured to automatically update any of the specified sites if the content changes. These tools may be of use to the one-to-one Web marketer in connecting clients to a site. Rather than having your customers remember to return to your site to check changing content, you can push those updates to them. Through the use of offline browsing and intelligent agents, your customers can have the flexibility and freedom of viewing at their convenience.

One-to-One Application Idea: Software Companies Can Build Push into Applications

PowerCerv Corporation (NASDAQ: PCRV) (www.powercerv.com), a leading supplier of client/server business applications, integrates push into its sales applications to allow companies to broadcast live updates to their mobile reps. They chose to use this self-service delivery model and selected FirstFloor Smart Delivery system (www.first-floor.com) to bring targeted Web-page and document delivery to PowerCerv's customer support and sales force customers worldwide. The integration of push with PowerCerv's products will provide PowerCerv's customers with an organized and targeted document delivery solution for distributing price lists, competitive information, and support documentation.

FirstFloor Smart Delivery

FirstFloor allows users to personalize their information environment, controlling how, when, and what information they receive. It uses intelligent agents to automatically notify users when content has been changed or updated.

FirstFloor does not sell its software directly to consumers, rather it licenses it to other software vendors to integrate into their applications. For example, according to Mark Bonacorso, director of marketing communications at FirstFloor Software, "Since FirstFloor is in the business of licensing Smart Delivery to other software application vendors, the pricing is below "list"; that is, more than likely the pricing is negotiated at the time of the sale." The list price for the Smart Notification Server is $9,995 per server, the Smart Subscriber (client) is $150 per client, and the Smart Delivery Application Developers Kit (ADK) has a $25,000 licensing fee.

Figure 5.4 Downtown's user interface.

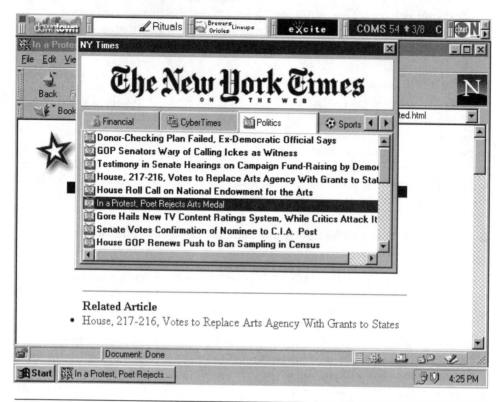

Bonacorso goes on to explain the different categories of push vendors and where FirstFloor fits in. "Some vendors specialize in software distribution, like Marimba and BackWeb, others in broadcast, like PointCast and AirMedia, FirstFloor specializes in document distribution. We are able to distribute files in their native formats to target users." If document distribution is a critical need of your company, this could be a useful tool for a Web marketer.

Other products that fall into this self-service delivery model are Incommon's Downtown, Netscape's In-Box Direct, and Verity's IntelliServ for Windows NT.

InCommon's Downtown

InCommon's Downtown automatically downloads updates to the user's favorite Web sites. Downtown resides on the user's desktop as a channel toolbar. Downtown is very unique in its interface. Its toolbar is a nonintrusive way of providing notification and access to information. Users customize the toolbar with the Web sites that they want to keep track of.

Web marketers may want to distribute a product like this to their prospects, customers, and vendors with certain Web sites already customized on the toolbar. Many enterprises are using this "private label" method to customize Web browsers and send them out to their prospects. Why not customize a push tool?

InCommon licenses Downtown to publishers of Web information—news, corporate information, e-commerce, and so forth. For publishers of information on the Internet (large, unrelated volume of viewers/users), they license the Downtown Server for $10,000 plus either a small per-user fee or a share of advertising revenue derived from the use of Downtown. For publishers on an intranet (small, known quantity of users), they license Downtown on a per-seat basis. This product is free to users.

According to Rob Caplan from InCommon's marketing department, "Downtown is a publishing system that provides publishers with a direct relationship to their viewers/users. With information notification and delivery directly to users' desktops, publishers are able to quickly and efficiently communicate with their users. Using Downtown's QuickCache technology, publishers are able to utilize larger files without concern for network performance constraints. QuickCache will download in the background only those files and objects that are new. This minimizes network traffic and keeps objects and files local for quick access by the user (see Figure 5.4). Downtown's interface is a small notification bar that scrolls key new information in an always-present task bar. And the popup windows provide summary information and user navigation into Web sites and corporate data stores."

Netscape In-Box Direct

Netscape In-Box Direct is a free subscription service to publications like *The Wall Street Journal*, *USA Today*, *Elle*, *Sports Illustrated*, and more. Each publication is automatically delivered directly to users' e-mail in-boxes. Users must use Netscape Mail 3.0 to receive this graphically rich content. Content providers include CNE, HotWired, *The New York Times*, Yahoo! and ZDNet. In-Box Direct is the first hybrid push solution, combining push content with e-mail distribution. For Web marketers who want an easy entry into push, this hybrid solution may be a good place to start.

Verity's IntelliServ for Windows NT

Verity's IntelliServ for Windows NT automatically delivers filtered information to users based on their preferences. Its one-button installation means that it is easy to install and ready to run right out of the box. Users can have information pushed to them from any source regardless of the file type or data format. Through customized notification, users can be notified of changes by e-mail, ticker, pager, or custom start page.

QUALCOMM, creators of the popular e-mail package Eudora, has announced its plans to bundle Verity's KeyView technology with Eudora. The KeyView 5.1 Plug-In for Eudora will allow users to view and print more than 25 popular file types directly from within Eudora Pro v3.0.3 for Windows.

Aggregated Delivery

The second model of push is called "aggregated delivery." Aggregated delivery systems act like TV networks or commercial online services in that they provide users with a wide variety of content and advertising choices packaged in a single offering.

This type of push would be of special interest to Web marketers of content sites. Again, you can "private label" and offer content specifically to a targeted group of consumers. For example, a national pet store can use this aggregated model to push all kinds of pet information directly to its audience. Users can choose channels on birds, cats, dogs, or whatever they have an interest in.

One-to-One Application Idea: Healthcare Providers Can Use Push for Managed Care Processing

Perot Systems (www.perot.com) has an agreement with Health First Health Plans, Inc. (HFHP) in Florida, to implement a pilot Web-based managed care processing and healthcare information environment that will make it easier for the company's healthcare providers to access information. Perot Systems will implement its Healthcare Solutions Model—a suite of technologies designed to streamline the electronic exchange of information—on top of Health First's existing intranet. Perot Systems will also use the PointCast Business Network Healthcare Insider to enhance functionality by broadcasting these capabilities along with world and industry news directly to the desktops of Health First's healthcare professionals.

"The Healthcare Solutions Model installed on the backend of the Healthcare Insider will add real value to Health First's daily operations," said Joe Boyd, Perot Systems' vice president and director of the Healthcare division. "Our Solutions Model is more than an application, it is the combination of data processing and Internet technology that creates an electronic work environment that has greater benefits than a simple Web site."

The terms of the initial six-month pilot project involve the integration of HFHP's existing intranet, InteliHealth's national content resources (such as news, education, databases), and a suite of EDI transactions, including interactive member eligibility, physician referrals, authorizations, and online access to provider directories.

During the pilot phase, Perot Systems will document the savings potential for plans of various sizes, and create modeling tools for future engagements. Immediate benefits to HFHP include reduced operational expenses in member and provider services as a result of decreased paper and mail handling, increased communications between providers, and improved administrative efficiency—with the ultimate goal of increasing member satisfaction.

PointCast's I-Server

The granddad of push is staying in the game. PointCast's proxy server allows companies to set up their own channels. Users can view their news as "Smart Screens," which will automatically engage when the computer is idle; or as a customizable scrolling ticker that can be viewed while running other apps; or as a "Channel Viewer," where the full text of all articles is displayed.

Other products that fall into this aggregated delivery model are Airmedia Live's Internet Broadcast Network, After Dark Online, and AlphaConnect StockVue.

Airmedia Live's Internet Broadcast Network

Airmedia Live's Internet Broadcast Network allows users to receive breaking headline news, sport scores, weather alerts, and financial updates.

This product is one of the few subscription-based services, but it may be well worth it for those who would rather not be deluged with advertising messages. The NewsCatcher wireless receiver costs $99.

Airmedia's content includes news, business, games, and sports information from providers such as CNN, Quote.Com, and Sportsline USA. Content is usually presented in scrolling marquees, which can be minimized to become a small stock ticker.

Of special interest to the Web marketer is that Hewlett-Packard and NEC are bundling the receiver with their newest computers.

After Dark Online

Berkeley Systems' After Dark Online is a lightweight version of their popular screensaver. Obtaining news from such popular sources as *USA Today* and *Sports Illustrated Online*, a user's screensaver is activated to receive headlines and summaries based on the user's preferences. It is also available in a stock ticker format. This product is free to users.

AlphaConnect StockVue

AlphaConnect StockVue Lite provides users with financial information and stock quotes from their choice of the following sources: Infoseek, Money Quick Quotes, MSN Investor, PC Quote, Quote.com, and Yahoo! Users can track up to three different portfolios (the $39.95 version lets users track up to eight), entering company names, symbols, and any holdings a user may have.

StockVue queries the user's preferred site either manually or automatically as often as the user specifies and delivers detailed information and any news on the chosen companies. Other features include the ability to calculate how stockholdings are performing through a minispreadsheet and alarms that signal the user if stocks fall below or go above a certain price. This product is free to users.

Mediated Delivery

The third category of push is what The Yankee Group calls "mediated delivery." These systems let Internet users control what information they receive from participating marketers and publishers by selecting from a menu of choices on the mediator's Web site.

This category probably has the most opportunities for Web marketers. While these vendors do offer channels, many specialize in more customized applications that can meet a variety of business-to-business as well as consumer needs. While many of these have been focusing on the consumer, mediated and the next category of intranet will show you some examples of the power of push for vendors, partners, and customers of the one-to-one enterprise.

BackWeb

One of BackWeb's (www.backweb.com) claims to fame is that it has more diverse content and delivery capabilities than its competitors. It is able to send personalized information from any content source, including legacy databases with real-time options. BackWeb currently has about 30 channels available, including Infoseek, iWorld, and the NetRadio Network. BackWeb provides software distribution but doesn't provide an entire framework for distributing and running applications as Marimba's Castanet does.

BackWeb acquired Lanacom in 1997 and will integrate its Headliner technologies to extend BackWeb's capabilities for Internet push channels. (Headliner won IW Labs' "Best of the Test" in the September 1997 Internet World.) BackWeb says the combined solution will make it easy for Internet publishers and service providers to build powerful channels for their audience that incorporate a variety of sources and viewing options. This product is also fully integrated with TIBCO for real-time multicast solutions and with AirMedia for real-time wireless solutions.

BackWeb is pioneering a new approach to push called "Polite Push," which is respectful of other work that is happening within the organization and minimizes the impact on the enterprises' Internet bandwidth and network. BackWeb's Channel

Software is also the engine behind Lufthansa's pushed airfare-discount alert service mentioned in the introduction to this chapter.

 Go to the companion Web site for "One-to-One Application Ideas: Companies Can Use Push to Send Virus Updates," which discusses how BackWeb, a leading push company, uses this mediated delivery model to create a secure-cast channel for McAfee and Associates.

House of Blues Internet Case Study

Background

House of Blues Inc. (HOB—hob.com) is an entertainment company whose mission is to deliver the "blues" to music enthusiasts using a variety of technologies. Divisions include a record label, a radio programming arm featuring a syndicated show starring Elwood Blues (Dan Ackroyd), a tours and talent unit that sponsors shows and events, a publishing wing, and a series of clubs and restaurants around the world.

Its audience includes the very young, who follow hip-hop artists such as Cypress Hill and Erykah Badu (participants in HOB's Smokin' Grooves event) all the way through to adults whose interests range across the history of blues and embrace stars like Buddy Guy and James Brown. The Internet user base is equally eclectic because of the diversity of music and information that is delivered.

Goals

House of Blues' marketing goal is to build a community of interest around the House of Blues brand. To start establishing the community, the marketing team created an Internet site that allows surfers to participate in what is happening at their clubs. Their next step was to reach out to the community, pulling them in rather than waiting for them to visit the HOB site.

Why Push?

According to Marc Schiller, vice president of New Media at House of Blues, "We had been evaluating ways to actively reach our fans, including e-mail. We thought the next logical step was push technology." Marc's group is responsible for digital distribution of content, researching and implementing new technologies, and developing new forms of entertainment. Marc comments, "We want to extend our brand and the community behind it in innovative and interesting ways. We want to 'push the envelope,' using a whole new model of content delivery for existing fans and to attract new people."

Implementation

House of Blues serves BackWeb on a Sun UltraSparc running Solaris, which is also used for all of its Web hosting. It creates its content using Windows NT. "Everything is in-house," explains Nick.

To assist in their internal development of the channel, a House of Blues engineer attended BackWeb's training session. "After attending only the first day of the two-day class, we were able to do it on our own. We have a good staff and learning to author was a small learning curve. Frankly, I was surprised to see how quickly we could put the channel up," said Nick. "One week after attending training, we were rolling. It was very fast. Being able to quickly repurpose existing content for the channel allowed us to get it running in time for Internet World and keep it going thereafter. We were helped by BackWeb's documentation, which is very thorough."

Channel Content

House of Blues carefully chooses the content it sends. Its goal is to send valuable, stimulating material that is significantly more appealing than can be delivered through other mediums, such as e-mail. Therefore, House of Blues frequently sends sound and multimedia clips to users, ensuring that both the message and the delivery are memorable. In addition, it wants the content to be highly meaningful to users, so a customizable framework was set up.

"The best way to make the content exciting and relevant is to make it very specific, so we set up content to correspond to the geographic region of the clubs. For example, you can sign up for the House of Blues channel and get pushed the schedule of events for the club near you. So, if you are in Chicago, you can get the contest for the John Fogerty show, which is taking place only in that region. Or if you live by the Myrtle Beach club, you get pushed schedules and promotions for that club only."

Customer Reactions

House of Blues is pleased by the customer reaction. After only a few months of operation, more than 10,000 users have registered for its channel and approximately 3000 tune in during a typical four-day span. According to Marc, "There has been a steady growth in the numbers. A lot of people are surprised by the power of what they get. We advertise a link to our schedules, then besides that we also deliver information on our new media projects. We've had great feedback from people who were unaware of the other activities the House of Blues supports.

"I get e-mail all the time. People love our channel. They are amazed this can even happen on a computer," Marc continues. "The first time something really cool like an HOB golf ball bounces across their screens, they say 'give us more.'" Nick adds, "We have a large international following who tune into BackWeb and we are working to improve our visibility. In fact, we just distributed 50,000 CDs with presubscribed BackWeb software through Connect, an Internet music magazine in the UK. We plan to do more promotions like this in the future."

Other products that fall into this mediated delivery model are Marimba's Castanet, NETdelivery, and Intermind Communicator.

Marimba's Castanet

Marimba's Castanet (www.marimba.com) is designed to distribute and manage applications automatically. When updating, Castanet delivers only the data that has changed, thus lessening traffic. The present program is built around Java, but future versions should support non-Java applications. Castanet focuses on full-blown application deployment rather than simple content push.

Software marketers have a significant interest in Castanet for the deployment of software updates and bug fixes. Other Web marketers may wish to deploy applications to partners or offsite sales representatives. Castanet is being used in OnSale Inc.'s pushed auction bid system mentioned earlier in this chapter.

NETdelivery Corp.

NETdelivery (www.netdelivery.com) is a Web-based delivery service that ties communities with common interests to providers of relevant content, merchandise, and services. They call it "Community Marketing" because it allows communities to obtain relevant information, facilitate decision-making, and engage confidently and easily in online commerce with NETdelivery's corporate partners and community partners via the Internet.

NETdelivery provides content from such sources as Inc. Online, NetGuide Live, and The Weather Channel. Catalog providers get 300 free deliveries per month and then pay 5 cents per delivery on volumes from 301–5000. Users can choose to receive notification of vendors' special offers. Notifications are delivered discreetly to a simple mailbox icon that raises the flag when there are messages. This product is free to users.

Intermind Communicator

Intermind Communicator (www.intermind.com) not only provides over 200 channels of personalized content but also specializes in intranet solutions. It is able to integrate intranet information notification and delivery with Lotus Notes/Domino applications and legacy data systems. Some of its most popular content publishers are Addicted to Noise, CBS News Up to the Minute, Discovery Online, Excite!, Live, HotWired, Popular Science, and iWorld's Netday News.

Intermind Communicator can also provide personalized delivery of technical support over extranets for companies communicating with their customers. It has the ability to customize products for large intranet and Internet customers.

By using Intermind's Dynamic Publisher, the server extension to Intermind Communicator that automates the creation and updates of channels, anyone is able to publish and subscribe to an unlimited number of customizable communications channels. The Publisher is free for noncommercial use. Commercial sites pay $5,000 per server to use Communicator and pay a monthly fee to view demographic information.

Intermind has the ability for private branding. Most businesses wish to retain and build as much brand equity as possible. Because of their architecture, it is easy for them to create private label and OEM versions of Intermind to serve these businesses. Intermind's strategy is to enable businesses with the power of its system, but under the branding of each individual company. By doing this, companies are able to maintain a one-on-one relationship with their customers and partners—especially now that companies can private label Intermind with their own graphics, buttons, and preloaded channels.

Direct Delivery

The fourth model of push is "direct delivery." This allows the PC desktop interface itself to pull information from the Internet. The best examples of direct delivery to date are the new browser offerings from Netscape and Microsoft.

Soon a majority of the people accessing the Internet will be doing so on push-enabled browsers. The vendors establishing premier channel status with both Microsoft and Netscape will be in a supreme position for market leadership just on the pure distribution mechanism. According to a September 1997 Zona research report, Netscape Navigator has 62 percent of the market and Microsoft's Internet Explorer has 36 percent.

Netscape

Netscape contends that push hasn't obtained widespread adoption yet because of a certain barrier to entry for average users to access push technologies. But now, for the first time, all Internet users can have access to the benefits of push technology. As a component of Netscape Communicator, Netcaster, the first open-standards-based, cross-platform push client, makes push technology a widely available commodity. With Netcaster, instead of having to go out and find information, applications, and images over the Internet, users can subscribe to their favorite Internet-based "channels" and have personalized content come to them automatically.

"The rapid dissemination of push technology can be expected to create huge demand for push solutions in the consumer, business, and education arenas," says John Doe, director of marketing communications.

"Even in the consumer market," Doe continues, "experts assert that the main competition for all media is the television. Netcaster will make a computer far more like a television, providing animations and other dynamic content that often occupy the entire screen; users merely subscribe to a channel, then sit back and watch (with a few clicks of a mouse or remote control). Once they discover just how easy and enjoyable push technology can make their computing experiences, users will create a voracious demand for channels and content that can be delivered through them."

In business, as well as in education and other institutions, version control of applications has been a constant problem. It has always been a challenge to ensure that all users are equipped with the same version of an application—upgrading users with bug fixes or new versions can be a tedious, unreliable process that usually depends on a great deal of work from an administrator, and it can be expensive. Netcaster and the Marimba Castanet technology that's part of it can help change all that, and can lower the cost of owning computer systems for businesses and other institutions. Institutional users can all subscribe to a channel within their intranet and receive automatic software updates.

Again, once businesses and schools begin to understand how much time and money this can save, there will be great demand for the Netcaster-based software distribution scheme. Presenting a true shift in the way content and applications are distributed, Netcaster enables a new class of solutions that lower costs, make content more dynamic and personalized for users, and open new markets. Best of all, Netcaster is based on existing open standards and is easy to use for millions of users on intranets and the Internet.

 We spoke with Dave Fester, group product manager for the Microsoft Internet Explorer 4.0 Team, concerning Microsoft's involvement in the push arena. Go to the companion Web site for a transcript of our interview with him.

Intranet Delivery

The fifth model for push tools is one that we've added called "intranet delivery." Recently, more push vendors are seeing the potential in targeting enterprise users. There are big opportunities for one-to-one marketers to help companies communicate with their employees via an intranet and with their customers via an extranet. More push vendors are realizing that mission-critical data distribution is a real, practical, and needed application of push.

 Go to this book's companion Web site to read "A One-to-One Application Idea: Companies Can Use Push to Service Customers More Effectively." You'll find a case study from Starburst Communications (www.starburst-com.com). It's a great example of how one-to-one Web marketers can use push to improve customer service issues both internally and externally.

StarBurst Multicast

Based on the company's Multicast File Transfer Protocol (MFTP), StarBurst Multicast is a multiplatform, cross-platform client/server application that transfers data files of any size simultaneously to multiple receivers over local and wide area networks supporting broadcast and multicast. According to Steve Collins, vice president of marketing, the newest software for most common network routers and switches (such as Cisco or Bay Networks) has multicasting support built in, no extra hardware required. Pricing for StarBurst Multicast starts at $39,900 for a server supporting 25 clients.

Other products that fall into this intranet delivery model are DataChannel's ChannelManager, Wayfarer's INCISA, Compassware's InfoMagnet, Diffusion's IntraExpress, NETDelivery, and TIBCO's TIB/Rendezvous.

DataChannel's ChannelManager

DataChannel's ChannelManager (www.datachannel.com) is the next generation of Webcasting. This product is the first and only tool that allows information systems administrators to manage Web channels, external newsfeeds, PC applications, and legacy corporate data—all within a customizable desktop environment. It also has customizable employee productivity tools as well as custom desktop templates for departments, workgroups, and individuals.

"This is the start of a new era in event-based Webcasting," says David Pool, president and CEO of DataChannel. "The ChannelManager environment allows a publisher to have an unprecedented level of delivery control, allowing the mixing of any Web-enabled content to be presented in a unified, customizable framework, where all the content is immediately updated in real time."

Wayfarer's INCISA

Wayfarer's INCISA (www.wayfarer.com) is specially designed for Intranets and includes no advertising. It employs a multicast approach by sending one message to all recipients instead of requiring users to keep checking for new content.

Wayfarer says INCISA's intelligent management and filtering of information ensures that the relevant, ad-free business information is narrowcast directly to the

Figure 5.5 INCISA—bridging the gap.

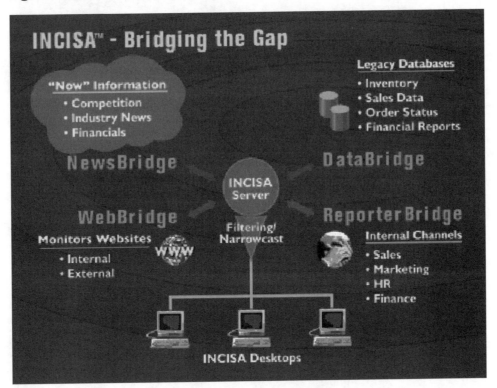

desktops of targeted users. Bandwidth requirements are minimal, ensuring that the network traffic doesn't come to a standstill, and firewall and data security are maintained and strengthened. Unlike consumer Webcasting, information can be provided not only from public Internet sources but also from internal legacy and corporate data systems, and through internal company channels such as sales, marketing, HR, and finance. Figure 5.5 shows Wayfarer's INCISA bridging the gap.

> **TIP** "Marketers can uses these tools to filter news and outside sources (wireservices, etc.). One of our larger customers is tracking four key competitors, three key suppliers, and about six top customers in real time. This means that anytime a news story or wire service event includes their names, the customers are immediately notified of the outside news." Rich Mironov, director of product marketing for Wayfarer.

Another application idea for using push is as an alerting system for manufacturing/sales systems. A major manufacturer added INCISA to purchasing and sales tracking systems, allowing it to signal when various kinds of events take place. For example:

- Your purchase requisition is entered/approved/disapproved (for materials managers).
- Your supplier delivers goods against your purchase requisition (for materials managers).
- Scheduled deliveries are more than one day late (for materials managers).
- Your customer order is entered (for sales rep).
- Your customer order is shipped (for sales rep).
- Your customer order is rescheduled/backordered (for sales rep).
- New master production schedule is posted (variety of departments). Advantages for the manufacturer:
- Real-time notification from Oracle financials/MFG system.
- Alerts are directed to the specific people/groups who need them (not broadcast).
- Yellow-flag and red-flag alerts go to different audiences.
- Reduced phone call load to order admin/tracking staff.
- Reps able to (proactively) manage customer delivery issues rather than waiting for customers to call.
- Can anticipate parts shortages better, so there are fewer line shut-downs due to backordered parts.

Figure 5.6 Wayfarer's Diet ZAP Cola demo.

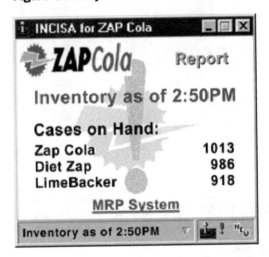

Wayfarer also shows another way that INCISA can be used in its ZAP Cola demo, as seen in Figure 5.6.

Compassware's InfoMagnet

InfoMagnet (www.compassware.com) is designed to help manage interaction with corporate databanks. It has intelligent real-time search and powerful filter capabilities. *NetGuide* chose InfoMagnet as the product it would most recommend for corporate information distribution (August 1997). The server software cost $4,995 and each user's license is $100. Figure 5.7 shows InfoMagnet in action.

 "Since a company's employees essentially determine a company's success or failure, it is important for them to be aware of everything that is happening in their industry. Push technology is a great new way to distribute information, but information is only valuable if it is relevant to the user. Push technology often overwhelms the user with too much irrelevant information, making it difficult to manage. Obviously, employees do not need the extra burden of wading through all the information that is pushed to their desktops. The answer is to combine push technology with intelligence and enable the users to manage their personal information flow. When employees have the ability to determine the importance of the information being pushed to them, they will have a better user experience and will be more productive. Supplying employees with the

Figure 5.7 InfoMagnet.

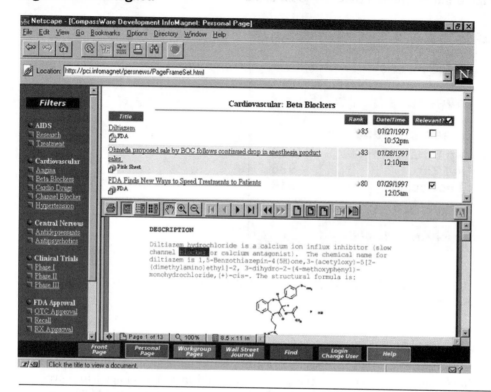

right tools to access relevant information is the key to a company's success." Scott S. Gatz, product manager, CompassWare Development, Inc.

Melissa Fabel, Marketing Communications Manager at Compassware: How Marketers Can Use Push

Pharmaceutical Company ABC has over 20,000 employees in different departments including research and development, sales, and competitive intelligence (CI). InfoMagnet can be used to integrate all of the information sources each department generates and deliver personalized, relevant information to all the employees. For example, the R&D department adds three reports to its database about Phase III clinical trials: one report about antihistamines, one about NSAIDS, and one about antacids. An employee in CI is tracking all the products of Pharmaceutical X and has developed a personal profile to specifically filter all new drug information regarding Pharmaceutical X.

After the R&D department submits its Phase III clinical trials reports, the competitive intelligence employee is alerted on his or her desktop that Pharmaceutical X's new antacid is now in Phase III clinical trials. Upon reading the report, he or she writes an MS Word memo to his or her boss, analyzing the effects Pharmaceutical X's new antacid may have on their own antacid product and creates an Excel spreadsheet comparing the two products. Both documents are saved in the Competitive Intelligence file server. A sales employee whose target market is gastroenterologists checks his or her personal page and learns about Pharmaceutical X's new antacid. He or she studies the Excel spreadsheet and formulates a sales strategy accordingly. Now three employees in different departments with different concerns have gained new knowledge by using InfoMagnet.

Since InfoMagnet allows each knowledge worker to create a personal profile, each employee receives only the information that is important to him or her. Using InfoMagnet, the employees from three different departments did not have to search each information source and wade through potentially irrelevant information. InfoMagnet delivered only the relevant information they needed. InfoMagnet saved these enterprise users valuable time and enabled them to make more-informed business decisions.

InfoMagnet essentially combines push technology with intelligence by allowing users to set up personal profiles to determine which information is relevant to them. Knowledge workers access InfoMagnet via a standard Web browser on their desktops and then create personal filters to access information across the enterprise, including real-time news feeds. They can access, navigate, and view MS Office documents, Lotus Notes, PDF, and HTML in their original format. By using InfoMagnet, pharmaceutical employees can stay abreast of the research or competitive intelligence that is being performed both inside and outside of their organization.

Diffusion's IntraExpress

IntraExpress (www.diffusion.com) was founded by a group of dedicated individuals experienced in solving corporate information problems. Realizing the potential of intranet and extranet, this team created IntraExpress to allow people within a company to use the company's communications channel to deliver information to their communities of interest.

Diffusion's IntraExpress users access the IntraExpress server and request documents immediately or in a subscription fashion. The document that the user sees is based on profiles stored on the server. This gives the publisher the ability to target particular users with custom information.

Ascend Communications, Inc., uses push to send a corporate newsletter that was, until recently, printed every four weeks and mailed. They also use IntraExpress to push new product updates and price lists to 1300 VARs across the globe. IntraExpress is more of a message-broadcast system rather than pushing dynamic content.

Diffusion also touts itself as being the first company to provide a comprehensive extranet-based solution to the complex issue of information delivery between a company and its employees, partners, and customers. IntraExpress acts as an "information broker," giving senders one central point of control for all information delivery, including e-mail, fax, pager, traditional mail, network printer, Webcasting, and the Web.

Beth Lee, Director of Marketing Communications for Diffusion, Inc: Meet Your Business Challenges with IntraExpress

Sales and marketing professionals must communicate regularly with many different people—direct customers, prospects, channel partners, third-party partners, and, of course, their own sales and support force. Information makes or breaks sales opportunities. Without the right information at the right time, partners will just as easily sell a competitor's product, so the cost of not communicating regularly and with impact is high.

Of course, the easier it is for partners to receive information, the more likely it is that they'll read it and use it to close sales. However, trying to satisfy customers' and partners' information needs creates enormous challenges, and sales and marketing professionals must deal with these challenges every time they send out information that's critical for sales or marketing success. Listed here are suggestions of how to address each of these recurring challenges using IntraExpress:

1. *Send information to everyone who needs it, the way they want it.*
Information that's vital to representing your products can't wait, yet this information, such as price lists, inventory status reports, competitive analyses,

and product updates, comes from everywhere. It may be in word processing files, spreadsheets, presentations, HTML, or a range of other application-specific formats. You need to send it to many different recipients, each of whom has specific file format and media preferences. Should you fax, e-mail, or Webcast it? How do you ensure that each recipient receives it in a format useful for him or her?

With IntraExpress, you can quickly and automatically send information from common desktop applications, Web servers, and application servers to everyone who needs it using any, or all, of your communication channels—e-mail, fax, Webcast, pager, or network printer—and also simultaneously post it to your Web site. IntraExpress can even convert files from common desktop applications so that they can be delivered in the recipient's preferred electronic file format. Automatic handling of multiple media and formats eliminates time-consuming, duplicate delivery efforts and format conversions.

2.   *Make information instantly accessible.* Timely access to the right information can make or break a sale. IntraExpress provides each recipient with a secure, personalized information library, where everything relevant to that person is stored and accessible. By providing recipients with around-the-clock access to their personal libraries, IntraExpress virtually eliminates the barrage of ad hoc requests you receive for previously distributed material. Recipients can retrieve their information from anywhere, via the media channel and format they prefer at the time—they are no longer limited by the sender's availability or original file format.

3.   *Leverage your Web site.* Your Web site contains valuable company and product information, and you want as many appropriate people as possible to use that information on a regular basis. However, not everyone is Internet enabled. IntraExpress can extend the reach of your Web site to your targeted recipients who do not have access to the Web—information can be delivered to them via common business media such as e-mail or fax. IntraExpress can also leverage your investment in the Web by enabling subscription delivery of information. By simply clicking a button on your Web site, users subscribe to important information, such as product announcements, and will automatically

receive updates as they are available. Recipients can also be notified when new information is added and then be brought to your Web site to view it at their convenience.

4.   *Keep up with change.* People change jobs, change roles, and change preferences. As new partners, employees, or customers come on board, IntraExpress ensures that they have immediate access to all of the information they need to perform effectively. People who leave no longer have access to your confidential business materials. Recipients manage their own personal profiles so, at any time, information delivery will reflect changes in their schedules, locations, or preferences. You no longer have to track individual delivery requirements, and everyone who needs information receives it.

According to Karen Styres, Vice President of Marketing for Diffusion, There Are Some Interesting Customer Applications Planned for the Future.

Documentum develops, markets, and supports a family of enterprise document management products that improve organizational effectiveness based on a company's business-critical information and proven processes. The Documentum Enterprise Document Management System (EDMS) automates and accelerates the creation, modification, and reuse of business-critical documents, Web pages, and other unstructured data and all of the collaborative efforts involved.

Documentum's customers are Fortune 1000 companies in a wide range of industries, including top worldwide pharmaceutical, manufacturing, and engineering firms. These companies are using the Documentum EDMS to reap dramatic improvements in their business-critical document processes for greater productivity, shortened time-to-market, and heightened competitive advantage.

Documentum and Diffusion are working together to provide customers with a complete solution, from content creation to information delivery. By combining Diffusion's information delivery solution with Documentum's document management solution, customers can not only efficiently create documents but manage the distribution effectively so everyone who needs to see or use the document, inside or outside the organization, can. In addition to

Documentum's rich functionality for creating material, the addition of Diffusion's information delivery functionality allows customers to deliver in multiple media format, create user profiles for preferred information, create personal information libraries for each user, and develop audit trails and reporting functionality.

TIBCO's TIB/Rendezvous

TIB/Rendezvous (www.TIBCO.com) doesn't really fall into any of these categories. It is a developer's tool for building scaleable distributed applications. Its publish/subscribe technology is the foundation of TIBnet, a family of push products. A number of partners are TIB-enabling their applications, including 3Com, AirMedia, BackWeb, Cisco Systems, CyberCash, DataChannel, Diffusion, EarthWeb, FirstFloor, Hewlett-Packard, IBM, Intermind, and Sun.

The Future of Push

In 1996, total push revenue was approximately $10 million. According to a recent white paper from The Yankee Group, by the year 2000, desktop delivery systems will account for $5.7 billion in Internet advertising revenues—nearly 30 percent of the projected 19.1 billion total (*NetGuide*, May 1997).

Right now push is being used for a lot of entertainment channels' deployment. The real money will be made in business–to–business information deployment.

Eric Greenberg, founder and chairman of the Internet consultancy Silicon Valley Internet Partners (SVIP), believes that ultimately, business will realize that push's true killer app is its ability to distribute software within corporations and to customers. "Companies spend millions on software distribution," says Greenberg. "It's one of the greatest costs of the client server system. Push will allow you to send changes to every desktop with a script that installs and implements the software automatically." (*Webmaster Magazine*, August 1997)

Push can also be used to monitor the enterprise data warehouse and notify appropriate people when significant changes occur. D2K Inc. recently launched a product that can deliver legacy and data warehouse information via the Internet. Users can schedule when they want to receive the information on their desktops as a Java-created chart or Excel spreadsheet.

The information that is available via the Web is only a small fraction of what most companies have internally. Linking legacy data systems with end users via the Internet will be a powerful business application. Presently, companies are reentering much of their internal data into Web format because they don't know of any other vehicle to port the data. Push can be that vehicle.

While some critics have been pessimistic about the true viability of push by offering e-mail as the only safe and effective form of push, others can see a bright future for push.

> *"Push has the potential to transform the Internet into a powerful online marketing tool, but the efficiency of multicast technology will be required to enable the large-scale deployment of push solutions."*
>
> *Steve Collins, vice president of marketing at Starburst*

As Paul Boutin said in Webmonkey-Geek Talk, "Push media isn't really the result of new technical specs or breakthroughs in software. It's the result of rethinking the way we interact with the content our networks can already deliver. That is really how one-to-one Web marketing fits into all of this. Marketers need to rethink how to deliver their messages to their customers one at a time, and if implemented correctly, push can be the way to get that message across.

Web Site Go to the companion Web site for a one-to-one case study on push, "PointCast Is a Perfect Fit for Fruit of the Loom."

Chapter 6, "One-to-One Web Community," discusses the role online communities will play in one-to-one Web marketing. The chapter shows you how virtual communities can be used for entertainment, consumer retail, and business-to-business applications, and discusses the heritage and future of online communities.

ONE-TO-ONE WEB COMMUNITY

6

"The new electronic independence recreates the world in the image of a global village."

Marshall McLuhan

Online community was one of the earliest uses of the Internet. Although most of these communities were noncommercial or even anticommercial, members took refuge within these communities to share thoughts and ideas, discuss controversies, get advice, and generally socialize. It was the ultimate in one-to-one communications.

These communities were based on *chat*. Realistically though, participants weren't *chatting* in the true sense of the word. They weren't really talking to anyone, just reading messages that other chat participants had posted. Once they entered a chat *room*, which was really just a Web page, they could choose to only read the exchanges, known as *lurking*, or they could join in and post their own messages.

Today companies are forming communities to better serve their customers. Advertisers are able to better target their messages within focused communities. Investors are putting millions of dollars into community-based technologies and touting it as the next big use for the World Wide Web.

In this chapter we discuss how one-to-one communities are being created by marketers to build relationships, solve problems, and collaborate with their customers and prospects. We briefly review the history of online communities, discussing two successful business models for creating these communities, and the basis of interaction needed for success. We examine some of the benefits, controversies, and applications of community. Finally, we explore some online community resources and also some concepts on the future of one-to-one Web community.

Impact of Community on the Internet

Online community has had a great impact on the Internet in the past. In this chapter, we examine its path in history. We also look at its impact on the future, which will become apparent through the support and enthusiasm of the financial community, the sociological and economical impacts shown in the book *Net Gain* (1997, Harvard Business School Press), by John Hagel and Arthur Armstrong, and the many one-to-one Web marketing opportunities.

History

Online communities such as chat rooms have been around for years. Chances are that if you meet a *real* Internet guru, he or she will tell you war stories about bulletin boards, posting and flaming, and all the fun he or she had in the *pre*-Web days.

For many of us who cut our teeth on the World Web Wide with a graphical-based browser like Netscape (or even, God forbid, Mosaic), let's run through a bit of the history of online community. With 3-D virtual worlds and avatars coming into mainstream now, it will be helpful to take a look back at where we have been in order to fully appreciate the richness of where we are about to go in the world of one-to-one online community.

The Well

One of the earliest examples of an online community was The Well (www.Well.com). Stewart Brand and Larry Brilliant founded the Whole Earth 'Lectronic Link in 1985. This community was started with a dialog between the intelligent, creative, and articulate writers and readers of *The Whole Earth Review*.

The Well started as purely a conversation space, but from 1992 to 1996 The Well provided its members with both Internet access and the legendary conferencing environment. In 1996 The Well consolidated the connectivity part of its business with the San Francisco Internet Access Provider, Hooked, forming the new Whole Earth Networks. Whole Earth Networks maintains The Well's servers and billing operations, while the conferencing, content, and cultural aspects are still supported by The Well's staff in Sausalito, California.

The formation of The Well in 1985 set the tone for the open but remarkably literate and uninhibited intellectual gathering that continues today. Over the years The Well members have been able to do traditional business networking in an untraditional environment and have provided support and mentoring to other members.

The Well members have also founded organizations like the Electronic Frontier Foundation and The River, and documented what was emerging in books like Howard Rheingold's *The Virtual Community* (1994, Harper Perennial Library), John Seabrook's *Deeper* (1997, Simon & Schuster), and Tom Mandel and Gerard Van Der Leun's *Rules of the Net* (1996, Hyperion).

Bulletin Boreds—Oops, We Mean Boards

The Well led to the rise of many garage bulletin board systems where basically, if you had a computer, a modem, and a phone line, you were in business. Net enthusiasts began to set up their own bulletin board systems (BBSs) where they could post messages and others could read them and/or respond back. These systems mainly focused on subject matters that were of interest to the *sysop* (the person administrating the bulletin board). They were highly specialized in microtopics and were extremely niche oriented.

Some were actually quite interesting, like discussions of movies and politics, while many could be quite boring—Who would be interested in what time mail messages should move on the network? However, that is the true beauty of the Internet—there is something for everyone. What's the saying? One man's trash is another man's treasure? Well, the same holds true for the Internet in that if you are searching for *any* topic, there is a pretty good chance that someone has a bulletin board system dedicated to that topic and people are chatting about it.

Many BBSs are in operation today but often pale to the graphical excitement of community that is now available on the Web.

MUDs, MOOs, MUSH, and Quack?

As early as 1978, MUDs and the world of fantasy gaming captured the hearts of thousands of dedicated techno-adventure seekers. Despite the funny names, these MUDs can be quite addictive.

MUDs are role-playing scenarios of the online game Dungeons and Dragons. MUD originally stood for multi-user dungeon; now it stands for multi-user dimensions. Players can interact with one another over extended sessions, even years. Variations on this concept are MUSHes and MUCKs, which extend these programs by including a usable programming language. MOOs, which weren't born until 1990, include a usable object–oriented programming language.

In order to play, users have to telnet into the MUD's Internet Protocol Port. For some MUDs, you may have to register. Some resources to help you find MUDs are

Resource	URL
The USENET newsgroup	rec.games.mud.announceColin Moock's 51+ Places of Note in the MUD World watarts.uwaterloo.ca/~camoock/mud_list.html
The MUD Resource Collection	www.godlike.com/muds/
Yahoo!'s List of MUDs	www.yahoo.com/Recreation/Games/ Internet_GAmes/MUDs_MUSHes_MOOs_etc/

Lost Souls (telnet: ux.tcs.uh.edu (129.7.2.110) 3000), a Dungeons and Dragons-based MUD with a large, open base world—terrains ranging from arctic to desert to jungle. Proclaimed to be possibly the most realistic combat system in existence, Lost Souls uses stats, skills, race, and guilds to enhance a player's individuality.

Commercial Online Services

Quick to follow were content community providers such as America Online (AOL), CompuServe, and Prodigy. AOL is the most successful of these three, being that it strongly focused on the community/communications model straight out of the gate. AOL also started with an attractive user interface for its content and communities, while CompuServe continued to use a text-only interface. In addition, AOL knew that its success depended on connecting its members to each other. It encouraged chat sessions among its members, and would set up chat rooms that focused the conversation on specific topics, such as love, money, gardening, waterskiing, and more. That way, people could get together with others who had similar interests.

Because of this philosophy, AOL has had one of the highest growth levels. "AOL had grown its subscriber base by nearly 3.6 million in the two years from 1993 to 1995, while CompuServe grew by 1.9 million members, and Prodigy grew barely at all, adding fewer than 200,000 members (net). Prodigy was slow to adjust its business model from a broadcast content model to a community model. As a result, it has been left behind (1997, *Net Gain*).

Be All the Mall that You Can Be

The next progression of online community as we know it was the creation of the online mega mall. These malls catered to everyone for every need. These malls, like Spectropolis (www.spectropolis.com), Minnesota Virtual Mall (mnvirtmall.com), The WholeSale Mega Mall (members.aol.com/wwwpro/wholesale/index.htm), and The Internet Mall (www.internet-mall.com), with over 20,000 stores have millions of products and services available to the consumer. While they can be very impressive, they can also be overwhelming, especially if you are "mission shopping."

Mission shopping is when you are on a mission to find one certain thing. You don't have time to mess around and browse or window shop. You are on a mission! Quite often these mega malls have lots of choices, but when it comes to honing in on one specific item, that ability can be almost impossible to master. And unfortunately these venues are not effective in the approaches of one-to-one Web marketing. They are way too general in their breadth and scope and try to be all things to all people.

For many consumers, however, these malls were their first introduction into the world of electronic commerce, and this opened the doors for other companies to follow this buying/selling online model but with a bit more focus. The most successful malls are those that are tightly focused in on meeting the specialized needs of a specific group of consumers.

Targeted Consumer/Vendor Malls

A good example of this type of site is SciQuest. Its tag line further conveys its mission of "Connecting Buyers and Sellers." SciQuest is a comprehensive, timesaving, scientific "buyer's guide" on the Internet. The SciQuest database consists of over 100,000 product categories from over 10,000 scientific vendors. So, if you are in the scientific sector and need any type of equipment, instrument, software, product, or service for scientific, laboratory, research, or development work, this is a good place to look.

SciQuest's mission is to streamline the purchasing and communication processes among scientists, buyers, and vendors by leveraging the efficiencies of the Internet and information technology for the maximum benefit and productivity enhancement of the scientific community.

The key features of this site are its search engine and SciMail (a smart e-mail system), which save users time by allowing them to find, qualify, and communicate with multiple vendors in just a few minutes. SciQuest's database has over 13,000 domestic and international suppliers of analytical, biotechnological, biomedical, clinical, and critical environment equipment, supplies, software, and other services. Searches can be conducted via product keywords, supplier location, geography served, distributor of choice, and ISO certification level.

SciQuest was conceived by the first-hand experience of its principles as laboratory supply distributor sales reps in the scientific industry. Their customers at that time were scientists. An example of one of their biggest frustrations was when a scientist was conducting a research project and had to find some new chemical, antibody, instrument, or supply. It was an unbelievably time-consuming task to find out who made the item, how much it cost, how to get the product, and how to communicate with the specific vendor.

The scientific industry is very segmented, with more than 10,000 vendors who sell in excess of $18 billion to over 500,000 laboratories. Scientists may spend two to six hours per week finding and communicating with this fragmented vendor population. SciQuest chose to use the Web as their vehicle because of the high level of Net sophistication among scientific researchers.

A final impetus that really made SciQuest want to pursue this business model was the lead management process within the scientific industry. In the traditional world of journal advertisement or trade show marketing, a scientist can fill out a bingo card or inquiry form. This document is normally processed through several people, often taking three to four weeks to arrive on the desk of the person who can take action (sales representative contact, literature fulfillment, sample department, etc.). SciQuest created the SciMail system so that an inquiry would instantaneously route to the appropriate person inside the vendor's organization. This has had tremendous impact on the ability of the vendor to quickly service a customer's request.

Before starting this venture, SciQuest conducted over 400 one-on-one surveys with researchers who were their customers at the time, from such large companies as Glaxo Wellcome, University of North Carolina at Chapel Hill, and many of the biotech companies.

Following is a copy of that original survey.

SciQuest Pre-Launch Survey

1. Please give us your typical information needs and the processes you use to ascertain the information (as they pertain to products and services).

2. How do you find out about new products and services? What journals, catalogs, magazines?

3. How often do you communicate with manufacturers and distributors directly?

4. Does your lab have Internet access?

5. What type of access? Browser?

6. How often do you use the Net? For what purpose?

7. Would you take the time to go on line if you could go to one site for your product and service information needs?

8. What would you like to be able to do at the site?

9. Would you use a site like SciQuest? Why, or why not?

10. How often do you or your lab:
    a. Search for a product for a specific application
    b. Request pdt samples
    c. Request pdt literature
    d. Request quotations
    e. Register complaints
    f. Request returns
    g. Request demos

h. Request cross references to equivalent pdts

I. Contact sales reps

j. Request pdt catalogs

k. Place orders

11. Do you think you or your company will purchase scientific pdts via the Net?

12. If yes, what types of pdts?

13. Does your company limit the use of the Net?

SciQuest's one-to-one Web marketing business model could conceivably be used across thousands of other niche industries. Figure 6.1 shows the entry into the SciQuest search engine and SciMall at www.sciquest.com/catalyst/welcome.cgi/catalyst/welcome.cgi. Note the groupings by product segments and by scientific disciplines and techniques that make it easy for scientists to find exactly what they need.

Figure 6.1 SciQuest search engine and SciMall.

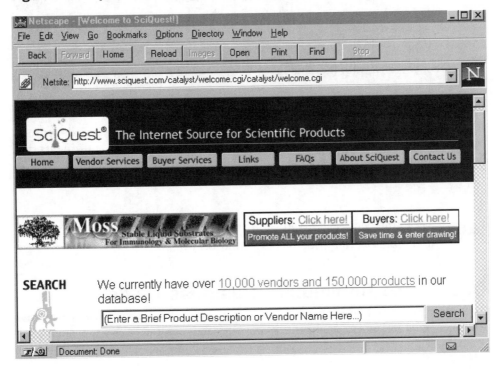

Advice from Bobby Feigler, Director of Sales and Marketing

1.   The best advice I could give to marketers would be to make sure that their target market uses the Internet on a very regular basis and that these prospects/customers are Net-savvy enough to understand the benefits. We at SciQuest spent a lot of time making sure that the market need really existed, both from the scientific user perspective and the vendor perspective (the people who pay us).

2.   Research your competitors!

3.   Another important issue is business model development. Basically ask yourself: Is this business structured in a such a way that you are going to make money?

4.   Make sure you have the right people in place, in the right numbers. Sales and marketing requires professional marketers and salespeople, and not necessarily a bunch of techies. We tend to enable existing, industry-standard technology for a specific business need.

5.   Lastly, be prepared financially. Raise your money up front, and do not be conservative with the amount. It will take a lot more than you forecast.

We're into Money!

As mentioned earlier, early forms of online communities were mainly social, noncommercial exchanges. Today the concept of online community and chat is taking its first baby steps into World Wide Web market success, as illustrated in an article in *USA Today* (3/19/97), which you can find on the companion Web site.

 Go to the companion Web site to find the article, "3-D Chat Rooms Generate Big Net Investments," from *USA Today*.

One-to-One Community Business Model

The newest and most effective forms of online community from a one-to-one perspective will be targeted consumer commerce/resource sites and corporate Web site communities.

Targeted Consumer Commerce and Resource Sites

We feel that the most effective one-to-one Web communities will be targeting consumers with specific and focused needs (like SciQuest). Another example of this type of site is The Herp Mall (www.herp.com). This mall is dedicated to information about Herpetology, a branch of zoology having to do with reptiles and amphibians. The site has animal dealers, exporters, supply dealers, food dealers, books and information, upcoming events, and even information about Herp Societies. If you want to buy a snake, this is the place to go.

This Targeted Consumer Commerce and Resource business model will be effective because there are literally millions of niche markets out there that need access to:

Information. Consumers need resources to be able to research, investigate, and compare the specialized niche products that they are looking for. Where else are they to find this information except online?

Products. Consumers need access to the highly specialized niche products that they wish to purchase. It's not like they can go up to the corner store and pick up these items.

Corporate Communities

Another very effective one-to-one community business model will be the corporate community. Corporations that take the time to communicate with their customers and then *react* by modifying and customizing their offerings will be the big winners in the next decade.

We are rapidly moving into the new business model of one-to-one community as revenue-generating and loyalty-enhancing tools for businesses.

"Web publishers have begun to use chat in ways that extend the application's original purpose as a social medium between users. While a Jupiter study shows that about 16 percent of top consumer Web sites have user-driven chat environments, increasingly chat will be used as a publisher- or merchant-to-consumer medium...Every Web publisher should consider chat as a customer support channel. Shopping sites and service-oriented sites such as travel and banking ventures have been missing a crucial element thus far: live merchant-to-consumer interaction. Companies that use chat in this capacity will form the most profitable online communities in the future," says Kate Doyle, Jupiter Communications analyst.

Following are some examples of companies integrating chat in a customer support capacity courtesy of Jupiter Communications:

Egghead. In an upcoming virtual store, salespeople will greet and help potential customers with computer questions (www.egghead.com).

NetMarket. NetMarket will provide weekly live auctions in chat rooms (www.netmarket.com).

Sprynet. Sprynet's customer service reps are available to answer questions about configuring Sprynet's service on line. They are currently helping about 15,000 people each month. This solution has been extremely cost effective for Sprynet in that 1-800 call center numbers cost a company 33.6 cents per minute while a chat room attendant's time is less than 1 cent per minute (www.sprynet.com).

Virtual Emporium. A Live Help area is planned in which representatives will answer questions about products in this mall site. Representatives, in this case, are actual floor-persons monitoring the chat room in shifts from Emporium's brick and mortar store (www.virtualemporium.com).

What Is Community?

In the past, communities were defined by regional areas, such as neighborhoods, cities, or geographic locations. Online communities have redefined that definition of community. Online communities are based on the need for people to interact with others with shared interests and commonalties. The physical boundaries of the world aren't applicable to the Web. Physical location has little to do with the thousands of communities that are actively prospering on the Internet.

In their book, *Net Gain: Expanding Markets through Virtual Communities* (1997, Havard Business School Press), John Hagel and Arthur G. Armstrong discuss that the basis of interaction in communities is based on people's desires to meet these four basic needs:

Interest. Many early online communities targeted the interest need by aggregating a dispersed group of people who share interest and expertise in a specific topic.

Relationship. Through online communities, people are able to form meaningful and personal relationships because they are free of the constraints of time and space.

Fantasy. Fantasy games like MUDs and MOOs allow people to escape from their daily lives into these online communities.

Transaction. Most people consider online transactions to be electronic commerce exchange, but for many communities, transaction means the giving or receiving of information.

Interest

Communities built around specific interests appear to be the most popular today and probably the easiest for the one-to-one Web marketer to create. If consumers have an interest in something, they will *want* access to as much information as possible because of that interest. Too often, marketers try to get their messages heard by people who simply aren't interested.

Communities built around the basic need of interest have a ready-made audience. These users are sitting on the edge of their seats waiting to get current, reliable information about their interests. The challenge for the one-to-one Web marketer will be locating these communities and participating in them. Or, if a specific community that you wish to target is not yet created, then take the initiative and go ahead and create it.

Much of this information can be garnered by interviewing your clients and prospects to see where their interests lie and if your product or service can be tailored to meet those interests. Even if your product or service does not directly mesh with your customers' primary interests, you may be able to create a community based on a related interest that could still give you an audience.

For example, if you sell windows for new houses, it is unlikely that you are going to find a community of people with a window fetish who want to have in-depth conversations about glass thickness, durability, and so on. However, you may find an audience who would love information about how to properly select windows. You could provide:

- Energy-saving tips
- Tips on how to make sure windows are fitted correctly or need replacement
- A guide for checking to see if homeowners are losing heat or air-conditioning out of their windows
- Instruction for homeowners on how to clean their windows without streaking

You could link your community to other complimentary community sites like home buyers' guides, newcomers' sites, relocation sites, home builder and general contractor sites, and Home Depot or Lowes Web sites that target the home buying or home-improving consumer. The possibilities are endless.

Relationship

In *Clicking* (1996, HarperBusiness), Faith Popcorn talks about the newest trends of this and future decades—one of them is *clanning*. She defines clanning as "the inclination to join up, belong to, hang out with groups of like kinds, to provide a secure feeling that our own belief systems will somehow be validated by consensus."

The need for relationship is primary and fundamental to all of us. Even in Maslow's hierarchy of needs, the need for belonging is ranked right up there with the need for food and shelter. We are a society of relations, be it through work, school, church, or family.

This need is so strong that many online communities have been popping up solely to fulfill this need. AOL's chat rooms were designed to get people to meet, interact, and

Figure 6.2 Match.com's relationship community.

form relationships. The Well was an intellectual-networking and relationship-building community. Many BBS community participants formed close relationships with others within those communities. They received advice, both professional and personal, and created relationships and contacts that lasted for years. Total-relationship services are being born on the Web. A good example of this is Match.com, the site for online matchmaking. This community's primary goal is to build relationships. Figure 6.2 shows Match.com's.

From a business perspective, relationship building takes on a whole new meaning. Companies need to build relationships with their customers. Gone are the days of the nameless, faceless consumer. Customers want to be remembered, catered to, and made to feel that their needs are being met by their vendors.

The bottom line is that people do business with people (and companies) who they like. There is too much competition out there for their business to have to tolerate mistreatment by their vendors. After all, *they* have the upper hand in this relationship in that they can always walk away. It is your job as a one-to-one Web marketer to delight your customers so much with your service and price and to know them so well (by asking them their needs and predicting their wants) that they wouldn't dream of leaving you!

Fantasy

Escapism is big business on the Internet, and users have the ability to "have it all" either through virtual reality or 3-D chats. The ability to step into another world and experience things even as another person is sure to intrigue even the most cautious Net user. Marketers can cater to this need by creating virtual spaces or "rooms" that are intellectually challenging (for gamers), graphically pleasing, and exciting. The graphical enhancements that have taken the Web by storm have made this a truly satisfying Web experience.

As we discussed earlier, MUDs, MOOs, and MUSEs were the early applications addressing this need. Now fantasy-seekers have their choice of 3-D environments in which to fulfill their every dream. Visit places like Honjo Jidai Mura 3D Chat World where you can walk and see the Japanese old city of Honjo Jidai Mura using Sony's 3-D VRML browser (www.gcoj.com).

Transaction

There is and has been a growing interest in gathering and exchanging information, especially concerning the purchasing of products. People like to hear what others have to say about a specific product that one consumer is using and another is considering purchasing.

In Barnes & Noble's online community (www.barnesandnoble.com) users can get personalized book recommendations from other readers. Online book groups have also been launched that will be run by BarnesandNobles.com's editorial staff or created and led by readers.

Technology Overview

You may be asking, "How does this chat work anyhow?" It's actually quite simple in the basic free solutions and can be more complex in the graphical solutions that are being popularized today.

Most Web-based chat systems automatically download a small Java applet into a Web page that handles all of the user functions. The Java applet prompts the user to log in using a unique name and identifies the "channel" or topic associated with the Web page accessed by the user. Once the Java applet connects with the chat server (which can be located practically anywhere on the Internet), the applet displays new chat comments and sends the user's comments to the chat server for broadcast to the group. Since the Java applet interacts directly with the chat server and doesn't communicate with the Web server that served the Web page, the chat server does not need to be located with the Web server—they are two independent operations.

This independence is what allows chat server companies such as ichat to use a centralized chat server to serve thousands of topics associated with thousands of Web pages—without having to interact with the Web servers on the Net. Many chat sites are available off of people's Web sites; participants don't need any special software, or if they do, often times it is free.

Getting Started

Once you come across a community that you'd like to participate in, you will probably be asked to register. You can use your real name, but most people make up a name. By concealing your identity, you are protecting your privacy, and it also allows you to get more into some of the role-playing that occurs on some fantasy sites.

After you select a login name, you may also be able to select an icon to represent you. These icons, known as *avatars*, can be any kind of character—some are cute and some are ugly. Sometimes, you can even create your own avatar. Avatars were created to give chat a bit more of a personality than the simple text-only chat of earlier days. Once you have your name and avatar, click the Enter button and follow the instructions to choose a room.

Once inside, you may be alone or you may find yourself in the middle of someone's conversation, so take your time and get your bearings. Scroll through the list of postings to understand what the conversation is about.

You don't have to jump right into the conversation. In fact, many more people watch and listen or *lurk*, as it is called, and then participate. If you are ready to participate, simple type in your comment or question and hit the Talk button to submit it. Your post will then be put up for others to respond to. The same rules of behavior apply in chat rooms as they do in other online communications, so be sure to review the basic rules of Netiquette to avoid offending anyone. You can also use emoticons and abbreviations to minimize the amount of typing.

Benefits of One-to-One Community

Online communities have the potential to be very strong candidates for one-to-one Web marketing. If companies start implementing community correctly with the one-to-one philosophies in the forefront of their plans, they are sure to see rapid return-on-investment (ROI). ROI has been a concern among marketing managers in that over the past few years, they have been making huge investments in the Web and seeing little return. This is partially because marketers haven't been implementing one-to-one methodologies.

The Web as a medium was made for one-to-one marketing. Too many marketers are still trying to fit the square peg of mass marketing into the round hole of the Internet, and it just won't fit. No matter how hard you hammer it or throw money at it, mass-marketing techniques do not fit the Web.

Once Web marketers embrace and start to implement these one-to-one Web marketing techniques, they will see the results they are looking for. One-to-one communities have particular marketing advantages in their ability to target an audience, gain access to information to better *customerize* their offerings, and act as a loyalty-building and communications vehicle. *Customerize* was coined by Peppers and Rogers, meaning to customize your products and service to your individual customers. Some of the benefits of one-to-one community are having a targeted audience; being able to customerize your offerings; and creating long-term relationships, better loyalty, and better communications with your customers.

Targeted Audience

By gaining customers one customer at a time, the one-to-one Web marketer is able to target very specific audiences with very specific needs that only a few vendors can meet. If you are one of the few and the proud, you need to take advantage of this position. Communities that are very focused can appeal to a specific audience. That gives you the ability to be *the* resource for this group.

Someone who collects sharks' teeth may want to buy, sell, or trade them, or just share the story of what beach they were on when they found that really big one. These kinds of targeted communities—from pencil buyers to antique car collectors—all need a *place*. And that place can be an online community.

Ability for Better "Customerization"

By creating online communities, marketers are able to interact with their prospects and customers on a daily basis. Through this interaction, you can gain a better understanding about exactly what your customers want. And when you know what your customers want, you're one step closer to figuring out how to give it to them. With this new insight about your customers, you are better equipped to "customerize" your offerings to your specific audiences. By talking with your customers individually via your community, you are armed with the knowledge to meet their very specific and individual needs.

One-to-one Web marketers will also have access to integrated transaction histories of their audiences. You can learn to predict and anticipate your customers' future needs by analyzing the data that you have gathered from them from their participation with you in your community. For example, say that you are Lands' End and you have a customer who always buys sweaters from your online catalog. The next time he or she visits your site you can give him or her a message like, "Hello, John Smith, we have this new fisherman's sweater on sale today for $59.99. Would you like us to check and see if your size is available?" This can be accomplished through one-to-one personalization, previously discussed in Chapter 4, "One-to-One Web Site Personalization."

Be an Agent for Your Customer

By tabulating and storing your clients' specific needs, you, as a one-to-one Web marketer, in a way become an agent for your customers. No longer are you a simple vendor, but truly more of a partner. You are able to work *together* with them to come up with a solution that meets their needs. By having the opportunity to collaborate with your customers to find the best solutions for them, you will be a trusted member of their team.

Warning: Sometimes you are not the best solution for your customer. Have the integrity and courage to send your customers somewhere else if that is the best thing for them. They will remember and be loyal to you for life because you put their needs in front of your own self-interests. Reach out and touch someone.

No longer confined by regional constraints in servicing clients, Web marketers can communicate and interact with customers via their online community. As a communications vehicle, online community has been very effective in helping numerous companies, especially in the areas of technical support and sales.

Providing customer-to-customer communications has proven to be most beneficial to many corporations. It's as if you have your own champion of your products, an evangelist who can lead others to experience the greatness of your companies' offerings. Most satisfied customers are more than happy to talk to others about their success, but unfortunately, most marketers (both Web and traditional) don't think to ask them. Isn't that crazy? Start to seek out your existing satisfied customers and get them together with some of your new customers. Your one-to-one community can be a gathering place for both veteran and new customers. The results can be very satisfying for all parties involved.

Some Community Controversies

Since the early days of chat rooms, there was some stigma associated with this type of online community. The rumors of sleazy chat rooms left many users with a bad taste for chat. In the last few years, companies have been focusing on the need for community in our society and have implemented more wholesome communities for the purpose of meeting others with similar interests, forging valuable relationships with a company, or exchanging information. Companies like Talk City position themselves as a "clean, well-lighted" community for chat on the Web. Since we are examining community from a one-to-one Web marketing perspective, the controversies discussed next are mainly from a management perspective including letting customers openly compare you against the competition, issues on the maintenance of content, and lack of control over discussion.

Bad Reputation

As we discussed earlier, many chat rooms are not family or business oriented. You should also be aware that some chat rooms are adult in nature. "Conversations" can be sexually oriented. That stigma is still on some chat rooms, but more companies are setting up communities so that perception will soon be a thing of the past.

We use the word *community* instead of *chat room*. A chat room is just a place to go and chat. What we are encouraging you to do, as one-to-one Web marketers, is to build communities—total places and worlds of useful content, information, and communication for you and your customers. One-to-one community will be the marketing tool of the next decade. You can count on it.

Open for Competition

If you are a community organizer and not a buyer or seller, this won't concern you. If you are a vendor, however, and you would like to set up a mall where customers can learn about your products, you have two choices:

1. You can create a corporate community at your Web site where it is understood by customers that they will only receive one side of the story because you are conveying your products' features and benefits from your perspective.

2. You can create a targeted consumer commerce/resource site in which you and your competitors have equal footing in the race for customers.

This second option is a scary proposition for most marketers. "What you mean you want us to help our competition access our customers?" says the concerned marketing communications manager. "Are you crazy?"

Well, actually, we aren't. Allowing for free comparisons of prices and features as well as customers' opinions on your products (and your competitors') has its advantages. Customers will appreciate being able to access this information in one central location and will respect your honesty in putting it out there on the line for everyone to see.

Content and Members Must Stay Fresh

As a community organizer, you have an obligation to your customers (or members, depending on what type of community you maintain, be it content or corporate) to keep your content, meaning articles, news stories, and product information, current. In the last few years, marketers have been dumping thousands of dollars into Web site development and then letting their sites grow stale because no one updates them. This can also happen to online communities if marketers aren't careful.

 When you put together your plan for your online community, at the same time create a maintenance plan and budget for at least one year. This will ensure that your content will stay up to date and that you won't lose your customers to a better-maintained community.

Also create events and forums that will draw people to your community. By promoting your community correctly, you always have fresh faces on line to keep the community alive (see Chapter 8, "One-to-One Advertising and Promotion").

One of the reasons that Apple's eWorld failed was that there was no one there. Online communities can fall prey to the same fate that makes a once-popular restaurant close within the first six months: *the fickle public*. Organizers are tasked with always keeping conversations, content, and events both current and engaging.

Control

Many companies are concerned with the control that they may relegate if they actually let their customers talk to one another. The sad truth is that people talk, and wouldn't you rather have them talking *to* you instead of *about* you. If someone is displeased with your product or service, wouldn't you rather he or she share that information with you rather than 30,000 users on a different virtual community?

If you provide your customers with a forum where they can openly discuss both the pros and the cons of your product, you will be surprised at how much you will learn. Be prepared, the truth hurts; however, there is no way that you can correct or improve on your product without knowing what is wrong. It is worth it to give up a certain amount of control to receive candid, valuable feedback from your customers that you may not have gotten otherwise.

Another issue to consider is the legal implications of moderated discussions. If you choose to moderate your chat or online posting forum, you could be considered a publisher and can be liable for what your participants say.

 Go to the companion Web site for "Online Services—Could You Be Found Liable?—Defamation lawsuits raise troubling issues for providers and users of online information and services."

Applications of Community and Products

Hagel and Armstrong, in their book *Net Gain* (1997, Harvard Business School Press), define five criteria in establishing a successful virtual community business model. Those criteria are

Distinctive focus. Communities that revolve around a special interest.

Capacity to integrate content and communications. Communities that blend chat with articles, ads, and commentary that are appropriate for the specific community.

Appreciation of member–generated content. Community participants can be a great resource for the most interesting and timely content. Their contribution should be nurtured and encouraged.

Access to competing publishers and vendors. The best commerce-based communities will be built by nonpartisan organizers presenting all options to the consumer in an unbiased manner. One-sided, one-vendor malls will be short lived.

Commercial orientation. Commerce communities will be very successful in organizing products, services, and information in a way that will make it very enjoyable, time saving, and *convenient* for people to buy.

While many of the community examples discussed next can fall into several of these categories, we have focused on each community's strongest traits in order to more clearly illustrate the criteria for successful community building.

Distinctive Focus

Whether it's roller-skating or cooking, clock making or golf, if you have a special interest you are sure to find information on it on the Web. Unfortunately you may find too much information. That is why communities with a distinctive focus are popping up all over. Users want their information to be organized in a way that is useful for them. The smart one-to-one marketer should look for ways to be *the source* of information within a specific niche. Again, this is a loyalty-building proposition. If you are meeting all of your users' needs, then why would they look somewhere else?

A good example of this type of site is *Go, girl!*

Go, girl!

Go, girl! is a biweekly magazine dedicated to getting women of all ages and fitness levels involved in sports. Launched on September 9, 1996, by Melissa Joulwan, *Go, girl!* has received numerous accolades from such noteworthy sources as *NetGuide* LIVE Spotlight, Netscape What's New, *USA Today* Hot Site, WebCrawler Select, the Way Cool Award, and Yahoo! of the Day.

Tips from Melissa Joulwan Editor of *Go, girl!* **Magazine**

The sense of community that's available on the Web is what convinced me to create an Internet magazine as opposed to a print publication. Although *Go, girl!* is based on a print metaphor, the driving philosophy behind it was to create a resource that women felt was interactive. Every page of the magazine includes a link to e-mail so that readers can communicate with us immediately upon finishing a story—and every e-mail we receive is answered by a real person. No form

---

letters, either. Yes, it's time-consuming, but our readers are very loyal—and they tell their friends about the magazine. I received a note from a reader recently who thanked me for responding personally to her request—and expressed her disappointment that larger companies had ignored her messages.

The key to building a sense of community on a Web site, I think, is to give the site a "voice." Take a stand and create a personality with the graphics and tone of the copy. Too many sites leave viewers "cold" because there's no sense of a person behind them. Even corporate sites can foster a sense of personality that will convince viewers to return again and again. Feedback links, chat groups or bulletin boards, and e-mail newsletters are all great ways to involve readers in a Web site—and make them feel like they're getting something in return for their attention to the site.

Our e-mail newsletter is very successful in returning people to the site on a regular basis. Subscribing to the magazine is free—and allows us to collect demographic information about our readers. In return, we send them updates whenever we publish a new issue of the magazine, and also include them in surveys and invitations to submit materials to the magazine. It's a great way to connect with the readers, and form a community. We plan to add a bulletin board in the future that will also go a long way in creating a more cohesive *Go, girl!* group.

As far as the future of the Internet is concerned, I think the notion of community is only going to keep expanding. That's what sets the Internet apart from other forms of communication. Where else can you read an article and send a note to the author in a split second? Or find other people who share your interests—without having to be introduced by a third party, join a club, or spend money? Or order in seconds the product about which you just read a review? The possibilities are amazing. And they also help tear down some of the boundaries that confine us now.

Go, girl! has readers all over the world—that's amazing. I've heard the arguments that e-mail and "virtual communication" are driving people away from each other, but I strongly disagree. I think that the communities being built on the Internet are helping make the planet smaller. They give people a forum in which to express themselves and learn from others. And they level the playing field a bit, so that everyone's voices can be heard. (Figure 6.3 shows *Go, girl!)*

Capacity to Integrate Content and Communications

Another criteria for creating a successful community is the organizer's adeptness at supplementing the discussion with useful articles and advertisements. One company who has mastered this skill is Well-Engaged.

Well-Engaged

Well-Engaged was formed in September 1996. It was spun off from The Well, the world-renowned pioneer in online community. It offers Web-based discussion group software and consulting services to leading companies committed to establishing conversation and community on their Web sites.

Figure 6.3 *Go, girl!* **Web community.**

In speaking with Sylvia Lacock, director of partner development, she said, "One of the first issues we discuss with our clients is how this will affect their bottom line." Well-Engaged is very focused on the building of community to better serve customers and integrating it as a marketing application.

Its customers have the ability to track individual users and then they can tailor content and advertising based on the information they get *about* their users and not just *from* their users.

We are an information society bombarded daily with messages. Anything a community organizer can do to make logic of all this data will be greatly appreciated. People don't want many choices, they only want *their* choice. It's great that all this information is available but it can be very overwhelming and frustrating for users when all they are looking for is one simple fact.

That is why search engines were created, but unfortunately, even they are too broad in scope and breadth. A focused community is a person's best bet in getting the targeted information that he or she is looking for, that has been specifically tailored to his or her needs.

| TIP | "The biggest mistake I see marketers making is not modifying their content appropriately. There are many tools available (Well-Engaged being one) that will allow the community organizer to tailor both links and ads around the discussion. As a service to your customers, you want to make your content as relevant to their needs as possible. People have the power, it is just changing the mindset and setting the priority to implement it effectively." Sylvia Lacock, director of partner development at Well-Engaged

Well-Engaged spends a great deal of time consulting with its clients about how to use the information that they glean. The cost of its product is a $3,500 license fee plus a service fee for its server. Some sites that are presently using Well-Engaged are:

Warner Music	www.elecktra.com	Enter Elektra/What's Hot/ Half-way down the page you will see the list of BBS topics
Lifetime Lounge	www.lifetimetv.com	Free to register
The Wall Street Journal	www.wsj.com	A subscription site with moderated discussions
CornerTalk	www.holyfieldtyson.com	Free to register

| Minds | www.minds.com | Free to register |
| Gamepower | www.gamepower.com | Free to register |

Talk City

Talk City is brought to you by LiveWorld Productions, an Internet content company specializing in online programming that brings together people in shared social, cultural, educational, and recreational experiences. LiveWorld was founded in April 1996, and has focused on building a reputation for Talk City as a "clean, well-lighted" community for chat on the Web.

Talk City is a live chat environment on the Internet for people who believe in the power of conversation. Its founders share the conviction that communicating ideas with people around the world promotes global understanding and global progress. The Talk City chat network is a community of communities, groups of individuals with specific areas of interest who can entertain and enlighten the rest of us about those interests in hosted chat rooms and on Web pages.

An intriguing example of the practical implementation of community: Talk City and Seismic Entertainment run virtual tours of Mars every evening at 5:30 P.M., PT. Imagine the possibilities!

Appreciation of Member–Generated Content

A good community organizer not only organizes and creates good content but also encourages users to create content. Organizers can help their users to help themselves, by enlisting them to keep the content current and interesting. This also reduces some of the cost of maintaining an online community. By collaborating with your members, they feel ownership of their community, again contributing to the loyalty factor.

GeoCities

GeoCities is dedicated to offering rich and dynamic content for members and visitors alike. The centerpiece of that strategy is providing free Personal Home Pages in one of its 38 theme communities to anyone with access to the Web. It also offers a free GeoCities e-mail account to everyone who signs up for a free homepage. GeoCities has more than 700,000 individuals sharing their thoughts and passions with the world. Users can also subscribe to GeoPlus, the premium service of GeoCities, to have more space for their homepage, get a personalized URL, and lots of free stuff.

GeoCities' philosophy has always been that locations on the Internet become easier to relate to when they are rich with content and closely identified with an actual idea or location. In support of this belief and in keeping with the culture of the Internet, it has developed this free Personal Home Page program, and built theme communities to accommodate thousands of homepages.

GeoCities was named the fifth most-visited site on the World Wide Web in the most recent PC-Meter report. According to the report, which measured Web traffic for the month of April 1997, GeoCities continues to increase its percentage of all "at home" users, while each of the other sites in the "top 10" witnessed a decline in their share of the same audience.

Tripod

Tripod (www.tripod.com)—one of the hottest Internet destinations for twenty-some-things, with membership reaching more than 500,000, and the nineteenth most-visited site on the Web—launched Screenlife in 1997 as a special section of its site devoted to communities and self-publishing. This personal publishing arena hosts more than 750,000 personal homepages created by members with the help of the site's industry-leading homepage-building technology and how-to advice. Tripod's innovative Internet community-building approach emphasizes freedom of choice, self- expression, and the ability for anyone to start an online group.

Unlike many Web communities on other sites, the communities within Tripod, called "Pods," feature professionally created content integrated with Tripod members' self-published pages, clustered around topics and issues of interest. In addition, Tripod members can join and participate in as many Pods as desired and can suggest the creation of new Pods. In effect, Pods can be much more cohesive and focused than many other Internet communities.

Each Pod has its own "Poderator," who encourages high-quality expression and interactivity on the site through scheduled weekly chat sessions and/or quizzes on the relevant topic. The weekly chats are well attended and host some spirited debates—everything from women in Hollywood films to the best way to break through writer's block. The Poderator also presents top personal publishers. "Best of Pod" awards are proudly displayed on the Pod's front page to celebrate the most savvy pages or the most thought-provoking content.

Tripod's new democratic approach to community building has already proved a success since the initial launch in July of three Pods: Film Buffs, devoted to the Siskel & Ebert in all of us; Alt.Music, for alternative music freaks; and Freebies!, for those who believe everything is best when free. Five more Pods have been added and all eight Pods are drawing thousands of site visits weekly. Also, more and more members are devoting pages to one or more of the Pods. Additions to the original Pods include Carburetor Junction for car enthusiasts; Gamesta', for gaming fans; Writer's Block for avid writers; and Page Slave, a commune for the most-fervent personal Web page publishers. "Pod Publishers" with pages dedicated to one or more Pods, as well as nonpublishers, flock to the sites to learn about links and resources or read about diverse opinions on subjects most dear to them. The most recent addition, X-Squared Pod, is devoted to women's issues. Attracting a variety of well-designed personal pages addressing a variety of women's topics from breast cancer to motherhood, X-Squared Pod was formed out of the Tripod's Women's Room, a major gathering place for people to learn about and explore women's viewpoints.

A dozen more Pods—most of which were suggested by Tripod members—are under development. Over the next few months, watch for communities to spring up around extreme sports, television, small businesses, work at home, beauty and fashion, cats, dogs, cooking, holistic health, martial arts, sci-fi, and humor. The cohesiveness of the Pods makes them attractive to advertisers seeking to effectively target campaigns to select groups of GenXers.

Access to Competing Publishers and Vendors

As mentioned earlier in the chapter, SciQuest is a good example of this criteria type in that it brings together all buyers and all sellers within the scientific industry. SciQuest is a true community organizer. It is neither a buyer nor a seller, but had the vision to bring these two groups together within this niche market.

This works fine when there is a neutral party acting as the community organizer or when a company creates a community for their customers, partners, and employees on their Web site, intranet, or extranet. The problem arises when a company, for example, a vacuum cleaner manufacturer, decides to create a community where consumers can learn about and purchase vacuums but it is the only company represented on this "solution" site. Or, it only allows inferior competitors to participate on the site, giving the host preferred standing. Consumers are smart, they can see through this. Marketers: Do not use the shield of one-to-one for self-congratulatory displays; you must truly be looking to assist your customers in making the best purchasing decisions. You must be an agent for them.

Commercial Orientation

Communities can be built for commercial purposes. There are many advertiser-supported online communities as well as communities sponsored by major advertisers.

iVillage

iVillage (www.ivillage.com) is a good company to examine for successful commercial orientations. Three of iVillage's most popular communities—Parent Soup, About Work, and Vices and Virtues—command advertising rates of $75,000 for six months or $150,000 for one year. Advertisers have the choice of a banner ad that will connect customers directly to their existing Web site, or a *bridge site*.

A *bridge site* is a minisite built within the iVillage channel. It is heavily branded to the advertiser and often links to specific areas within an advertiser's existing Web site. When a visitor clicks on an ad banner, he or she is brought into the bridge site, which

Figure 6.4 Advertising via bridge site example: Sears.

contains information that is complementary to the channel. iVillage believes that bridge sites are particularly useful when an advertiser

- Has an existing site with broad appeal but wants to attract a more specific demographic group through advertising on an iVillage channel

- Has a corporate Web site with good information but little consumer appeal

- Wants to direct consumers into various specific areas within its existing site, not just through the front door

- Wants to align closely with the iVillage channel identity

- Wants to test the latest technology employed on the iVillage channels

- Wants to try a new platform, be it the Web or America Online

- Doesn't have an existing Web site at all

A bridge site can be as small as one page or as large as hundreds of pages. Costs are assessed on a case-by-case basis, but sponsors own any content that is developed for use within its area. Figure 6.4 shows a bridge site for Polaroid that is off of iVillage's About Work community.

iVillage's goal is to create and build targeted communities on line that help people with the real issues of their real lives. The communities are owned by their members who are the driving force behind the subjects they are most passionate about.

Parent Soup

iVillage describes Parent Soup "like the neighborhood's favorite kitchen table—the coffee is great and the conversation is better. iVillage supplies the table and treats, and their members create a warm ring of laughter, wisdom, information, and love. Every person who joins the Soup enriches it by bringing a unique perspective on parenting, a fresh set of stories, a new question."

About Work

About Work was designed to help people cope with the ever-changing workplace. Subscribers can participate in communities targeting job hunters, those who work from home, entrepreneurs, and people who want advice on career planning.

Vice & Virtues

Vice & Virtues was created to enhance users online and real-world lives through the unconditional support, shared wisdom, comic relief, and camaraderie they find in talking with others who share similar interests and life challenges.

The Palace

With more than 2 million users, The Palace Inc. (www.thepalace.com) is the leading provider of tools for graphical virtual communities on the Internet. The 1000-plus Palace sites that let people chat, attend events, and participate in online games, lectures, and events include Egghead Computer, Syracuse University, 3Com, GameSpot, Merrill Lynch, NEC, The Dallas Cowboys, Sony Pictures, *Entrepreneur Magazine*, *Playboy*, House of Blues, and Fox Broadcasting Network.

The Palace also has strategic relationships with Sun Microsystems, FireFly Network, Microsoft, Intel, and Time Warner. There are also many noncommercial palaces available for users to visit, but in this section we are going to focus on the commercial applications of The Palace.

Palace Commercial Servers

The Palace provides organizations with tools to develop multimedia virtual communities on the Internet. PalaceServer software allows companies to design and author visually rich environments or "Palaces" that bring users together.

PalaceServer includes PalacePresents, a feature that adds the capability for organizations to host live, moderated auditorium events, including streaming audio and video and an embedded Web browser all within the familiar Palace user interface; and InstantPalace, their new Java client that allows visitors to InstantPalace-enabled Web sites to instantly participate in multimedia virtual communities with no download or installation.

Companies can also leverage the rest of the rich, vibrant, and growing Palace community. With nearly half a million Palace users and over a thousand PalaceServers in place, and an average of a thousand Palace users logged in at any given moment, marketers can see where the people are and where the places to go are.

MGM Uses Community to Promote New Movie

For quite some time, major studios have been using World Wide Web sites to publicize upcoming films. The Web site for Independence Day, (www.id4.com) was one of the most popular sites of its time even before the release of the movie. Now, MGM is one of the movie companies taking this innovation a step further by using a multimedia, real-time discussion environment called "The Palace" to create buzz for "Hoodlum," the highly anticipated film released on August 27, 1997.

Starring Laurence Fishburne, Tim Roth, Vanessa Williams, Cicely Tyson, and Andy Garcia as Lucky Luciano, "Hoodlum" is the dramatic story of the battle against the mob's attempt to take control of Harlem's penny numbers racket during the 1930s. The Web site promoting "Hoodlum" has its own special Palace where movie fans can fully experience the feel of the movie by visiting distinct rooms that mirror the sets used in the film. Site visitors adopt special graphical representations (avatars) to be their onsite personas as they participate in chats and events relating to the movie.

"We are excited to be part of this revolutionary advance in developing real-time discussion areas on film marketing sites," said Mark Jeffrey, vice president and cofounder of The Palace, Inc. "It's fitting that films are pioneers in using this advanced communications technology. The Hoodlum Palace is the perfect tool to leverage movie goers' interest in the film, planting seeds for the development of a community based around the movie."

OnLive!

OnLive! Technologies' product line includes client and server software with all the elements necessary to enable any Web site to support group voice chat in an immersive, 3-D graphical environment.

The OnLive! Traveler is end-user client software that allows real-time voice communication in 3-D virtual environments. With OnLive! Traveler, users are able to navigate through communities of 3-D environments, represented by their own 3-D avatars, and converse naturally with other users in real time. OnLive! Traveler works as a standalone application or as a helper application to World Wide Web browsers. The OnLive! Community Server operates in conjunction with any Web site HTTP server and can dramatically enhance any site by turning it into a community where groups of people can talk and interact in 3-D environments.

MTV: Music Television

One company that is using OnLive! is MTV: Music Television. MTV: Music Television, a unit of Viacom Inc., announced that MTV fans now have access to online technology that, for the first time, enables groups of people to talk in 3-D virtual environments over the Internet.

OnLive! has developed the breakthrough technology that turns MTV Online or any Web site into a community by enabling groups of people to use their *voices*, not text, to talk on line. This virtual environment, called "MTV TikkiLand," can be accessed via MTV's Web site at www.mtv.com. Modeled after the Tikki God theme featured on the MTV Beach House, a variety of MTV TikkiLand 3-D settings let users bask in the warm glow of a virtual sunset by the beach and explore an exotic Tikki God cybertemple.

Anyone with a multimedia Pentium and a basic 14.4 modem connection to the Internet can access the OnLive! experience through this site. Users simply select an OnLive! avatar, an onscreen persona, and then navigate a range of interconnected 3-D communities, including the premiere MTV TikkiLand. Communicating with other people is easy since participants talk, listen, and respond as they would in any social gathering.

MTV introduced viewers to OnLive! Technologies by broadcasting segments of their VJs interacting in TikkiLand on July 11, 1997. MTV viewers saw the VJs as OnLive! avatars introducing videos, segueing to various programs, and bantering among themselves. The broadcast element marked the first time an Internet technology was launched on national television. Additionally, music and celebrity talent appearing at the MTV Beach House throughout the summer entered the MTV "Webabago," signaling that they were available for online users to join them in MTV TikkiLand.

"Whether it's in television or online mediums, MTV is about challenging traditional programming formats," said Matt Farber, senior vice president of programming/new business. "MTV's innovative approach to entertainment, coupled with OnLive!'s revolutionary software, creates a powerful partnership that will redefine the way we think about the entertainment experience."

"MTV allows OnLive! to reach a market audience that has already embraced the Internet as a means of communication, information, and entertainment," said Betsy Pace, CEO of OnLive! Technologies. "What better showcase destination than MTV to demonstrate how OnLive!'s group voice-communication capabilities compliment cur-

Figure 6.5 MTV's 3-D virtual environment.

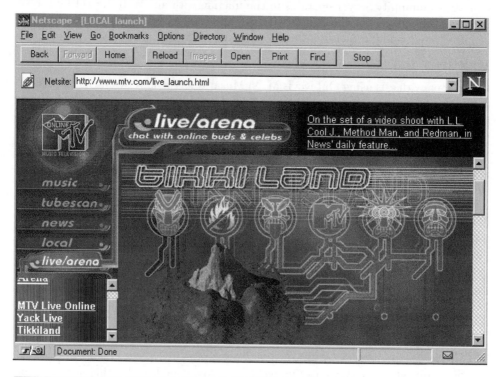

rent programming content and add value through personalized interaction among users." Figure 6.5 shows MTV's 3-D virtual environment.

ichat

Founded by Andrew Busey in 1995, ichat is the leading supplier of interactive, Net-based communications software. ichat delivers several products focused on quick, affordable, online communications.

In a corporate context, ichat's software facilitates low-cost internal collaboration and increases the quality of interaction between customer and supplier. On Internet content sites, ichat's technology enables Web-site community building by increasing user interactivity and promoting repeat visits.

ichat's ROOMS is an integrated, scaleable chat server with a feature-rich user interface. ichat's Message Boards is a robust, chat-integrated discussion forum that allows users to search for and post topical messages. The ichat Pager is an Internet paging application providing real-time connections among Internet users. By providing a common directory structure and shared user experience, ichat's ComHub integrates ichat's Pager, Rooms, and Message Boards. All ichat client products are available for free.

ichat's partnerships with premier Internet technology innovators such as Netscape, Progressive Networks, NetGravity, FireFly, and I/PRO integrate chat with best-of-breed products to create an interactive communications medium that meets the needs and interests of end users, Web site developers, ISPs, corporations, and advertisers.

Universal Chat

Universal Studios On-Line and ichat announced the launch of the first live Hollywood chat program created by a major studio on the World Wide Web. Universal Chat, located on the Universal Studios Web site (www.universalstudios.com), is equipped with ichat's Web-integrated chat software.

"Building on Universal's tradition of innovation and creativity, this strategic partnership with ichat enables Universal to offer interactive, real-time chat to entertainment enthusiasts," said Paul Rioux, president of Universal Studios New Media Group. "Visitors to the site can become true participants in the Hollywood community, with unprecedented access to the creators and stars of the movie and television industry."

"ichat is excited to work with Universal in creating the first Hollywood online community, which will allow entertainment buffs everywhere to connect with leading celebrities, writers, and producers," said Andrew Busey, founder and chief technology officer for ichat. "It's truly a one-stop site, where users can interact with the entertainment community, sharing their views, insights, and information."

Drawing from Universal's extensive pool of talent, Universal Chat will feature both moderated and unmoderated scheduled evening programming, from 6:00–11:00 P.M. (PST) every Monday through Friday. Highlights scheduled during the debut week of April 14, 1997 will include live chats with Tom Arnold, star of Universal Pictures' action-packed caper comedy, *McHale's Navy*, and the acclaimed director Carl Reiner, who will discuss *That Old Feeling*, his romantic comedy starring Bette Midler and Dennis Farina. Universal Chat consists of several open rooms, offering visitors a variety of online experiences: Hercules: *The Legendary Journeys* and *Xena: Warrior Princess*, with non-stop action; *Crimestoppers*, featuring such hit television series as *Law & Order*, *New York Undercover, Feds, Sliders*, and *The Burning Zone*; the *SciFi Ground Zero Chat Station*, featuring classic videos from Universal Studios Home Video; and *Comedy Corner*, focusing on television sitcoms including the series *Mr. Rhodes* and *Something So Right*.

Additional behind-the-scenes and inside information is available in the Backlot Café, with forums including Getting to Know the Hollywood Business, exploring everything from acting tips to selling scripts; and Writer's Workshop, where aspiring writers can meet, exchange ideas, and learn from some of Hollywood's top screen and television writers.

Ideas for Implementing Community as a Marketing Function

We as marketers know that we must build community with our customers or someone else will. Up until now it has been a challenge with geographical barriers of distance and language. Community was historically built with customers either through phone calls or sales visits.

Today, technology provides us with a new tool for building community. If marketers are creative in their implementations, their customers will reward them with their purchases and feedback. Following are some examples of how companies can use community to grow and nurture their existing customer base, as well as create budding relations with future customers.

Online Customer Support

Companies can now begin to help their customers help themselves. Through offerings like product-centric chat, customers can answer each other's questions, and endorse and recommend products based on firsthand experience. By creating online manuals and FAQ sections, companies can save time and money by lessening the calls into their help centers. Technical support departments can create a series of technical tutorial workshops that address frequently asked questions, problems, and issues that their customers have. They can schedule them as moderated online events.

Intranet

More and more companies are realizing the urgency of creating effective intranets within their firewalls. Some applications of intranets are:

Departmental meetings. Marketing can have worldwide weekly strategy meetings on line.

Salesforce communications. Sales representatives can access information only they would need.

Project tracking. Multiple layers of management and team members can get immediate status and schedule updates.

Extranet

Many companies are using the community of their extranets to garner valuable customer feedback. For example, Kaiser Permanente has chat in its member services section that nurse practitioners actively participate in. Companies are allowing their key customers access to valuable information that they have gathered for them.

Others are using extranets to provide online presentations to prospects in this secure area, giving the prospect a passcode to enter. This allows them to protect some of their sensitive information that would impress a prospect but also would be of interest to their competition (if they had access to it).

Other Community Resources

Here are a few resources to help you with your exploration of online communities:

The WebChat Broadcasting System. WebChat features all sorts of subject-oriented rooms, with thousands of participants (www.wbs.net).

NandoChat. From one of the pioneers in electronic journalism, the Nando Times, comes Nando Chat, where you can discuss news, sports, and entertainment with others (www.nando.net/xwebchat/chat.html).

The Center for the Study of Online Community. This is an academic resource dedicated to the study of online communities (www.sscnet.ucla.edu/soc/csoc).

The Future of Community

One-to-one communities will grow and prosper once marketers begin to see the benefits of collaborating with their customers. Services such as PlanetAll (www.planetall.com) are popping up to help people keep in touch. You'll be able to send your kid "away" (not really) to an online camp like Kid's Web Camp '97 (www.kidswebcamp.com). The first annual Kid's Web Camp, which ran from July 15 to August 15, 1997, had over 1000 kids from all over the world signed up for the first-ever "virtual Web summer camp." In camp, kids are teamed up with kids from all over the world to learn how to make their own Web sites, upload them to a server, use the Web to do online research projects, and go on Web field trips. Online "camp counselors" and "technical aides" assist kids every step of the way with individual attention. Plenty of chat rooms, team activities, and contests make learning about the Web fun—all from the convenience of home.

Educational Uses

We see a number of future applications for one-to-one community in the educational forums for both children and adults.

Kids, Parents, and Teachers

Other targeted communities for kids (and teachers) are coming into sight and this is just the beginning. PlanetK-12 (www.planetk-12.com) is the first targeted community site and is geared specifically to meet the needs of K-12 educators and students. PlanetK-12 is part of PlanetSearch Networks. "Our goal for PlanetSearch Networks is to build various online communities where people, with similar interests and professions can share their experiences and information," said Steve Leventhal, general manager, PlanetSearch Networks. "PlanetSearch and the targeted community sites provide pertinent and quality information, from a number of well-known sources, to people who want to expand their personal and professional horizons through online contact with others."

PlanetK-12 offers all of PlanetSearch's features and benefits, a wide range of educational tools and resources for curriculum planning and professional development, as well as a community environment. Special features include Curriculum Corner, which offers lesson plans, instructional projects, and materials arranged by subject, grade, or theme. The Research Desk provides curriculum-related support materials and information. Technology 101 offers a technology glossary, product reviews, technical support, and planning guides. The community environment is fostered through the Teachers' Lounge, a rich, interactive meeting place. Through bulletin boards and project posting areas, educators can share ideas and classroom experiences and support each other in common interests and causes. In the School Store, educators can purchase school resources, curriculum guides, and equipment. The School Store also offers products from key online, software, and book publishers.

Universities

Georgia Tech has created a pilot study by the university's innovative School of Literature, Communication, and Culture (LCC). The experiment will involve the use of multimedia virtual community/chat room software from The Palace Inc. and extend to 7 of the 42 sections of freshman English. For the first time, Georgia Tech is requiring all entering freshmen to bring their own computers and has equipped dormitories with high-speed Internet access lines. Students involved in the Palace endeavor will supplement their English studies with real-time Internet discussions of class material.

Over the summer, a group led by faculty member Greg Van Hoosier-Carey, LCC's computer coordinator, prepared online areas decorated as meeting halls, classrooms, offices, and cafés. Using their computers, students will congregate in these virtual rooms wearing graphical icons called "avatars," which will be generated from photographs of the students' faces. They will collaborate on writing projects, meet with professors during non-office hours, and view and discuss sample writing materials. At the end of the school year, the progress of these students will be compared to those in more traditional sections.

"The goal of our pilot study is not simply to get freshmen to produce better compositions of the kind currently produced in our traditional classrooms, but to provide them with the opportunity to develop the kind of collaborative, dynamic, and interactive communication skills necessary for the complex social and technical demands of the contemporary workplace," said Richard Grusin, chairman of LCC. "In looking over the software options currently on the market, we felt that The Palace would help us prepare students to communicate orally, textually, and graphically over the Internet, synchronously and asynchronously, in nonlinear, multimediated formats," Grusin said. Kent State and Syracuse University are also planning to use this form of innovative community. We're certain that it won't be long before other universities will follow.

Client/Partner Education

QED is a human resources consulting firm. Recently, we spoke with its president, David Hertz, about QED's plans for a new community initiative. QED has chosen to create a community in order for themselves and their clients to be able to participate in forums, conferences, and learning programs. The goal is to break down the wall between client and service provider.

This community will be an extension of QED's corporate Web site. The site will include:

- Information about, from, and delivered to QED
- The community as a forum for the exchange of ideas
- A virtual university dedicated to skills building, managerial effectiveness, individual coaching, and career development.

Conferencing

A recent special to *The Wall Street Journal* Interactive Edition (NGIB) by Jane Costello notes that the National Federation of Independent Businesses has begun sponsoring

Fig. 6.6 VCOT—Virtual Community of Tomorrow.

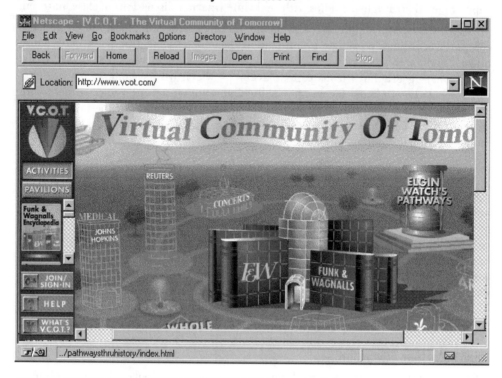

satellite conferences across the country. Last year NFIB held three conferences in states across the country with as many as 52 sites set up for the gathering.

The article continues, "Many experts view the Web itself as a kind of ultimate convention center, allowing small businesses to have access to information and issues beyond their local enterprise zone. Small-business Web sites often come equipped with chat rooms, bulletin boards, and guest speakers who address issues that keep small-business owners plugged in, even if they are not able to leave the comforts of their home office.

Future Fun

Check out VCOT—Virtual Community of Tomorrow (www.vcot.com). This site (see Figure 6.6) includes:

• The complete, unabridged Funk & Wagnall's Multimedia Encyclopedia, with thousands of pictures, hundreds of sounds, and loads of animations.

- The Bridgeman Art Museum, now exhibiting "The Fleeting Moment," an interactive journey into the world of impressionism.

- Click-to-Play Arcade, with some of the Internet's most popular single- and multiuser games.

- The Gibson Arts & Crafts Pavilion, where you can send out animated greeting cards plus create your own avatar for chatting.

- Elgin Watch's Pathways Through History Pavilion, featuring "In Time for Technology!"

 Go to the companion Web site for a one-to-one case study on "Edmund's Town Hall," a computer-mediated conferencing system where users gather to discuss automobile purchasing decisions.

Chapter 7, "One-to-One Web Presentation and Conferencing," discusses the Web presentation and conferencing in your one-to-one Web marketing programs. With the advancements in audio and video transmission, you can now conduct presentations for your customers using the Web. The chapter includes discussions about the technology, applications, product and service providers, and some examples of presentation and conferencing happening now.

ONE-TO-ONE WEB PRESENTATION AND CONFERENCING

7

"Man's mind, once stretched by a new idea, never regains its original dimensions."

Oliver Wendell Holmes

People have enjoyed the feeling of one-to-one communication since the beginning of time and have always looked for ways to enhance that feeling. Since AT&T demonstrated the videophone at the World's Fair in 1964, the expectation of communicating with people who are at a distance has remained one of the "future" benefits of this technological age—until now.

A number of improvements in computing and communications technologies now allow us to apply one-to-one marketing concepts using real-time audio and video on the Internet. Although it is still very new, and it requires more coordination than just sending e-mail, the value is there now.

In their report, "Teleconferencing Markets and Strategies: From Novelty to Necessity," analysts at the market research firm Forward Concepts expect the amount of videoconferencing equipment and services to grow dramatically from the estimated $300 million in 1996 to $3 billion in the year 2001. Why after all these years are we seeing this level of growth? The maturity and convergence of the various technologies is now allowing the growth in online conferencing, much like the growth in PCs that was experienced in the 1980s and 1990s. The current strong demand for PCs with enhanced processor chips capable of better graphics and video shows that the market is looking for the technologies that will allow it to communicate better and faster.

The first question is, "Why use multimedia when *monomedia* would work?" The answer, of course, is that the type of media used should fit the type of presentation you are making—and that depends on the audience and its needs.

This chapter helps answer questions about what multimedia technologies are available to deliver a marketing message to individuals and how to help sales and support personnel communicate directly with online users, prospects, and customers. You'll see that the blending of graphics, audio, and video allows Web marketers to make maximum use of the sometimes limited Internet bandwidth to build relationships using one-to-one Web marketing techniques.

Benefits of One-to-One Web Presentation and Conferencing

All new technologies require frequent review to see when they should be used in an organization. In the case of videoconferencing, the cost of installing equipment for a single location has dropped from over $10,000 to well under $1,000. When compared to the travel costs of sending a person to a meeting, the lower cost of using videoconferencing produces a quick return on investment. The real challenge of deciding when to use Internet-based conferencing today is not cost, but other issues of time, content, and group dynamics.

How do you measure the value of a timely response? Most of the time it's easy—the prospect or customer says he or she needs information *now* and your experts are located in multiple locations. Telephone conference calls can meet most of these needs for focused information, but Web conferencing can enhance many of the electronic meetings we have now and replace some of the one-on-one presentations without losing the personal communications dynamics.

In the 1980s and early 1990s, 3M sponsored research conducted by the Wharton Center for Applied Research and the University of Minnesota's Management Information Systems Research Center. The research indicates the value of using dynamic presentation materials to help an audience understand the presenter's material.

- When visual aids are used in a presentation, the audience remembers as much as 10 percent more of the information presented.

- Using visual aids can reduce the length of the average meeting by as much as 28 percent.

- Use of visual aids increases audience attention (7.5 percent) and comprehension (8.5 percent).

With the various technologies available today for audio, video, and collaboration using the Internet, the type of meeting and its content are key determiners of what technology to use. Gregg Keizer described the new possibilities using the Internet for meetings in his article, "Meeting of the Minds" (*CNET*, 5/21/97):

"And while at one time accomplishing this teamwork required you to spend four hours in a stuffy conference room sitting next to a smelly guy named Vinnie, the

Internet has shattered that shackle. Net-based conferencing software lets you take part in group meetings from the comfort of your own desk, from whatever corner of the world you happen to be in. You can collect opinions from several people simultaneously, throw ideas on a whiteboard, work on shared documents, type chatty comments back and forth, and even watch the Young Turks smirk while they trash others' ideas."

While it's obvious that the public setting of online conferencing should not be used to criticize others, this technology can be used very effectively in certain key situations:

- Audio and video can be used together, with a presenter responding to questions from the audience.

- Group brainstorming is enhanced by seeing calculated results of scenarios displayed instantly.

- Collaboration of a group strengthens development of a document (text, tabular, or graphic).

- Training on the use of computer-based systems is improved with immediate feedback and participation.

In their book, *Net Gain* (1997, Harvard Business School Press), John Hagel and Arthur Armstrong discuss how virtual communities can reshape companies:

"Within businesses, they [virtual communities] may improve management effectiveness by speeding up the emergence of 'communities of process' that link together cross-functional teams that are focused on the same set of business processes...The answer in the past was to get all the relevant managers together for meetings. In practice this led to organizational paralysis, as capable managers spent hours in meetings where their contribution could have been limited to minutes. Applying the principle of the virtual community to this problem by establishing electronic billboards, and meeting areas, supplemented by e-mail and even videoconferencing facilities that allow people to communicate electronically without leaving their desks, could reinforce informal networks that already exist and strengthen integration across organizational divides."

This idea can also be applied to relationships with prospects, customers, and suppliers. It doesn't take too much imagination to figure out the benefits of bringing people together using the Internet and its conferencing capabilities.

Types of Presentations

So let's make sure we know the type of presentation we are making so we can make effective choices for media, content, and presentation. In his book, *Effective Business and Technical Presentations* (1975, Addison-Wesley), George Morrisey describes many techniques for effective communications, but he first sets the stage, so to speak, by describing four types of presentations commonly used to motivate an audience:

Persuasive. Selling an audience on the credibility of the material in order for the audience to feel that the material is worthwhile (i.e., worth its time and worthy of its belief). This form of presentation is used to *sell* members of the audience on believing the material being presented so they will *act* upon that belief. This action could be investing time to research a product, persuade others in their organization, or actually buy the product being presented. The commonality for all of these objectives is for an *action* to be taken by the audience. The persuasive form of communicating on the Web is most applicable for helping visitors feel that your products are *exactly* what they need.

Explanatory. Providing a general familiarization of the topic being presented, sometimes used to present information about recent developments, new products, or other new information. Here, the primary objective is *not* to try to sell a product, but rather to provide the audience with new or renewed knowledge and understanding and problem solving. This works well on a Web site for strengthening a one-to-one relationship with customers who already know the value of your products but are looking for additional information.

Instructional. Teaching the audience about how to use a tool, process, or procedure. This requires greater involvement on the part of the audience than other types of presentations. With Web-based training, you can engender your company to customers by providing personalized training on demand, wherever they are in the world.

Briefing. Bringing the audience up to date on a topic it is already familiar with. This type of presentation may or may not involve heavy detail, based on the needs and interests of the specific audience. The wide range of Web-based multimedia techniques available can be used to strengthen the one-to-one relationships between partners, whether those partnerships are with customers or vendors.

The recent trend in companies to adopt Internet-based *collaborative* techniques builds upon Morrisey's Explanatory type of presentation and becomes an effective approach to actually getting work done, which we'll see later in this chapter when we cover the latest collaborative tools.

Building Relationships with One-to-One Web Presentation and Conferencing

Throughout this book, we've covered techniques and technologies that can provide words written by one individual to be sent to another individual (plus the associated graphics, audio files, etc.). In this chapter we help you integrate audio and video into your one-to-one Web marketing in order to help you build relationships, provide information more quickly, and satisfy the needs of your audience.

First, let's define your audiences and who can benefit from the different Web-based multimedia technologies. In the world of the Web there are, in general, two types of Web sites: content Web sites and marketing Web sites. While content sites market their material, and marketing sites have content, Table 7.1 shows that the general distinction is that content Web sites provide information that leads to other Web sites that sell products.

Table 7.1 Characteristics of Content Web Sites Versus Marketing Web Sites

Attributes	Content Web Sites	Marketing Web Sites
Articles with links to other Web sites	Yes	No
Advertising links to other Web sites	Yes	No
Comparison of different products	Yes	No
Product description sheets	No	Yes
Products available for sale	No	Yes

Content Web sites have the same dilemma that other news media organizations face, how to attract an audience that will eventually leave the media presentation and go buy the advertiser's products—then later return to the media's presentation for more news and information! The other almost schizophrenic characteristic of content media is the need to serve two masters: advertisers and the audience.

For example, Figure 7.1 shows the homepage for CNet's Web site of Internet news (www.news.com) that contains links to both exceptionally high-quality articles within the site as well as banner ads that take the reader away from CNet to the advertiser's site.

Web marketers whose goal is to sell products that meet customers' needs face similar challenges, but the path to success is somewhat more straightforward since a product company's audiences are

- Prospects
- Customers
- Employees
- Vendors
- Financial community

Figure 7.1 Homepage for CNet's News.com Web site.

Each of these audiences has different interests, needs, goals, and—something that is important in one-to-one Web marketing—relatively short attention spans!

TIP

James Jeffries and Jefferson Bates deal with adult attention spans in their book, *The Executive's Guide to Meetings, Conferences, and Audiovisual Presentations* (1983, McGraw-Hill), by offering tips to remember on how attention cycles up and down during a presentation.

They point out that attention initially increases during the first third of the presentation, then declines significantly during the second third, and gradually returns to its peak during the last third. Jeffries and Bates suggest that presenters not try to fight the natural ebb and flow of attention.

As one-to-one Web marketers, we need to take all of these—plus the benefits and constraints of the technologies—into consideration when creating multimedia material for Web marketing.

Table 7.2 shows how the depth of content and amount of interaction enter into your decision on what type of multimedia technology will help you effectively convey your message.

Table 7.2 Use of Content and Interaction in Types of Presentations

Depth of Content	Content	Instructional
High	Persuasive presentation	Collaboration
Low	Low interaction	High interaction

Prospects

Individuals who are gathering information about your products and services move from a general information-gathering state to a very specific questioning state. In fact, when the purchase price is high, the amount of presale technical information you need to provide is much greater than for less-expensive products. In addition, the number of people involved at a prospect's organization increases when impact on their organization is high.

A recent study by CommerceNet and Nielsen Media Research confirmed that most people using the Web are looking for products. In fact, of the 220 million people over 16 years old in the United States and Canada, only 17 percent use the Web. Of those people, 73 percent of them use the Web to search for information about products and services. At the other end of the statistics spectrum is the small number of people who actually purchase products on line. In fact, only 5.6 million people (15 percent) have purchased on line. More than half of these users—53 percent—have searched specifically when making a purchase decision. This indicates that many people are using the Web to gather information to help them, and their companies, make informed decisions about the products they buy.

One of the ways you can minimize your sales expenses while providing personalized, real-time answers to prospects is to conduct meetings and conferences using the Internet. For years, McGraw-Hill has published its research results on the cost of an in-person sales call to demonstrate the value of advertising. Recent studies show the cost is approaching $500 for each sales call. As the number of sales calls needed to make a sale increases, the pressure mounts to reduce time and costs.

Prospective customers have a set of needs that are very different from other groups with which your company communicates because they know the least about your products and have the least commitment to buying them. While other groups might give you a second chance to communicate clearly, prospects need to be led through the process of learning about you in terms they can relate to.

If you've seen an audience in a dark room slowly sink in their seats as the speaker drones on and on about a mundane topic, then you've experienced the compete antithesis of dynamic one-to-one marketing!

One of the reasons audiences have a hard time keeping their attention focused on speakers is that presentations aren't customized for each individual in real time, nor do they take the audiences' needs into consideration or match the presentation technique to the needs of each individual.

Customers

Customers who buy from one supplier over and over are the life's blood of most corporations because the cost of selling to an existing customer is much less than the cost of obtaining a new one.

Customers who have purchased your product or service need more detailed information than prospects in order for them to use your products better—and this allows you to grow the relationship.

Most industries have experienced changes in how products are sold and distributed. More time is being required to provide personalized service to customers in order to maintain the relationship and help ensure that future orders will be received. This has traditionally meant that salespeople and their support people have been spending more time making smaller sales.

This trend has sales managers looking for ways to increase the efficiency of their sales team. One-to-one marketing techniques are being explored in both new sales and customer support.

Vendors

One of the support groups your company depends upon is its vendors. Each company has its own way of dealing with vendors, but with today's economy it's important to develop "partner" relationships with vendors. This means you need to update vendors on your needs and help them understand how they can effectively help you meet your challenges.

With the growth of electronic data interchange (EDI) that connects the purchasing computer of one company to the order entry computer of another, it's becoming important for the employees of both to develop ways to work well together.

Steve Young, director of the electronic commerce research program at INPUT, a Mountain View, California-based research firm, has observed that the industry is composed of established EDI companies, who are all pretty aggressive and technologically astute, but growing at quite handsome rates according to most standards—25–35 percent—and then you've got this enormous tidal wave of the Internet companies moving ahead at much faster growth rates and with a history behind them of much quicker adoption of standards."

The firm's recent study, "Electronic Commerce Markets and Forecast, 1996–2000," forecasts that in the year 2000, Internet access network revenue for commerce will reach $860 million, as compared with $930 million in EDI network revenue. Commerce-related Internet software sales will reach $284 million compared to $342 million in conventional EDI software sales.

The growing reliance on vendors as partners requires a new level of information sharing. With vendors using the Internet to transmit orders, it's clear that the Internet can be used to allow people at both vendor and customer locations to update each other. The types of communications that can help two companies coordinate their activities include research updates, new product briefings, sales training seminars, prospect presentations, customer training, and project coordination.

Selecting the Right Web Conferencing Technology

With the combination of Internet technologies for making presentations and traditional multimedia presentation technologies, one of the early challenges is in selecting the right technology for the right audience. As Tim Tully points out in his survey of presentation tools ("Net-Savvy Tools for Dynamic Presentations," *Netguide*, 5/97):

> *"These tools allow you to bolster your presentations with live links to the Net. For example, by clicking on a button, you can dynamically update those humble pie charts with information from your database back at headquarters. Or you can prepare relevant bookmarks ahead of time and seamlessly transition to the Web to glean additional information."*

Many of us like to use the "latest and greatest" presentation tool to wow the audience, but there are times when a tool gets in the way of the message. Web-based presentation tools range from the simplest approach to complex, real-time video extravaganzas—slides, near real-time video images, streaming video with audio, Internet telephony, and videoconferencing.

A basic approach that can help you decide which technology to use is to compare the strength of the need for the information on the part of the individual with the effort he or she must go through to obtain that information. In the case of viewing static Web pages, the effort is next to none. Compare this to the effort required to download and install a plug-in in order to participate in a videoconference. When considering the technology, consider the appropriateness to the specific audience by applying George Morrisey's "six A's" for selecting the appropriate technique:

Audibility or visibility. Can the use of audio or video enhance the message?

Accessibility or availability. Can members of the audience access the presentation?

Adaptability. Does the presentation technique enhance some particular point you are making?

Appropriateness. Does the technique match the subject (e.g., audio to sell music CDs, video to highlight a DNA string, interactivity to conform audience attentiveness)?

Arresting quality. Will the presentation technique gain attention and keep it on the subject matter rather than on the technique itself?

Auxiliary nature. Does the presentation technique strengthen the message?

Applying Morrisey's "six A's" to your selection of the right technology for effective one-to-one Web marketing requires applying the right combination of interaction and depth of material. Table 7.3 shows our recommendations for the technology appropriate for a particular type of presentation to a particular audience.

Table 7.3 Communication Technologies and Appropriate Target Audiences

	Prospects	Customers	Employees	Vendors	Financial
Slides	Sales presentation	Briefing	Training		
Telephone		Support			
Audio	Promotion		News	News	News
Images (Web cameras)	Information	Information	Status		
Streaming video	Promotion	Training	Training		News
Videoconferencing	Large complex			Briefing	Briefing

As we've seen, the right technology can enhance meetings by encouraging one-to-one communications, so let's take a look at the different types of Web-based presentation technologies for one-to-one Web marketers.

Using Slides on the Net

One of the easiest ways to incorporate "multimedia" into your presentations is to take advantage of those existing presentations in your library!

For the last few years, most business presentations have been created in presentation design programs such as Microsoft's PowerPoint or one of its competitors. Most of these programs have some way—although its not always easy—to convert these for use on the Web.

We've all seen presentations that are comprised of still-frame slides with an individual presenting to a single person or an audience, using a standard telephone line to present the speech portion of the presentation. Why not use the Internet for the audio? Most of the occasions when you want to present a set of slides will involve an audience that does not want to go to extra effort to view your Internet-based presentation, and the Internet connection is likely to be 28.8 kbps. In order to keep the presentation looking good and moving quickly, you won't want to try to combine displaying pages and audioconferencing on the Internet.

A better approach is to use an ordinary telephone connection for the audio portion of your presentation. Just arrange for a speakerphone in the room with the audience and a computer with a connection to the Internet. You'll be in constant touch with the audience and can utilize good one-to-one Web marketing techniques to build your relationship with the audience. This use of two technologies is more reliable and flexible than stressing one technology to its fullest potential. Keep in mind how to create a fast, seamless communication setting.

> **TIP** When using Web-based slides to enhance a telephone call with a prospect (or anyone else for that matter), you will need to have some way to let the other person know when to change slides. It's best to have someone from your team physically present who can watch the audience for clues that you need to alter your presentation on-the-fly (such as when an executive briefs a salesperson's prospect remotely). If someone from your team is not able to be in the audience, be sure to work out in advance how you will indicate when to change slides.

Products for Producing Presentations

Now let's look at two of the more popular presentation programs used to create slides for use on the Web.

Microsoft PowerPoint (www.microsoft.com)

Recent versions of this product allow you to save presentations in HTML format. It creates both a graphical version of what's seen on the screen and a text-only version.

Figure 7.2 PowerPoint slide for the Web using the default graphical template.

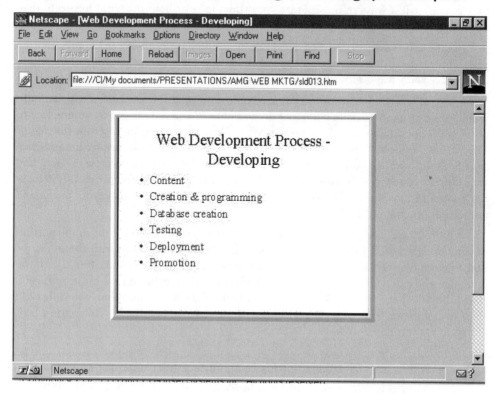

Figure 7.2 shows a typical example of the graphical version that includes a mini screen shot of the whole slide with navigation graphics to move forward and backward in the presentation. Although this resembles the original slide, it doesn't fill the browser window and takes time to download.

The text version of converted PowerPoint slides is not much better since the default template doesn't use any art to enhance the look of the slide. When planning to convert a number of PowerPoint presentations for use on the Web, consider modifying the default text template to make slides that are more professional and more like your original slides. Figure 7.3 shows one of our training slides that has been converted to HTML using a modified version of the template file. Notice how the heading and bullets fill the window. In addition, these bullets can easily be turned into links that access other Web pages.

Figure 7.3 PowerPoint slide for the Web using a modified text format.

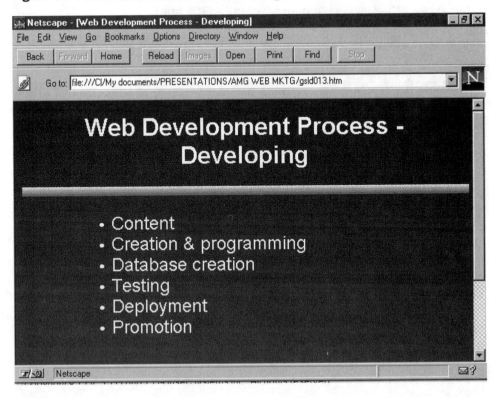

Astound (www.astound.com)

This product has been used for many years to create high-end presentations, but recent enhancements to PowerPoint have eroded this product's appeal in the market for most business presentations. The company has enhanced its high-end products to make them more powerful and more attractive for creating fancy Web presentations.

In order to use your traditional Astound presentations on the Web, you can use the Astound Web Installer to place presentations on a Web page to be viewed by other Web users. The Installer formats the presentation for Web playback by breaking the file into small files that load while the project plays, so it begins quickly.

Unfortunately, Astound presentations require the use of an external viewer program, which your audience needs to download and install prior to your presentation. If you are

Figure 7.4 Mark Gallagher's opening slide about intranet usage. (http://www.gallagher.com/intranet/vision/sld001.htm)

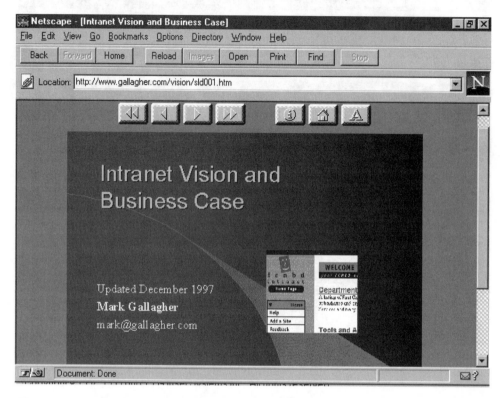

looking to develop new Web presentations, be sure to check out Astound WebMotion. It uses Java applets to deliver presentations without plug-ins or programming.

Examples of Presentations on the Web

There are many PowerPoint presentations on the Web—a search with AltaVista (altavista.digital.com) lists over 4000 slide presentations in its index. Here are some examples of presentations available on various Web sites that can give you an idea of how they look to an audience:

- To view a variety of slides used by Mark Gallagher to help companies understand intranets, visit www.gallagher.com (see Figure 7.4).

- Asante, the manufacturer of computer networking equipment, has an extensive set of slides about its products, including photos of its equipment with callout descriptions. Visit www.asante.com/choosing/ for a list of presentations. For an example, go to www.asante.com/choosing/section4/sld005.htm.

- Conferences and trade shows on the Internet are the topic of this presentation on the Web site of Lehman Associates, a consulting firm. Visit www.ansible.com/asae1296/sld001.htm.

Using a Web Camera

One of the most popular ways to incorporate video on your Web site is with "semi real-time" video, showing frequent updates of a live video feed from a changing scene. As one-to-one Web marketers looking for ways to communicate directly with an audience, we need to remember to give them just what they're looking for!

If you're looking for a way to get started with video but don't want to invest in producing video programming and publishing it with a video server, a *Web Cam* can get you started.

Technology Overview of Web Cameras

Until recently, the process of connecting cameras to a Web site involved custom software and complex electronics. Now there are a number of off-the-shelf products that make using Web cameras very easy.

The technology needed to display instantaneous photos on the Web requires two pieces: Web server software and a camera that is designed to respond to requests from the Web software. Many of the video cameras on the market require the use of a *video capture board* in the PC that can convert video into the digital files we are accustomed to using when creating Web sites.

The software that runs on the Web server is designed to receive requests for images from the browser and then send a signal to the camera requesting an image. The camera then takes the current image, converts it into the format needed for the Web, and passes it to the software on the Web server where it is served to the browser.

Some Web developers use refresh commands to cause the browser to request periodic refreshment of the image automatically, while other Web managers prefer to serve images only once per visit.

Web Cameras Helping Tourism Industry

Tourist destinations that depend on favorable weather conditions are using Web cameras to provide customers with a look at actual conditions at their locations. By providing tourists with an actual look at up-to-the-minute conditions at their locations they are able to provide better information than weather forecasts.

For seasonal resort areas, live cameras showing the current weather are a real boon to the local economy. For the North Carolina Outer Banks area, the tourist industry frequently experiences a significant number of cancellations when a hurricane is reported in the Atlantic. By providing a current look at the beach (www.rsn.com/cams/hattys/), along with current weather conditions and forecasts, tourists can see for themselves when a hurricane is actually approaching or will not affect their vacation plans.

The Resort Sports Network (www.rsn.com) has a number of other Resort Cam Web pages that show how many resort areas around the country look at any given time.

Web Camera Products

There is a wide range of products available to display still images on a Web site, from inexpensive cameras designed for the Web to near broadcast-quality cameras. In this section, we've chosen to focus on an inexpensive camera and software combination that are proven to work well together, leaving the high-end products for the videoconference section later in the chapter.

Connectix (www.quickcam.com)

One of the most popular low-cost cameras used to create video on the Web is the QuickCam from Connectix. While the quality of the image created with the QuickCam is not as high as professional video cameras, the under-$300 cost makes it very affordable.

Installation of the QuickCam is easier than other cameras because the PC version connects to the parallel port (the Macintosh version connects to the serial port). This means that no special video board is required, so you save the cost of adding a board to your system.

Webcam 32 (kolban.com/webcam32)

Webcam32 is a Windows 95/NT application that allows video camera images to be displayed within a Web page. This product can deliver images to your Web audience in a number of ways, such as periodic updates to a Web page or continuously pushing images to users.

Webcam 32 can provide instantaneous images on the server or it can be configured to only show the last image it uploaded, so it works in a wide variety of environments.

Examples of Web Cameras

It will be helpful to experience Web cameras so you can understand their value in one-to-one Web marketing, so here is a list of a few *sights to see* on the Web:

- The Arizona Department of Transportation wants you to see the traffic situation, such as this Web camera showing Durango Curve—watch out, partner! Visit www.azfms.com/Images/Cameras/camera33.html.

- Want to know what's shaking in Los Angeles? When the Earth moves in Southern California, you can see it live on the NBC 4 Seismo-Cam. Visit www.knbc4la.com/seismo/index.html.

- If you are planning a vacation—or want to remember one—take a look at Front Street, Lahaina, Maui, Hawaii. Visit www.mauigateway.com/~video/.

Using Streaming Video on the Web

Since we live in a *TV age* it's natural for marketers as well as Web users to expect that video will be the next big technology to become available. The difficulty, of course, is in overcoming the bandwidth limitations of today's Internet and the modem speeds used by many people. This makes it important to consider not only the value of video to convey your message, but also the bandwidth available to members of your audience. Some of the uses for video include training materials, news broadcasts, and product demonstrations.

Technology Overview

The first few videos used on the Web were large files that needed to be completely downloaded before they could be viewed. Once the technique of *streaming audio* became a proven technology, companies went to work on applying the same technique to video so that motion could be viewed as the file is being downloaded.

When video files were just downloaded and played locally, a variety of network problems were hidden because a 5-minute increase in download time from 30 minutes to 35 minutes wasn't very noticeable. With streaming video, those delays could cause havoc with the program. Part of the solution is to compress the files by identifying repeating patterns and sending each pattern only once, but that doesn't solve all of the problems.

In his White Paper, "Broadcasting Video on the World Wide Web," Tom Arnold provides a detailed explanation of the difficulty of producing and distributing streaming video on the Web (www.inproduction.com); for example, the amount of data being sent, network traffic, and the speed of users' computers and connections.

After the technical challenges of compression have been dealt with, the other two challenges deal with the variability of the Internet to deliver a continuous flow of data. The original design of the Internet allowed small groups of data, called "packets," to move through the network of computers at whatever speed the network would allow. That was okay when the Internet was used primarily for e-mail because it didn't matter if an e-mail message was delayed a few seconds (or in some cases, a few minutes). Now that we're trying to push a continuous stream of data, it's critical that the flow of video frames be seen as continuous.

Figure 7.5 RealVideo player showing streaming video broadcast.

How is this done? The same way most municipal water systems deliver water today—accumulate water in storage tanks during low usage and empty the tanks during high consumption.

With streaming video, the storage tank is a temporary storage buffer at the viewer's computer. The trick, of course, is to store enough in the buffer so that the display is continuous, but not so much that it takes too long to start displaying the video. Each streaming video product has its own way to adjust the speed, balance of audio versus video, buffer, and other factors that make each product unique.

Streaming Video Products

The streaming video products available to serve video on your Web site generally have three major components: a creation software tool, Web video server software, and browser plug-in software.

RealVideo (www.real.com)

Real Networks started with the RealAudio streaming audio product and then added streaming video. The screen shot in Figure 7.5 shows the size of the video.

Web Theater (www.vxtreme.com)

VXtreme's Web Theater is more than one product, it is a suite of products for the creation and encoding of material for the Web. In addition, the products provide a number of configurations that allow the producer to balance quality of video, audio, and speed.

VDOLive (www.vdo.net)

The VDOLive family of products includes On-Demand and Broadcast server products, LiteVDO for streaming video through any firewall, and a set of developer tools for capturing and compressing video.

VivoActive (www.vivo.com)

Like the other major vendors in this market, Vivo Software's line of products includes a number of products to meet the various needs of Web marketers and video producers.

Creating video for the Web

So where is all this video going to come from? From you, of course! As the compression technology has developed to deliver streaming video on the Web, so has the technology to *create* video programming.

If you are looking to emphasize content over image, then you'll be interested in acquiring the camera (don't forget the tripod!), a high-speed PC, and the associated video software tools needed to create your own content.

Ken Raley, publisher of the online magazine *Jump Cut* (www.raley.com), makes available a number of documents that detail the steps in creating video as well as technical summaries of products he has used. If you're a "first-time video producer," you will want to follow Ken's guidelines:

1. Write a detailed script.

2. Line up preproduction.

3. Obtain camera equipment.

4. Tape the production.

5. Digitize the video.

6. Edit the video.

7. Compress the finished video file.

8. Publish the video on your Web site.

What about the need for using video in one-to-one Web marketing that emphasizes image? There's only one answer: Hire professionals. The amount of detail required to create and produce broadcast-quality video requires a team of experienced video producers who can help you convey your marketing message in a powerful video.

Examples of Streaming Video on the Web

As we've discussed, the lack of bandwidth to deliver full 30-frame-per-second (television quality) video makes the use of streaming video for marketing somewhat difficult.

At the present time, streaming video is used mostly by content providers, those journalistic Web sites that provide the news, information, and entertainment that allow the rest of us to see the innovative edge of what can be done today. Who else is better equipped to create lots of video content than a television network! One of the early news content Web sites to display streaming video was the special Web site of CBS called "Up to the Minute" (uttm.com).

TIP | The great quest for more bandwidth takes on many forms. Even though corporate LANs can deliver most of the bandwidth needed for the organization (is there *ever* enough bandwidth!), delivering video to people in other companies can be a problem. In order to achieve high bandwidth between your Web server and an audience at another company (such as your customers or vendors), arrange for everyone to use the same ISP. Large ISPs such as UUnet and MCI have very high-speed backbones (i.e., main network pathway), which means companies using only their service, and not moving network traffic through other ISPs, can achieve a higher bandwidth.

By elimininating the chance for traffic to travel through ISPs with slower connections, you can have some control over the bandwidth available to deliver your video.

For those of us who are awake at early morning hours, UTTM is a source of news and information, and the Web version of the show provides additional information that is not included in the broadcast version.

Here are a few other examples of streaming video you can experience. Just be ready to download and install the proper plug-in for the program.

- CMP, the publisher of a number of computer and technology publications, operates a Web site dedicated to video using VIVO. Visit www.first-tv.com/.

- Braas Company provides video demonstrations of their automation solutions for industry using VDO. Check out their fluid-handling equipment, then schedule a visit from the Mobile Products Center. Visit www.braasco.com/mobile.html (Figure 7.6).

- Check out the latest movie promo from Hollywood using VDO. Visit infos-eek.vdo.net.

Figure 7.6 Streaming video using VDO at the Mobile site.

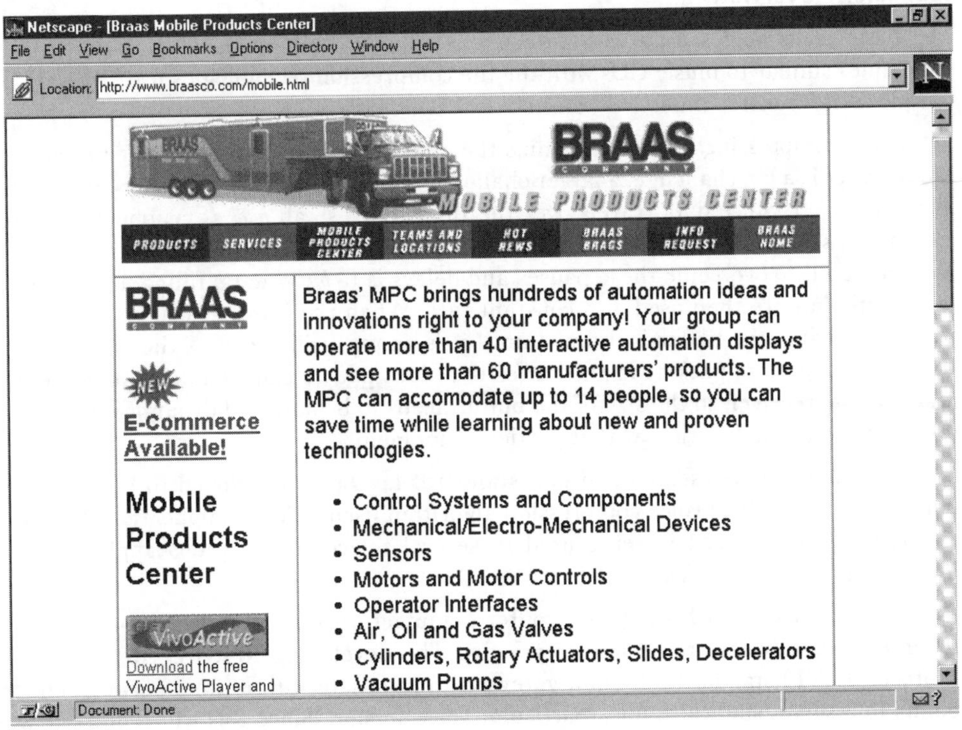

- Live news from Fox News is available using RealVideo. Visit www.foxnews.com.

- News from CNN/fn using VXtreme

Internet Telephony

Using the Internet to carry voice conversations has had its share of appeal but, until recently, has been slow to take off. However, now that standards have been adopted and vendors have begun selling second-generation VON (voice over the Internet) products, voice over the Internet is becoming much more doable.

Benefits of Internet Telephony

The most striking benefit of using the Internet to deliver telephone-type audio conversations is the lower cost. Companies that can install compatible equipment in remote offices are already reducing long distance charges. As these companies install products adhering to international protocols, conversations between companies via the Internet will become commonplace.

Technology Overview

The basic technologies used with Internet telephony combine the analog-to-digital techniques similar to music CDs with the file compression technologies used for years to reduce file transfer time.

While compressing files to maximize the amount of information transferred over the Internet is a big challenge, a larger challenge is managing network delays inherent in the Internet. Since data travels over the Internet in small *packets*, as opposed to a continuous stream of data, there are frequent pauses and delays. The technique that has been used to overcome these pauses and delays is to *buffer* data, filling a reservoir of packets that are then used at a constant rate. When the Internet causes delays in packets arriving, the buffer is drained until it is empty (which causes the pause). Of course, storing more packets in the buffer to reduce pauses causes a delay in content reaching the receiver, so the size of the buffer needs to be adjusted dynamically based on the speed of the Internet at that particular moment.

Fortunately, new research and new standards are being developed to help eliminate this problem. The voice-compression algorithm used in VON applications known as the G.723.1 standard is being used in several telecommunications applications, including private networks.

Now that a standard is in place, router manufacturers are creating prioritization schemes to give voice traffic higher priority. The developing Resource Reservation Protocol (RSVP) standard will allow gateways to negotiate with routers between endpoints to reserve bandwidth for a particular voice session. Since this will require new network hardware to be designed, manufactured, and installed, it will be some time before the Internet will be ready to move streaming traffic faster than ordinary traffic (e.g., e-mail, Web, etc.).

Internet Telephony Products

Internet telephony products include products that connect people when one or both people are using the Internet. Some products just connect two individuals, and a new category of products is starting to arrive on the market that handles the switching usually performed by corporate PBX systems.

Jeff Pulver's Voice over the Net Web site (www.von.com) has a continually updated list of Internet telephony products, but you can start by reviewing the following products to get an idea of what is available:

Internet Phone from VocalTec (www.vocaltec.com).

WebTalk from Quarterdeck (www.qdeck.com).

Intel Internet Phone from Intel Corp (www.intel.com).

Videoconferencing on the Internet

We've all been enamored with the stars we see on television, so it's no wonder that we want to see ourselves on television, too. While today's videoconferencing can't deliver broadcast-quality video without tremendous expense, we can experience conversations with people, individually or as a group, that are as productive as face-to-face meetings.

The recent growth in desktop videoconferencing demonstrates that the technology is becoming usable and affordable. Elliot Gold, president of TeleSpan, a publishing and consulting company that focuses on videoconferencing, would predicted shipments would grow from under 200,000 units in 1995 to at least 2.5 million units in 1997.

In the past, dedicated videoconferencing systems were so expensive that they were usually installed in conference rooms that could be used by a large number of employees. Equipment compatibility restricted who you could talk to, so most videoconferencing was done within a company.

In addition to corporate meetings within a company, other typical uses of these dedicated videoconferencing facilities have been in health care, where doctors consult with patients in another part of the state, and distance learning, where students can watch an instructor in a centralized facility.

The growth of videoconferencing—within companies and between companies—will continue to increase, according to Jim Hebert, executive director of the International Teleconferencing Association (www.itca.org). The ITCA estimates that 50 million conferencing-ready PCs will be in use within a year. This prediction is based on research conducted by Infonetics Research, that found that 59 percent of companies surveyed plan to use videoconferencing using their corporate LAN within a year.

Technology Overview

Videoconferencing technology can be divided two ways: the type of use and the equipment needed to implement it.

Until recently, desktop videoconferencing products could only display one other location on the screen, which limited its use to a little more than a telephone call—hardly a group collaboration technology.

Recent advances in desktop videoconferencing technology now allow what's sometimes called "continuous presence," which is the ability to handle audio and video channels from multiple locations. These signals are mixed by a videoconference server and sent to all participants so that everyone can be heard and seen at the same time on the screen. Steve Nill, chief financial officer of VideoServer, Inc., says continuous presence is just one advance that will help bring about large-scale acceptance of video-conferencing.

An additional technology that has been added to videoconference products is the ability to experience the use of a computer application by all participants in the conference. By displaying the changing elements of a computer window—including mouse movements—and allowing each participant to control the application being run, members of the audience can become involved in ways that have not been possible in the past.

Standards for Videoconferencing

Advances in computer design are just one reason for today's popularity in videoconferencing. Another reason for acceptance is the use of standards of handling audio and video data over multiple types of networking systems.

For instance, the International Telecommunication Union, an international telecommunications organization, has helped set standards that many manufacturers and software companies are agreeing to use. The standard, called "H.324," establishes how videoconferencing will take place over standard telephone lines. And, yes, there is a generally accepted acronym for plain old telephone service—POTS.

In order to videoconference with multiple locations, vendors have agreed to use the H.323 standard, which covers Internet videoconferencing. So, with H.323 and H.324, videoconferencing has taken a new turn to pull people together.

If you're looking for a few more acronyms to toss out at the next party of people who couldn't gather over a videoconference, try saying that you look for high QoS, and then explain that means *Quality of Service*. And if the guy next to you tries to one-up you and starts talking about things like G.711, H.263, or the old H.320 standard, just remind him that they all got rolled up into the new H.323 and H.324 standards.

Equipment for Videoconferencing

Now that we have the standards out of the way, let's talk about cameras ("Makeup, get the shine off this guy's head") and how they're connected to the computer screen at the other end of the line. In general, the products needed at each location for a video-conference include a camera, video capture board in the PC, videoconference software, and an Internet connection. High-end video cameras need to be connected to a specialized video capture board that converts video signal into the digital signal that can be transmitted by the videoconference software to compatible (thank goodness for standards) software at another location.

As we saw earlier in the chapter in the section on Web cameras, not all cameras require a specialized video capture board. The QuickCam from Connectix plugs into the parallel port of computers, so it doesn't need a video capture board. Steve Cross, vice president of Connectix, estimates they are selling cameras at the rate of 3 million units per year.

Evaluating Products for Internet Videoconferencing

The number of products on the market today for use in videoconferencing using ordinary telephone lines as well as the Internet is growing. Some of the products are individual pieces that need to be combined with other products, while some products are sold as complete systems.

In addition, not all videoconferencing products have all of the features—or support all of the standards—that you may need, so here are a few features to keep in mind when evaluating these products:

Audio-only versus audio and video. Some conferencing products support sharing of applications, whiteboards, and other handy features, but don't support video. If video is important, make sure it's included.

Interaction with other brands. While manufacturers may say they support certain standards, their products may or may not work well with products from other manufacturers. Until interaction with other brands becomes common, be sure to evaluate which products are compatible.

Multiplatform support. If your organization uses both Windows 3.1 and Windows 95, or if you use Macintosh or Unix computers, take these multi-platform needs into consideration.

Ease of setup. Plan for how you will install and set up equipment at each of your company's locations, as well as those of your customers who will be using the system. Sometimes the extra cost of complete turn-key systems is outweighed by the savings in time and resources to install systems across an enterprise.

Multiperson conference. Some videoconference products allow for multiple people to participate in text-only "chats" without video or audio, while other products support full multiperson videoconferences (splitting the screen into multiple views).

Application sharing. Allowing the audience to see how a particular computer program looks as a presenter uses it gives the audience a real sense of interacting without having to overcome the initial concern about training everyone. Some videoconference products allow for easy sharing of practically any computer application(i.e., software program), while others require each location to have a copy of the shared program installed.

Collaboration. Whiteboard sharing of applications and notes is one of the most valuable features of videoconferencing, but it is handled in different ways by different vendors.

As you can see, evaluating videoconference products requires careful consideration of the features you will need now, as well as those in the near term, in order for your trials and full implementation to be successful. When starting to evaluate Internet-based videoconferencing, please visit our companion site, One-to-One Web Marketing Online (www.1to1web.com), for new and updated information and resources.

Software Products for Internet Videoconferencing

Now let's discuss some examples of the software products on the market and take a brief look at their distinctive features.

CU-SeeMe 3.0 (www.cuseeme.com)

Originally developed and provided by Cornell University (thus, the CU) and now available as a commercial product from White Pines, CU-SeeMe was the first popular Internet product to allow for multipoint audioconferencing and videoconferencing. While it has a whiteboard, look carefully at the application sharing features to see if they meet your needs.

NetMeeting (www.microsoft.com)

Microsoft has provided this product free of charge on its Web site for some time and has generated a considerable user base experienced in using this product. It has the most popular features used in business today: audio, video, file transfer, chat, application sharing, and whiteboard, so it meets the needs of many people looking to conference over the Internet. The product is only available for the Windows 95 and Windows NT platforms, so take that into consideration.

Internet Phone (www.vocaltec.com)

The Internet Phone product from VocalTec Communications Ltd. has a set of features similar to NetMeeting in that it supports audio and video, whiteboarding, and text chat. In addition, its audio conferencing allows up to 100 people to participate in an audio conference when used in conjunction with the VocalTec Conferencing Server. The product also allows PC-to-phone calling through direct online links to Internet telephony service.

Hardware Products for Internet Videoconferencing

Here are some examples of more hardware-based products, some of which include computers, cameras, and everything you need for plug-and-play installations.

ProShare

The Intel ProShare Video System is a PC-based desktop videoconferencing solution that brings full video, audio, and data conferencing capabilities to business PC users. It works over ISDN phone lines or LAN connections and operates on either Windows 95 or Windows 3.1. The technology complies with H.320, H.323, and T.120 interoperability standards.

Internet Video Phone (www.intel.com)

The Intel Internet Video Phone allows Internet users to see and talk to each other while using other Internet applications, such as browsing the Web. The Intel Internet Video Phone works on Pentium processor-based PCs running the Windows 95 operating system, and it complies with the ITU H.323 interoperability standard.

Complete Videoconference Systems

Complete videoconference systems that include the computer, monitor, camera, and other equipment save time and reduce the opportunity for misconfiguration. The three complete systems discussed next illustrate the type of products available.

Intel's TeamStation (www.intel.com)

Intel's TeamStation system, a PC-based multifunction videoconferencing solution, delivers video/audio/data conferencing and presentation capabilities, plus Internet and corporate network access. The Intel TeamStation system's standard configuration includes a 233 MHz Pentium II processor, Intel ProShare technology, and an auto-tracking, high-resolution camera. The TeamStation system supports the H.320, H.323, and T.120 international communication standards, as well as Microsoft NetMeeting for interoperability.

PictureTel's LiveLAN (www.picturetel.com)

The LiveLAN videoconferencing system (see Figure 7.7) works on corporate LANs and delivers full-screen and full-motion video. It runs on a Pentium PC running Windows 95 and is H.323 and T.120 standard compliant. Like other complete solutions, it pro-

Figure 7.7 PictureTel's LiveLAN on the screen.

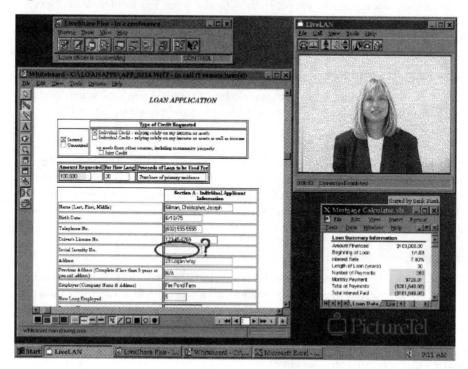

vides for data collaboration, application sharing, shared whiteboard, file transfer, and messaging. And since LiveLAN's application sharing is interoperable with Microsoft's Net Meeting, you can conference with Net Meeting users in your LAN.

PolyCom's ShowStation IP (www.polycom.com)

ShowStation IP allows for both formal and ad hoc Web presentations involving 10 multipoint conferences. ShowStation IP can connect to any number of remote sites that have either a ShowStation or a PC via the Internet, an existing corporate intranet, or ordinary analog phone lines. Conference participants at any number of sites can use ShowStation IP's electronic pen to write, draw, highlight, or erase on the unit's display just as with an overhead transparency, and all notes and comments are immediately visible at all sites simultaneously. ShowStation IP supports common software such as Microsoft's Net Meeting, which allows users to load and store presentations directly from the ShowStation IP's floppy disk drive. ShowStation IP also supports printing of the presentation and can read Microsoft Office 97 files.

Videoconferencing Service

When you need special features that are part of the network itself, such as encryption or extremely high speeds, then an outside service may be the best solution. One service that is pioneering a new set of features is discussed next.

PictureNet (www.picturetel.com)

PictureTel has joined with an Internet service provider to work on what it calls "a major trial network" called PictureNet, a Virtual Private Data Network (VPDN) that uses encryption technology to create a private network over the public IP network.

The objectives the two companies want to achieve with PictureNet are to demonstrate the commercial viability of conferencing over the Internet, capture and collect performance and data metrics, and obtain feedback from users and proactively address issues.

PictureTel has said that PictureNet is Phase 1 of a broader plan for the implementation of videoconferencing over the Internet. In Phase 2, PictureTel will extend the trial to work with six to eight customers who will conduct intracompany videoconferences over the Internet. In Phase 3, PictureTel will broaden the trial to include intercompany and business-to-consumer conferencing.

Group Conferencing for Training

The high cost of in-person training is causing many companies to look more closely at using Internet-based training techniques.

Cisco Systems, the leading provider of Internet routers (the devices that decide which path to take through the maze of possible Internet connections), faces the challenge of growth and training everyone on their new technologies. The audiences they communicate with start with prospects, customers, and market analysts and include everyone inside the company—from salespeople to engineers and manufacturing personnel.

While their internal television network provides the capability for real-time broadcasts, their training needs extend beyond the set schedule that is inherent in live broadcasts. Steve Anthese, program manager of applied technology at Cisco, recently started using a video-on-demand product that delivers prerecorded video programming directly to the desktop of individuals via their internal intranet.

By allowing a person to select the material, the time of delivery, and the location of delivery, one-to-one communication is put in the hands of the individual.

Videoconferencing with Prospective Customers

One of the benefits of the work to make videoconferencing equipment compatible with multiple standards is the ability to have conferences using the Internet and ordinary telephone lines (POTS) depending on the need.

For example, Mentor Graphics is using Intel's ProShare conferencing systems at its trade shows to increase customer communication and to "bring the factory to the conference." At the 1997 Design Automation Conference, Mentor used videoconferencing systems in its product demo suites so qualified customers could communicate directly with the software developers at the company headquarters.

Videoconferencing with Customers

There are many opportunities to use videoconferencing to interact with customers to provide better customer service and reduce costs; however, each of these opportunities must be approached with care. It is important to understand how customers feel about replacing in-person experiences with videoconferencing experiences.

For example, customers of the Swiss CoOp bank are conducting their financial affairs from a Zurich shopping mall using an interactive multimedia banking kiosk. Using the kiosk, customers can view a range of multimedia presentations about the bank's insurance services and use a live video link, based on Intel's ProShare conferencing software, to contact a financial counselor. The installation is one of a series of trials by the CoOp to test the concept of remote banking using kiosks, in a variety of locations, to deliver an enhanced range of customer services.

Since many banking services are almost identical to the services provided by other banks, the key is to maintain a relationship with the customer through the introduction of new technologies such as videoconferencing.

In another banking example, Flagstar Bank, a large wholesale lender, uses videoconferencing to approve more loans more quickly and with less hassle. Flagstar has installed Intel ProShare conferencing systems at more than 600 mortgage broker sites in 30 states. Underwriters can review a borrower's application with the borrower during a videoconference and get important questions answered on the spot.

Information gathered during the personal interview is then sent to a Freddie Mac automated underwriting system and a response comes back within minutes. The entire approval process can take an hour. This use of videoconferencing won the 1997 Computerworld Smithsonian Award for its use of information technology in the Finance, Insurance, and Real Estate categories.

Flagstar Bank was selected by a panel of distinguished judges who sought projects that were based on innovative uses of information technology that bring about improvement to society. The system will become part of the Smithsonian Institution's Permanent Research Collection of Information Technology Innovation at the National Museum of American History.

As you can see from these two examples, using videoconferencing technologies with the public today requires that you provide the hardware and network connections in places convenient to the public in order to achieve the near-broadcast quality the public expects.

Conferencing within an Organization

One of the easiest approaches to introducing videoconferencing is to use it within an organization where you have control over the computing environment and the training and support environments.

Judges in the U.S. District Court in Houston, Texas, use videoconferencing to meet with judges in remote areas. Instead of traveling there on a regular basis, the judges located outside Houston join the meetings using desktop conferencing units. This way, the court saves valuable working hours and money.

In another example—on the other side of the bench—the law firm of Arnold, White & Durkee uses personal conferencing for such meetings as linking a patent inventor directly with a firm lawyer. The two parties create a rough draft of the patent application together in real time by pulling a word processing document into a shared, onscreen notebook for collaboration. Using this method, the difference in cost from an in-person meeting in another city can be dramatic.

By using videoconferencing within an organization, you gain experience with the many technologies involved and also have an opportunity to understand how people interact with these systems.

Designing/Developing Interactivity with the Audience

Each of the technologies we've explored relies on the same basic communication need: Move information into the minds of individuals in your audience. This communications need hasn't changed over the ages, but our understanding of how to impart information has grown. Human factors research has identified a number of details about how the human brain absorbs information.

In his book, *Multimedia Authoring* (1994, Academic Press), Scott Fisher reviews the findings of research into developing interactive presentations that truly communicate. He lists several key points to consider when you create your presentation:

- Most people can keep track of five items of information in short-term memory.
- The length of time these five items can be retained is about 15 to 30 seconds.
- Short-term memory works best when the information is in the form of visual and textual material.

These concepts have different impacts in different types of presentations. For example, prospects looking for general information can be expected to remember five general benefits of your product. On the other hand, customers in a technical training session might have a hard time remembering five detailed steps to using your product.

As Fisher points out, information that requires the audience member to turn away from the presentation to perform the task consumes the retention time and makes it essential to reduce the amount of material presented within a given time.

Applying these concepts to presentations requires carefully following the steps to preparing and presenting presentations, which George Morrisey covers in his book, *Effective Business and Technical Presentations* (1975, Addison-Wesley):

1. Establish objectives for the presentation.

2. Analyze your audience.

3. Prepare a preliminary plan for the presentation.

4. Select the right resource material required for the message.

5. Organize material for effective presentation.

6. Practice the presentation.

It seems that most of us know these steps, we just don't always follow them! As presentation technology has become more complex, the need to practice using the technology has become more important. You've probably sat through the executive's speech where the slides didn't match, or the microphone wasn't loud enough, or the lights were too bright for the slides. With Internet presentations, just think of all of the *additional* problems you can face when trying to impress your audience, and then rehearse until you can deal with any eventuality.

The Future of One-to-One Web Presentations and Conferencing

One of the keys to improving relationships with prospects and customers is increasing the attention, involvement, and interaction of the audience whether that audience is 1 person or 1000 people. The appeal of television and movies is the combination of motion and audio. The immediate challenge for using Internet-based multimedia is obtaining sufficient bandwidth for all users to allow full-motion (i.e., 30 frames per second) video and CD-quality audio. Corporations with high-speed internal networks are currently achieving near-broadcast quality video, but the bandwidth consumption limits the availability.

After bandwidth limitations are overcome, the next breakthrough will be greater audience involvement. One type of audience involvement will be real-time voting, much like presenters do now when speaking to an audience. Additional techniques to attract and hold an audience's attention will be 3-D graphical environments for individuals to interact, personalized multimedia on demand, and improved workgroup collaboration. While it's clear that the technological products will continue to be developed at a quick pace, the greater challenge is providing presenters with training on these technologies so that they are effective in delivering their presentation with Internet-based multimedia.

 Go to the companion Web site for a one-to-one case study on Lakeview Engineering, a company providing videoconferencing services on the Net.

Chapter 8, "One-to-One Web Advertising and Promotion," shows you how to create targeted and one-to-one Web advertising campaigns. Since the inception of the ever-present Web banner, many strides have been made to provide Web marketers with the ability to target advertisements to groups and even individual members in the online audience. Web advertising has moved from static Web banners to online advertising that looks and acts like dynamic television ads. The introduction of advertising networks and ad management products will change how advertising is done on the Web.

ONE-TO-ONE WEB ADVERTISING AND PROMOTION

8

"Propaganda ends where dialogue begins."

Marchall McLuhan

Mass advertising. Direct marketing. Now the next paradigm shift: one-to-one marketing. The computer has enabled this awe-inspiring transformation of the marketing discipline. In 1970, computers were becoming more prevalent and the cost of computing was declining. At the same time, *market segmentation* and *demographics* were the buzzwords of the day. Add to this lifestyle data, *psychographics*, and a computer at the end of each marketer's fingertips, and we now have a direct-marketing business in excess of $100 billion dollars annually.

No one could have predicted the opportunity for marketers to target their messages to a single user on the World Wide Web. Peppers and Rogers, leaders in the one-to-one marketing arena, had alluded to the possibility of an electronic medium that could individually address the needs of each customer in their first book, *One to One Future* (1993, Doubleday). Only a very few short years later, the World Wide Web has revolutionized the way we advertise. For example, people cannot click on a magazine advertisement and receive instant information about products or offers—you can do this on the Web. Also, most traditional advertising offers some targeting and response-tracking capabilities, but the Web can target ads and track users in a much more granular and one-to-one manner. For example, the InfoSeek search engine offers advertisers the UltraMatch service, which targets ads to online users most likely to respond based on confidential user profiles and user interaction behavior. UltraMatch uses advanced neural networking technology that is used in the banking industry to detect credit card fraud.

In Joseph Turow's book, *Breaking Up America* (1997, The University of Chicago Press), he discussed the popular notion among advertisers in the 1980s and early 1990s—signaling. *Signaling* was the practice of trying to reach targets using traditional advertising and publicity methods that would engender affinity among people and the identities of those advertisers. With the emergence of relationship marketing, this practice was an inefficient way to build loyalty among brands. Mr. Turow states, "Relying on signaling was no longer enough to ensure loyalty to the company and its output, practitioners generally agreed. What was needed was an ongoing conversation with every desirable customer. This approach to selling therefore implied two other efforts that were then getting much play in the advertising world: database marketing and interactive marketing." With this in mind, the Web is the optimum vehicle to accomplish this with its ability to fine-tune targeting efforts through tracking and user profiling.

In this chapter, we discuss how online advertising is evolving into a one-to-one marketing medium. We show how the Web and advancing technologies, such as tracking and intelligent agents, provide us with the possibility to deliver a single advertising message to each and every customer. In online advertising speak, an online ad reaches the right *eyeballs*. We also provide an overview of each type of advertising format and forum, and discuss which can be used for targeting and one-to-one advertising. We provide an overview of services and tools, such as advertising networks and ad serving software, that ease the process of creating and managing a targeted advertising campaign. Finally, we take a peek at what is coming in the future of online advertising.

The State of Online Advertising

Online advertising had a rocky start with the old guard of the Internet using harsh retaliatory tactics against anyone who put commercial advertising messages on newsgroups. Before the World Wide Web, the Internet community prohibited and abhorred commercial advertising messages and often responded to the person who sent the message with an angry *flame* message.

Now online advertising has become acceptable to most online users. According to an April 1997 online survey conducted by *BBDO TechSetter Magazine* (www.techsetter.com), almost 72 percent of the respondents said they pay attention to the advertising banners within an online edition of magazines on the Internet. There are still exceptions to the growing acceptance of online advertising, including unsolicited e-mail ads (a.k.a. spam) and commercial postings on newsgroups or discussion groups that expressly forbid the practice. Here are a few major milestones for online advertising with some information from an October 1996 article appearing in *Advertising Age*:

November 1993   GNN introduces advertising to the Internet.

October 1994   HotWired site launches with ads from AT&T, Sprint, and others.

March 1995	Ragu is the first packaged-goods marketer to open a Web site.
July 1995	Forrester Research reports total online ad spending for 1995 will total $37 million.
October 1995	Poppe Tyson spins off its Web ad sales unit to form DoubleClick.
January 1996	Microsoft pays $200,000 to sponsor Super Bowl Web site.
May 1996	iVillage receives $800,000 in ad commitments.
October 1996	CASIE introduces proposed Web banner ad guidelines.
January 1997	Hewlett-Packard introduces interactive "Pong" banner ad campaign.
August 1997	Jupiter predicts online advertising will total $7.7 billion by the year 2002.

Analysts believe that Internet advertising will reach $1 billion by the end of 1998. IBM (www.ibm.com) placed online advertisements in over 500 sites in 1997. A major trend in online advertising is the convergence of brand advertising and direct marketing. Jupiter Communications (www.jup.com) believes that online advertising will move "from an awareness device to an action instigator." In fact, there have already been new advertising formats that bring the online ad, and transaction, to the audience instead of whisking the viewer off to another Web page or site to complete the transaction cycle.

Benefits of One-to-One Web Advertising and Promotion

In their 1997 book, *One to One Enterprise* (Doubleday), Peppers and Rogers present the necessity of building learning relationships, which means, "Give your customer the opportunity to teach you what he wants. Remember it, give it back to him, and keep his business forever."

One-to-one Web advertising and promotion have the capabilities to form a loyalty-building relationship with your online customers or users. Loyalty has the benefit of increasing advertising return on investment (ROI) and profitability through increased transactions from existing customers and a lower marketing cost. What could be more compelling?

The benefits of one-to-one Web advertising include the ability to put the right message in front of the right audience at the right time, encouraging dialog with customers, taking advantage of one of the lowest costs available to provide hundreds of different messages to different audiences, and the ability to track, report, and actually know if an online ad is successful.

The Right Message to the Right Person at the Right Time

Jack Powers, well-know Internet insider, wrote an article titled "Tempting The Click," in July 1996 on his Electric Pages Web site (www.electric-pages.com/articles.tempt.htm). In that article Mr. Powers stated, "Tempting the click means replacing the 'one-to-many' flow of conventional advertising communications with a 'one-to-one' relationship that tunes the message to each prospect."

Undoubtedly, the Web has the capability of targeting an ad based on, at a minimum, the user's computer, Web browser, time of day, past purchases, past clicks, geographical location, IP address, and other criteria. With other methods that capture actual user profile information or infer things about one group of users based on another group of users who have *like* attributes and characteristics, online advertisers can finely hone their ad campaigns.

Imagine that you have identified 15 different target markets for your new Web content site. Each target has several idiosyncratic demographic and psychographic attributes. Without doing sophisticated math, you can see that there is the potential for creating hundreds of banner or other online ad types that could be served up on hundreds of Web sites. Not only is it possible, it is a reality with the Web.

The Web is beginning to cluster, where information is being accessed through specialized Web sites, also called "channels" or "communities," that cater to groups with narrow demographic or psychographic characteristics. There are supersites or directories dedicated to specific markets or industries. For example, Manufacturing Marketplace (www.manufacturing.net) is a directory and online community that is solely dedicated to the professional who buys products from the manufacturing industry. C|Net introduced Snap! (www.snap.com), a site dedicated to presenting Web information that is targeted to the user. When a first-time user arrives at the main site, Snap! requests the user's zip code and then presents a Web page that is tailored to the user—plus users can create a personal page. Snap! offers advertisers many opportunities to present ads in a targeted way. There are several channels, including business, computing, health, living, money, shopping, and travel. There has also been significant growth in localized sites where national, regional, or local advertisers can present localized advertising. Hot Coupons! (www.hotcoupons.com) and CitySearch (www.citysearch.com) were pioneers in enabling ad targeting based on local geography. This clustering of the Web will provide advertisers with the ability to locate and market to specific target groups and measure the success of each ad within each target group. This microanalysis is what makes the Web attractive to direct marketers and advertisers.

Encourages Customer-to-Advertiser Dialog

One-to-one Web marketing requires interaction, or dialog, between customer and advertiser. Translation: *customer loyalty*. When customers tell you about themselves, and what they like/don't like about you and your competition, you can increase revenue from each customer and increase your ability to compete. The Web has opened up a worldwide opportunity but it has also changed the competitive landscape. It is easier than ever for customers to shop around on the Internet.

In 1991 Regis McKenna wrote *Relationship Marketing* (Addison-Wesley), which had a significant impact on changing marketing's focus to be customer centric. He states, "Technology is transforming choice, and choice is transforming the marketplace." There are so many choices that customers have become less loyal and more confused. The challenge for online advertisers is to form one-to-one relationships with customers through dialog—what customers tell you about and how they interact with your advertising. This dialog opens the door to encouraging ongoing relationships with all of your customer and market segments. It has been said that it is about five times more expensive to acquire a new customer than to get additional business from an existing one. All customers are not created equal, and you can only find this out by establishing a dialog with them.

Low Cost to Deliver Multiple Messages to Multiple Audiences

A face-to-face sales meeting can cost thousands of dollars. The fully burdened cost to reach a prospect via a targeted ad in a specialized magazine can cost hundreds of dollars. A highly targeted direct-mail piece can cost several or hundreds of dollars. A highly targeted Web banner can cost a few cents to several dollars to reach a likely-to-buy online customer. If you have hundreds of ad messages, the cost to create and place them on the Web is significantly less than traditional media. The cost to create online ads will be increasing in the future with the increasing use of animation, video, and audio, but the cost will still not come close to producing TV or magazine ads—especially if you need to create 15 different ad campaigns.

Recordability and Accountability

Ad networks, ad management products, and Web traffic analysis products can give online advertisers more data than they ever dreamed of or, in many cases, could ever have the time to deal with. This is where the Web leaves traditional advertising's and direct marketing's attempts to reach individual customers in the dust. What has been needed is a way to measure advertising ROI. When your objective is oriented to direct response or sales transactions, recordability and accountability is a critical element to the online ad process. If your objective is to build brand awareness among online customers, then a more mass advertising model is appropriate where measuring impressions, click-throughs, and resulting transactions are not as critical. However, tracking and analyzing online advertising and promotional campaigns is important—how much data you capture and what you analyze will vary depending on your campaign objective. If an online ad is not working, you can change it in a matter of a few hours, but first you have to know if the ad is not working. The bottom line is, if you want to measure something from numbers of clicks on an ad to what type of ad works best within a particular Web site that reaches a particular target market, you can do it on the Web.

Figure 8.1 Roadblocks to one-to-one advertising according to Jupiter Communications.

Source: Jupiter Communications

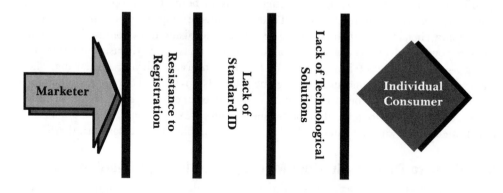

Better Sales Leads

An October 6, 1997, *Business Week* article stated how Toyota's (www.toyota.com) number-one source for leads is their Web site, overtaking its 800 number. From May 1996 to May 1997, Toyota received 152,000 Web leads. Toyota later matched the online leads with the names of buyers at dealerships to find that the Web ads led to the sale of 7329 cars, which is a 5 percent conversion rate. The more targeted you make your advertising, the more qualified the sales leads. Direct marketers have found more return on their direct-marketing budget by trying to increase the response rate through targeted offers. Mass marketers can only go so far in targeting, so they receive lots of unqualified prospects which requires more resources to sift out the truly qualified sales prospects. So highly targeted Web ads can increase the likelihood of response and conversion to purchase, and can decrease the cost associated with qualifying the prospects to determine if they are likely to buy.

Hurdles to One-to-One Web Advertising and Promotion

Internet advertising industry analysts, authors, and practitioners all agree that the biggest potential the Web brings to advertising is its one-to-one capabilities. They predict that online advertising will allow Web marketers to realize this dream. However, according to a Jupiter Communications "Online Advertising Report" (August 1997), it is a benefit to know more about an individual customer, but it may not always be worth

Figure 8.2 The pros and cons of targeting according to Jupiter Communications.

Source: Jupiter Communications

	Advertisers	Publishers
Pros	Increased Response Less Waste Increases Creative Impact	Higher CPMs Builds Relationship with Advertiser
Cons	No Clear Proof of Increased ROI after Certain Point	Premier Inventory Shortage Lack of Reach Inventory Management Problems

paying a lot of money for the information. Figures 8.1 and 8.2 show some of the road-blocks to the fabled market of one and the pros and cons of targeting.

The primary conditions existing in the online advertising medium that will present challenges to one-to-one Web marketers include privacy concerns, the higher cost to implement one-to-one online ad campaigns versus nontargeted campaigns, accuracy of user information, and the size of the online market in general.

Privacy Concerns by Online Users

Creating personalized ad messages is dependent on technology and the gathering of information that most online customers are currently not comfortable with. According to an April 1997 *Business Week*/Harris Poll, 65 percent of respondents were not willing to share personal and financial information so that online ads could be targeted to their tastes and interests. Many marketers and technology companies are frustrated by the misinformation about the cookie technology and other techniques that identify users to online publishers. Some online consumers think that online marketers can get their social security numbers from a cookie file without the consumer's consent. Not true.

Figure 8.3 Turning privacy problem into a plus, according to Jupiter Communications.

Source: Jupiter Communications

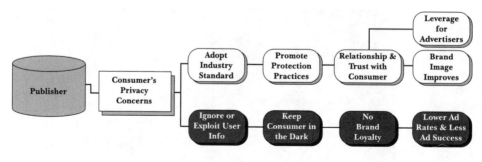

In order to turn this situation around and realize the benefits of one-to-one online advertising, Web marketers will need to embrace privacy standards (and also educate the market!) and practices brought forward by organizations such as the World Wide Web Consortium (www.w3c.org), Direct Marketing Association (www.the-dma.org), and TRUSTe (www.truste.org). Many Web marketing leaders believe that the industry should be self regulating in order to keep the government, particularly the Federal Trade Commission (www.ftc.gov), from regulating the industry. See Chapter 11, "One-to-One Web Privacy," for an additional discussion about online privacy. Figure 8.3 shows how to turn the privacy problem into a plus.

Higher Cost to Implement One-to-One Online Ad Campaigns

There are some online advertising industry representatives who believe that the cost of creating one-to-one advertising on the Web outweighs its benefits.

On One Hand

The cost-per-thousands (CPMs) for placing online ads can very from $1 to $200, depending on the Web site and the level of targeting desired. There is usually a charge for each additional target selection chosen when buying an ad placement. There are also additional creative and production costs associated with each additional ad or campaign versus one Web banner created for one audience as a whole.

On the Other Hand

According to Wenda Harris Millard, executive vice president of marketing and programming at DoubleClick, "People don't laugh at John Wannamaker's famous statement: 'Half the money I spend on advertising is wasted, and the trouble is, I don't know which half,' because the Web provides tracking and accountability that solves this mystery." She believes that one-to-one Web marketing isn't cost prohibitive because it is more efficient and, in the long run, less expensive than other traditional methods that can cost hundreds of dollars per qualified lead.

Accuracy of Target Information

With the fears over online privacy, many online consumers have not provided information to online marketers, which has limited the ability to target messages. Or consumers have not given accurate information about themselves, and many online publishers have no real way to verify the information. With software that enables users to block cookies, targeting is further limited. Web sites that have fee-based subscriptions or take online orders have the ability to verify most user information such as address, phone number, credit, and purchases. However, even these types of sites cannot verify more qualitative data such as user preferences.

According to the GVU 7th WWW User Survey (www.gvu.gatech.edu/user_surveys/), approximately 40 percent of respondents have provided false information, and a little more the 14 percent gave false information over 25 percent of the time. According to Bill Irvine, director of interactive media at The Wolf Group (www.wolfgroup.com), targeting on the Internet is based on limited information that can be unreliable or incorrect. However, Irvine does see a promising future for one-to-one marketing on the Web.

Size of Online Advertising Market

To some of the largest advertisers, the Web itself looks like one big target market of 82 million personal computers connected to the Internet in 1997 and more than 268 million by 2001, according to Dataquest (www.dataquest.com). There are currently only about 1000 Web sites selling advertising. To put the Web ad market in perspective, online advertising (U.S.) is expected to reach $4.4 billion in the year 2000, which will be a significantly small portion of the total ad spending of $131 billion.

The good news is that the adoption of the Web continues at a breakneck pace. More people are using the Web more times per week and spending more time than ever before. Here is the time it took for each type of media to reach 50 million users, according to a Morgan Stanley Technology Research report:

Radio   38 years

TV   13 years

Cable   10 years

Internet 5 years (est.)

Although the online market is still relatively small, the types and numbers of Web sites are vast. There are more than 1 million Web domains and there is a Web site for almost any subject you can think of (and many you would have never thought of!). With this in mind, online targeting makes good marketing sense.

The Nuts and Bolts of One-to-One Web Advertising

To understand the nature of online advertising and its emerging targeting and one-to-one marketing capabilities, we will provide the foundation: the types of advertising, where to advertise, and which online formats and locations are best for mass marketing, target marketing, and one-to-one advertising. First let's take a look at the dynamics of the online advertising market and technologies.

The Online Audience

As mentioned earlier, the Web market could be considered a very large target market to some large advertisers. To many marketers, the online ad will be considered a segment of their total market. To other marketers, such as a business or publisher that is *only* on line, the Web audience will be their whole market. For both types of marketers, it is important to understand the uniqueness of the online audience. It has been rapidly changing and will continue to evolve. Here are some important facts about today's online audience:

- It is the *World Wide* Web. The number of online households will rise from 23.4 million in 1996 to 66.6 million in 2000 (Jupiter Communications, 9/96).

- Daily use of the Web grew from 36 percent of adult online users in 1995 to 49 percent in 1997 (Find/SVP, 5/97).

- Use of traditional media has declined among adult online users as a result of the Internet (Find/SVP, 5/97).

- The gender, age, income, and educational characteristics of online users have changed:

    —Women, 40% ; Men, 60% (Find/SVP, 5/97).

    —40–49 years of age, 23%; 30–39 years of age, 18%; 18–24 years of age, 14%; 25–29 years of age, 14%; 50–64 years of age, 14%; and 65 years of age or older, 5% (Lou Harris/*Business Week*, 5/97).

    —Have annual incomes in excess of $75,000, 21%; have annual incomes between $35,000–$50,000, 20%; have annual incomes between $50,000–75,000, 12%; have annual incomes between $25,000–$35,000, 12%; have annual incomes below $15,000, 12%; have annual incomes between $15,000 and 25,000, 6% (Lou Harris/*Business Week*, 5/97).

—Have some college education, 27%; have high school education or less, 23%; have a college diploma, 23% have post graduate education, 18% (Lou Harris/*Business Week*, 5/97).

- Most popular activities online:

    —Gathering information (86%), searching (63%), browsing (61%), work (54%), education (52%), communication (47%), entertainment (46%), and shopping (18%) (GVU Study #7, 5/97).

- The majority of online users access the Web primarily from home, followed by work and school (GVU Study #7, 5/97).

The iVALS (Internet Values and Lifestyles Survey) segments their online survey respondents to the following categories based on their survey located at future.sri.com:80/vals/ivals/ques-nt.html:

Immigrant. Represents 16% of respondents, and is highly skeptical of Internet's usefulness.

Seeker. Represents 11% of respondents, and focuses on work and specific online tasks.

Surfer. Represents 9% of respondents, and is active with leisure online orientation.

Mainstreamer. Represents 12% of respondents, and patterns online usage after work and personal requirements.

Sociable. Represents 9% of respondents, and has strongest orientation to social aspects of the Internet like movies and computer games.

Worker. Represents 5% of respondents, has utilitarian view of the Net, and watches less TV than the average Internet user.

Pioneer. Represents 10% of respondents, and is a power user of the Internet.

Upstreamer. Represents 14% of respondents, is an Internet generalist like the Mainstreamer, and is a prime target for personalized online services.

Socialite. Represents 9% of respondents, is a prominent participant in online discussions, and has multiple, well-defined online personae.

Wizard. Represents 6% of respondents, and is the most active and skilled Internet group with a median age under 30 years old.

The bottom line is that people behave differently and have particular expectations on line. Web marketers should be aware of the online audience's idiosyncrasies. We should address online users with different visual and textual cues, offers and content than what would be provided in traditional media.

Branding or Direct Response?

Both! As the Web population is growing, there are sites, directories, and search engines emerging as mass-marketing vehicles. There are also more and more highly targeted sites coming on line. Web sites span from sites that are simple awareness vehicles to full-blown, mail-order commerce sites. Depending on what business you are in, and the primary reason for your online presence, you can use Web advertising for building your brand or for generating direct response.

Brand-building certain online locations, such as a high-traffic Web site, and certain ad formats, such as the animated interstitial, can be very effective ways to generate brand affinity among online users. For direct response, the interactive and hyperlink nature of the Web allows advertisers to generate traffic and transactions. For example, a Web banner that is promoting a free offer will get people to respond. The more the ad is targeted, the higher the response rate.

Mass, Targeted, One-to-One

The Web allows some level of mass marketing, target marketing, and one-to-one marketing. Before proceeding, let's go back to the basics and define each type of marketing:

Mass marketing. One-to-all or one-to-many communications without specialization of message or medium. For example, a company image advertisement in *Life* magazine.

Target marketing. One-to-many or one-to-few communications with specialization of message and medium for each identified segment of the whole market. For example, Ford Motor Company's sport utility vehicle advertisement in *The Ladies Home Journal* with images and copy geared to womens' needs for this type of vehicle.

One-to-one marketing. One-to-few or one-to-one communications with individualized message and medium for each highly targeted market or individual customer. For example, a personalized e-mail advertising message with content geared to that individual's stated preferences, or by other targeting criteria such as browser type, computer type, geographical area, prior interactions or transactions, demographic data, or lifestyle data.

According to a 1997 study by Forrester Research (www.forrester.com), "Targeted advertising to individual consumers via Web sites will become an industry standard in three years." There is an ever-widening range of online advertising options that one-to-one Web marketers can choose from depending on the objectives of their advertising campaign, from simple banner ads on a search engine to interstitial advertisements that behave like television advertising with animation or full-motion video. Many Web marketers are using a combination of online advertising formats within one campaign. Figure 8.4 shows the spectrum of online advertising.

Figure 8.4 The online advertising spectrum.

One-to-All	One-to-Many	One-to-Few	One-to-Fewer	One-to-One
1 : 1,000,000	1 : 10,000	1 : 1,000	1 : 100	1 : 1
Search Engine Home Pages	Targeted Web Sites/ Directories	Personalized Web Sites/ Directories	Personalized Web Sites and Push Channels	Highly Personalized Web Sites and Push Channe
High Traffic/ Mass Appeal Web Sites	Push Channels	Push Channels	Web Sites With Collaborative Filtering	Chat
	Search Engine Keywords	Advertising Networks	Personalized Push	Personalized E-Mail
	Advertising Networks	Targeted E-Mail	Advertising Networks	
	E-Mail		Chat	
			Targeted E-Mail	

Targeting and One-to-One Advertising Technologies

The market for targeting and one-to-one Web technologies is booming. Just imagine serving up hundreds, thousands, or millions of unique banner ads to each online user within your prospective market. There are new technologies and applications being developed to make this a reality in terms of implementation and affordability. Here is the recipe:

1. **Combine one or more of the following ingredients:** cookies, user profiling, content personalization, intelligent agents, and neural networking.

2. **Add one or more of the following ingredients:** databases, data mining, interaction log files, transaction log files, demographics, and psychographics.

3. **Blend the above with savvy direct or one-to-one marketers in partnership with database, information technology, and Web wizards.**

Seriously, in order for one-to-one Web marketers to successfully realize the potential of the Internet, they need to bring forward experiences in direct marketing to the Web but apply them in a new way. Also, one-to-one Web marketers will need to work in concert, like never before, with their information technology and Web development counterparts to understand the potential, and drawbacks, of the new (and in many cases, unproved) one-to-one technologies such as intelligent agents and data mining.

Today's One-to-One Web Advertising Technologies

Web technologies that enable the delivery of targeted or individualized advertisements are making many marketers excited, but they are also making many online consumers nervous about their privacy. Most of the current technologies involve some level of personal data; therefore it will be a precarious future for these types of technologies. With self-regulation and building trust among consumers, these one-to-one Web technologies will become the norm. The current technologies include cookies, profiling/personalization, and intelligent agents.

Cookies

Cookies work in conjunction with the Web browser and extend HTTP (HyperText Transfer Protocol) by allowing a Web server to pass information (a cookie) to the browser, as long as the user has not turned off the cookie capability in his or her browser or has purchased *cookie cutter* software to block cookies. Each time a user returns to a Web site, that site's Web server can search a cookie file for only the information that the user had placed there earlier and send it back to the Web server. This is what allows Web sites and advertisers to provide some level of personalized information or messages. Cookies can store user interests via a unique ID tag. Web sites correlate this unique ID with a database on the Web server. Each time the user visits their Web site, the server looks for the associated information in the database (e.g., clickstreams, transactions, survey answers). Editorial and advertising can then be served up to the user. Cookies can also allow advertisers to limit advertising based on frequency and to rotate ads based on the first, second, or third time the user visited the site or saw a particular ad. Figure 8.5 shows information from the cookie file of one of this book's authors.

There are some downsides to the use of cookies in one-to-one marketing. First, users can block out cookies by changing the configuration in later versions of popular Web browsers, including Netscape Navigator 3.0 and Internet Explorer 3.0. There is also software that allows users to block cookies. Second, users can easily delete the

Figure 8.5 Sample cookie file.

```
cookies - Notepad                                          _ □ ×
File  Edit  Search  Help
# Netscape HTTP Cookie File
# http://www.netscape.com/newsref/std/cookie_spec.html
# This is a generated file!  Do not edit.

.cnn.com          TRUE    /customnews    FALSE    946627200         CNN_CUSTOM
.musicblvd.com    TRUE    /cgi-bin/tw    FALSE    946645199         MBNV_SID
www.dummiesdaily.com  FALSE  /cgi-bin/    FALSE   901681743         dumm
www.1800flowers.com   FALSE  /flowers     FALSE   944035200         SHOP
.dummiesdaily.com     TRUE   /cgi-bin     FALSE   908124685         dumm
customnews.cnn.com    FALSE  /cnews  FALSE   946627200    PNAA      :Ktu
customnews.cnn.com    FALSE  /cnews  FALSE   946627200    PNAB      :121
customnews.cnn.com    FALSE  /cnews  FALSE   946627200    PNAC      :DXB
.netscape.com     TRUE    /       FALSE   946684799    NETSCAPE_ID  1000
.focalink.com     TRUE    /       FALSE   946641600    SB_ID    084954720100
.focalink.com     TRUE    /       FALSE   946641600    SB_IMAGE     9.1.
.hardwired.com    TRUE    /       FALSE   946684799    p_uniqid     yM6d
.adobe.com        TRUE    /       FALSE   946684799    INTERSE 207.69.165.1
.isn.com          TRUE    /       FALSE   946684799    session 21732676
.internet.net     TRUE    /       FALSE   946684799    session 21580643
.bmgt.umd.edu     TRUE    /       FALSE   946684799    BMGT    user-37kbsmn
.cyberatlas.com   TRUE    /       FALSE   946684799    IPRO_TAG     32a7
.infoseek.com     TRUE    /       FALSE   881610389    InfoseekUserId  386E
www.microsoft.com     FALSE  /       FALSE   937422000    MC1       GUID
.msn.com          TRUE    /       FALSE   937396800    MC1      GUID=38dd6eb
.disney.com       TRUE    /       FALSE   946684799    DISNEY  207.69.165.8
```

information in their cookie file. Third, proxy servers that allow many users to connect to the Internet through one gateway can block cookies or can make many users appear as one on the Web server. Finally, cookies identify computers and not people. This means that cookies will have targeting and one-to-one online advertising capabilities. For further discussion about cookies, see Chapter 9, "One-to-One with Web Site Tracking."

Profiling/Personalization

Industry analysts predict that Web site personalization will be evident in at least half of commercial Web sites by the end of 1998. Beyond Web site tracking and traffic analysis, the benefit of Web site personalization allows Web publishers to provide in-depth audience information beyond a user's clickstream. With a profile tool, site owners ask users for demographic and psychographic information that can tell more about each user. Since personalization products also have tracking components, the Web publisher can associate clickstreams with individual user profiles, or groups of people based on a single profile characteristic (e.g., gender, favorite type of movie, profession, marital status, and more).

Some of the products and/or services that incorporate user profiling or personalization include Broadvision One-to-One, FireFly, GuestTrack, LikeMinds, MicroMass, and NetPerceptions. See Chapter 4, "One-to-One Web Site Personalization," for an in-depth discussion on Web profiling and personalization techniques, products, and services. See Chapter 9, "One-to-One with Web Site Tracking," for a discussion on Web tracking and traffic analysis products and services.

Intelligent Agents and Ad Servers

Intelligent agents are software applications that make decisions based on user input and a community of users or other data. Intelligent agents make predictive responses based on prior Web activity and/or user profiles that include demographic and psychographic information. The agent sifts through information to find relevant information such as content or advertising. The information is then delivered to the user. Agent-based ad networks, online ad serving, and other software products or services that assist the process of targeting can cost a few thousand dollars to hundreds of thousands of dollars. Some of the products and services that incorporate intelligent agent technology include:

Accipiter Ad Manager (www.accipiter.com) is working with WiseWire (www.wisewire.com) to provide advertisers with user profile information.

Aptex (www.aptex.com) created SelectCast for Web sites that sell advertising to provide targeted ad delivery using an affinitiy modeling process.

Cyber Dialogue (www.cyberdialogue.com), in conjunction with its sister company Yankelovich Partners, created the Dialog Telescope to categorize individual Web site visitors into target market segments based on intelligent agent, predictive, and psychographic models.

DoubleClick DART (www.doubleclick.net) began as an advertising network and is now making its DART technology available as an ad server that enables marketers to target advertisements.

FireFly (www.firefly.net), the pioneer in using intelligent agent technology for Web sites, is now working with other companies to apply the technology to advertising. FireFly also uses collaborative filtering, which matches data from a user with data from other users that have similar likes and dislikes, and other preferences.

Infoseek Ultramatch (www.infoseek.com) is an ad network that is using the advanced neural networking technology from Aptex Software to serve up ads based on users' behavioral interaction.

Starpoint (www.startpt.com) developed its Affinity Engine to help advertisers customize ads based on clickstream, demographic, geographic, psychographic, collaborative filter, digital ID, and HTTP information.

Important One-to-One Web Advertising Concepts

Cookies are limited to watching the behavior of a computer user. Intelligent agents can make judgments based on user input and input of like people. Profiling and personalization can deliver custom information based on input given by the user on the Web site. Web server log files can give marketers general ideas about which Web pages are the most popular, peak time of day, and percentage of unique visitors who placed an order. Which technology makes the most sense? It depends on budget and objective. As we said earlier, the more targeted an ad message and placement, the more expensive the ad campaign. The more granular you want to track performance, the more expensive this endeavor will be. Not every online ad campaign needs to be defined so tightly, especially when the size of the online market is still *relatively* small. It is also important to consider the concepts discussed next when deciding on how you will develop your online ad campaign.

Behavior Versus Declaration

Is it better to know how users act or what they tell you about themselves? The answer should be that we want to know a bit of both! Online users may not be all that honest, depending on how much they have at stake relative to the offer, content, and so forth. On the other hand, behavior tracked using cookies or tracking software doesn't necessarily tell you what is in the hearts and minds of each user. Guestbooks, registrations, profiling, and surveys are techniques that will enable users to tell you about themselves.

Inferred Versus Known

Cookies and intelligent agents, such as FireFly, enable advertisers to take behavior to new heights where the preferences and actions can be determined based on something that it inferred rather than known. When products involve emotions, tastes, likes, dislikes, and lifestyle data, an inferred model may be best. Movies, food, clothing, recreation, cars, music, and other lifestyle-oriented interests are very subjective. Thus a marketer cannot draw a *black or white* conclusion on what an online user may be interested in based on what he or she has told you or how he or she has behaved in the past. This is where a strict set of logic, based on what is known, may not work as well. For example, you operate an online music store. If a particular user has purchased three country music CDs, does this mean he or she will only buy country music? Not necessarily. Most music enthusiasts' interests tend to span several music genre, even if they have a strong affinity toward one. And people change over time as they are exposed to more people and interests in their lives.

Types of Online Advertising

The world of online advertising has grown very quickly in dollars and Web sites, and new types of advertising are being created. In just a short few years we have moved from static Web banners to full-blown multimedia ads that fill up the entire browser. Users can now interact with banners and some advertisers have built comprehensive Web sites that have the sole purpose of promoting their brand or brands to the online audience.

Web Site as an Advertising Vehicle

For many companies, the primary objective for a Web site is advertising. Web sites are used to increase awareness of a company or brand in the online market. There are two types of sites: *whole Web sites* and *microsites*.

Whole Web Site

Many companies have built Web sites to build their brand image among online users. They aren't necessarily electronic commerce Web sites or corporate image sites—their main objective is to advertise their products and increase brand awareness and brand loyalty. Proctor and Gamble (www.pg.com) has built the Tide ClothesLine (www.tide.com), which is a Web site dedicated to promoting the Tide brand of clothing detergent. The Web site encourages users to "interact" with the Tide brand. The site contains very comprehensive information about laundry and fabric care with several content areas and interactivity. For example, the Tide Stain Detective is a personalized, interactive problem solver for getting stains out of clothing. The site also has contests, product information, and an online store that allows customers to purchase laundry-related merchandise (not Tide products), and it cross-promotes the company-sponsored NASCAR racing team. The site is a good balance of useful content and brand promotion, where the user receives a lot of benefits from the site rather than just a lot of advertising messages. If you have, or plan to have, a brand-building Web site, then the Tide site is a good model for credible brand promotion.

There are many brand Web sites on the Internet. Here is just a sample of sites that do a good job of customer-brand bonding:

Budweiser Beer	www.budweiser.com
Clinique Makeup	www.clinque.com
Disney Online	www.disney.com
Kellogg's Planet K	www.kelloggs.com
L'eggs Pantyhose	www.leggs.com
Levi's Jeans	www.levi.com
Nike Athletic Wear	www.nike.com
Pampers Diapers	www.pampers.com
Ragu Spaghetti Sauce	www.eat.com
Toyota Cars	www.toyota.com

A Web site has the unique ability to provide individualized marketing messages and information when the site uses cookie or HTTP header information. For targeted or one-to-one marketing on your Web site, you can deploy a user profiling mechanism such as site registration, guestbook, or using personalization technology such as BroadVision's One-to-One, GuestTrack, and other software or services. (See Chapter 4, "One-to-One Web Site Personalization," for more information on Web site personalization.)

Microsites

Microsites are Web sites that are specifically designed to build relationships between an online customer and an advertiser's brand. There are many benefits to having a microsite—many of the benefits already discussed include flexibility, interactivity, and delivery of personalized content and advertising messages. The unique value is that the Web marketer can build a relationship with the customer less clandestinely and more credibly. Here are some examples of microsites:

Toyota built a special Web site that is geared to car enthusiasts. Car Culture (www.carsandculture.com) features games, road-trip itineraries, maps, auto culture, garages of famous people, chat, bulletin boards, and, of course, advertisements for Toyota cars and trucks.

A special microsite was developed and placed on the PC Week Online Web site. Managing Customer Information Systems (www.managingcis.com) is a special-interest, online advertorial geared to information technology managers in customer support departments. The microsite has a few sponsors that are linked (see Figure 8.6).

Banners

Web banner advertisements are rectangular graphical images that carry advertising or promotional messages that link to other Web sites or pages. The most common size is about seven inches in length and about one inch in height. Many people refer to Web banners as "billboards," because they are similar to the billboard ads found along the roadside in that they can only convey limited information. The goal of the Web marketer is to provide enough advertising information to get the user to click on the ad, which takes them to a Web site or a special section within a Web site.

According to Tara Calishain, author of several Internet books and the publisher of *Skywriting: The Internet Advertising Newsletter*, "...it's impossible to call banner ads "billboards" any more. A banner ad can be a static display ad, sure, but now it can also take orders, gather demographic information, and interact with the viewers. And the more they can do, the more valuable the real estate they take up becomes." Each type of banner advertisement format is discussed next.

Figure 8.6 shows a microsite on _PC Week Online_.

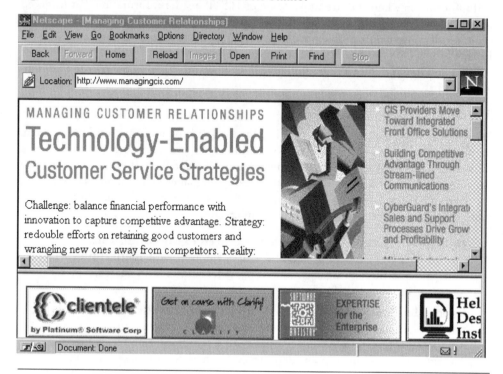

Simple Banners, or "Billboards"

Simple banners, a.k.a. billboards, were the first forms of advertising on the Web. There are a few unique benefits of Web banner advertising versus other forms of traditional advertising. You can control who sees which banner advertisement. If a banner ad is not performing, you can change it the same day! You can easily test multiple advertisements and receive rapid or even real-time performance data. The flexibility and accountability of Web banner advertising is what makes the new online medium very attractive to Web marketers.

The aim of the advertiser is to receive maximum "click-throughs," which are the number of times an online user clicks on the Web banner ad. In general, banner ads typically receive about a 2-percent click-through rate. This means that 2 percent of the time the ad was served (a.k.a. impression), it was clicked on by users. There are many techniques available to improve click-through rates on simple banners, such as adding the phrase "click here," using certain colors (brighter colors versus black and white), providing "free" offers, and introducing something "new." Figure 8.7 shows a variety of Web banner ads.

Figure 8.7 A variety of Web banner advertisements.

Buttons

Buttons and *hot corners* are an abbreviated version of Web banners. A button is usually rectangular or square and measures about one-half or one-quarter the size of a banner. The most prevalent button advertisement to date has been the "Netscape Now!" and Microsoft's Internet Explorer buttons. Although the message is extremely limited, the buttons can be designed and placed according to each target audience you want to reach.

Targeted Banners/Targeted Sites

If your advertising campaign goal involves reaching several segments of your customer or prospect base, then develop banners for each targeted site or groups of target sites. The ability to target messages enables one-to-one Web marketers to reach just a few customers with a specific marketing message. Many online advertisers have also experienced the higher click-through rates associated with target Web ads. For example, if you sell a sport utility vehicle (SUV), then you probably have several types of customers, or target markets, to which you would like to direct advertising messages. The markets for SUVs can include several groups within the commercial market and consumer market, such as:

Commercial Market for SUVs	**Consumer Market for SUVS**
Construction managers for home building	People who own boats
Construction manager for commercial buildings	Large families
Automobile parts retail store chain	Young, high-income couples interested in outdoor activities

As you can see, the list for specialized markets for SUVs can include several types. When you design and place targeted Web banner advertising, you will want to create a different message for each type of customer.

On the Web, you have some options when you want to place targeted advertising:

Search engines or online directories. If you want to reach potential buyers of SUVs on a search engine like Yahoo!, then you can purchase general keyword selections such as "sport utility," "sport utility vehicle," and "four-wheel drive." Your Web banners are served up to your audiences when they type in the same keywords. You can also try to reach your target audiences by buying keywords that meet the interests or attributes of each target market. For example, to reach the outdoor enthusiasts, you may want to buy keywords such as "camping," "skiing," and "hiking." If you want to reach people who have boats, then you could choose "boating," "boats," "waterskiing," "fishing," and so forth.

Online magazines, or E-zines. There are thousands of online editions of print magazines, or E-zines. You will be able to place advertising within these sites whose audiences meet your targeting criteria. For example, if you want to reach the young couples interested in your SUV, then you may want to place advertising, with an outdoor adventure theme on SkiNet (www.skinet.com) and Adventure Sports Online (www.adventuresports.com).

Advertising networks. Ad networks, such as DoubleClick, allow you to build a media plan that spans numerous sites that are geared to your target markets. (Advertising networks are discussed later in this chapter.) Targeting banner ads will become a mainstay of online advertising campaigns. For example, Quote.com (www.quote.com), the Internet's leading provider of financial market news and information, created the Target Audience Ad Package. Advertisers are able to display targeted advertising banners based on a stock-ticker symbol.

Links to "Side Doors" or "Back Doors"

One way to enhance response rate measurement is the use of *side doors* or *back doors*. This means that you can direct banner ads to bring users to a specific area on your site, instead of the homepage, when they click on your ad. This approach can help you increase the response and conversion rate of ads by bringing the audience directly to the information related to a particular ad. Online users want instant gratification, so having the promotional information linked directly to the ad, enhances the likelihood that these users will convert from prospects to customers. You can build promotional areas on the Web site that map to special target markets. This can help you measure ad campaign effectiveness by isolating the measurement of ad performance to sections of the site versus trying to evaluate a particular campaign's success over the entire Web site, which can be very cumbersome.

Figure 8.8 Intel's Animated Web advertising campaign.

Animated and Interactive Banners

Animated and interactive Web banner advertisements have the benefit of becoming more intrusive and attention getting. They also can increase click-through rates and allow one-to-one marketers to lengthen the attention span of the online audience long enough to begin a dialog or enhance a relationship with the prospect or customer. Since you can apply the targeting methods we mentioned previously (and mention again later in the chapter), here is just a simple overview of each type of animated or interactive banner:

Animation. According to a study by ZD Net (www.zdnet.com), animation improved click-through rates 15–40 percent over static Web banners. There is a trade off between bandwidth constraints and the ability to tell more of your story. Also, animation is not a replacement for good creative content and call-to-action—both are still required. Figure 8.8 shows how Intel (www.intel.com) uses animation in a recent advertising campain for the Pentium II microprocessor.

Pull-down. This is a simple, relatively low-bandwidth, interactive banner. It begs users to select something in the list that is "targeted" to their wants or needs. Figure 8.9 shows the Beatrice (www.bguide.com) Web ad that allows users to select specific topics from a pulldown menu.

Games. Hewlett-Packard engaged users in a game of pong with a Web banner ad. At the time, it was one of the first uses of interaction in a banner. Other

Figure 8.9 Pulldown menu in Beatrice Web ad.

engaging games within banners could include word puzzles, tic-tac-toe, Pac Man, manipulating a game character or logo, and others. Figure 8.10 shows an interactive game ad promoting Narrative's Enliven advertising product.

Tickers. News tickers have been adapted to include marketing messages. They are eye-catching and since they are text, you can easily target messages to viewers. To enhance interactivity, these tickers also can be clicked on and users are hyperlinked to associated Web sites or pages. Figure 8.11 shows BD Interactive's (www.bdinteractive.com) Java-based TickerLINX technology on the Internet Advertising Bureau's (www.iab.net) Web site.

Audio/video. The use of audio and video is increasing as connection speeds are improving. The use of audio and/or video enables Web marketers to enhance the effectiveness of banners since the ads become like radio and TV. They are more eye-catching, engaging, and can involve more of the user's senses. Figure 8.12 shows use of video in a Web banner using InterVU's (www.intervu.net) V-Banner technology.

Here are some companies working on taking Web banners to the next level:

Digital Pulp (www.digitalpulp.com) created the Nano-Site service, which allows Web marketers to create anything from interactive and one-to-one advertising banners up to fully functioning Web sites. Advertisers can create multimedia ads and sites and track user interaction, including demographic and psychographic information.

Narrative Communications Corporation (www.narrative.com) has developed the Enliven software to offer advertisers animation, audio, support for multiple URL targets within a single ad, and logging and reporting.

Zapa Digital (www.zapadigital.com) created the MicroSite product suite to allow advertisers to create banners with sight, sound, and animation. There

Figure 8.10 Enliven "catch the eyeballs" campaign.

Figure 8.11 BD Interactive's TickerLINX Java-based advertising ticker showcased on Internet Advertising Bureau Web site.

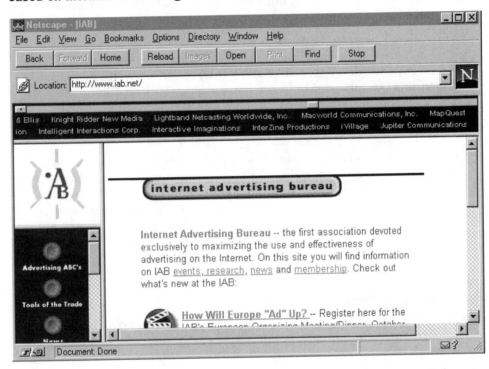

is also a logging server to track user interaction with the banner, not just whether they responded, but how they responded.

Direct-Response Banners

With the inherent ability of the Web to allow users to respond immediately to advertisements with a simple click of a mouse, direct-response banners will become a more prevalent advertising choice among Web marketers. Direct-response banners flip the banner model upside down, where the ads and offers are brought to the user instead

Figure 8.12 interVU's V-Banner technology used in banner ad.

of having the user go to the ads by hyperlinking to another Web site or page. Target and one-to-one Web ad methods can be applied to these types of banners as well. Plus, many Web marketers conveniently bring the transactions to the user. Here are a couple of examples:

- There was a banner for Casio's Remote Control Watch that allowed users to place an order for the watch from the actual banner. The banner used a VirtualTAG, which is a Java-based animated interactive advertising banner. The VirtualTAG allows advertisers to promote, provide information, and accept orders using First Virtual's VirtualPIN, which is the First Virtual Internet Payment System. Visit www.vtag.com/ main.html for more information.

- K2 Design, an advertising agency, developed a Java-based "interactive Direct Response" (iDR) application that produces a banner called a "Vampire." With just one click on a Vampire banner, a user interacts with self-contained forms or other interactive options that have been embedded into the banner. Users immediately have the option to quickly reply to an offer without having to click through and wait for a Web page to load. Vampire banners also allow surfers to navigate inside the banner environment. Visit www.k2design.com/vampire.html for more information.

Banner Advertising Resources

Here are a few places to visit on line that will be helpful in your Web banner advertising pursuits. There are additional online advertising resources listed near the end of this chapter.

Mark Welch's Banner Ad Directory	www.markwelch.com
Internet Advertising Bureau	www.iab.net
CASIE	www.commercepark.com/AAAA/

Next-Generation Web Advertising Types

It didn't take long for marketers to yearn for more than static Web banner ads. First, advertisers stretched the Web banner to its interactive limit. Now, online ads are taking many shapes, sizes, and behaviors. The benefit of all of this technological and creative advancement is the ability for the Web marketer to establish dialog with the user or customer. The next generation of ads are going out and grabbing eyeballs, encouraging clicks, provoking thought, and eliciting response—at a very low production cost and instantly modifiable. The new ad models are more intrusive (in a good way!), engaging (more time spent with ad, higher click-throughs), transactional (money, ongoing relationships), and one-to-one marketing (the right eyeballs see the right ad). Let's take a look at these promising new ad formats.

Figure 8.13 Sample popup ad.

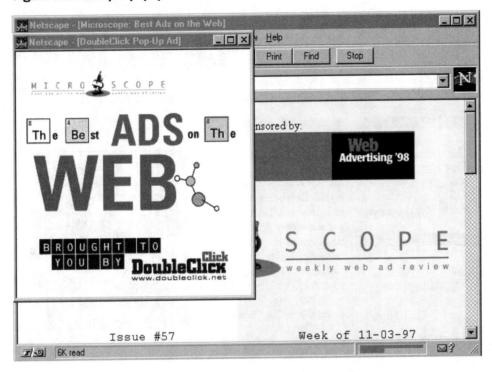

Popup Windows

Popup windows are online advertisements that are launched when a user goes to or interacts with a Web site. The popups are separate, self-contained windows that are smaller than the browser. In general, these ads are more attention getting and increase click-through rates; plus, they don't wisk users away from the original Web site, which is very user friendly. Figure 8.13 shows an example of a popup window advertisement.

Advertorials and Info-ads

Advertorials and informational ads are not new ad vehicles in the real world, but are emerging in the Web world. These ad formats blend advertising messages with editorial content. This allows advertisers to tell more of the story, which enables higher qualification rates. In other words, the viewer has more information to make a decision of whether to further pursue the offer. This gives advertisers higher quality and serious sales inquiries rather than what we marketers know as "tire kickers." Many Web marketing gurus already advocate not using vague messages, so the advertorial and info-

Figure 8.14 Golf.com advertorial.

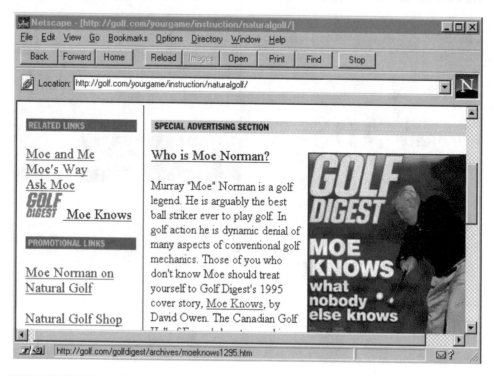

ad are ways to take this philosophy to the farthest extent. Figure 8.14 shows a sample advertorial.

Roadblocks

High impact and high click-throughs are the attraction of roadblock Web advertisements. Roadblocks require the user to pass through the full screen to get to the Web site. This is an intrusive ad type that will only work if the advertising is compelling and useful to the viewer; otherwise, savvy Web users will be frustrated when they are required look at the advertisement before they get to the content. This type of ad has been used on the Riddler.com game site. Figure 8.15 shows a sample interstitial advertisement on Riddler.com (www.riddler.com).

Interstitials/Intermercials

Hailed as the next best thing to come across Web browsers, interstitials (a.k.a. intermercials) are animated banner and full-screen online ads. Interstitials look much like television advertisements. If you have experienced PointCast (www.pointcast.com),

Figure 8.15 Roadblock ad on Riddler.com.

then you have seen intermercial advertisements. Jupiter Communications estimates that by 1999, 5- to 10-second animated interstitials will be commonplace. Berkeley Systems (www.berksys.com), an entertainment software company, reported impressive results on an ad campaign it conducted on its BeZerk Web site. They found that interstitials were twice as effective as traditional Web banner ads.

Sponsorships

Sponsorships allow users to *bond* with brands. Instead of outright, in-your-face promotional messages, you can add credibility to your advertising by being associated with a respected company or Web site. Sponsorships typically have a higher impact when coupled with useful content and interactivity. In 1997 Delta Air Lines sponsored a special business travel section on *The New York Times* Online Edition (www.nytimes.com). This type of promotion enabled Delta Air Lines to build relationships with prospects and customers because it was a mini Web site within the travel section on the newspaper's online edition. Users could spend time reading helpful travel information and the site provided convenient links to the Delta Air Lines site. Web marketers could monitor the

Figure 8.16 Jupiter Communications rates the targeting capabilities of various online ad models.

Ad Model	Ratings
Banners	● ● ●
Sponsorships	● ●
Advertorial	● ●
Product Placement	● ●
Interstitials	● ● +

● = LOW VALUE; ● ● ●= HIGH VALUE

performance of referring links to see if the sponsorship was successful. Web marketers could also provide special offers where they capture user profile information in order to facilitate future promotions based on user demographics.

Ad Types That Are Best for Target and One-to-One Advertising

In a 1997 Jupiter Communications' (www.jup.com) study titled "Banners and Beyond: Ad Strategies for Branding, Driving Traffic and Sales," it stated that the Web has the potential for highly accurate tracking and online advertising, making one-to-one marketing a reality in terms of technology and cost. Figure 8.16 is Jupiter's online ad model ratings in terms of targeting.

Web banners are still the best way to target sites or ad networks that have targeting at the heart of their technology and marketing missions. Many publishers and ad network companies can target banners based on browser type, domain, ISP, computer platform, geographical location, SIC code, and time of day. Many are enhancing the targeting capabilities with demographic and lifestyle information. One-to-one Web marketers will want to seek online advertising opportunities where the Web publisher has collected accurate user or profile information. Guestbook registration, billing information from subscription-based sites, cookies, and intelligent-agent technology are some of the sources for user information. The best information is from the users themselves, as long as they don't give false information.

Places to Advertise On Line

Mary Meeker, a managing director at Morgan Stanley, authored *The Internet Advertising Report*. In this report she classified Web sites as aggregated, content provider, commerce, and hybrid. Each type of site has a different revenue model and therefore advertising model. Here is a discussion of each classification:

Aggregated. The best-known aggregated Web sites are search engines such as AltaVista, Excite, InfoSeek, WebCrawler, and Yahoo! Their main reason for existence is advertising and, while not unexpected, they are at the top of the charts in terms of ad revenue. Typically search engines are better for mass marketing or branding. One-to-one Web marketers can target Web banner ads by keyword, but search engines are advancing in terms of how they can target. For example, InfoSeek created Ultramatch that allows advertisers to display banner ads to the people who will most likely respond. Other examples of aggregated Web sites include push channels such as PointCast, supersites such as @griculture (www.agriculture.com), and virtual tradeshows such as ChemExpo (www.chemexpo.com).

Content Provider. Online publishers and traditional publishers with online editions are examples of content providers. These types of sites will provide the best targeting capabilities in the future. There are no-fee content providers such as C|Net (www.cnet.com), HomeArts (www.homearts.com), Bonus.com (www.bonus.com), and Internet.com (www.internet.com), and fee-based provides such as *The Wall Street Journal* Interactive (www.wsj.com). The fee-based online publishers will be able to get very detailed and accurate user profile information because users will not only be required to give name, address, and telephone number, they will give additional information—all of which can be verified using billing data. No-fee publishers that have highly valued content can also get users to register on the site. The registration process is where online publishers can obtain demographic and geographic data.

Commerce Sites. Commerce sites are important to your online marketing program if your goal is to support the sales of your product on these sites. Like content providers, commerce sites can target messages based on product categories and search keywords. The advantage a commerce site has in targeting is in the transaction history and billing information. This information is highly accurate and can be used to provide cross-selling advertising. Commerce sites include Quote.com (www.quote.com), Insight Direct (www.insight.com), and CDNow (www.cdnow.com).

Hybrid. The Quicken Financial Network (www.qfn.com) is a support site for its financial software products Quicken and TurboTax and services such as online banking, but it is also a financial information supersite. These sites have the combined targeting capabilities of content providers and commerce capabilities.

Advertising Networks

There are over 1000 Web sites that sell advertising—the sites are very disparate and most have relatively small audiences to provide to advertisers. For example, ad networks are good if you are trying to reach as many prospects as possible within a narrow target (i.e., women who are between the ages of 18 and 34, have incomes in excess of $80,000, are married, and have kids). You will want to enlist an advertising network to aggregate all sites that offer this kind of targeting in order to have a large enough audience. This enables the one-to-one marketer to only reach the target markets that will be interested in your advertising message, with minimal ad-impression waste. This is where advertising networks are attractive. Add to this the ability for ad networks to track and report results and you have a highly effective online advertising tool.

If your primary marketing objective is to build brand awareness, ad networks enable you to provide separate targeted messages to each segment you want to reach. This allows you to cost-effectively increase brand penetration within segments. Here is a small sample of advertising networks:

General

Burst!	www.burstmedia.com
Commonwealth Network	commonwealth.riddler.com
DoubleClick	www.doubleclick.net
Petry Network	www.petrynetwork.com

Barter

LinkExchange	www.linkechange.com
LinkMedia Network	www.linkmedia.com

Auction

Adbot	www.adbot.com
Flycast Communications	www.flycast.com

Specialized

BannerWomen (sites with at least 80% women users)	www.bannerwomen.com
Digital Music Network (Popular music and entertainment sites)	www.dmnmedia.com

DoubleClick (www.doubleclick.net) is one of the leading ad networks with a unique user database in excess of 28 million. It represent more than 70 highly branded Web sites, including Dilbert (www.dilbert.com), BillBoard Online (www.billboard.com), and *U.S. News and World Report* (www.usnews.com). According to DoubleClick's Wenda Harris Millard, online advertising can provide highly qualified leads at an impressive

ROI, which is the most important yardstick to advertisers. Ms. Millard also believes that Web advertising answers all the criteria that is of concern to advertisers that traditional media cannot do as effectively:

How can I reach my target?

What is the optimum reach and frequency equation?

Which creative works best?

Is the advertising effective?

The Web does a unique thing that traditional advertising cannot. Because of its technology, you can cap the frequency of a particular Web advertisement or banner, which minimizes *banner burnout* and waste. An I/Pro study showed that by about the third or fourth time a banner ad was displayed to a user, its effectiveness diminished. Imagine that you are reading a magazine and you have seen the same BMW ad for the fourth time. Now, what if someone came up and turned the page so you wouldn't see that particular ad? The Web can do this with its tracking and database integration capabilities. An online ad system can know if you have seen a particular banner one time, two times, three times…Oh, the possibilities.

Heineken (www.heineken.ni/index.html), the Dutch beer company, enlisted the DoubleClick ad network for a Valentine's Day promotion. Heineken wanted to generate traffic and build a brand that was "hip and sophisticated." They used a special Valentine's Day E-Card to generate Web site traffic. They used an animated banner and wanted to target the ads to an adult audience. In order to reach the adult target, but not the underage drinkers. DoubleClick's DART (Dynamic Advertising Reporting and Targeting) technology allowed Heineken to exclude all users from the educational (.edu) Web domains. Heineken saw a 50 percent increase in entries to a game that appeared on the E-Card entry form, and they achieved a click-through rate of 8.77 percent.

DoubleClick's DART is a patent-pending system that dynamically delivers targeted banners. It allows advertisers to target by

Affinity

Geographic location

High-level internet domain type

Organization type (SIC code)

Organization name

Organization size or revenue

Control ad frequency and ad banner series

Service provider

User's operating system

Browser type

Days and hours to display an ad banner

Ad banner distribution

The DART system also has a feature called "Darwin" that naturally selects which ad to display in order to produce the highest response. Even with the higher cost for highly targeted advertising, one-to-one Web marketers will gain the advantage of putting the right message in front of the right person, and reduce wasteful ad impressions.

Alternative Web Advertising Forms

Jupiter Communications' "Banners and Beyond: Ad Strategies for Branding, Driving Traffic and Sales" report stated, "The best targeting opportunities are currently not on the traditional publisher sites but on alternative ad platforms." Figure 8.17 shows how each alternative advertising model rates in terms of targeting, branding, driving traffic, driving sales, and reaching low-bandwidth consumers.

Chat/Community

Chat and community sites are natural relationship- and loyalty-building vehicles. Although a *Business Week*/Lou Harris poll showed that only 26 percent of the respondents interact with other people via chat, chat users spend more time on line while they are on a chat site or online community. There are more than 1000 sites that have chat. Some high-traffic online communities with chat include iVillage (www.ivillage.com), Women's Wire (www.womenswire.com), and Yahoo!. Since many chat sites and online communities serve a target market of their own, this enhances a Web marketer's ability to find a highly targeted audience. With most chat sites requiring registration, this information can be used to target ads by demographics, psychographics, and even by discussion topic. Figure 8.18 shows an ad that is targeted to the participants of ParentSoup's many chat sessions.

Figure 8.17 Jupiter Communications' rates alternative ad models.

Platform	Targeting	Branding	Driving Traffic	Driving Sales	Reaching Low-bandwidth Consumers
Chat	● ● ●	● ● ●	●	●	● ●
E-mail	● ● ●	● ●	●	● ●	● ● ●
Push Technology	● ● ●	● ● ●	● ● ●	● ● ●	● ●
ISPs	● ● ●	● ● +	● ● +	● ● +	● ● ●

● = LOW VALUE; ● ● ● = HIGH VALUE

Figure 8.18 Targeted advertising on ParentSoup's chat schedule page.

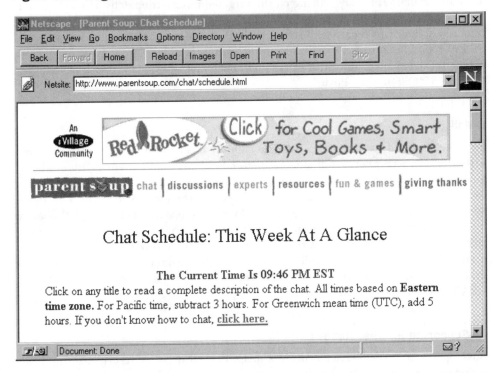

For a detailed discussion about online communities, see Chapter 6, "One-to-One Web Community."

Push

Push advertising can be many-to-one and one-to-one in nature. PointCast is a pioneer in aggregating and pushing content and advertisements to users. Since PointCast is advertiser supported, it is free to users. Because users select and personalize the information they want to receive, advertisers can target advertising based on these selections. Push (a.k.a. Webcasting, channel) is already targeted in that a certain segment of the online population chose to sign up for the service. PointCast can also target based on local and regional markets and special interests.

In April 1997 Taylor Made Golf used two channels on PointCast to promote a new golf club. Taylor Made chose to advertise on the Sports and Weather channels. Since the ads within PointCast can link to Web sites, Taylor Made received 1500 to 2000 consumers daily to its Web site from the PointCast ads.

Many online publishers and companies are adding push channels, which starts to open up the market for advertising on the targeted information delivery mechanisms. For example, TechWeb (www.techweb.com) offers users of its online computing resource a choice to receive information via PointCast, inCommon, Downtown, and BackWeb push channels, as well as by e-mail in text and HTML formats. For a more detailed discussion on how push works and how to set up your own push channel see Chapter 5, "One-to-One Push."

E-Mail

E-mail is emerging as an inexpensive, yet highly targeted advertising vehicle. Even with the controversy surrounding unsolicited e-mail ads (a.k.a. spam), e-mail is being quickly adopted as a main ingredient in online ad campaigns. E-mail reaches more users than the Web, is intrusive, and doesn't require the user to go to the Web to see advertising. E-mail technology is advancing with the support of HTML tags that allow for multimedia e-mails and the integration with database technology. When people sign up for e-mail they fill out a registration form that captures some personal information. There are also free e-mail services such as Juno.com (www.juno.com) that give users free e-mail if they view advertising. For more information on e-mail marketing, see Chapter 3, "One-to-One E-Mail."

Ad-Supported Internet Access

Ad-supported Internet service providers such as FreeRide (www.freeride.com) provide Internet access for free or at a discount in exchange for delivering ads to their users. Users of FreeRide collect points when they visit sponsoring Web sites, fill out online surveys, and other activities. The points can be redeemed for products such as magazine subscriptions, Internet access, games, CDs, and more. Free Internet access gives advertisers the ability to target much like they would for e-mail advertisements.

The Role of Ad Management Software

Advertising management software products have the power to revolutionize Web advertising campaigns. They target, they track, and they even slice and dice...information, that is. The reporting capabilities of ad management software systems make it possible for Web marketers to know which ad Web site, or Web page worked well or didn't work so well. They can tell you if the ad worked better in the morning or at 2:00 P.M. They can juggle multiple ad banners to ensure that the appropriate ad was delivered to the correct eyeballs. These products will become standard among most, if not all, Web sites that sell online advertising; and they will be an essential element in one-to-one Web advertising.

Advertising managers typically can target ads based on the users' computer platform, browser, date, time, hostname, geographic location, and the Web site that the user just came from (a.k.a. referrer). The ad management systems are now incorporating additional targeting data. For example, NetGravity's AdServer 3.0 can target ads based upon standard user demographic data, including zip code, age, gender, or any other data gathered by the site. AdServer has the ability to integrate a Web site's user profile information and incorporate this data in their reports. AdServer can also limit the frequency of an ad to a particular user based on the number of times the advertiser wants the ad to be shown. The AdServer can also deliver ads based on associated editorial content. For example, if the feature story is about automobiles, then only auto and related ads will be shown. The software can also prevent the display of competing ads on the same page! Advertising agencies, ad networks, and ad management software products all provide advertising performance data and analysis. For information on Web tracking and analysis and related products, see Chapter 9, "One-to-One with Web Site Tracking." Figure 8.19 shows the management capabilities of Accipiter AdManager.

Figure 8.19 Accipiter AdManager provides an administration and user-tracking interface.

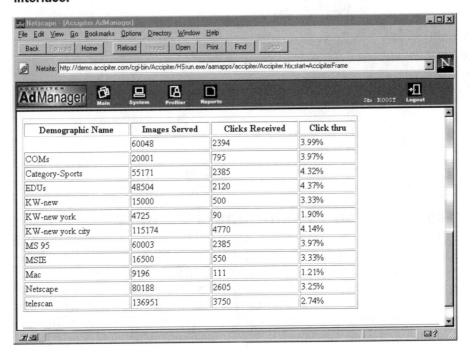

AdServer and Management Products/Services

Each advertising server and management product has its own bells and whistles, but most provide targeting and reporting capabilities. Table 8.1 lists a variety of ad serving and management software products.

Table 8.1 Ad Management Products and Services

Company	Products	URL
Accipiter	Admanager	www.accipiter.com
Bellcore	Adapt/X Advertiser	www.bellcore.com
Clickable	AdClick Pro	www.clickables.com
DigitalNation	Adjuggler	www.adjuggler.com
DoubleClick	DART	www.doubleclick.net
Focalink	SmartBanner	www.focalink.com
Intelligent Interactions	Adfinity	www.adfinity.com
NetCreations	Ad Magic	www.netcreations.com/admagic/
NetGravity	AdServer	www.netgravity.com
Networking Wizards	On Target	www.networkingwizards.com
RealMedia	Ad Stream	www.realmedia.com
Victory	Information Management Ad Master	www.ad-network.com/ad-master/
W3.com	AdOptimizer	www.w3.com

One-to-One Web Promotions/Publicity

Online promotions are great advertising and publicity interactive events, and they can be done in a targeted or one-to-one manner. Like what was discussed for advertising earlier in the chapter, promotions can be done in a targeted fashion and can be even more powerful in that the user interacts with the promotion and is identified in the process. The benefit of promotions is that the Web marketer can acquire user profile information from online users that participate in the promotion. This information can be used in additional ongoing communications beyond the promotional event itself.

Keep in mind that online promotions can only kick-start the one-to-one Web marketing process. Promotions are often like a light switch in that while promotions are running, you have a lot of activity (light is on), and as soon as they are over, activity plummets (light is off). In your promotional plans, you should already have the *after-marketing* plan well thought out and ready to execute at the close of the promotion. Keep in mind these attributes shared by great promotions according to the author of *Publicity On The Internet* (1997, John Wiley & Sons) and publicity expert Steve O'Keefe:

Integrity. A promotion grows out of the product being promoted.

Appeal. The promotion is irresistible to the target market.

Scope. The scale is perfectly suited to the product and the audience.

Timing. The right gimmick at just the right time.

Novelty. The concept has a unique twist to it.

Preparation. You must be ready to capture the lightning.

Web marketers can use targeted promotions on a Web site, across the Internet, and within special online promotion services.

On Your Web Site

When you launch, relaunch, or want to increase traffic among particular target markets, you can use an online promotion to drive the desired traffic. Within your site you can craft contests, loyalty programs, and offers for free information or classes that will kick-start your Web site marketing. No doubt Web site promotions increase your site's traffic, but can you keep them coming back for the duration? As with other advertising types, promotions can be advertised and promoted in a targeted manner.

Contests

Contests are one of the most popular forms of Web site promotions. Contests provide marketers with the ability to increase site traffic and obtain user profile information. Both the contest and site should provide the online users with enough excitement and content to make it a memorable experience. Here are some examples of Web site contests:

    iQVC Goldrush. In August 1997, the TV shopping network QVC launched a special contest on its Web site. iQVC (www.qvc.com) sponsored an online treasure hunt within its 100,000-plus Web pages. Users, or "gold diggers," who found five hidden gold cybernuggets were entered into the drawing for a gold necklace and bracelet set. The online contest was held in conjunction with the company's television program and celebrated the 101st anniversary of the 1896 discovery of gold in the Klondike region of Alaska. The purpose of the contest was to drive traffic to the Web site and promote a large gold sale.

The Palace Avatar Costume Ball. The Palace (www.thepalace.com), a popular online community and software company, relaunched its new Web site with an online costume ball featuring avatars, which are graphical representations of online personaes. The Bring Your Own Avatar (BYOA) inaugurated the launch of a new Web site for The Palace. Cash prizes and free memberships were awarded to the most creative avatar costume.

The Weather Channel. The companion Web site for the Weather Channel (www.weather.com) conducted an online contest, "Click, Click and Away," to allow visitors to win a chance for a grand prize of a vacation a year for 20 years. Each contestant who entered the contest received an electronic version of a scratch-off game card. Using a mouse, online contestants used their computer's mouse to virtually scratch off the online gamecard to reveal a potential prize.

Loyalty Programs

Web marketers can build loyalty among their customers with quality products and quality service. You can add special reward programs that facilitate loyalty among the best customers. This idea was best practiced by the airline industry with its frequent flyer programs. This method takes into account the basic marketing assumption of "all customers are not created equal." When a customer invests time and effort into a loyalty program, they provide Web marketers with a lot of information. Your Web site can conduct affinity programs where users receive electronic content, or traditional rewards such as discounts, affinity merchandise (e.g., watches, T-shirts, and other items with the company or product logo to be earned or even paid for by the customer), and free products and services using a frequency program. These types of programs help you identify and nurture who will be your most loyal and/or profitable customers. The programs can help you delineate segments within your entire customer base and even pare the program down to the individual user.

Free or Low-Cost Information or Classes

Free information can keep customers coming back as long as it is useful to the target audience. For example, Reel.com (www.reel.com), an online video store, offers low-cost ($9.95 to $14.95) film classes to online users featuring well-known film industry insiders. Cinema U. offers classes such as film theory. The folks at Arial Software (www.arialsoftware.com) give away a multistep e-mail marketing class that comes directly to the recipient's e-mail box. It contains very useful information about how to conduct a successful e-mail marketing campaign.

The online registration process for free or low-cost classes or information allows Web marketers to get more personal information from users than they could with guestbook or site registration because these types of promotions provide a level of value in exchange. The online user will happily provide information for something of value in return, especially if you inform them of what you will be doing with the submitted information. C|Net offers their free *Digital Dispatch* weekly electronic newsletter and they have over 850,000 subscribers. The e-mail newsletter model gives the Web site owner the ability to gauge success since users sign up to receive the newsletter and, more importantly, users can take themselves off the list just as easily if they do not find the information of value. When signing up for the Digital Dispatch, C|Net has several registration questions that capture user profile information. For an additional discussion on e-mail marketing, see Chapter 3 "One-to-One E-Mail."

Across the Internet

Internet-wide promotions can provide a lot of excitement among users as well as the opportunity for a company to build a database of prospects and learn more about their target markets. An Internet promotion can be sponsored by several companies in order to make a bigger impact and facilitate cobranding.

Contests

There are many types of contests you can use to promote your Web site, products, or company. Contests are great ways to build marketing lists and prospect databases because users must provide some information in order to participate. Three contest types include

Events/activities. The Software Publishers Association (SPA) (www.spa.org) hosts CyberSurfari, a yearly online contest for students. According to the SPA, the contest's mission in "CyberSurfari '97 is a World Wide Web treasure hunt designed to help individuals, families, and school teams learn about and enjoy the Web. The CyberSurfari challenge is to submit as many treasure codes as possible during the contest by finding specific pieces of information on fascinating Web site 'outposts' around the world."

Games. Games can consist of single player or multiplayer games, quizzes, treasure hunts, trivia, surveys, and so forth. ESPN SportsZone Fantasy Hockey is a contest in which a fan buys a ficticious hockey team for $19.95 (or $29.95 for non-SportZone subscribers) and drafts pro hockey players. The team owner wins points based on accumulated player statistics from timely reports.

Frequency programs. WebFlyer.com (www.webflyer.com), a site that refers to itself as the ultimate source for frequent flier programs, ran a 30-day promotion called "ClickMiles," where users could earn frequent flyer miles on airlines such as American Airline's AAdvantage and Delta Airline's SkyMiles programs by surfing the Internet.

Check out the following directory on Yahoo! for a list of contests: www.yahoo.com/Entertainment/Contests__Surveys__Polls/Indices/ to see a current collection of online contests.

Online Promotion Networks and Services

Much like the free Internet service and e-mail services, there are online promotion networks and services that reward users when they take part in online advertising and promotion. This online promotion category looks more like targeted direct-response marketing than targeted advertising. They interactively involve the online user into building a relationship between user and advertiser. Some Internet marketers have questioned the value of the user involved in these types of promotional services. However, Web marketers could think of the participants as a target market, enlist these companies in building these campaigns for their own sites, or at least learn from them. Plus, these promotion companies use a pay-for-performance model that can be quite attractive to online advertisers who must measure response and transactions versus general awareness. CyberGold and FreeRide are two such free services that reward users who view advertising. Yoyodyne is a promotional company that works together with advertisers to build online promotions on your Web site, or you can participate in their special online game promotions that will drive traffic to your site.

CyberGold. CyberGold (www.cybergold.com) is a direct-marketing company and the creator of CyberCoin, an Internet payment currency. The company's CyberGold program pays users cash rewards starting at 50 cents for reading ads and answering questions. The rewards are transferred to the user's bank account or donated to a nonprofit organization. The company conducted a test on Time Warner's Pathfinder Network where incentive-based advertising produced up to 13 times more click-through responses over traditional banner ads. CyberGold is enabling its technology to match ads and other online information to users based on information like personal interests and demographics. In their words, "Eventually we envision a whole marketplace for attention in which every ad is a wanted ad."

FreeRide. FreeRide (www.freeride.com) is a brand-loyalty marketing program that rewards users with free Internet service and other services or products. Users who participate in surveys and view ads receive points that can be redeemed. Some of the sponsors/brands who have participated in the FreeRide service include Duracell Batteries, Quaker Oatmeal, Oreo Cookies, Kodak Fun Saver Camera, Advil, and over 100 Internet service providers.

Yoyodyne. Yoyodyne (www.yoyodyne.com), a company that calls itself the premier relationship-marketing company on the Internet, provides promotional services that are based on push technology, licensing (e.g., Dilbert's online trivia game), sweepstakes, and customer games they can implement for your Web site, in a one-to-one manner. In the process of participating in the games and other promotions, users provide demographic and psychographic information.

The Future of One-to-One Web Advertising and Promotion

The buzzwords for online advertising and promotion into the near future include *interactive*, *intrusive*, *one-to-one*, *intelligent agents*, *neural nets*, and *local market targeting*.

Many advertising pundits are making predictions that the Web will be able to provide more intrusive advertising like the television. Video and audio are already making their way onto Web banner ads. InterVU (www.intervue.net) has created the V-Banner to incorporate 15-, 30-, and 60-second ad spots. Early results have shown these banners to increase click-throughs considerably.

Other advertising gurus are predicting that online advertising will be able make every ad delivered to be an ad that online users want, because it is targeted to their likes, dislikes, what neighborhood they live in, what car they drive, what college they went to, and so on. Jupiter Communications sees that online ad budgets will incorporate more local advertising, moving from 100 percent of ad budgets going to a national audience in 1995 to 54 percent of online ad budgets going to local marketing advertising in 2002.

Another key trend in online advertising is Web audience measurement and auditing. Organizations such as the Audit Bureau of Circulations (ABC) (www.accessabc.com) perform audits on Web sites that sell advertising. ABC already verifies the circulation data for advertisers and has begun to incorporate audience demographics information in its reports.

We will close with this discussion about the future of online advertising with this profound thought:

> "...one thing is certain: In the 1:1 future, the consumer will be the one in the driver's seat, and the advertiser will be thumbing a ride." Don Peppers and Martha Rogers, Ph.D., "Advertising in the One-to-One Future" (InfoWorld, 2/12/96).

 Go to the companion Web site for the case study, "Don't Forget the Offer," taken from a "Who's Marketing Online" article by Charles Sayers.

Chapter 9, "One-to-One with Web Site Tracking," provides you with an in-depth understanding of tracking and analyzing your online audience. The chapter covers tracking technology and products. It also discusses ways to begin to get to know your audience better by using onsite registration. The chapter helps you to understand how tracking data can give you insight into what is of interest to your online customers. Tracking and traffic analysis are important activities for all Web marketers, but only part of the one-to-one Web marketing equation.

ONE-TO-ONE WITH WEB SITE TRACKING

Much of this book deals with how to understand the information-gathering process your prospects go through as they learn about your products and services. But there is more to one-to-one marketing than providing the right information in the right place at the right time. You need to be both a good marketer and a good listener, so it's important to know how to observe what your prospects and customers are doing on your Web site, how to ask for information about them, and what to do with that information once you have it.

This chapter covers two techniques you can use to gather this information. First, we cover the "behind the scenes" look at analyzing the log files created by your Web server. Next, we take a close look at the very "public" registration process of gathering data from people who visit your Web site. We also discuss how to capture and track sales leads and information inquiries.

Before we start observing our Web site visitors, however, we need to know what we want to learn from our observations. As we've talked about in other chapters, prospective customers who come to your Web site are looking for something. Perhaps they are looking for a product to meet an unfilled need. Perhaps they are looking for information to satisfy some curiosity. Perhaps they have arrived at your site accidentally while searching for something else.

Most of the people coming to your Web site will be somewhere along the traditional path of making a purchase decision, so it's important for you to be able to identify which stage in this process people are in so you can satisfy their individual needs.

As we move from mass marketing to one-to-one marketing, we need to look for ways to apply what we know about "clusters" of people—what we sometimes call "market segments" or "niche markets"—and learn how to adjust our marketing to meet the needs of individuals. Only by concentrating on individuals can we truly take advantage of the potential that the Web has to offer.

Marketing research over the years has identified several distinct steps in the purchase of products that require evaluation:

1. Recognition of need
2. Search for information about alternatives
3. Evaluation of alternatives
4. Purchase
5. Evaluation of purchase

By using the traffic data we can collect on a Web site, we can spot clusters of behavior that are related to the purchasing process. This means we can adjust the marketing communications process to meet those information needs, and hopefully meet the product needs of the prospect, too.

Traffic Analysis

As pages on your Web site are being seen by thousands or perhaps millions of people, you will naturally become curious about who is seeing your Web site content. In fact, more than curiosity should be driving your interest in learning about your Web visitors because a great deal can be learned about the viewing patterns and habits of your audience, such as why they came to your site, how they got there, and what information they are looking for.

"There is a wealth of information in the log files that many Webmasters don't make use of," said Rick Stout, author of *Web Site Stats* (1997, Osborne McGraw-Hill). "As the traffic at a Web site increases, there is greater interest in finding out what Web visitors are doing on the site—and that's when they turn to Web traffic analysis programs." The constantly changing needs for traffic analysis are reflected in the popularity of Stout's Web site that is dedicated to this topic (www.webstats.com).

As we move from wanting to use a Web site to broadcast to the masses to using it to focus on individuals, we need to know more about the members of the audience so we can apply the principles of one-to-one Web marketing. It's an overwhelming task to think about the needs of each of the thousands of people coming to your site, but it is possible to think *about the individuals* coming to your Web site. Part of being able to think with a one-to-one marketing mind set requires that you have the tools to analyze data, but another part is the process of how we think about the people behind the data.

While it would be great to be able to correlate Web traffic to demographic or psychographic information on individuals, there are very few tools available to help us do that (see Chapter 4, "One-to-One Web Site Personalization," for information about building user profiles and the ability to track users based on their profiles). Before we explain how to glean this level of information from the Web server, let's take a look at traditional Web traffic analysis tools and techniques and then cover some advanced technologies and techniques.

Most Web marketers start by asking the question "How many people saw my pages?" and then progress to more in-depth questions. Many of these questions can be answered by tabulating the data found in the log files that are constantly being updated by your Web server software.

This chapter answers many of the questions asked by Web marketers:

What type of data is stored in the log files?

How can it be tabulated?

Can I make graphs of the data?

What can I learn from the Web log analysis?

What products are available to create log analysis reports?

Will the log tell me exactly who is coming to my Web site?

Can I get a profile of the individuals coming to my Web site?

As you can see, there are many questions that can be answered about Web site activity from the log files that can help you tailor your Web content to the individuals in your target audience, so let's dive right in and review just what's available and how to use it.

Technology Overview

In order to gain the most benefit from your Web server log files, it's important to know what files are available and what data they collect. Then, as we get into specific Web analysis tools and techniques, you'll know exactly how the different products do their analysis, and why there are limitations on what can be garnered from the logs.

Definitions

In order for the answer to make sense, we need to define the terms used in dealing with:

Hit. A "hit" is generally thought of as accessing any file on your Web site, including the HTML files, graphics files, and any other material you provide. For example, if your homepage has nine different graphic images, then viewing your homepage results in 10 "hits" to your site. Because of the potential misuse of this measurement, many Web managers prefer to measure other activities.

Page view. A "page view" is just what it says: The viewing of a single Web page. This is generally the number of HTML pages that have been served and it excludes the number of graphic images served.

Visits. A "visit" is also called a "session" because it represents all of the material an individual Web visitor sees during one visit. Since standard Web logs include the IP address for each computer coming to your site, it is easy for the analysis programs to count the number of visits by counting the number of different IP addresses in the log. Of course, inaccuracies can creep in because an ISP can give an IP address to a second person later in the day, and that second person would be seen as continuing the first person's visit.

Visitors. A "visitor" should be the number of unique people who came to your site. In other words, it should be a nonduplicated count of visits. Of course, it may be hard for a log analysis program to determine that someone with a different IP address is the same person who visited your site the day before. The use of *cookies* to identify when a particular computer returns to your site can help improve the accuracy in counting visitors. Some inaccuracy can creep into these numbers, too, because different people can use the same computer to visit the same Web site. Normally this is not a problem, but as families start visiting the same Web site (parents looking for guidance, students looking for homework help, kids looking for games), you could soon face the problem of identifying different people using the same computer—which some of the newer Web browsers handle.

Organizations. The number of different "organizations" coming to your Web site is based on the domain name used by visitors. Of course, with so many people using dial-up services, this measurement may not be as useful as you would like. For instance, the millions of people using America Online are all seen as coming from the same organization.

Data in the Logs

Most Web server software generates a standard set of logs, using a standard file format, so the logs created by your Web server software should match the information and illustrations found in this chapter.

There are a number of changes taking place in the tracking of visitors to Web sites, so it will be good to understand the initial tracking ability so we can cover the latest developments in tracking.

The original Web server programs created a number of log files, including:

access_log. Filenames, IP addresses, date, and time

referer_log. URL of Web site providing links to your site

error_log. Incompleted requests for files and other error messages

Figure 9.1 shows the directory of log files for Allen Interactive's Web server (www.allen.com).

Figure 9.1 Directory listing of Web server log files.

```
-rw-r-r-   1 root      root      739940 Jul 26 15:41 access_log
-rw-r-r-   1 root      root      279024 Jul 26 12:29 agent_log
-rw-r-r-   1 root      root      173746 Jul 26 12:29 error_log
-rw-r-r-   1 root      root      411224 Jul 26 12:29 referer_log
```

Access Log

When Web server software was initially being created, the National Center for Supercomputing Applications created what is known as the "Common Log Format," which has been used by most Web server software developers. The fields of information stored in the access_log file using the Common Log Format includes

- IP address
- ID field (generally not used)
- AuthUser field used when ID/password authentication is used for security
- Date, time, and offset from Greenwich Mean Time (GMT)
- Method of request: "get" indicating a request for an HTML file; "post", data being supplied from a form; or "head," usually a request from an "agent" program on the Internet requesting just the header information about a file
- Filename
- Status or error code
- Size of file

The portion of the access_log file in Figure 9.2 shows the information stored in the main log file.

Address Field

There are two ways that a user's Internet address can be stored in a log file: as the IP address or the domain name of the computer being used. Figure 9.2 shows IP addresses (e.g., 207.171.21.62), but you may find it helpful to see the actual domain name using the nslookup command, such as that shown in Figure 9.3. The reason many Web managers don't include the domain names in log files is that extra processing power and network bandwidth are used to look up that domain—a task that can be done more efficiently by another computer processing that data in non-prime time.

The first thing you'll want to know is how many different people are visiting your site. The closest estimate is the number of "unique sessions," which is determined by how many different IP addresses are in your access log. The addresses of people com-

Figure 9.2 Web server access_log.

```
207.171.21.62 - - [01/Jul/1997:04:57:53 -0400] "GET /images/hp-
wostars.gif HTTP/1.0" 200 36055
143.117.49.17 - - [01/Jul/1997:04:58:09 -0400] "GET
/images/microsoft-5.gif
HTTP/1.0" 200 57139
143.117.49.17 - - [01/Jul/1997:04:58:50 -0400] "GET /succ_04.html
HTTP/1.0" 200 2762
143.117.49.17 - - [01/Jul/1997:04:58:52 -0400] "GET /images/cg-med-
1t.gif HT
TP/1.0" 200 3137
143.117.49.17 - - [01/Jul/1997:04:58:52 -0400] "GET
/images/microsoft-1t.gif
 HTTP/1.0" 200 5163
143.117.49.17 - - [01/Jul/1997:04:58:53 -0400] "GET /images/cg-
saguaro-1t.gif HTTP/1.0" 200 5434
207.171.21.62 - - [01/Jul/1997:05:01:43 -0400] "GET /meet.html
HTTP/1.0" 200  7157
207.171.21.62 - - [01/Jul/1997:05:01:45 -0400] "GET /images/gray.jpg
HTTP/1.0" 200 1536
207.171.21.62 - - [01/Jul/1997:05:01:45 -0400] "GET /images/b-
meet.gif HTTP/ 1.0" 200 21551
204.62.245.166 - - [01/Jul/1997:05:03:02 -0400] "GET /webdev.html
HTTP/1.0" 200 9850
```

ing to your Web site are very important in determining the number of distinct people and distinct visits, or sessions. Making these determinations is not as easy as you might think because of a number of factors.

IP addresses used to always be assigned to individual computers, so it was easy to assume that a unique IP address was associated with a unique computer. Since most

Figure 9.3 Results of the nslookup **command.**

```
cliff> nslookup 199.171.201.14

Name:    winet.wiley.com
Address:  199.171.201.14
```

people always use the same computer to go on line, the number of unique IP addresses would equal the number of unique people. A number of changes in the Internet world have made this method of estimating people less accurate. These changes include

- Dial-up users are usually assigned a different IP address each time they connect to their Internet service provider (ISP).

- Users of commercial online services (e.g., America Online, CompuServe, Prodigy, and MSN) access the Internet through a limited number of Internet "gateways," each with its own IP address.

- Corporate users connect through proxy computers, each with its own IP address.

- Community terminals, in libraries and cafés, allow many people to use the same computer.

As the Internet becomes more popular, the number of IP addresses in a log file will have less and less relationship to unique people, so we should use the term "unique sessions" instead of "people." You can do that by adding a profile tracking system to your Web site that identifies individual people.

After determining the number of unique sessions from the Access log, the next information we're interested in determining includes

- The number of accesses to the homepage.

- The number of times a graphic unique to the homepage is accessed. This indicates how many people came to the site with graphics turned on.

- The number of times the intermediate index pages were accessed from the homepage, which shows the interest areas of people. For example, if you believe that a certain link should be popular but it is not accessed often, check to see if the link is visible when the homepage is initially displayed or if the user has to scroll down to find it. If it's low on the page, try moving it up and watch the log to see if it makes a difference.

- The order pages are accessed by individual IP addresses. This shows the "train of thought" people are going through in visiting your site.

- The time spent on each individual page, which can be calculated for individual IP addresses.

Date and Time Field

The information in the date and time field looks rather obvious and, for the most part, it is. However, there are a few potential *gotchas* with this that can cause difficulty in tabulating logs for large sites that use multiple servers.

Figure 9.4 Form submission to AltaVista using the POST method.

```
altavista.digital.com/cgi-bin/query?pg=q&what=web&kl=XX&q=GuestTrack
```

As Web sites become larger, it is customary to add multiple computers to the "cluster" of servers and display various pages from different servers in the group. Sometimes a load-balancing front end is used to direct each server request to the system that is least busy. Other large Web sites dedicate certain servers for certain services, such as database requests, transactions, and so forth. Still other Web sites "mirror" the pages of one server at another server, perhaps in a different part of the world. When users are directed to servers in a different time zone, the time zone data can be used to help synchronize log files to a common time, say, GMT (Greenwich Mean Time).

Since it is almost impossible to keep the internal clocks of multiple servers completely synchronized, there will frequently be slight differences in the times for pages. This means that an individual who accesses a series of pages that are served by multiple servers could result in log entries that are out of order, which can affect tabulations for such things as the path through the site.

Method Field

For the most part, the method field will provide you with little information because static HTML files result in a GET, while most form data results in POST entries in the log.

There are a few things to be aware of regarding form data and the use of GET and POST, including a potential security problem for your users.

Without getting into the technical aspects of creating forms and the CGI programs that process form data, we can generalize that forms can use either the GET or POST method of sending data to the server. When the HTML command in the form specifies "method=post," then the form data is passed "behind the scenes" to the CGI program. On the other hand, when the HTML file includes "method=get" in the form tag, then form data is passed in the URL to the server , and can be seen in the Location box in the browser. For example, Figure 9.4 shows the results in the browser's Location box after searching for the product GuestTrack.

Figure 9.5 shows the referer_log entry after clicking on the links to the GuestTrack homepage displayed by AltaVista.

Figure 9.5 Entry in the referer_log showing the URL of the user's prior Web page.

```
altavista.digital.com/cgi-bin/query?pg=q&what=web&kl=XX&q=GuestTrack -> /
```

As you can see, the URL contains the search criteria plus various other internal data used by the search engine. Just imagine if the form had contained sensitive information (such as a credit card number or password), which is now visible to anyone looking over the shoulder of the user. Of course, there isn't much of a security risk with this because most of the time you know who is looking over your shoulder—in the *physical* world. Unfortunately someone could be looking over the shoulder of your user in the *virtual* world.

One of the two potential security risks involved in sending confidential data with the GET method involves bookmarks. Since the confidential information is in the Location window, a user could decide to bookmark the URL and inadvertently store the information on his or her hard drive in an insecure manner.

The other potential security risk comes from accidentally transmitting confidential information to another Web site. If the Web page that is displayed as a result of the GET command contains links to pages at other Web sites, then any confidential information from your users will be transmitted to the Web site you are referring them to, and the data will be stored in that other site's referrer log. We'll cover more details about the referrer log in the next section, but be aware of the potential security risk you expose your audience to if you create a page with these two criteria:

- Form generated by the GET command
- Resulting page contains links to pages at another Web site

 TIP   In order to avoid the potential security problems for your audience of passing confidential data into another Web site's logs, consider having your CGI programs written to use the POST method, which passes data to the server directly without being displayed in the URL.

Status Field

Web server software generates a variety of status codes that indicate specific results of requests for Web pages, but they fall into a distinct set of categories:

200   Successful delivery of the file

300   Redirect to another file

400   Failure to deliver the file

500   Server error

Of course, most files served by your Web site will result in one of the *success* codes, so let's turn our attention to the other codes that indicate potential problems.

The redirect code results when one page is requested but the user is redirected to another page. This occurs for a variety of reasons, although they are almost all good.

You've probably experienced redirection on the Web when you've gone to one Web page that automatically sends you to another Web page. That type of redirection is accomplished by a special tag in the head area of the HTML document. Sometimes Web developers use redirection to create a "slide show" effect by taking you through a series of pages without you clicking on any links. At other times Web developers use redirection when a Web site moves or is reorganized and a previously available page has been replaced with another page. Instead of just displaying a link to the new page, the use of redirection can automatically take the user to the new page.

There are other ways a Web administrator can invoke redirection, usually within the configuration settings of the Web server software itself. For instance, when a complete Web site moves from one URL to another, it is easy for the Web administrator to make an entry in the server to redirect users who access any page within the moved site.

While redirection sounds very good, Web managers need to watch for log entries showing redirection because it can indicate that links to your site from a search engine or content site are out of date. If your site moved some time back and you are still receiving redirection, you might want to be concerned that the referring site will eventually discontinue redirecting people to your site.

Size Field

The size of the file served is reported differently by different Web server software, so be sure you understand what the value represents for your Web server. Some Web servers report the size of the file requested without regard to the amount of data actually served, while other server programs report the actual amount of data served.

As you can imagine, if your audience is frequently choosing not to receive all of a page or a graphic file, then you need to look into why they might be aborting the display. Some common reasons for people to not receive all of a file include

- The page is not relevant to them and they click Stop or Back.
- The page is not relevant and they leave the site through a bookmark.
- The page takes too long to download and they click Stop to read the text.
- Users found the link on the page they were interested in and clicked a link to another page.

As you can see, there are a number of reasons why the display of a page or a graphic would be terminated prior to completion—and some of them are good, such as the user quickly finding what he or she is looking for. But how can you tell which reason applies to a particular user? Many times you can determine which reason was the one motivating the user by looking at later entries in the log. Did that person go to another page a few moments later? If so, it probably indicates that he or she moved to another page more quickly than your graphic was displayed.

Referrer Log

The Referrer log tells how people found your Web site. For example, should you first discover that visitors are entering your Web site through content pages (which may have little image and few navigation buttons) instead of your homepage, you'll understand why those visitors link to so few pages.

The other key piece of information in the Referrer log is where people were as they linked to your site. Where did they start from to find you? Not only does the Referrer log show the URL, it indicates the search criteria used at the popular search engines, such as Yahoo!, InfoSeek, and others that include that information on the URL. One important action you can take is that after you determine the search criteria people are using to find you, perform those same searches yourself. See which competitor Web sites people are seeing in addition to the link to your site.

Figure 9.6 shows three referrals from InfoSeek and the words those users were searching for at the time.

In the first entry in the Referrer log, the person searching entered the three-word phrase "guest script web," which took the person to the Web page guest-track.html. (Ignore the other characters that are used to direct the database.) The second entry shows another person searching with the phrase "gt catalog" that took the person to the file gt-cat.html. The third entry shows someone linking from a page at an ISP to the Web page index.html that is stored on our Web server in the "thought" directory.

As you can see, there are many valuable pieces of data you can glean from your Web logs, but you also have to keep in mind just how they are determined and how accurate the data is.

Analyzing Logs

How do you analyze a log? Carefully!

Figure 9.6 Entries from the Referrer log referer_log.

```
www.infoseek.com/Titles?qt=%2Bguest+%2Bscript+%2Bweb&sn=503633203&lk=
ip-noframes&st=30 -> /guesttrack.html
www.infoseek.com/Titles?qt=gt%2Fcatalog&col=WW&sv=IS&lk=noframes&nh=1
0 -> /gt-cat.html
www.peterboro.net/page1.htm -> /thought/index.html
```

When you find people leaving a key page, such as your homepage, and going to another page on your Web site without seeing all of your graphics, you are losing an opportunity to establish an "image," or brand awareness. You may want to reimplement this part of your Web site to download graphics faster so these affinity audiences will see the same imagery as the newcomers to your site.

One easy way to make graphics appear to download quicker is to use the "low src" attribute which can be used to display a smaller graphic file prior to displaying a larger file. This technique is usually used to display a JPEG version of a graphic first, followed by a GIF version of the same image. If your graphics are used for navigation (i.e., have words describing links), then you may want to combine this technique with another technique: making the JPEG file a black-and-white version of the color GIF file. By restricting the JPEG file to only two colors (black and white), the size of the file is reduced even more.

These are just a few of the design techniques Web developers can use to display graphics to that most important group of Web visitors, those with whom you have a relationship and want to emphasize the relationship through graphics without delaying their moving through your Web site. For more tips on designing a Web site to improve the relationship with your audience, see our Web site at www.1to1web.com.

Seriously, the first question most people want answered from their Web server logs is, "How many people came to my site?" With current log analysis programs, you can actually answer that question.

In order to derive insights into your audience that can help you achieve one-to-one marketing success, it's important to know what questions to answer and what actions you can take to improve your Web marketing based on those answers. First, let's go over the things you can change and improve because those will lead us to asking other questions.

Situation

Too few leads being generated from the Web site.

Question:

How many people saw the inquiry form?

Action:

If many people are seeing your inquiry form but only a small percentage of people are filling it out, then you need to look at reorganizing the form, reducing the questions, or breaking the form into multiple, sequential forms. People like to be "guided" through giving information. A long scrolling form can keep people from filling it out.

Situation

Too few people are seeing the inquiry form.

Question:

How many people are seeing the pages leading to the inquiry form? How long, on average, do they read those content pages? Is the path to the inquiry form inviting?

Action:

If you just have a text link or a graphical icon linking to the inquiry form, consider adding the other type of link. Research into how people react to direct-mail pieces shows there are multiple types of people, and multiple ways they take action on what they learn. This means that you need to have both text links and graphical links in your site.

Another technique that pulls people through a Web site to the action location is to personalize the presentation of links and descriptive material. For instance, consider using personalization software to recognize why they would complete the inquiry form, and display text that will appeal to them. For instance, if your Web site sells a guide to earning more income and a guide to great vacations, use the information in your users' profile to determine which is more important to them and then display an inviting sales message.

Example #1: Let us send you the top 10 tips to earning more income.

Example #2: Let us send a set of colorful brochures about your favorite vacation spots.

By combining what you learn from your log analysis with what you want to accomplish in your one-to-one Web marketing, you can use your log analysis reports to pinpoint where changes need to be made in your Web site.

Benefits and Costs of Web Tracking and Analysis

Now that we've seen what can be learned from Web logs, let's see how we can evaluate the benefit of investing in the software, processes, and procedures necessary to perform these analyses.

The first element of performing a cost/benefit analysis is to determine the cost. The purchase price of most Web log analysis programs is only a few hundred dollars ($500–$1,000), while some analysis programs cost up to $6,500. In addition to software products, there are services that will generate traffic reports for you using their computers for as little as a few hundred dollars per month, going up as your needs go up. As you can imagine, most products can be installed rather easily, but the cost in terms of time to analyze log reports on an ongoing basis is where you need to focus your analysis of costs.

The primary benefit of investing in traffic analysis products and spending time analyzing your traffic is having information to measure the performance of your Web site. When you are armed with traffic information, you can have actual facts and statistics as to what sections of your Web site are popular among users. You can also see who visits to determine if you are attracting the most desirable target markets. If you have advertising or link campaigns on Web sites, you can assess whether these efforts are working for you. Knowledge is a powerful tool, and traffic analysis can help you easily acquire and assess site traffic.

Applications of Tracking and Analysis

Now let's take a look at how to apply the data you'll derive from a more detailed analysis of your traffic by reviewing what actions you might take based on the data available in the traffic tabulations as shown in Table 9.1.

Table 9.1 What Web Site Traffic Can Reveal and Action Steps

Traffic Information	Action
Popular pages indicate the appeal of your site.	Promote the popular topics in online and traditional promotion.
Less popular pages indicate lack of interest.	See if less popular pages are read by certain types of people (e.g., registered customers). Perhaps you should add links to those pages in other parts of the site.
Length of time spent on pages shows whether material is actually read or just skimmed.	Short durations on long Web pages indicate people found them too difficult to read or the material didn't meet their expectations. You may need to rewrite material into a more "Web friendly" style.

Table 9.1 *Continued*

Traffic Information	Action
Starting pages other than your homepage should be reviewed for "image."	Review starting pages to see if they tell enough of your story to newcomers or if you need to add more image graphics (e.g., logos, navigation bars, etc.).

Applying Direct Marketing to the Web

Traditional marketing people who have wanted to improve their ability to target prospective customers have done such things as rent lists of people who have been observed doing a particular behavior. For instance, if you sell safety equipment, such as lab coats to protect the person working in a laboratory, then you'll be interested in using a mailing list of laboratories that have purchased related products. By targeting your communications to people who have demonstrated an interest in an area in which you sell products, you can increase the likelihood that any particular person in that audience will buy your products.

The key aspect here is not to try to find people who have bought a competitive product in the past—they may be loyal customers of the other company—but to identify people who have a concern in an area in which you sell products. However, finding and targeting your competitors' dissatisfied customers may yield excellent results, and the Web is one of the best mediums to accomplish this. In the direct-mail industry, these mailing lists are called *hotline* lists.

The principles of excellent marketing don't change when the media changes; only how we apply those principles changes. With the Web, you can use traffic analysis to develop statistical analysis of *clusters* of Web visitors. What makes up a cluster? Common behavior. By using the analytical capabilities of your log analysis software, or by using a database, you can select the "hits" from all users matching a set of criteria.

Example #1

Suppose you have a daily newspaper Web site that covers national news, business news, and sports news. Within the business news section, you cover stock prices, commodity prices, and bond prices.

By identifying a cluster of users who spend above-average time with your stock price pages, you can infer that those individuals would be interested in seeing ads for stockbrokers and stock information services. These people are different from people who read only a few of your stock price pages but spend more time on company news pages and are less likely to be interested in ads related to buying and selling stock.

Example #2

Continuing our newspaper Web site example, we're now looking to identify people for an advertorial (sponsored articles) about management training products. In order to create a cluster of readers appropriate for this advertiser, we need to identify the types of pages we can use to identify these prospects. In this case we might look for people who spend an above-average amount of time with news stories dealing with changes in company management.

Since the key stories that we can use to identify this cluster might be located in different parts of your Web site, we may now be able to use the *sections* reports of many traffic analysis programs, so we will need to identify the filenames of stories appropriate for this cluster and create a *macro* or *mini* program to tabulate the logs for these people. What we are attempting to do by creating various clusters of people with different behaviors is to differentiate members of our audience.

Testing a Business Concept

Market testing is a fundamental technique in traditional marketing, and it's a fundamental technique of successful Web marketing as well. With Web marketing we have so much more data available on each individual—information that marketers using traditional mass media don't have—that it takes combining our traditional marketing techniques with this new source of data to become focused on the individual.

There are a number of ways that traffic analysis can be used in market testing. We've all probably heard the traditional admonition of "Ready, Aim, Fire" rearranged to represent a marketer's view: "Ready, Fire, Aim!" While no one would suggest investing millions of dollars in a business without having a clear goal, market testing of a concept or offer can be done very easily on the Web without expensive focus groups and delays.

You can do a similar type of "coding" with your Web site to identify which source of leads and customers is most valuable. Sevio Software, a division of Robert A. Sevio, Inc. (www.sevio.com), needed to know which uses of its MarketView software, a marketing analysis tool, were most important to its target market, so multiple introductory Web pages were created. Each introductory Web page highlighted a different application, or benefit, of the software product. By analyzing the hits to each introductory page, Sevio was able to easily identify which application descriptions were generating the most leads to its Web site. "We learned a great deal about which benefits people are looking for to help improve their own marketing analysis," said Bob Sevio, president of Sevio Software.

Of course, the real question we need to ask is whether those leads produce actual revenue, so it's important to track those individuals through their complete information-gathering process—perhaps over multiple visits to the Web site—to determine with precision which sources of traffic *really* pay off. By analyzing the path prospects took through its site, Sevio Software was able to identify not only the most popular uses for its software, but which uses generated the most leads and customers. "We've seen that the referrer log can tell us the search criteria used to link to our site, and we've seen that having multiple homepages can give us data on the source of links to our site," said Sevio.

If you have been wondering if your site is appealing to as many people as it can be, or if you have multiple target markets, here is a technique to test everything from a business concept to a special offer. This technique uses the metatags that describe your Web site to several of the leading search engines.

Here are the steps to follow to conduct this test:

1. Make a copy of the homepage. For most tests, you will want to keep everything the same except the description and keywords used by the search engines.

2. Edit the metatag for description to reflect the new benefit or concept you are testing. Make sure your description is short enough to be completely displayed by the various search engines.

3. Edit the metatag for keywords that will also appeal to the target group for this test. Be sure to include in the list of keywords any keyword that is not used in the description metatag or used close to the top of the actual Web page.

4. Store this test homepage on your Web site and test the page and its links to the rest of your Web site.

5. Submit the test homepage to a number of search engines that use metatags, such as AltaVista and Infoseek.

Since search engines such as AltaVista and Infoseek are now updating their databases very quickly, you should start seeing results within a few days. What results? By watching your traffic analysis reports for the number of hits to the test homepage you can see the popularity of the test concept and compare it to your original homepage.

If your traffic analysis program allows you to trace the path of visitors from page to page, then you can also determine the number of people who come in through the test homepage and reach an inquiry page and compare that to the number of people who reach that same inquiry page starting with your original homepage.

In addition to just counting hits to the test homepage, you can also review the referrer log to see the search criteria used to reach the test homepage. Once you see the search criteria that brings people to your test homepage, look for other keywords being used that you may not have included in your meta tags for description or keywords.

After you've gathered sufficient data on how well the initial meta tags did in bringing people to your test homepage, you can adjust the meta tags and repeat the process. Just be sure to resubmit the test homepage to the search engines again so they will use the new meta tags for the next test.

Once you know the search criteria being used by your audience, then you can see what they see by performing the same searches. Just enter the same keywords in the same search engines and see where your test homepage appears in the list of links. Are you on the first page or further back? To get a feeling of the mind set of your audience when they reach your test homepage, continue to use the same searching techniques they are likely to have used in order to reach your site. This means looking at the descriptions on the search engines results pages, determining if you (as a potential buyer) would click on the first link. If so, then go ahead and explore that site until you determine it doesn't meet your (as a prospect) needs. If your prospects normally compare multiple brands before they make a purchase, then proceed with the next site recommended by the search engine.

By the time you reach the link to your test homepage, think about what you (as a prospect) have learned. Have you been educated about how to buy this particular product? Have you learned some features that other brands have that you've added to your list of evaluation criteria? Are you seeing that many of the products in this category are so similar that it's hard to find criteria upon which to make a buying decision?

If you are feeling at this point in your test that your prospects may be confused and may randomly pick a vendor, then you're ready to apply more of the concepts of one-to-one Web marketing in order to build a relationship with your prospects. Just as a salesperson attempts to build a relationship with each of the individuals he or she deals with, you may quickly see that a relationship with individual prospects may be the only differentiating characteristic you have in order to rise above your competitors and bring in the sale.

Identifying Clusters of Individuals

Despite the quality of today's Web traffic analysis programs, sometimes you need to perform an analysis that is either unique to your situation or is beyond what current traffic analysis applications can perform. When this happens, it's best to switch to a comprehensive statistical analysis tool that you are familiar with in order to have complete control over the data and the statistical techniques you need.

Identifying Actual People

As we've seen, the Web logs do not actually track individual people; they track the Internet addresses currently being used. As one-to-one Web marketers, we need to know more about the individual people coming to our Web site, so it's important to use additional technology to track individuals.

Using Cookies to Identify Computers

Much has been written about the "cookies" that are stored on the computers of Web users by some Web servers. Some privacy advocates are concerned that personal information is being gathered about individuals in a way that violates their right to privacy.

The study on almost 60,000 Internet users at the University of Michigan for the Hermes Project (www-personal.umich.edu/~sgupta/hermes) indicates that over 81 percent felt cookies were undesirable. This very high negative feeling is a symptom of the media's coverage—sometimes incorrect coverage—of the potential for invading Web users' privacy without their knowledge.

Will Roger wrote in *Inter@active Week* about a survey presented by *Privacy and American Business Magazine* about the mistrust of cookies. Of 1009 people surveyed, 87 percent said Web sites should not use cookies without first getting permission, and 85 percent deemed it important to tell visitors how Web sites use cookies.

In fact, a "cookie" is usually just an identifying code the browser is instructed to save in a specially named file where all of the cookie information is stored. The specification that Netscape developed for cookies requires that only the Web server that originally sends a particular cookie can retrieve that cookie. This means that identifying codes written to your computer by one Web site are not allowed to be retrieved by a different Web site. In addition, cookies normally don't contain any more than an identifying code used by that site to identify your computer when you return on later visits. The last item on each line in Figure 9.7 shows the type of codes used to identify computers.

Advantages of Using Cookies

There are many reasons why you as a Web manager would want to use cookies, beyond the benefits of traffic analysis, such as in personalization and other services you can provide to your audience.

Neil Robertson, a software engineer for net.Genesis Corp., wrote in the April 1996 issue of *Internet World* about the value of cookies in accurate Web traffic log analysis. He said that cookies aid in analyzing Web traffic because they can identify individual sessions. Since IP addresses are reused by different people dialing into an ISP, trying to identify sessions using IP addresses doesn't always produce accurate results.

Figure 9.7 Typical entries in a browser's cookie file.

```
webcrawler.comFALSE   /      FALSE  1022364724    AnonTrack
3C488F3333899z34
www.sun.com:80FALSE   /      FALSE  978307200     AM_UserID
dq3b066a36693580
```

Limitations of Cookies

While cookies add a degree of identification, cookies are limited in that they identify only computers, not necessarily the people who use them. The reason it's important to make this distinction is that there are multiple ways to identify users other than with cookies, some of which overcome the limitations of cookies. Here are three types of projects where cookies won't work:

- Identify customers using a computer at home, office, or an in-store kiosk.
- Track customers across a group of Web sites to "cross-sell" products.
- Allow multiple employees to use the same computer to receive personalized notices.

"Tagging" and Tracking Individuals

There are several techniques used to identify individual people when cookies will not work, but all of them require the assistance of a system administrator who can add the necessary programs and system files to your Web site.

IDs and Passwords

The oldest method of identifying users on the Web is to require the user to enter an ID and a password to gain access to certain sections of a Web site. It's technically easy to activate this feature, but Web users generally are not able to remember their IDs and passwords. This means you should use this feature only for important, frequently accessed areas where the value to the user is much greater than the annoyance of having to remember an ID and password.

You'll recall that the Web server log files have a field reserved for user IDs, the AuthUser field, so if you decide to use IDs and passwords, you'll find that your logs can identify specific users.

Session IDs stored in URLs

A more popular method of identifying people when they return to your Web site is through the use of a "session" or "personal" ID that is embedded in the URL that they choose to store in their bookmark file.

Some Web catalog software uses session IDs while a person is shopping in order to know which person is adding products to his or her "shopping cart." These session IDs normally persist during only one session or visit to a Web site, but they can be helpful if your Web traffic analysis program is flexible enough to separate them.

Several of the Web personalization software products use IDs in URLs to identify people by having them bookmark pages on the Web site. When these people use their bookmark to return to the Web site, the personalization software automatically recognizes who they are and acts accordingly. The GuestTrack personalization and tracking software uses this technique:

```
www.intelli-source.com/cgi-bin/guesttrack?1234567890ab&index.html
```

The use of personalization is covered in Chapter 4, "One-to-One Web Site Personalization," so if your Web site uses this technique you will want to make sure your Web traffic analysis software can handle log entries with both an ID and a Web page on the same line of the log entries.

Products/Services

There is a wide variety of options available in selecting a Web traffic analysis program, so here are a number of features you will want to consider and rank before you make a decision on which product is best for you.

Platform

Some analysis programs run on the Web server itself; others require you to move the log files to your PC for processing; and others are services that process your log files on their computers. There are benefits to all methods, so you need to consider whether you are more interested in reducing the processing load of your server or keeping data files on the central server.

In addition, most programs are designed to run on only certain platforms, so you need to consider whether a product is a server-based program and if it runs on the type of server you use.

If your Web site runs in a shared server environment at a Web hosting service, then you will need to coordinate your selection of an analysis tool with its system administrator, because the hosting service may have policies against adding such programs to its equipment. Many Web hosting services provide their customers with some level of analysis reporting as part of their service. Since Web log analysis programs consume a great deal of processing power, they have found it's easier to manage this need than let each of their customers handle it themselves.

File Size

As your Web site receives more traffic, your log files each month will become very large, and may become too large for your analysis program to process. Therefore, take into consideration future growth of your site and its needs. If your site uses multiple dedicated servers, then you will want to be sure to evaluate analysis products that are designed to aggregate logs for a cluster of Web servers

Viewer Program

Some traffic analysis programs use a special viewer program that must be installed on your PC in order for you to view your reports, whether they are processed on your computer or at a service bureau. Other analysis programs use standard Web browsers to view files, and some have incorporated Java applets that can provide additional flexibility to selecting and viewing reports.

With a browser, you are more likely to be able to view reports remotely, whether you administer a remote server or just want to display reports to a group in the conference room. With products that use special viewers, you may be limited in how you access and view reports, especially when the log files have been downloaded to a specific desktop computer in another office.

In addition, some analysis programs are designed for you to access reports (with a browser or special program), while others automatically deliver reports to you via e-mail. For most needs, the viewing of reports on demand versus e-mail is a matter of personal choice, but high-traffic sites that need instant analysis can benefit from having reports delivered via e-mail. In situations where a group of people are interested in receiving traffic reports, such as marketing, sales, and the Webmaster, it is easy to establish a single e-mail address that forwards mail to the entire group.

Log Files versus Database

One of the latest features of Web traffic analysis programs is to build a database of traffic information as it is created, instead of processing a log file created by the server. While using a database to store information instead of a traditional text file may sound like some *whizbang* selling point, there are situations in which this is very beneficial.

Some analysis programs that use a database are able to reduce processing load using a database technique to process only certain data, and not process data that is not needed for a report.

There are a wide variety of Web log tracking products and services available to meet a wide range of needs. Some Web site managers need real-time tracking so they can make instant decisions on the content they are serving. Other managers are more interested in balancing the load between multiple Web servers in a cluster. The product summaries here are intended to help you prepare a "short list" of vendors to focus your attention on. In addition to the summaries in this book, be sure to take a look at the updated articles and links available to you on our Web site.

Questions to ask about log analysis programs that you consider:

- Can it handle data from multiple servers?
- Is it a service or a product?
- How often can it process data?
- Does it process data in real time or only when run?
- Will it run on a Web hosting company's shared server?
- What kind of customization is possible?

- Can demographic/psychographic data be integrated?

As you determine how you will use a Web traffic analysis program, you will also want to consider the types of preformatted reports available. Figure 9.8 shows a list of reports typically found in traffic analysis programs you can use to determine which ones you need, and then evaluate the products on the market.

Traffic Analysis Products

There is a wide variety of Web traffic analysis products on the market, and we've included short descriptions of a few of them to help you understand the types of products available.

WebTrends

The log analysis program that continues to win awards for its capability and flexibility is WebTrends. What started out as a program that created attractive charts and graphs from a Web server's log file has become a program that meets the needs of practically every Web manager, from individual business to large corporation and ISP.

Many of the recent enhancements to WebTrends are aimed at meeting the needs of Web managers who need instant analysis of a wide variety of data (see Figure 9.9). Since the program can run continuously, it can gather the newest data from extremely large log files and process that new data quickly. Suffice it to say that the program gathers a great deal of data and processes it quickly.

It can also handle several formats such as the new Extended Common Log File, which includes the browser information and referrer field.

The wide variety of report formats and file formats shows that WebTrends understands the needs of Web managers. In addition to reports you can view with a browser, the program can produce Word documents, spreadsheets, and data for your systems to bill for advertising on your site.

If cookies are available in your log files, WebTrends (www.webtrends.com) will use them to calculate user sessions more accurately because it doesn't have to rely on just a user's IP address, which may change from session to session.

Usage Analyst

This product was originally called "Market Focus" from a company named Intersé before it was acquired by Microsoft where it is now part of its BackOffice suite of products. The product runs on Windows 95 and NT (which explains its value to Microsoft) and has a number or preformatted reports and modules that allow almost complete flexibility in designing tabulations to meet your specific needs.

Figure 9.8 Typical reports available in many Web traffic analysis programs.

Reports Available from Traffic Analysis Products

Top referring sites

Top requested pages

Top requested directories

Visits by day/time

Most active countries

Most active organizations (i.e., domains)

File activity by hour of day

Activity by day of week

Errors and abandonment

Most used browsers and versions

Most used platforms (i.e., operating systems)

Number of visits

Average number of pages displayed per visit

Average length of visit

Top entry pages for visits

Top exit pages for visits

Top referring URLs

The product is based on Microsoft's database technology and has been integrated into the BackOffice line of products, so if you use Microsoft's Web server products you will be interested in evaluating Usage Analyst as well.

net.Analysis Pro UX

The traffic analysis products from net.Genesis were among the first on the market, so they are better known than some others—which is not always good. Early users of these products found they needed greater speed and flexibility; features that the company says have recently been added.

The recently released net.Analysis Pro UX provides three reporting options: a "reporter" program, a browser-based display of reports, and the ability to publish reports in HTML for your internal Web site.

Figure 9.9 WebTrends' log analysis program.

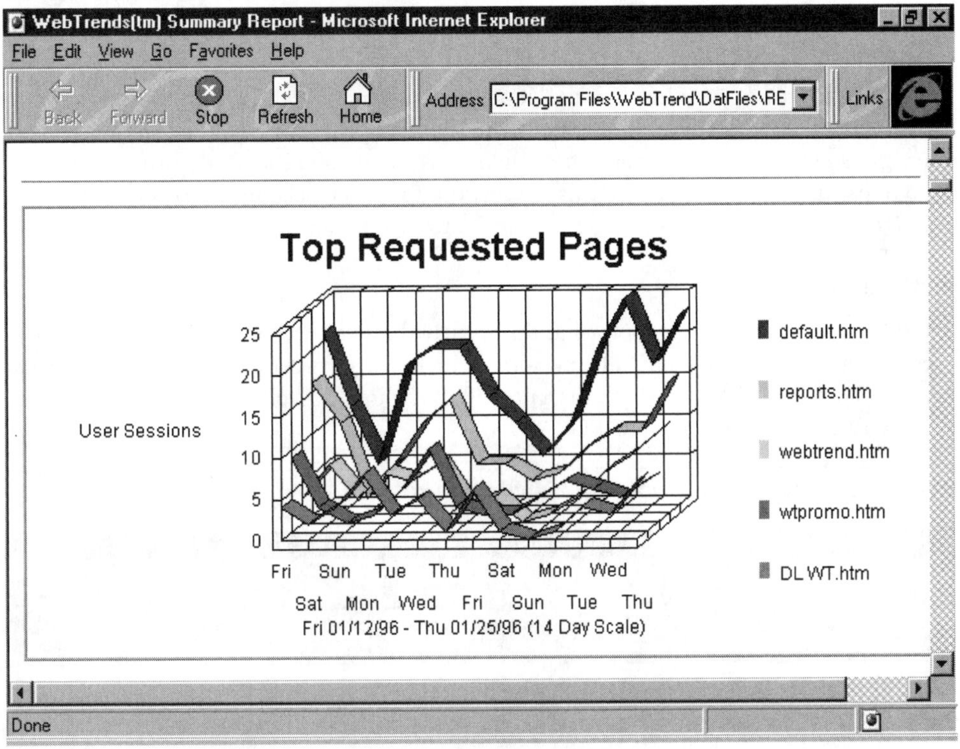

The customization capability of net.Analysis Pro UX goes beyond the standard set of reports by allowing the user to use the data within one report to select a further evaluation using another analysis/reporting format.

Like other popular traffic analysis products, net.Analysis Pro UX runs on both Sun Solaris (Unix) and NT Web servers (www.netgen.com/).

Traffic Analysis Services

Most Web managers will want to have their Web server logs processed on their own computers, either on the server or on a desktop computer connected to the server. However, there are situations in which you may find it beneficial to use an outside service to process your log data.

The two main log analysis service companies, I/PRO and NetCount, provide more than just reports. They describe their reports as "audits" that can be used to assure advertisers of the number of people, visits, and impressions a Web site has delivered. For sites that depend on advertising and sponsorship revenue, being able to tell an advertiser that he or she can trust the log reports because they were processed by an outside company is sometimes very valuable.

In addition to providing independent verification of Web traffic, the other main advantage of using an outside service is the reduced processing load on in-house computing resources. As a site grows to receiving over 200,000 hits per day, the computing resources and management of this important function become more of a drain on resources, and therefore become a candidate to be outsourced.

NetLine by I/PRO

I/PRO handles log analysis somewhat differently than other vendors because it is a service and not a product. The NetLine service includes software to automatically transfer your log files to I/PRO, which then processes the log files, creates reports, and delivers the finished reports to your PC.

Figure 9.10 NetLine software for viewing log reports.

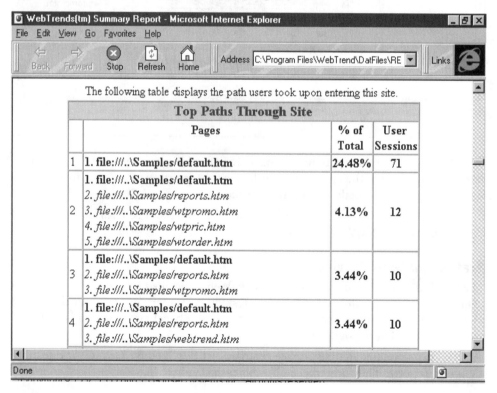

Another difference between the NetLine service and software products on the market is that special software is provided for you to view your reports (see Figure 9.10), which is different from most other log analysis products that create traditional Web pages with tables and graphs (see Figure 9.11). I/PRO's primary focus is on providing an independent analysis of a Web site's log files that can be provided to advertisers and others who need assurance of your traffic.

NetCount

NetCount (www.netcount.com) is one of the other services that provides Web traffic analysis using its computers to perform the tabulation. One of the big advantages of NetCount is its association with the accounting firm Price Waterhouse, which has provided traditional auditing services for many years.

The NetCount/Price Waterhouse products deliver what they call "tamper-resistant" measurement of Web site traffic and online advertising performance on a daily or weekly basis. In addition, their association with BPA International provides additional certification of the quality of their effort to measure Web traffic. BPA's nonintrusive third-party audits provide confirmation of site traffic on a monthly or quarterly basis. The combined services provide online advertisers and content providers with additional assurance of the traffic reports because the processing is performed at NetCount facilities and not at the Web site.

With the move toward learning more about the Web audience, NetCount is preparing to provide traffic information tied to demographic information with their HeadCount service. HeadCount will track individual users in a seamless manner (no user passwords or ID codes required). Household and/or business demographic data will be provided.

Enhance Web Site Data with Guestbook Registration

Many Web sites encourage people to use a form called a "guestbook" to provide information about themselves so they can receive additional information, register for contests, and for a wide variety of other purposes. If you are selling products on your Web site to consumers who make quick purchase decisions, then you may not need to capture registration information because you are more interested in them completing the order form and making a purchase. On the other hand, if you are marketing products that require evaluation, it's important to identify prospects and work with them during the evaluation period.

How to Use a Guestbook on Your Site

Many marketing Web sites have general product information that is freely available to the general public, plus additional information that is ordinarily given only to well-

---

Figure 9.11 Report produced by I/PRO's NetLine service.

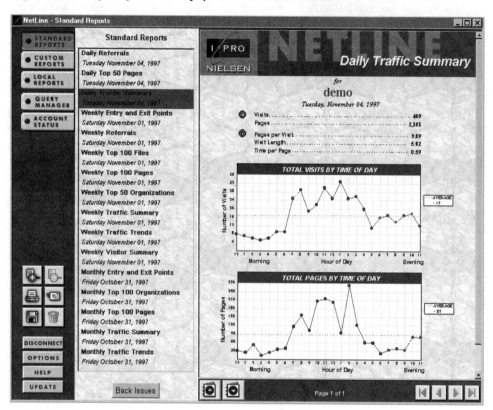

qualified prospects. In order to restrict access to the additional information to those people who are qualified prospects, you can use a registration form to gather information about their needs and purchase plans. Based on the answers, your Web site can then deliver information appropriate to their needs and current situation, and you receive valuable information that can help your salespeople.

The traditional process for processing inquiries involves many steps and takes a considerable amount of time.

1. Advertising generates an inquiry.

2. Product literature is mailed to the person inquiring.

3. Prospect mails back a "bounce back" postcard indicating preliminary interest.

4. Salesperson telephones to schedule an appointment to review the prospect's needs.

5. Salesperson meets with prospect to review needs, tour the plant, and ask "qualification" questions.

6. Proposal is prepared based on the needs and other insights gained from the plant tour.

7. Prospect receives the proposal and reviews specifications, prices, terms, etc.

8. Purchase order is prepared and sent to the salesperson for processing.

This is the traditional one-to-one approach to selling products, which is called "considered decisions"–ones where the purchase is based on analyzing and weighing a considerable amount of product information. This is also an approach that can be used on Web sites to accomplish the same flow of information between you and your prospect in a much shorter and much more efficient process.

One example of a company that is benefiting tremendously from having a good inquiry form on its Web site is Pall Corporation, a manufacturer of specialized filtration devices (www.pall.com:8080/www/webforms.nsf/ContactPall?openform).

When an engineer is searching for a solution to a problem, the Pall Web site can answer many questions about filtration in general by using examples from a wide variety of industries.

The Web site is working extremely well," said Claire Zinnes, interactive marketing manager. "Pall sells into practically every industry so practically anything that is manufactured needs filtration somewhere in the process."

Since Pall's Web site gives the complete story about its products that can be used across many industries, it is important for the inquiry form to allow prospects to provide information about their need. Zinnes says new sales leads generated by the Web account for many new clients around the world.

Pall typically sees over a 50-percent increase in visits to its Web site each month, with approximately 3 percent of the visits resulting in an inquiry. These inquiries are automatically stored in a Lotus Notes database where the interactive marketing staff at Pall's headquarters reviews each lead and forwards them to the appropriate salesperson within a few hours.

"When you have someone who needs a specialized blood filtration product for an operation, or has an airplane that can't take off until we supply the part, it's important to our customers that we react quickly," said Zinnes.

Capturing and Tracking Leads

Today, you can automatically move Web-generated inquiries directly to the lead tracking software used by salespeople, which can reduce the response time of salespeople considerably. One lead tracking program, GoldMine Software (www.goldminesw.com), now offers an enhancement that handles the task of transferring Web leads to salespeople.

Whether this is done with an "off-the-shelf" sales force automation package or with an integrated Web server/database system, as Pall Corporation does using Lotus Notes, it's important to quickly move inquiries to the salespeople so they can respond quickly.

The traditional approach to handling leads results in long delays in responding to inquiries, sometimes after the need has already been met by a competitor's product.

As you can imagine, this process is very labor intensive and time-consuming because material has to be mailed back and forth, and the salesperson must travel to the prospect, prepare the proposal, present it to the prospect, and answer follow-up questions.

While Approvers (people who can approve purchases) are the final decision makers, Recommenders play an important function in the evaluation process, so their needs must be taken into consideration as much as those of the Approvers.

Recommenders are generally looking for projects that will help them "shine" and advance within an organization, so they are looking for the most positive benefits possible for their organization. Approvers, on the other hand, are already in a more senior-level position within their organization than Recommenders, and are usually more concerned about the potential problems with new products and systems.

The other primary qualification criteria you can obtain is the expected time frame of the purchase. Table 9.2 shows our recommended action plan for Recommenders and Approvers based on their expected time for the purchase.

Table 9.2 Proposed Action Matrix

Review	Purchase over 6 Months	Purchase Less than 6 Months
Recommender	Mail material	Contact by phone, follow up monthly
		Contact by phone, conference with Approver
Approver	Mail material	Contact by phone, offer evaluation
		Contact by phone, identify the people evaluating products

Many corporate purchase decisions take place within a six-month window of time starting with the notification of the team members of the upcoming project and ending with the purchase of products needed to start the project. Of course, many products are purchased during the life of projects, but you have a much greater chance of making a sale if you are being considered during the pre-project information-gathering period.

If prospects indicate they are just reviewing product material, then it is not likely that they will be involved in a purchase within the next year, but that they have an interest for a future project. These people may not fit our qualification profile today, but they are clearly forward-thinking people who should be contacted periodically. In fact, leads like this are generally worth following up for approximately two years. After that time, many people have changed positions, companies, projects, interests, and so forth.

If a purchase is expected to take place after six months, it can be a sign that there truly is a project (and that someone will eventually make a sale), but that the time frame is uncertain. If a Recommender says the purchase will be after six months, that may be a "hopeful" time estimate—they are hopeful that the project will be approved and that they will be on the team. If an Approver says the purchase will be after six months, that may indicate the project is in his or her plans for the upcoming year—and there is much more likelihood of a purchase.

If either the Recommender or the Approver say a purchase will take place within the next six months, there is a strong likelihood that there will be a purchase and your salespeople should contact the prospect frequently to ensure that your product is one of those being considered. If an inquiry comes from a recommender, then it's important for your salespeople to identify the approver as quickly as possible and qualify him or her regarding budget, time frame, and need. (It's frequently difficult to obtain information about the second qualification item on our list—ability to purchase from you—until you've established a personal relationship with the individuals involved in the purchase.)

As you look for ways to qualify a prospect using data from the inquiry form, you will usually find that you will make more sales when the person completing the inquiry form is a recommender than an approver. While this may seem backward, consider the motivations of each person and you'll see how this fits within the corporate political structure.

While it's generally thought that you want to "sell high" into an organization, the reality is that when a senior executive inquires about a particular product, they usually pass the material down through the organization to others for evaluation. This gives the recommenders at the lower level an opportunity to include their favorite products in the evaluation and to give those products higher grades than the product suggested by the executive. This is why we suggest that if an approver makes an inquiry about a product to be purchased within the next six months that you actively identify the people handling the evaluation and work closely with them to make sure your product has a fair chance of being recommended. The old maxim of "sell high" needs to be modified to be "Sell concepts high—sell products low" within an organization.

The evaluation period for many products extends over several months. It should be emphasized that there are two very important parts of the traditional sales process that must be incorporated into the Web version for this to be successful:

1. The prospect must be given more than he or she is giving at each step in the process.

2. The prospect must be given the time to digest and absorb the information you are providing so he or she can make a considered decision in your favor.

This means that in order for you to successfully use one-to-one marketing, you need to qualify prospects using data from the inquiry form and then apply sound sales techniques to build the relationship and help move the prospect to making a purchase of your product. While many enthusiasts of Web marketing like to use e-mail to contact prospects, you shouldn't forget the value of the telephone to maintain and build relationships with the individuals you do business with.

Cost and Benefits of Using Guestbooks

There are a variety of ways to add a guestbook to a Web site: from having a programmer develop a simple script within a few hours to using off-the-shelf personalization software with these features.

The cost of creating simple scripts for your Web site is just the few hours it takes your programmer or system administrator to write the software and install it on your Web site. Personalization software starts at $1,000 for products such as GuestTrack and can cost upwards of $50,000–$100,000 for products that require substantial customization.

The benefits of using guestbook software are closely tied to how you use the data. When your salespeople are able to contact prospects faster than your competitors—and close more sales faster—then the benefits will be clear.

The Future of Tracking

The tracking techniques covered in this chapter can help you improve your success on the Web by showing what people are doing on your Web site, as well as allow you to gather information from individuals.

The Web personalization software covered in Chapter 4, "One-to-One Web Site Personalization," points the way to improved one-to-one marketing, but the Web traffic software companies will need to quickly catch up so their products will continue to be helpful.

One of the challenges facing vendors of traffic analysis software is how to track the "intrapage" activity. In other words, personalization software can display different content to each user, but the traffic analysis software shows that the same page was accessed by these different people. Since pages are created "dynamically" on the fly, making content decisions based on each person's profile, these activities are not included in the log files. As Web personalization becomes more common, look for the Web traffic analysis software vendors to find ways to track individuals with greater precision so you can meet the needs of the individual.

Chapter 10, "Integrating One-to-One Web with Other Marketing Systems and Processes," discusses how databases can be integrated with Web sites. It also provides an understanding of how databases are important to one-to-one Web marketing. The chapter also gives an overview of data mining and data warehousing and their roles in one-to-one Web marketing.

INTEGRATING ONE-TO-ONE WEB WITH OTHER MARKETING SYSTEMS AND PROCESSES

10

> "The companies best equipped for the 21st century consider invest-
> ment in real-time systems to be essential to maintaining their com-
> petitive edge and keeping their customers."

> Regis McKenna in *Real Time: Preparing for the Age of the Never Satisfied
> Customer* (1997, Harvard Business School Press)

Databases are everywhere. It seems that everything we do goes into a database that collects data on where we go, what we do, and what we buy. When used correctly, the integrated systems of computers that we interact with can help make our lives much more fulfilling. That's the focus of this chapter: To help you help your customers through the integration of databases and other computing systems into your Web site.

In an article written by Lee Marc Stein for the Direct Marketing Association, "The Whys and Hows of Prospect/Customer Self-Qualification," he said, "Being relevant is of increasing relevance." He went on to point out that our customers want to be part of the information flow. He said, "The benefits go beyond getting relevant answers: Consumers want to be part of the marketing process from the beginning, and answering questions makes them a part of this process."

With one in every four American adults (47 million people) now on line, according to a recent survey by IntelliQuest, the number of people looking to buy products on line is growing at a rapid rate. In fact, IntelliQuest found growth was up 34 percent in one year. In addition, its survey estimated that another 11.2 million U.S. adults would log on in 1997.

The focus of this chapter is to help you integrate your one-to-one Web marketing activities with other marketing systems in your company, and to integrate these systems into the processes your company uses to help customers and generate revenue and profits. We cover some of the new database technologies that are now ready to help you pull your systems together into an integrated approach to building a relationship with your online audience.

The reason it's important to integrate your Web site with your existing computing environment is that people are looking to gather information and make purchases on line. This means you have an opportunity to learn about the needs of your customers and provide just the information they need.

One of the interesting changes in shopping that the Internet is bringing about is the shift in where people are making their purchases. According to a survey by NFO Interactive, nearly one-third of online shoppers spend less money in retail stores and on catalog items as a result of shopping on line.

What are people buying on line? About 24 percent of Net users have made a purchase over the Internet, according to Deloitte & Touch LLP/National Retail Federation. Top purchases are software (31%), CDs/tapes (24%), women's apparel (17%), men's apparel (17%), sporting goods (17%), toys (14%), electronics (13%), jewelry (12%), and computers (12%).

As intriguing as online shopping is for companies, most people use the Web as they use other media: to gather information. According to the Seventh Graphics, Visualization, & Usability (GVU) Center's World Wide Web User Survey (www.cc.gat-ech.edu/gvu/user_surveys/), information gathering was the most popular reason for using the Web (86%) followed by searching (63%), browsing (61%), work (54%), education (52%), communication (47%), entertainment (46%), and shopping (18%).

The story behind these statistics is that the Web audience is growing and looking for more sophistication in the sites they visit and use. This means that more and more sites will use a variety of database technologies in order to manage the vast quantity of data that allows them to apply one-to-one Web marketing techniques and principles.

State of Web-to-Database Integration

Database technology is typically used when manual methods of managing data become, well, unmanageable. One of the more difficult decisions to make is to determine that the effort and investment of moving to a database outweighs the cost of continuing with the manual process.

With Web site content, many companies find that practically all of the content on their Web site is "static," in that it doesn't change from day to day, or week to week. For high-traffic media Web sites, however, the content changes daily, and sometimes hourly, so manual methods of creating Web pages are out of the question.

For companies wishing to provide access to a selected portion of a large body of information, a searchable database on the Web server will suffice. For other companies to provide access to order entry and order status systems, a fully integrated Web-to-database system is needed to provide instantaneous results of the query.

There are other ways database technology can help achieve the benefits of one-to-one Web marketing, such as in analyzing data collected about Web visitors and customers. This data can be used to identify ways in which to serve the audience better on the Web site and in the back-end operations of fulfillment and customer service.

Many of the traditional database software companies have added capabilities to their core products that allow a data processing organization to integrate a Web site into their traditional server environment. For instance, Oracle (www.oracle.com) and Sybase (www.sybase.com) provide several Web development tools, while PowerSoft (www.powersoft.com), a subsidiary of Sybase that sells advanced database development tools, has incorporated the Web into its tools.

Other companies sell products that help companies turn their mainframe legacy applications into Web applications, which not only reduces the need for expensive mainframe terminals but also allows more employees to have access to essential mainframe applications.

Benefits of Web-to-Database Integration

The growth of economies has led marketers to look for more efficient ways to reach their target audience with sales messages. The move to reach a mass audience with a small number of media vehicles had several effects on marketing:

- A small number of media outlets were being used, such as the three leading broadcast networks and a small number of high-circulation publications.

- The marketing message became more general and emotional because it was inefficient to target the message to small clusters of customers.

- Selling to individuals, at home and at work, became an effective, although expensive, way to deliver a customized sales message to individuals.

As computer technology became inexpensive enough for marketers to use, other forms of marketing communications became cost effective, which led to the use of direct mail and specialized catalogs—and fewer salespeople making individual sales calls on customers. The problems with direct mail are the same as mass media advertising, just not as large. Direct mail, like mass advertising, is a one-way form of communication that is aimed at a large number of people.

Even with today's large number of cable television channels, most television advertising budgets are spent on commercials that reach millions of people each time they run. Not what we'd call targeted advertising! Even direct-mail campaigns are aimed at tens of thousands of people.

As we've seen in every chapter of this book, true one-to-one Web marketing provides the benefits of communicating with people as individuals, much like a salesperson does in customizing a sales presentation based on the needs, wants, and desires of the prospect. This chapter describes several ways to use database technologies, internetworking, and statistical techniques to improve communication with prospects and customers, and provide products and services that meet the needs and expectations of customers. By applying these techniques, businesses can meet the needs of their Web audiences, but since the technique of database marketing is integral to a discussion of using databases on the Web for marketing, we need to understand the basics of database marketing.

The idea of storing information about consumers has been in use since there were customers. Salespeople have kept notes on cards, in notebooks, and now in computers that help them tailor their sales message to the customers they see.

Even though personal selling is augmented through the use of Web-based presentations, the need to store information about your customer hasn't gone away. In fact, the more a company applies computer power to understanding and serving customers, the more it uses the concept of database marketing.

What Is Database Marketing?

The term "database marketing" has been used to mean many things, because there are many ways to create a database. Although no single definition is necessarily more correct than another, Swanson Russell Associates, a marketing communications firm in Lincoln, Nebraska (www.sramarketing.com), has developed a definition that works well for most companies:

> **Database marketing.** Creating a computer file of a company's customers and/or best prospects and then marketing to those people as individuals.

In addition, the executives at Swanson Russell Associates also define the term "database marketing communications," which they use to refer to all the communications (letters, mailing pieces, newsletters, brochures, telephone calls, company magazines, videos, faxes, electronic mail, etc.) directed to the people whose names are stored in a database.

Since the reason we are engaging in one-to-one Web marketing is to sell our products and services, then it's appropriate for us to cover traditional database marketing systems and see how they can be integrated with our Web marketing activities.

For many years salespeople have used contact manager software which collects name and address information, next contact dates, and comments about recent sales calls. For individual salespeople, this may be enough use of a database to help jog their memory about their prospects and customers in order to build a relationship. With the decline in personal selling and the increase in selling through a distribution channel it has become hard to monitor and track customers. With database tools, marketers now have the ability to use the massive amounts of data that can be accumulated to learn the needs of at least clusters, or groups, of customers, and sometimes about individuals themselves.

As the demographics of Web users approaches that of the general population, data gathered on a Web site will more nearly represent a company's total market, not just those customers who are also Internet users. Even before the online and offline markets become homogeneous we can gain tremendous benefits from current database marketing techniques.

In their book, *Strategic Database Marketing* (1994, Ntc Publishing Group), Rob Jackson and Paul Wang identified several benefits of database marketing techniques that apply to the one-to-one Web marketer:

- The ability to target marketing efforts only to people likely to be interested.

- The ability to create long-term relationships.

- The ability to offer varied messages to different prospective customers.

- An advantage in product distribution.

- Increased knowledge about customers.

Each of these benefits is based on developing a database of customer information, some of which you can obtain directly from visitors to your Web site, but some data you may need to obtain from other sources. Before we cover sources of external data, let's go over several specific projects you can conduct using database marketing techniques.

Identify the best customers. Use RFM analysis (see sidebar) to determine which customers are profitable to market to and which ones are not.

Develop new customers. Obtain data files from companies that develop comprehensive databases of potential customers that you can incorporate into your master database.

Tailor messages based on customer usage. With a complete history of each customer's purchase profile you can tailor your mail or e-mail based on the types of products he or she uses, frequency of purchase, combinations of products, etc.

Recognize customers after their purchase. Reinforce the correctness of a purchase decision by letting them know they made the right decision and that you appreciate their business.

Cross-sell related and complementary products. Some products are naturally used with other products you sell, so use your customer purchase database to identify opportunities to suggest additional products during the buying session.

Communicate with customers without telling your competition. Some forms of marketing communication, such as advertising and mass mailings, notify your competition about your plans before the message reaches your customers. By sending messages directly to good customers in your database you eliminate the possibility of the competition to countering your campaign.

Conduct product research. The more information you have about how customers use your products, the better equipped you are to create better products. Data such as time between repeat purchases, warranty work, and other contact with customers indicate how your products are being used.

Personalize customer service. When customers contact your customer service operation, an online database of purchasing history can help the service representative show you are interested in solving their problems and meeting their needs.

Eliminate conflicting or confusing communications. It's important to present a single image to customers, even if you treat groups of customers differently. For example, you don't want customers who purchase frequently to receive a "get acquainted with us" offer because it looks like you have forgotten what good customers they are!

Rob Jackson, senior vice president of KnowledgeBase Marketing, Inc., illustrates the underlying concept of serving your customer through one-to-one Web marketing principles with his Customer Driven Strategy. Table 10.1 shows the distinctions he makes between the traditional approach of *inside-out thinking* where the company decides what to sell to the customer versus the approach of *outside-in thinking* where the company listens to the customer.

Table 10.1 Customer Driven Strategy

Inside-Out Thinking	Outside-In Thinking
What we want the customer to buy	What the customer wants to buy
How we want to communicate to them	How they want us to communicate with them
What we want them to hear/see/understand	What they want us to say, show, and tell

Source: KnowledgeBase Marketing, Inc.

Using RFM Analysis to Identify Clusters of Customers

RFM is a technique that has been used for many years by large direct mail operations, such as national consumer catalogs. With over 50,000 customers, companies have a monumental task identifying the needs and desires of groups of customers because several factors influence each person's buying behavior.

Direct marketers discovered that three factors taken together were helpful in identifying clusters of customers and predicting future behavior. These three factors—recency, frequency, and monetary—can normally be *coded* in a database and tabulations run to help marketing managers learn which groups are important to the company.

Arthur Middleton Hughes described how to code a customer database in his article, "Coding for RFM," in *Marketing Tools* magazine. Basicall, the process is to assign each customer to one of five groups for each of the three characteristics.

1.   *Recency* is the date of the most recent purchase.

2.   *Frequency* is the total number of purchases that person has made since he or she started doing business with you.

3.   *Monetary* is the total amount of money the customer has spent with you since he or she started doing business with you.

You might think that by knowing the oldest date, the largest order, and the customer with the most orders, that the customer database could be coded in one pass; however, it is not quite that simple. The reason multiple passes through the database are needed is that each of the five groups is not an even distribution of customers over its range, but an equal number of customers in each group.

The first step is to sort your entire database by the recency date, with the most recent at the top. Then, code the top 20 percent with a "5," the next 20 percent as "4," and so on. Each customer then has a 5, 4, 3, 2, or 1 recency code in his or her database record. Be sure that each of the five groups (called "quintiles") are the same size (i.e., has one-fifth of the total file).

Next, code Frequency the same way, with the top 20 percent coded with a "5," and so on. Then, code monetary with its code.

The next step is to create a three-digit number from the three codes we've created so that each customer has a number from "555" down to "111" in the RFM field of the database for a total of 125 groups, or *cells*.

To use the RFM codes to predict results, you will need to select a portion of the total customer database and send those people the next mailing you plan to send to the entire customer base. After the test customers have had an opportunity to respond to the test mailing, determine the response rate for each RFM cell. You can then use a variety of analysis techniques to determine whether to contact particular cells of customers in the master database, such as response rate, average order size, average profitability, and so forth.

The use of this technique in one-to-one Web marketing needs to be adjusted based on whether all of your customers use the Web or whether a large portion of your customers haven't told you about their online capability.

Since the RFM technique doesn't use any advanced statistical calculations, it can be implemented very easily with simple database updating procedures. Statisticians sometimes feel this technique is subject to error because recent customers also have a small number of orders and, of course, your oldest customers have more orders than average. This reduces the predictive ability of these two characteristics; however, from a practical standpoint, RFM provides a great deal of predictive ability for very little investment.

Modeling Your Market

There are a number of statistical techniques that can be used to improve upon the accuracy of RFM to predict the behavior of customers. In his book, *Database Marketing: The Ultimate Marketing Tool* (1993, McGraw-Hill), Edward Nash suggests that the traditional statistical method called "regression analysis" is a better tool for prediction than RFM because it can take into account more elements that are probably in the customer database.

In order to illustrate how the results of a regression analysis are used in a formula to predict behavior, let's use two of the data elements used earlier in the RFM analysis:

Recency. Number of months since last order.

Frequency. Number of orders placed by the customer.

A typical model used to predict behavior has *coefficients*, or weights, that are multiplied times the data element. Then the results of these multiplications are added together along with some base value (i.e., starting point):

Order Size = $25 + (–2.50 x Recency) + (+1.50 x Frequency)

This model says that for each month that has passed since his or her last order (i.e., Recency), a particular customer's order will be $2.50 lower, and that for each additional order placed (i.e., Frequency), that customer's order will be $1.50 higher. For example, a customer with a Recency of three months and a Frequency of six orders, the model predicts their next order will be

Order Size = $25.00 + (–2.50 x 3) + (+ 1.50 x 6) = $25.00 – $7.50 + $9.00 = $26.50.

For a customer who placed one order 10 months ago, the model predicts that the next order will be

Order Size = $25.00 + (–2.50 x 10) + (+1.50 x 1) = $25.00 – 25.00 + 1.50 = $1.50.

Obviously it is not profitable to even try to market to an old customer like this because the expected order size is much lower than is needed to make a profit.

By using additional data elements commonly found in the master customer database, the accuracy of the regression model and other statistical techniques goes up dramatically. While most businesses do not sell directly to consumers, the types of data that can be obtained through a consumer-oriented Web site illustrate the types of data that can be used in creating database marketing models:

- Age
- Gender
- Income
- Education level
- Occupation
- Marital status
- Home location (e.g., urban, suburban, rural)
- Lifestyle characteristics (e.g., hobbies, interests, community concerns, etc.)

Where this type of data may not be available directly from individuals, consider purchasing data from companies that gather demographic and psychographic data about consumers and similar data about businesses, such as

Claritas	www.claritas.com
Acxiom	www.acxiom.com
CACI Marketing Systems	demographics.caci.com

Designing a Relational Database

One of the biggest advances in database technology in recent years has been the almost universal adoption of *relational* databases. In a relational database, multiple sets of data, called "tables," are connected to one another by their common elements.

The Relational Database Model (RDM) was created by Dr. E. F. Codd in the 1960s when he was with IBM. His approach to storing and retrieving data improved upon previous techniques by reducing redundancy in the data files. Just as in an office where each person keeps his or her own paper-based list of customer telephone numbers, the effort to update everyone's list is significant. In addition, during the time when the master list is being updated and when each employee receives his or her new list, there is a possiblility that someone will use an incorrect number. It's the same with database techniques used prior to relational databases—multiple occurrences of the same data used excess space and required extra effort to update each occurrence.

Designing a relational database requires examining the data to find sets of data that are used in multiple places, then identifying a unique way to reference an individual group of data. The basic elements of a relational database are tables, records, and fields. Table 10.2 has a typical customer table with two records, one for each customer. Each customer has seven fields of information.

Table 10.2 Customer Table in a Relational Database

Cust ID	Company	Address	City	State	Zip	Phone
001	ABC Co.	1234 E. 56th St.	Anywhere	ST	11100	555-333-2222
002	Smith & Co.	853 S. Main St.	Evergreen	CO	87654	301-777-6666

Each customer's address and telephone number are kept in only one place and are retrieved as reports are produced. This allows up-to-date information to be included.

In order to show how multiple tables in a database can be related, a typical customer order database is shown in Figure 10.1. Notice that the Customer table is related to the Invoice table by the Cust ID, and that the Invoice table is related to the Product table by the Product Number.

The software programs used to create relational databases are typically called a "relational database management system" (RDBMS). Many of the products available today use *Structured Query Language* (SQL), which uses English words to describe how to retrieve and calculate data, as well as what to report.

While each RDBMS product provides its own set of tools and techniques, it's more important to understand how data can be grouped and related in order to create a relational database. As Michael Hernandez said in his book *Database Design for Mere Mortals* (1997, Addison-Wesley), "People who are familiar with the fundamental principles of proper database design have a better comprehension of the RDBMS software and the tools it provides than whose who know little at all about database design." For this reason it is a good idea to learn the fundamental design principles that authors such as Hernandez cover in their database design books.

Types of Systems and Processes Can Be Integrated with the Web

There are many ways to use databases in one-to-one Web marketing, from managing the Web site content to taking orders and providing specialized services for customers. There are so many approaches to using databases, and different technologies associated with each use, that we've divided the uses in to different categories:

- Content management
- Customization
- Commerce
- Customer service

The process of providing information to your Web audience and obtaining information from them is similar to traditional marketing and selling techniques; it's just

Figure 10.1 Data tables in a typical customer order database.

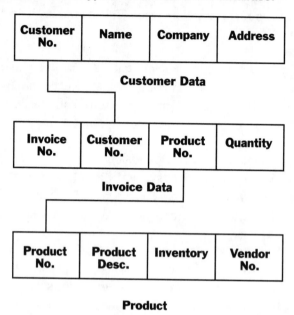

Customer No.	Name	Company	Address

Customer Data

Invoice No.	Customer No.	Product No.	Quantity

Invoice Data

Product No.	Product Desc.	Inventory	Vendor No.

Product

speeded up considerably. For instance, Edward Nash in his book *Database Marketing, the Ultimate Marketing Tool* (1993, McGraw-Hill), refers to the *two-step selling* process of using mass media to generate inquiries from people who think they may be interested in the product being advertised. These people then receive more information than could be provided in an advertisement, along with a reply card that asks a few qualifying questions. Based on answers on the reply card, these people may be elevated to *prospect* status and receive a telephone call from a salesperson, or they may be placed on a mailing list for periodic mailings.

On the Web the whole process is accelerated dramatically because a Web site can deliver the full range of information—from the general benefits found in an advertisement to detailed product specifications—in one session. While this is good for the prospect, it can be bad for the Web marketer who has provided a great deal of information without obtaining information about the prospect.

This means we need to go beyond having a Web site with just static Web pages in order to create an environment where we can learn about our Web audience. Don Peppers, a noted authority on one-to-one marketing, calls this a "learning relationship." In an *Information Week* article, "Market of One—Ready, Aim, Sell!" (February 17, 1997), John Foley describes how one-to-one marketing on the Web requires the use of three technologies working together to form relationships with customers: customer databases, interactive media, and systems that support mass customization. Peppers and Rogers popularized the term *mass customization*, the concept of using these technologies to provide customers with customized products and services that meet their individual needs.

In industrial manufacturing, design engineers learned early that by specifying components instead of custom manufactured parts, a wide range of products could be made from a small number of subassemblies. In the early 1980s, this became the basis for a class of software called "materials resource planning" (MRP) software which tied every department together with a unified database structure. Sales orders entered into an MRP system immediately influenced the purchase of materials that would be needed weeks later to assemble the product as well as production scheduling, accounting, and other parts of the company.

While later enhancements to MRP systems improved service at manufacturers with a relatively small number of customers, the concept of mass customization has been difficult to implement for a large number of customers until just recently. The easy access to the Internet for field salespeople and customers now allows companies to integrate information systems from the initial inquiry through the sales, manufacturing, and distribution processes.

Content Management

The area of content management on a Web site has started receiving attention because as Web sites become large, the issue of site maintenance becomes even larger. Jesse Berst, editorial director at Ziff-Davis' ZDNet AnchorDesk, is a proponent of using databases to separate the content of a Web site from the format of the Web site. In his article, "The Best Way to Build Web Pages" (www.zdnet.com/anchordesk/story/story_964.html), Berst made the point by describing how his online publication handles content management: "You create the content in a database (type in text, specify which graphics you want, etc.). Then the database pours that content into preformatted templates to create HTML pages. Since content and format are separate, you can change them independently. If you want to give all your pages a new look, you simply change one template. (Compare that to changing each page manually one at a time.)"

When you take a look at previous articles at some news sites, the old article is accompanied by current headlines.

Some of the benefits of using database-driven content Web site tools include

Consistent format. Each page of content is formatted the same way using a limited number of templates.

Content creation separated from graphics creation. Individuals on a Web management team can focus on their skills without concern for interfering with others on the team.

Easy to maintain. Since only a few template pages need to be updated when the format changes, the job of updating a site requires less work.

With different browsers—and different versions of the same browser—supporting different sets of features, it's always been a challenge to develop Web sites that a majority of the audience can see. With the advent of the new Extensible Markup Language (XML) that will be used in place of HTML for many Web sites, it is more important to separate content from format and then let the Web server determine which browser someone is using and which template to use.

Since the whole topic of how XML will affect the format of Web sites is ongoing, be sure to periodically review our One-to-One Web Marketing Online Web site (www.1to1web.com) for updates.

Customization

In addition to maintaining text content, a database is perfect for Web sites that use a significant amount of customized information. An excellent example displaying information in a table form is a television schedule that is customized for each market.

For example, GIST Communications, Inc., provides TV listings and related content at its Web site, GIST TV (www.GIST.com). GIST's software enables users to create a customized television listings guide on the Internet and links to sites related to individual television shows. Figure 10.2 shows an example of a typical television "grid" showing what's on each station at various times. Since the format of most of the pages is consistent, it is perfect to use a database and templates to display these Web pages on the fly.

Of course, when you gather the information from your audience needed to customized their Web experiences, you are also gathering information you can use off line in your traditional marketing activities. For example, Hewlett-Packard (HP) (www.hp.com) has been enhancing the accuracy of its customer database. Since many of its products are sold through resellers, it has been difficult to obtain accurate information about its end customers. Information about customers is gathered in a number of ways, including through its Web site. Periodically HP uses leads and customer data to mail a questionnaire requesting updated contact information that also includes cross-sell and up-sell promotions based on the products that had been bought in the past.

Another way databases of information gathered from a Web audience can be used is illustrated by the florist organization FTD. It has recently added a database system that can store a customer's billing information (except credit card information) and recipient information in its database for automatic order entry. This is in addition to the reminder service that stores information about holidays, business, and sends custom reminder e-mail messages. FTD expects to use this database to promote special offers to the tens of thousands of people in the database.

Figure 10.2 GIST TV Web site displays television schedules in a table format using a database.

Commerce

One of the most-talked about uses of a Web site is to take orders for products from consumers. When entrepreneurs first saw how inexpensive it was to publish a few pages on the Web, they thought they'd found the silver bullet to competing with large companies. In the early days of the Web, one of the most-used phrases was "level playing field."

Unfortunately for small entrepreneurs, the effort required to produce a Web site that can process customer orders is more complex, and requires more technical expertise than most do-it-yourself entrepreneurs can muster.

The good news is that tools are becoming available that make it easy to conduct commerce on the Web, and forecasts indicate that both consumer and business-to-business commerce on the Web will continue to experience tremendous growth. Although the leading analyst firms differ in their forecasts, one research group, e-Marketer (www.e-land.com), projects that consumer sales on the Web will grow to $6 billion by the year 2000, while business-to-business commerce on the Web in the year 2000 will reach $140 billion.

"While consumer online revenue is growing rapidly, all researchers agree that the big money in e-commerce will come from business-to -business sales over the Net. This mirrors the physical world where business transactions are worth 10 times as much as consumer sales."

The whole topic of commerce on the Internet is fraught with pitfalls that can catch you in its net (so to speak). Once you decide to take a perfectly good marketing Web site and add the one-to-one aspects of commerce, get ready to learn about databases, security, and federal laws dealing with financial transactions.

On the other hand, the potential for additional revenue is very high. The challenges of conducting commerce on the Internet are much the same as businesses face in the physical world:

Identity. Is the person or company placing the order really who they say they are or, in the case of orders from companies, does the person actually have authority to commit the company to the purchase?

Creditworthy. Does the individual placing the order actually have the funds available?

Security. Is the financial data transmitted protected all along the path so that no unscrupulous person can intercept it?

The process of meeting these and other challenges to electronic commerce have, for the most part, been overcome with standards, accepted procedures, and industry-accepted products and services.

Customer Service

One of the most effective uses of one-to-one Web marketing is helping customers by providing them with access to a variety of information as services.

A very easy way to add a database to a Web site that provides customers (and prospects) with a great deal of value is to add a search engine to make it easy to find help documents.

Agfa-Gevaert Group (www.agfa.com), a manufacturer of photographic and imaging products, uses a search engine within its customer support Web site to help customers locate documents based on search criteria. While this is the same technique as providing a search engine for an entire Web site, there are several benefits to restricting a search engine to just customer support documents:

1. A restricted search makes it easy to find documents specifically related to solving customer problems.
2. The marketing portion of your Web site remains presented in the order designed for it.
3. Old or semiprivate documents that are not linked are not accessible through the search engine.

Costs of Adding Database Technology

The cost of adding a database to an existing Web site varies according to the type of database being added, but a recent study published in *NetMarketing* indicates a budget of $10,000–$35,000 would be adequate. Web development firms across the United States were asked to estimate costs for three types of Web database functions. The median cost to add a registration database was $8,000; the cost for a searchable database of stock information was $23,000; and a database to manage content on a Web site was $35,000.

Products and Services

There is a wide range of products and services that use databases and real-time connectivity technologies in Web marketing. The few companies listed here are taken from the more comprehensive listing of resources on our One-to-One Web Marketing Online Web site (www.1to1web.com):

Content Management

Thunderstone	www.thunderstone.com
Vignette Corporation	www.vignette.com

Customization

BroadVision	www.broadvision.com
GuestTrack	www.guesttrack.com

Commerce

Electronic Authorization Systems, Inc.	www.easpays.com/
Electronic Card Systems	www.ecsworldwide.com/
Automated Transaction Services, Inc.	www.atsbank.com/
Anacom Communications, Inc.	www.anacom.com/

Customer Service

Oracle	www.oracle.com
Sybase	www.sybase.com

Data Warehousing and Data Mining Applied to One-to-One Web Marketing

As the amount and complexity of data continues to grow, new data management techniques have been developed that provide marketers with quicker access to analytical reports. Two of these techniques are *data warehousing* and *data mining*. Although one is for storing data and the other is a set of advanced analytical techniques, they work together to help manage large sets of data.

With the large amount of data that is generated by a Web site, such as tracking, purchases, and profile information, these advanced data management techniques will be used more and more to build one-to-one relationships with the Web audience.

What Is Data Warehousing?

What a term—"data warehousing." It sounds like we're boxing up old bills and hauling them off to an old brick building with broken windows.

Data warehousing is nothing like that, but it does involve storing historical data for use in analyzing business conditions and making decisions. In fact, making decisions should be the focus of creating and maintaining a data warehouse.

The staff and researchers at The Data Warehousing Institute (www.dw-institute.com) have included in their statement of purpose a succinct description of data warehousing: "Data warehousing is broad in scope, including: extracting data from legacy systems and other data sources; cleaning, scrubbing and preparing data for decision support; maintaining data in appropriate data stores; accessing and analyzing data using a variety of end-user tools and mining data for significant relationships. The primary purpose of these efforts is to provide easy access to specially prepared data that can be used with decision support applications such as management report, queries, decision support systems, executive information systems, and data mining."

The early attempts to build enterprise-wide systems to facilitate decisions used real-time queries into large corporate databases. In some cases, the real-time nature of these systems was so critical to the operation of the company that the processing delays caused by executives using the system caused more problems than they solved.

The solution has been to create a "snapshot" of the real-time database systems and warehouse this data on a computing system that is designed to perform analytical calculations without affecting the production computing systems. Since there are a number of ways that production computing can be affected when trying to perform an analysis, let's touch on the potential problems, including the difficulties of integrating data from the Web site.

As Michael Berry and Gordon Linoff point out in their book *Data Mining Techniques* (1997, John Wiley & Sons), a number of factors in large corporations can make it necessary to create a data warehouse in order to have an effective decision support system *and* a responsive production computing system.

For companies that have acquired various companies that must work together in the manufacture of a line of products, the various data processing systems in use generally don't use a common set of data. In order for management to have an overall picture of these business units, data must be collected from each unit and converted into a consistent format before trying to mine the data for information and insights.

In addition, many companies have added automation to various functions, from order processing to computerized manufacturing equipment, all creating data about their individual parts of the process. These different databases with different data formats were not designed to share data with a centralized analytical system, so data warehouse techniques are needed to pull this disparate data into a centralized location.

Berry and Gordon point out another important reason to use data warehousing—the one that is most important to those of us interested in one-to-one Web marketing—which is the change in emphasis that is taking place. As management realizes that the concept of one-to-one marketing is becoming the dominant approach to meeting customer needs, companies will devote the analytical resources needed to understand small groups of customers.

What Is Data Mining?

With the prediction models that are possible with database marketing techniques, you might think that you don't need any more tools, but such is not the case. In fact, the predictive capabilities of the linear regression model we developed earlier has several limitations that data mining techniques can overcome.

The main problem with the linear regression model is, well, that it's linear! The statistical principles behind this method depend on data being symmetrical: ups equal downs, the number of As equals the number of Fs, and other aspects of human behavior that just don't apply. In fact, have you noticed that the stock market goes down faster than it goes up?

While these calculation problems are significant, there are a number of data processing problems that data mining techniques can overcome as well, many of which we touch on in this section. In fact, since most of the techniques used in data mining have been in existence for many years, one of the main questions people have about data mining is, "Why is it becoming popular now?"

Berry and Linoff describe the influences that have come together to allow this set of tools to become one of the hottest quantitative developments in years:

- More data is being created.
- Data is being warehoused for easy access.

- Computing power is more affordable and accessible.
- Competitive pressure makes it essential to become more productive.
- Data mining software tools are becoming available.

As with other technologies that have become adopted after many years, data mining is an analysis technique that is being used by major corporations almost as fast as they are creating Web sites! In fact, a study of the usage of data warehouses by the META Group survey found that in 1995, 19 percent of the companies contacted had systems with over 50 gigabytes of data level, while the number of companies was expected to grow to 59 percent a year later.

Data Grows on You

One of the results in the growth in population and computers is that there is more data available now to describe what people are doing. Years ago, when a company purchased a product from a supplier, the paper purchase order, followed by a paper invoice and a paper check, were eventually boxed up and stored in a warehouse. In that situation, there was very little likelihood that data, as we know it, would have been created or tabulated.

Today, transactions like this are handled almost entirely through computers, using what's called *Online Transaction Processing* (OLTP). While it may seem that transaction represents a financial transaction, actually data processing people refer to the processes of storing and retrieving data from a database as transactions.

As we saw in the sidebar describing how a relational database system stores data, these OLTP systems are designed to quickly access individual data items in order to respond to customer orders, inquiries, and other needs. Data is stored in formats that minimize the amount of disk space needed, which assumes that any calculated value can be recalculated from the raw data anytime it's needed. For instance, a relational database system can be used to calculate the sum of orders in the Western Region.

Data Is Being Warehoused

As the amount of data about transactions has grown, so has the time required to run extensive analysis reports for management. The ability to store summarized data in a data warehouse for use in calculating extensive analysis reports now allows the intensive data mining techniques to be used.

The creation of a data warehouse for use in data mining involves reformatting data that makes it easier for these calculations to be performed in a timely fashion. Just imagine an executive requesting an analysis such as "Rank the average change in sales for each of the past three years by division." The steps to handle this with a traditional relational database system that is used for order processing (providing all of the data was still online) would be:

1. Sum all invoices for a region for the most recent year and store it in a temporary location.

2. Repeat the sum function for a region for each of the preceding two years and store the results.

3. Calculate the average change from year to year for a region.

4. Repeat steps #1 through #3 for each region.

5. Rank the results of each region.

As you can see, what sounds like a simple analysis results in every record in the database being accessed plus additional calculations to create the final results. OLTP systems are designed to access just a few records within the database—not the entire database—so it's clear that the decision analysis needs of management need to be handled by a system that is more efficient.

The approach to creating a data warehouse for use in data mining is similar to creating a spreadsheet where certain columns are used for summary data, while other cells contain zeroes to show that no data was available for that area.

In addition, since much of the data mining needs involve analyzing data over time, called "time series analysis," the structure of the data warehouse should take this need into consideration. For example, if you create a spreadsheet for data about products (rows) sold in each region (columns) for a particular period of time, such as a year, and then create similar additional spreadsheets behind the first one for past years, you have created a three-dimensional set of data. If you then turn the data cube one-quarter turn so that products are on the rows and each year's data is represented in the columns, then it is much easier to calculate a wide range of management analyses.

Since data mining techniques involve many more elements of data than just products, regions, and years, the complexity of data needed in the data warehouse grows quickly.

Competitive Pressure Makes It Essential to Become More Productive

The almost automatic growth that occurred in our economy in past decades has not continued into the present, which presents a challenge for corporate executives today. This has forced many companies to seek out new ways to serve customers, become more productive, and increase profits. This competitive pressure has given marketing executives additional motivation to explore complex procedures such as data mining.

The other motivating factor for using data mining is the move toward identifying smaller groups of prospects and customers that can be served profitably. The interest in one-to-one Web marketing is adding to this motivation as the Web presents an opportunity to compete on a new level.

Data Mining Software Tools Are Becoming Available

The statistical techniques and artificial intelligence techniques that are part of the data mining category have been used for many years by researchers who are accustomed to adjusting the many configurations that were necessary to obtain satisfactory results.

Today, the software industry provides a number of excellent data mining products that automate much of the work that used to require a Ph.D. in statistics or similar expertise. In addition, the advent of a *graphical user interface* (GUI) that most of us now take for granted has contributed to the approachability of complex products such as data mining.

Data Mining Techniques

As we said earlier, many of the statistical techniques used in data mining have been around for years, but have had limited use because they require lots of data and lots of processing power. Two of the most commonly used techniques in data mining include:

Neural networks. Nonlinear predictive models that learn (i.e., adjust the weights themselves) through training.

Decision trees. Tree-shaped decision points that represent a path to a solution or result. Each decision point uses a rule to analyze a particular data element (e.g., is Age over 30?). By using a large number of rules and data elements, a large number of paths can be handled, which allows for extremely complex groups of rules. Two decision tree methods include Classification and Regression Trees (CART) and Chi Square Automatic Interaction Detection (CHAID).

There are several reasons that data mining techniques require so much data. Several of the techniques require a tremendous amount of data for use in *training*, or adjusting the formulas, so that they accurately predict behavior. After a set of formulas has been trained, then another tremendous amount of different data is needed to test the predictive ability of the formulas.

Products

There is a growing number of data mining products available that provide easy access to these advanced analytical techniques. The products listed here are part of a continually updated list of resources on our One-to-One Web Marketing Online Web site (www.1to1web.com):

Thinking Machines	www.think.com
DataMind	www.datamindcorp.com
IBM	www.software.ibm.com
Angos Software	www.angoss.com
HNC Software	hncs.com
SAS Institute	www.sas.com
Pilot Software	www.pilotsw.com

Using Databases in One-to-One Web Marketing

Many of the database techniques we've covered in this chapter lend themselves to helping improve the effectiveness of our one-to-one Web marketing efforts. Some of these techniques can be implemented easily, while others, such as data mining, will require more effort.

For a Web site promoting products to consumers at home or to businesses, the process of integrating your Web site into your existing computing environment is similar:

Decide on your objectives. Are you looking to generate leads for salespeople, product orders, or some other item that needs "back-end" fulfillment?

Determine the process. Map the movement of data from the point of origin through fulfillment of the customer's needs (and back).

Design the implementation plan. Make sure that every department affected has ample opportunity to help make the project a success.

Develop the software to perform the integration. Allow sufficient time for the technical team to create a quality system because blending the different technologies is a complex process.

Deploy the system. Launch the new system, invite "friends and family" to test the system prior to its public launch, and then tell the world.

Direct E-Mail to Prospects and Customers

One of the easiest database techniques to implement is to collect names and e-mail addresses from people registering with your guestbook and automatically generate e-mails to those people. The content of these e-mails was covered in Chapter 3, "One-to-One E-Mail," so here we'll touch on the database techniques to manage that data.

Three Ways to Connect Your Web Server to Your Data center

There are a number of ways to connect a Web site to traditional computing resources, some of which respond instantly, while other methods don't involve real-time computing. In order to help keep these techniques in perspective, here are some of the ways we integrate traditional computing with one-to-one Web marketing:

E-mail. Data is converted to a special format and forwarded from the Web server via Internet e-mail to a computer program that can import that data in the special format. If the receiving computer is set up to receive mail instantly, such as an order entry system, it can process the data quickly. If the receiving computer belongs to an individual and is off line occasionally, then the e-mail is forwarded to that individual's mailbox and stored until it comes back on line (thus the descriptive phrase "store-and-forward" applies).

Store in a local database. Data is processed at the Web server and stored in a database with other transactional data at the Web server where it is later copied to a computer system that handles traditional processing, such as an order entry system or an inquiry fulfillment system. In this case, immediate processing is not required.

Real-time processing. Programs running on the Web server are connected directly to the same database being used for traditional processing. This is a more complex process than the other methods, but allows real-time updates to the master database system, such as inventory checking, credit validation, or near real-time control of equipment or processes.

You use a contact manager program such as GoldMine or ACT! that can select records based on criteria you specify, such as interested in certain products, live in certain areas, and so forth. The e-mail programs discussed in Chapter 3 can import these e-mail addresses and launch your e-mail campaign.

Sales Lead Management

One of the easiest ways to integrate a Web site with traditional marketing is to start with automating the process of processing sales leads generated by the Web site. The type of inquiry forms typically found on Web sites was covered in Chapter 9, "One-to-

One with Web Site Tracking," so let's take the next step and cover how to take the data entered by prospects and move the data to people who can respond to the needs of your prospects.

Sales contact programs such as GoldMine (www.goldminesw.com) now offer supplementary programs that move data from Web forms to their contact management system. GoldMine users can now direct GoldMine 95 to import and process contact data created from an incoming Internet e-mail message. The message can contain special instructions that direct GoldMine to check for duplicates, schedule activities, or create new records. This feature allows prospect data entered on a Web page to be collected and then automatically sent to GoldMine for importing.

Capturing Web Inquiries in Your Sales Automation System

It's a relatively easy way to automate the process of passing prospect data from your Web site to your sales contact system that has an Internet e-mail module that allows it to receive e-mail directly. When a prospect completes an inquiry form and clicks on the Submit button, the Web server runs a CGI program that receives the data from the form and formats it into an e-mail message. The CGI program determines the sales cycle tasks and sends the data to the contact manager via Internet e-mail. When the contact manager's e-mail module receives the data it automatically adds it to the database using the rules that have been customized for the company's sales process. Of course, this process requires that the form, CGI program, and contact manager database be programmed and configured to work together.

The first step is to design a Web form that captures data in the same fields used by your contact database designed to provide data for the fields in your contact database. Next, a Web programmer needs to create the CGI program needed to format the data to match your sales contact manager. Just imagine the pleasant surprise your prospect receives when he or she talks to the salesperson who has all of the detailed information at the ready.

One of the earliest uses of this technique of moving prospect data from a Web site to a fulfillment database was on the CORT Furniture Web site (http//www.cort1.com), where leads from the Web site's inquiry form (see Figure 10.3) are converted to CSV records and sent via e-mail to a fulfillment operation. They are then e-mailed to headquarters marketing staff. When the fulfillment operation receives the e-mails, the data is imported in CORT's database, where certain data fields tell which brochures and other material have been requested.

Figure 10.3 Cort Furniture Rental inquiry form generates data that is automatically imported into a fulfillment database.

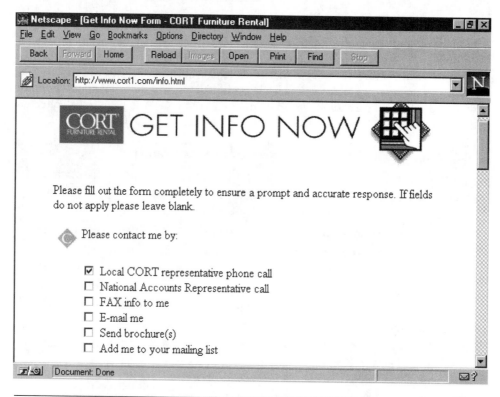

Turn Web Log Files into Predictors of Prospect Behavior

Until recently the log files created by Web servers could only be used for relatively simple tabulations, such as those covered in Chapter 9, "One-to-One with Web Site Tracking." By using the data mining techniques such as decision tree analysis, the almost infinite number of paths through a Web site can be analyzed to determine the patterns Web site users follow, and tell which patterns are used by customers versus the paths followed by people who don't make purchases or inquiries.

Some Web log analysis programs have difficulty in processing files larger than 50 megabytes, but data mining software can be used on files of several hundred gigabytes. For Web sites that receive 50,000 visitors per day who retrieve anywhere from 10 to 30 pages from the site, the log file will grow by several megabytes each day.

When the log file data is combined with the profile data collected on a personalized Web site, the opportunity to understand the behavior of Web visitors becomes possible using data mining techniques.

Moving Database Records Between Systems

The process of automatically importing inquiries into contact managers, databases, and spreadsheets has become easier with the use of a common data file format known as *Comma Separated Value* (CSV) format. This is the format a number of word processing programs have used for a long time for mailmerge processing to create personalized letters.

CSV files have each field of data enclosed in double quote marks and have a comma between fields. The following example shows a file with a *header* record that names each field, which is required by some word processing programs, but not always required by database and spreadsheet programs:

```
name,address,city,state,zip
"Peggy Kernahan","222 S. Main, #333","Bigtown","CO","87654"
"Bob Roberts, Jr.","543 E. 129th St., SW","Tulsa","OK","76543"
```

This example shows each name using a comma—which is why each field needs to be enclosed with unique characters—so the importing software can tell when the data begins and ends. One thing to keep in mind is that most software importing CSV files requires that the quote mark be the character with straight lines. The proper name for the character is double-ditto marks, since actual quote marks are curved in or out.

Since most programmers who have worked with CSV files already know the requirement to use double-ditto marks, you shouldn't have problems when you tell your technical staff you need CSV files!

Security on the Web

There are several technical challenges that face information technology executives in integrating Web servers, whether public or internal, into traditional data processing.

One of the problems inherent in the Internet is that it is a stateless environment, which means that the connection between the server and the browser is active only while a Web page is being served. Solutions to this are covered in Chapter 9, "One-to-One with Web Site Tracking."

Another challenge facing IT is security: how to allow access for only authorized users, and how to keep private data on the public Internet private. The technique of making data secure from unauthorized access on the Internet is called "encryption," which is done by substituting different characters for the actual characters and then reversing the process at the receiving end.

To illustrate how encryption works, imagine telling someone that you will be changing every letter in a message to the next letter in the alphabet, and that they should do the opposite. Of course, that pattern would be obvious in a document of just a few words, so it's important to use an encryption method that has a significant amount of difficulty.

When security on the Internet is being discussed, it's hard to avoid the current batch of acronyms, such as RSA, SET, SSL, and the like, all of which are TLAs (three letter acronyms!) that have important places in this topic. To learn more about what these acronyms mean and where you can learn more about security, take a look at the sidebar called "Deciphering Internet Security."

Decyphering Internet Security

Security on the Internet has become an entire industry—with it's own language—that will affect all of us, from merchant to consumer, so let's take a look at how to decipher the acronyms that dominate this subject.

SSL. Netscape Communications (www.netscape.com) created a security protocol called the Secure Sockets Layer (SSL) that is used in a variety of Internet applications, including Netscape's Web server and browser products.

RSA. The security software company RSA Data Security, Inc. (www.rsa.com) created a process of encryption that has been patented, then licensed to a large number of companies. Since the patent is about to run out, it is anticipated that other companies will start using the RSA methodology once it comes into the public domain. It was widely anticipated that the RSA method would become an official standard, but reluctance to use a technology owned by one company has made the standards groups reluctant to endorse RSA as an official standard.

SET. When the two leading credit card companies, Visa and MasterCard, agree on something, the whole industry pays attention. The Secure Electronic Transactions (SET) architecture has attracted widespread attention for several reasons. One reason is that a study by SRI Consulting (www.sriconsulting.com) shows that most consumers will use credit cards, not some form of electronic cash, to make purchases over the Internet. One of the limitations of SET in early trials is the delay in responding to an Internet user (as much as 30 seconds) because of the heavy encryption and data transmission that occurs.

ECC. The Elliptic Curve Cryptosystem (ECC) from Certicom Corp. (www.certicom.com) is a form of public-key cryptography that is calculated differently from RSA's approach which makes it quicker to calculate and potentially more appropriate for low-memory devices such as smart cards, cellular phones, and television set-top boxes.

Just as a chain is only as strong as its weakest link, so it is with security on your Web site. One of the most visible forms of security is the secure Web server software you use because individuals making purchases on the Web have come to expect to see the indicators in their browser window that a secure server is being used for their credit card and other private data. Netscape heavily promoted the idea that a blue bar across the top of the window and a solid blue key at the bottom meant *secure*.

Products

C2Net's Stronghold Web Server (based on the Apache Web server)	www.c2.net (www.apache.org)
Netscape Communications	www.netscape.com
Microsoft Corp.	www.microsoft.com
O'Reilly & Associates, Inc.	website.ora.com

As you might imagine, there are more secure Web server products on the market so before you restrict your decision to just these servers, be sure to review the updated list of features at the WebCompare site which is maintained by David Strom for Internet.com, Mecklermedia's electronic newspaper (webcompare.internet.com).

The Netcraft Web Server Survey (www.netcraft.com/survey) can give you an idea of the market share of each major brand of Web server software in use. Their survey of Web Server software usage on the Internet polls many servers with an HTTP request for the server name. In the September 1997 survey they received responses from 1,364,714 sites, and the results are in Table 10.3.

Table 10.3 Web Server Software Usage

Developer	Aug 97	Percent	Sep 97	Percent	Change
Apache	548990	43.23	600848	44.03	0.80
Microsoft	224577	17.69	242265	17.75	0.06
Netscape	149290	11.76	157283	11.52	-0.24
NCSA	67338	5.30	6686	14.90	-0.40
O'Reilly	41676	3.28	43018	3.15	-0.13

As you can see, the most popular server is the Apache server (44%), which runs on UNIX platforms, followed by Microsoft's servers (18%), which run on the NT and Windows 95 platforms. In addition to reporting overall brands of Web server software, the Netcraft Web Server Survey also reports on specific versions of Web servers. Table 10.4 shows the top secure servers including Stronghold, which is based on the Apache server, as well as Netscape's commerce server.

Table 10.4 Top Web Servers

Server	Aug 97	Percent	Sep 97	Percent	Change
Apache	548990	43.23	600848	44.03	0.80
Microsoft-IIS	209102	16.47228513		16.74	0.27
Netscape-Enterprise	63888	5.03	70185	5.14	0.11
NCSA	67338	5.30	66861	4.90	-0.40
Netscape-Commerce	37315	2.94	39122	2.87	-0.07
Stronghold	32021	2.52	35635	2.6	10.09

As you can see from Table 10.4 the usage of secure servers on the Internet is very low compared to Web servers as a whole, which indicates that very few sites are conducting secure commerce transactions.

Processing credit card payments

Provided by First Data Merchant Services

(www.firstdata.com)

Making purchases over the Internet involves four main parties: the consumer or credit card holder; the merchant who is offering products or services for sale; the merchant bank that has contracted with the merchant to enable the merchant to accept credit cards over the Internet; and the company that processes credit card payments for the merchant bank, known as the acquiring processor. (The acquiring processor processes merchants' credit card transactions through the financial network on behalf of merchant banks.) One other party is involved, the issuing bank that has issued the consumer's bank card.

The consumer interacts with the merchant's Web site by using a Web browser such as Netscape Navigator. To make credit card purchases, the consumer must obtain a bank card from an issuing bank and, when making a purchase, provide bank card information to the merchant's commerce application.

The merchant's commerce application makes goods and services available for sale over the Internet by payment-enabling the merchant's Web server application. To accept credit card payments over the Internet, the merchant must have an account with a merchant bank that offers Internet credit card processing. The merchant bank may also function as the acquiring processor to move the credit card transaction through the financial networks; or it may designate another company to function as acquiring processor on its behalf.

Steps In An Internet Credit Card Transaction

The diagram in Figure 10.4 shows how a payment-enabled Web server handles an Internet credit card transaction.

1. When the consumer decides to buy something, the merchant's commerce application prompts the consumer for credit card information, usually along with other information such as a shipping address.

2. The consumer enters payment information either into a form secured by the Secure Sockets Layer (SSL) protocol or into an application, such as Netscape Navigator, that is compliant with the Secure Electronic Transactions (SET) specification. With the secured form, the payment infor-

Figure 10.4 Payment process for a credit card transaction.

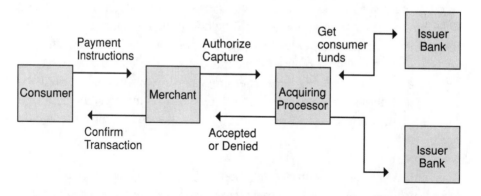

mation is protected by SSL as it is sent to the merchant. With SET, credit card information is enclosed in a "slip"—an encrypted, electronic analogy to a paper credit card slip. The slip is then sent to the merchant.

3. Using the payment software incorporated in the Web server, the merchant sends the encrypted transaction to the acquiring processor for authorization. The authorization is a request to hold funds for purchase.

4. The acquiring processor either authorizes a certain amount of money (and issues an authorization code) or declines the transaction. An authorization reduces the available credit limit but does not actually put a charge on the customer's bill or move money to the merchant.

5. If the transaction is authorized, a "capture" is the next step. The capture takes the information from the successful authorization and charges the authorized amount of money to the consumer's credit card. In line with bank card (Visa/MasterCard) association rules, the merchant is not allowed to capture transactions until the ordered goods can be shipped, so there may be a time lag between the authorization and the capture.

6. If the consumer cancels the order before it is captured, a "void" is generated; if the consumer returns goods after the transaction has been captured, a "credit" is generated.

7. The final step is to "settle" the transaction between the merchant and the acquiring processor. Captures and credits usually accumulate into a "batch" and are settled as a group. When a batch is submitted, the merchant's payment-enabled Web server connects with the acquiring processor to finalize the transactions and transfer monies to the merchant bank account.

(First Data Merchant Services offers a full range of processing services to its clients—financial institutions, independent sales organizations and merchants—including authorization, transaction capture, settlement, chargeback handling, reconciliation, reporting, prepaid card issuance and acceptance, and Internet-based transaction processing. In 1996, FDMS processed close to 6 billion transactions, serving existing and emerging merchant industries with an array of industry solutions.)

Before you start planning to add commerce to your site, be sure to experience online commerce yourself so you'll know just how it feels to a customer to search for the product you're looking for, entering your credit card number, and wait for the confirmation—and the product. If you haven't purchased products online yet, then it's time *you* did a little surfing for fun (or business) and bought your next book or hobby-related item on the Web.

And, if you'd like to get an overview of the consumer-oriented merchants using secure servers, go to the Virtual Emporium (www.virtualemporium.com). This site is an online shopping community with some 200 secure online shopping sites (Figure 10.5). In addition, the online stores are accessible from their retail stores, kiosk network, and their Web site.

A commerce-based Web server presents more technical and procedural challenges for a company than most other marketing activities it will undertake. This is because the system provides the one-to-one Web marketing function to customers while it is integrated with the internal computing environment that only employees have traditionally used. The combined need for a very high level of customer service on the Web site and tight security makes it essential that every department within a company that will be affected by the commerce operation be involved starting with the planning stages. As you prepare for adding commerce to your Web site, be sure to check out the latest information at our One-to-One Web Marketing Online Web site (www.1to1web.com).

The Future of Web-to-Database Integration

As we mentioned earlier, the cost to add database technology to a Web site is rather high compared to the cost of publishing a Web site using static pages. Why go to this

Figure 10.5 Virtual Emporium site with links to hundreds of online Web sites.

extra expense? Many marketing executives have a feeling that customizing the content and customer service of a Web site builds an attraction on the part of the prospect or customer, but they generally don't know *why* customization and personalization increases affinity.

In his article in *Forbes* (www.forbes.com), "Brands With Feeling," Joshua Levine showed that some marketers understand that there is an emotional aspect to the relationship between marketer and customer—that customers look for emotional satisfaction with their purchases. The two questions for marketers are, of course, what can we do to increase the emotional satisfaction and how can we do that with our Web sites?

The answer to the first question is to understand the personal motivations of your audience and to adapt your message so it is more understandable and accepted. In his book, *Taking Care of Business* (1985, Pocket Books), Dr. David Viscott wrote about having identified three main types of people, as well as the goals and driving forces of each type:

- To belong
- To own
- To win

Traditional direct marketers have used buying motives like this for years by providing multiple pieces of sales material in a single mailing, relying on the prospect to pick and choose the piece to read based on their personal motivations. This is, of course, an expensive route to "personalization," but for many marketers it has been effective.

Since most Web marketers have created their Web sites based on the assumption that every prospect has the same personal buying motives, it is hard to find examples of Web sites that recognize the personal difference between people. The first step is understanding the differences between people who appear to have the same needs.

Values and Lifestyles

SRI International (www.sri.com), an independent, nonprofit research institute, has conducted a series of research studies since 1978 that takes demographics to the next step—psychographics. Traditional demographic consumer-research techniques measure attributes such as age, gender, and income—an approach that is useful for understanding where people stand in society. A psychographic approach takes the analysis a step further, measuring people's attitudes and lifestyle characteristics. Such measurements are excellent indicators of how people are thinking and where they are going with their lives.

SRI's Values and Lifestyles (VALS) program groups people into eight categories:

- Actualizers
- Fullfilleds
- Achievers
- Experiencers
- Believers
- Strivers
- Makers
- Strugglers

The Impact of Empathy

As Web marketers add techniques such as personalization and advanced tracking, and data mining to their one-to-one Web marketing toolbox, a new understanding of the Web audience will emerge. By combing what we learn about each individual's psychographic profile with their Web behavior we will be able to tailor the Web experience more closely to each person's needs.

Our experience in developing highly personalized Web sites, combined with our experience in traditional in-person sales direct marketing, has led us to develop the Five E's of One-to-One Web Marketing:

Empathize. Understand the logical and emotional needs of each person

Enrich. Provide information about products and services that is based on what you've learned about the individual

Enhance. Give your message more impact by adding to the value they expected to receive

Encourage. Show how their quick decision can improve their situation sooner

Enliven. Support your customer with types of extra benefits that appeal to their individual motivations

One aspect of the future of Web-to-database integration will involve better data processing techniques, better security, and faster response to customer needs. An even larger impact will occur as Web marketers learn to use database technology to understand not only the obvious needs of customers, but also the emotional wants and desires that drive all purchase decisions.

| Web Site | Go to the Companion Web site for a case study about Peapod Online Grocery, a company that delivers groceries to over 40,000 households in six markets. |

The next chapter is dedicated to an important issue for one-to-one Web marketers which is online privacy. There has been a lot of heated debate regarding this issue. The chapter will give you a look at privacy from all sides. It will also recommend how to increase your customers' or user's confidence by creating a privacy policy. What makes one-to-one Web marketing possible is user information so if users are reluctant to give information, both the user and marketer loses out. The chapter also provides resources so you can monitor and participate in the industry's self-regulation activities.

ONE-TO-ONE WEB PRIVACY

"Good one-to-one marketers will become jealous guardians of their customers' privacy."

Martha Rogers, Ph.D., interview in *Wired* magazine, March 1996.

Although the direct-marketing industry is noted for buying and selling customer data without the customer's consent, the Internet is being held to a higher standard. Some privacy advocates are calling for Web marketers to seek the online customer's permission before being able to sell the data to a third party. Instead of using the *opt-out* model seen in the direct, telemarketing, and mail-order industry, advocates are fervently promoting an *opt-in* model where consumers have ultimate choice and control over their information and who will be able to use it.

The adoption of privacy practices and policies among Web marketers is still relatively new. In June 1997, the Electronic Privacy Information Center (EPIC) conducted a study of the 100 most frequently visited Web sites on the Internet as measured on the 100hot Web site (www.100hot.com). EPIC was looking to see what privacy policies and practices were in place. They found

- Sites had explicit privacy policies, and only a few were easy to find.

- Sites collected personal information.

- One site, FireFly (www.firefly.net), gave users control over their profile and allowed users to review and modify it.

- All sites allowed users to at least access the homepage without disclosing personal information.

- Sites enabled cookies, but EPIC only visited a few Web pages at each of the 100 sites.

The EPIC study of the top sites reveals that Web marketers have a lot of work ahead to make their Web sites privacy friendly. EPIC believes that good privacy policies explain the responsibilities of the organization that is collecting personal information and the rights of the user that provided the personal information. Also, some of the problems concerning online privacy can be attributed to Web site owners who collected information just for the sake of it without returning any value to the online user. Many users became very suspicious of this activity.

For one-to-one Web marketers to realize the benefits, they will need to convince customers of the value of providing personal information, and convince them swiftly and very publicly. As expected, marketers are strongly pursuing self-regulation in order to prevent government intervention. In this chapter we discuss the other side of one-to-one marketing's double-edged sword: privacy.

The Two Sides of the One-to-One Web Marketing Coin

The fact is, one-to-one Web marketing is not possible without the customer's participation. If the current negative perceptions of online marketers continue to persist, then both the customer and the Web marketer will lose. On the one hand, the benefits of one-to-one marketing to both the Web marketer and the customer are great. On the other hand, the online audience has spoken out against spam, cookies, and other tasty Internet privacy controversies. For both the Web marketer and the online customer to realize benefits, a lot of trust will need to be established.

The Benefits

There are benefits on both sides of the one-to-one marketing equation. In a March 1996 interview in *Wired* magazine with one-to-one marketing guru Martha Rogers, Ms. Rogers made the following statement about the benefits of one-to-one marketing to both the marketers and their customers: "Simply the more I know about you, the more I'm able to meet your needs—better than someone who doesn't know you. Ultimately, if I do it right, it's a great advantage to both of us."

Benefits to the Web Marketer

Throughout our book we discuss the incredible opportunity the combination of one-to-one and the Web brings to the Web marketer. Imagine being able to have information and insight into what makes each customer the most satisfied with your products and services. This information can help you repeat this success over and over at a lower and lower marketing cost each time. The information also reduces waste associated with mass marketing and even some direct marketing. A 2-percent response rate on online offers is not what Web marketers should be expecting. With the Web you have the power of matching offers with the people most likely to respond. In fact, savvy Web advertisers are already trying to increase response rates to 20 percent and higher, and we can expect even higher results in the near future as Web sites and marketing campaigns become more targeted and more user profile information is available.

In order to accomplish this task, one-to-one Web marketers need to know what makes our online audience, prospects, or customers tick, and click. The more you know about each customer, or groups of customers, the more you can tailor marketing and sales messages. You cannot distinguish between two online customers without some basic information. For example, how does a Web marketer know the gender of an online customer without asking?

All of this information-gathering activity translates into increased profitability and lower customer attrition and turnover. In some cases, personalized delivery of goods and services can be provided to the discerning customer at a premium—providing these specialized services at a higher rate.

Benefits to the Web Audience

Online customers will give information to Web marketers if they see value in it. The overall benefit of one-to-one Web marketing to customers is they no longer waste a lot of time wading through numerous offers to find the one most appropriate to their tastes or situation. With the Web adding to the information-overload problems in today's information society, customers will benefit from the assistance the one-to-one Web marketer gives them by providing personalized information. According to Brewster Khale, inventor of WAIS (Wide Area Information Server), at the end of 1996 over 2 terabytes (TB) of information were on the World Wide Web. Compare this to the Library of Congress, which has 20 million books that equal 20TB of data. According to Giga Information Group, the Web is expanding at over 100GB of data per week. Online users will appreciate help in making the time they spend more efficient and therefore more rewarding.

One-to-one Web marketing can also provide users with the benefit of convenience. When ordering books from Amazon.com, existing customers don't have to fill out the entire online order form every time they order. They simply type in their unique password, and verify or modify any information Amazon.com has stored from past orders. This makes it very convenient to order from Amazon.com; therefore their customers see the benefit of this ease and convenience.

Another benefit is how important the customer feels. Don't you feel important when you receive special, individualized attention when you go to your favorite restaurant or store? Feeling important is of great benefit to a customer. This feeling of importance by the customer translates into affinity and loyalty.

One spark of hope for Web marketers has been the acceptance of direct marketing. This acceptance will help set the stage for the acceptance of the online version of direct marketing. The 1996 Equifax/Harris Consumer Privacy Survey revealed that 73 percent of respondents said they would elect to have their names removed from *only some* mailing lists, and 15 percent said they would have their name removed from *all* lists.

The Challenges

With new opportunities come new challenges. One-to-one Web marketing efforts will be on an uphill slope on the information highway. Here are a few facts to give you a sense of the privacy challenges presented to Web marketers:

According to the "Internet Privacy Study" by Boston Consulting Group (www.bcg.com), over 70 percent of the respondents are more concerned about privacy and information exchanged on the Internet versus phone or e-mail. More than 41 percent of the respondents left Web sites that asked users to provide registration information. Twenty-seven percent of these online users entered false information on Web site registration forms.

The "1996 Equifax/Harris Consumer Privacy Survey" (www.equifax.com) found that 43 percent of Internet users disagreed strongly with this statement: "Providers of online services should be able to track the places users go on the Internet in order to send these users targeted marketing offers." A total of 71 percent of respondents disagreed somewhat or strongly, and only 4 percent agreed strongly with this statement.

According to Giga Group (www.gigaweb.com) and Arthur D. Little (www.adlittle.com), privacy was ranked second behind security in a ranking of barriers to adoption of electronic commerce.

The Graphic, Visualization, & Usability Center's (GVU) 7th WWW User Survey results showed that about 40 percent of respondents provided false information to a Web site when they registered. Also in this survey, the most prevalent reasons why users do not register on a Web site are that the terms and conditions of how the collected information is going to be used are not clearly specified, and that users feel that the information they reveal is not worth being able to access the Web site.

In July 1997 America Online (AOL), the popular commercial online service provider, had to reverse its initial stance on selling information about its 8 million customers to direct marketing firms. When AOL's plan became public, it caused a major uproar among its customers.

Cookies, spam, hackers, and other strange-sounding cyberphenomena are making Web surfers uneasy. Online consumers feel that cookies—technology that keeps track of what people are doing on line—violate a person's right to privacy. Unsolicited commercial e-mail, or spam, is an invasion of privacy and very unwelcome to many because the spammer did not ask the user's permission: the spammer covertly obtained the user's e-mail. There is the ever-present fear of hackers, people who take pleasure in finding the Achilles' heel of a Web server and breaking through security barriers just to lurk or sometimes even steal information from the computer. With this going on, and a lot of misinformation in the media, we can all agree that there is a legitimacy to the fears of online consumers. As you can see, Web marketers will not be able to hide from the inevitable, which is to build enough trust to alleviate the online population's privacy concerns.

Privacy Issues

Although there is much hype and media attention to privacy on the Internet, online users are skittish. Misinformation about cookies and missteps that led to private information that was too easily accessible on the Social Security Administration's Web site has escalated the privacy issue. Now there are several groups railing against online marketers, and the Federal Trade Commission has a pivotal role in ensuring that the marketing industry satisfactorily addresses the privacy needs of the online audience.

What Media Hath Wrought

During June 1997 Federal Trade Commission hearings, Dr. Alan Westin, publisher of the *Privacy & American Business Newsletter*, stated, "So the media, in a standard fashion, have emphasized to people that [the Internet] is not a safe place, this is not a secure place for your confidential information." This statement was a conclusion to a contradiction in findings in a study conducted by Dr. Westin and Lou Harris and Associates. The survey results indicated that the majority of Internet users see a need for privacy protection, while there has been a small percentage (5 percent) of Internet users who have actually suffered an invasion of privacy. The study also asked similar questions about privacy in the *off-line* world and upwards of 25–35 percent of respondents reported incidences of invasion of privacy. So, it will take privacy protection practices and significant public education to change this perception.

Perception Is Reality

Perception is reality. As we marketers know, this is one of the golden rules of marketing. More importantly, this is how Web marketers should approach the privacy concerns of the online consumer. Even if you may not agree that there is a legitimate basis for a lot of the media reports and opinions, Web marketers should consider the other golden rule: The customer is always right.

Figure 11.1 Sample cookie file.

```
cookies - Notepad                                              _ □ ×
File  Edit  Search  Help

# Netscape HTTP Cookie File
# http://www.netscape.com/newsref/std/cookie_spec.html
# This is a generated file!  Do not edit.

.cnn.com            TRUE     /customnews    FALSE    946627200      CNN_CUSTOM
.musicblvd.com      TRUE     /cgi-bin/tw    FALSE    946645199      MBNV_SID
www.dummiesdaily.com FALSE   /cgi-bin/      FALSE    901681743      dumm
www.1800flowers.com FALSE    /flowers       FALSE    944035200      SHOP
.dummiesdaily.com   TRUE     /cgi-bin       FALSE    908124685      dumm
customnews.cnn.com  FALSE    /cnews  FALSE  946627200      PNAA      :Ktu
customnews.cnn.com  FALSE    /cnews  FALSE  946627200      PNAB      :121
customnews.cnn.com  FALSE    /cnews  FALSE  946627200      PNAC      :DXB
.netscape.com       TRUE     /       FALSE  946684799      NETSCAPE_ID   100E
.focalink.com       TRUE     /       FALSE  946641600      SB_ID    084954720100
.focalink.com       TRUE     /       FALSE  946641600      SB_IMAGE      9.1.
.hardwired.com      TRUE     /       FALSE  946684799      p_uniqid      yM6d
.adobe.com          TRUE     /       FALSE  946684799      INTERSE 207.69.165.1
.isn.com            TRUE     /       FALSE  946684799      session 21732676
.internet.net       TRUE     /       FALSE  946684799      session 21580643
.bmgt.umd.edu       TRUE     /       FALSE  946684799      BMGT    user-37kbsmn
.cyberatlas.com     TRUE     /       FALSE  946684799      IPRO_TAG      32a7
.infoseek.com       TRUE     /       FALSE  881610389      InfoseekUserId  386E
www.microsoft.com   FALSE    /       FALSE  937422000      MC1       GUID
.msn.com            TRUE     /       FALSE  937396800      MC1     GUID=38dd6eb
.disney.com         TRUE     /       FALSE  946684799      DISNEY  207.69.165.8
```

All about Cookies

As you are probably already aware, cookies are bits of information collected and stored by a Web browser when a person navigates the Web. It can be an identification tags that Web sites have placed in the cookie file, and it can pick up your computer operating system, browser, and username. There is what is called the *bad cookie*, which is information that tracks and records user activity on the Web. All of this is going on without much notice to the user. Figure 11.1 shows a sample cookie file that is in Netscape Navigator's text file format.

The cookie technology was built with good intentions, but it has gotten a scarred reputation. Lou Montulli is an engineer at Netscape and was one of the inventors of the cookies. He states in a *Red Herring Hits* magazine article that "the only way cookies can contain personal information is if users freely volunteer information about themselves." According to Mr. Montulli, cookies cannot access other parts of an online user's computer hard drive. At one point during the cookie controversy, Microsoft and Netscape were considering releasing the next versions of their browsers with the cookies *turned off* as the default. Luckily for marketers, things have calmed down and this has not occurred.

The benefit to the user is that when he or she continues to visit a Web site, he or she can receive personalized information. There are limits to what a cookie can do for one-to-one Web marketing. Cookies track computers, not users. When cookie information, or other tracking technologies, are coupled with onsite registration, it can be a very powerful source of information for the Web marketer. The mixture of what is known (user profile) with what has been tracked (cookie file) can give Web marketers a clear and more accurate view of what is important to online customers. This information can also serve as an indication of what is successful in an online marketing campaign or within a Web site.

In their book, *Enterprise One to One*, Peppers and Rogers believed that for any cookie format to gain wide acceptance, the user should have a large degree of control over their information. For additional information about cookies, check out CookieCentral at www.cookiecentral.com.

Possible Solutions to Increase Consumer Confidence

Those involved with the Internet and online marketing have already taken steps to increase customer confidence, including privacy initiatives, legislation, practices, policies, technologies, and standards. The common wish of Web marketers is to swiftly implement self-regulation so the government will not step in with what could be very limiting privacy laws.

Privacy Initiatives and Legislation

In order to ensure that the Web becomes a viable commerce platform, governments and industry trade organizations have responded swiftly to the online privacy controversy and have proactively addressed the concerns of the online audience and vocal privacy advocacy groups. There have been initiatives and legislation around the world. Two notable privacy bills introduced in the United States Congress are:

Consumer Internet Privacy Protection Act of 1997. This bill was introduced by U.S. Representative Bruce Vento. The bill proposed to prohibit the disclosure of personally identifiable information without prior informed consent, and users should be able to change their mind and revoke their consent. The bill also proposed that users have the right to access their personally identifiable information for verification and correction of errors.

Data Privacy Act of 1997. This bill was introduced by U.S. Representative Billy Tauzin. The bill proposes the creation of a computer interactive services industry working group. The bill suggests that the group establish these voluntary guidelines:

"(1) limiting the collection and use, for commercial marketing, of personal information obtained from individuals through any interactive computer service; (2) relating to the distribution of unsolicited commercial electronic mail; and (3) providing incentives for such guidelines. Prohibits: (1) the commercial marketing use of government information regarding an individual that is obtained through the use of any interactive computer services without the individual's prior consent; and (2) the display of any individual's social security number through the use of any interactive computer service, with specified exceptions. Prohibits the commercial marketing use of any personal health and medical information obtained through an interactive computer service unless: (1) the person has obtained prior consent of the individual to whom such information relates for such use; or (2) such use is otherwise authorized by law."

Online privacy issues have been addressed in other bills as well. In addition to legislation, the Federal Trade Commission has held public hearings and many industry trade groups have presented their self-regulation proposals.

Federal Trade Commission (FTC)

In June 1997 the Federal Trade Commission (www.ftc.gov) sponsored the Workshop on Consumer Information Privacy. The workshop was hosted by FTC Commissioner Christine Varney. Online marketers, advocacy groups, and legislators discussed the many issues regarding privacy on the Internet. Shortly after the hearings, the FTC recommended that the online industry practice self-regulation rather than having Congress take regulatory action. In a letter to Senator John McCain, the FTC outlined the actions taken from the privacy workshop as publicized in the following press release (see Figure 11.2):

Figure 11.2 Federal Trade Commission outlines privacy actions in a press release.

FOR RELEASE: JULY 31, 1997

FTC OUTLINES STEPS FOR COMMISSION ACTION

ON CONSUMER PRIVACY ISSUES IN LETTER TO CONGRESS

In a letter to Senator John McCain, Chairman of the Senate Committee on Commerce, Science and Transportation, and Congressman Thomas Bliley, Chairman of the House Commerce Committee, the Federal Trade Commission summarized preliminary findings from the Commission's Public Workshop on Consumer

Privacy held in June, and outlined several steps the Commission will undertake in the next year to address consumer privacy issues. The letter addresses the four major topics covered by the Workshop.

Computerized Databases

The Commission's letter notes that a number of major database companies that operate as "look-up" services began to address the widespread concerns raised by the collection, sale, and use of computerized databases that contain identifying information about consumers. During the workshop, the companies offered a "preliminary self-regulatory proposal to limit the availability of sensitive information, to ensure the accuracy and security of this information, and to educate consumers about their practices." The Commission's letter identifies some key issues that Workshop participants and Commission staff believe still need to be addressed: "preventing misuse of personal information; providing consumers with sufficient access to their own information to correct inaccuracies; avoiding undue chilling of the free flow of information for legitimate purposes; assessing the effectiveness of self-regulatory guidelines and enforcement mechanisms; and examining the extent to which government action, if any, may be needed."

These issues will be examined in detail in a report of an ongoing study of computerized databases that will be submitted to Congress by the end of this year.

Unsolicited Commercial E-mail

During the Workshop, research was presented that indicated that unsolicited commercial e-mail is disliked by almost all consumers who receive it. One clear result of the Workshop was that a "disparate group, including senders of unsolicited commercial e-mail, technology experts, and privacy advocates, has committed to develop a voluntary response to consumer and industry concerns and to report back to the Commission in 6 months," the letter states. Commission staff will monitor this effort. Commission staff also is monitoring unsolicited commercial e-mail to see if it involves the fraudulent offering of products or services or other practices that could be unfair or deceptive and therefore in violation of the Federal Trade Commission Act.

Consumer Online Privacy

Consumers are concerned about the security and confidentiality of their personal information in the online environment, and as the Commission letter points out "they are looking for greater protections, preferably from voluntary efforts by industry, but if necessary from government." The Workshop produced a great deal of interest and participation by industry members who demonstrated different approaches to protecting online privacy. However, as the Commission points out, "Self-regulatory approaches and emerging technological tools will be effective in protecting online privacy only to the extent that they are widely adopted by Web sites and, in the case of technology, are readily available to consumers and easy to use." Commission staff is committed to assisting industry and consumer groups in educational efforts that will prove essential if consumers are to have confidence in the World Wide Web. Commission staff also will "monitor the [Web] . . . to determine the extent to which commercial Web sites are disclosing their information practices and offering consumers choice regarding the collection and use of their personal information online," the letter states. The letter notes the Commission's hope that by "March 1, 1998 . . . a substantial majority of commercial Web sites are clearly posting their information practices and privacy policies." The letter adds that Commission staff will be looking to see whether Web sites are honoring consumers' privacy preferences.

A follow-up report on these online consumer privacy issues will be submitted to Congress on or before June 1, 1998. "Our recommendations, if any, will take into account whether the initial efforts demonstrated at the Workshop are translated into broader industry progress toward effective self-regulation," the Commission said.

Children's Online Privacy

The Workshop revealed that online information collection from children poses unique problems. Discussion at the Workshop produced important information about: parents' attitudes about children's privacy concerns; Web sites' information collection practices; industry proposals and technological responses. The Commission's letter to Congress presents a summary of the survey data presented at the Workshop and concludes that "[i]nformation presented at the Workshop indicates that numerous Web sites are collecting a variety of personal information from children without providing effective notice to parents, although there was less information about how and in what form the data is used once collected." The testimony at the Workshop from the FBI and Justice Department also revealed that online activities that allow children to disclose personal information are "rapidly becoming one of the most prevalent sources used by predators to identify and contact children," the letter states.

Recently released self-regulatory guidelines are the beginning of an industry effort to educate Web sites on collection and use of children's information. The Commission points out in its letter, however, that while the guidelines do require notice and some choice over disclosure of personal information to third parties, "the guidelines do not make clear what specific steps would satisfy these obligations." In addition, the letter noted that the "extent and speed" of compliance are essential elements in analyzing whether the government should act. According to the letter, "the staff will continue to pursue a dialogue with industry about the desirability of FTC guidelines in the area of children's online privacy."

The Commission also reported on the importance and development of technological *tools to protect children's privacy online noting that the effectiveness of these tools "will depend on their widespread adoption by industry and parents."*

In order to address concerns about online information collection practices from children, the Commission said that its staff will continue to review these practices by commercial Web sites in order to ascertain if any are engaging in deceptive or unfair practices that would be illegal under the FTC Act. The FTC's Bureau of Consumer Protection's response to a petition from the Center for Media Education provided guidance to the industry with respect to what would constitute deceptive or unfair collection practices from children online. (See FTC News Release dated July 16.)

The letter also states that the Commission staff will continue to monitor and assess self-regulatory efforts, as well as technological responses to these concerns. The June 1998 report to Congress will analyze the "percentage of sites providing notice to parents, whether the notice meets the criteria set forth in the staff's response letter to CME, what information is being collected from children, and how Web sites are using this information." Finally, the Commission pledged to work with all interested parties in developing education materials for parents and children regarding children's online privacy protections. The need to educate parents was deemed an important goal of the participants at the Workshop.

The Direct Marketing Association

The Direct Marketing Association (www.the-dma.org) has historically taken the initiative to give consumers a way to *opt out* of marketing. The organization is an advocate of self-regulation and has taken these steps in order to prevent government intervention. The DMA created the Mail Preference and Telephone Preference Services to enable consumers to remove their names from nonprofit and commercial marketing lists. It plans to create a similar service for online marketing called the e-Mail Preference Service (e-MPS). Here is an excerpt from its online privacy guidelines:

> **Online notice and opt out**. All marketers operating online sites, whether or not they collect personal information on line from individuals, should make available to consumers their information practices in a prominent place. Marketers sharing personal information collected on line should furnish individuals with an opportunity to prohibit the disclosure of such information.

> **Unsolicited marketing e-mail**. Online solicitations should be posted to newsgroups, bulletin boards, and chat rooms only when consistent with the forum's stated policies. To facilitate adherence to this principle, forum operators should publicize their policies regarding solicitations in their forums. For example, "We would like to send offers for valuable services and products that may be of interest to consumers." Marketers should inquire about the

forum's policies before directing online e-mail solicitations to the forum. Online e-mail solicitations should be clearly identified as solicitations and should disclose the marketer's identity. Marketers using e-mail should furnish consumers with whom they do not have an established business relationship with notice and a mechanism through which they can notify the marketer that they do not wish to receive future online solicitations. Marketers using e-mail should furnish consumers with whom they have an established business relationship with notice and a mechanism through which they can request that the marketer suppress their e-mail addresses from lists or databases rented, sold, or exchanged for online solicitation purposes.

Online data collection from or about children. Marketers should be sensitive to parents' concerns about the collection of their children's names, addresses, or other similar information, and should support the ability of parents to limit the collection of such data for marketing purposes through notice and opt-out. Marketers should encourage children to consult with their parents before furnishing data. Marketers should also support industry and other efforts to help educate parents about ways to protect their children's privacy online, including informing them about software tools and parental access controls that prevent their children from disclosing their name, address, or other personal information.

For additional information and updates visit their Web site.

Recommendations

The common theme of the online industry is self-regulation. Everyone involved prefers to build the trust with their online audience instead of government legislation. For Web marketers, there is no single solution to preserve online privacy while enabling one-to-one online marketing. There are common beliefs that will help a one-to-one Web marketer succeed in protecting his or her customers' privacy. Web marketers who ask for too much information will be suspect. People are savvy and they can figure out if the information you are asking for is related to your business. The following is a sample of potential online privacy solutions.

Addressing Online Privacy Directly

Jupiter Communications (www.jup.com) has these recommendations for preserving the balance between online privacy and building relationships with consumers:

Online marketers should offer more for less in exchange for their personal information. Online marketers should offer incentives in exchange for accurate information and permission to use it.

Online marketers need to come together to agree upon and promote the acceptance and usage of privacy standards. A unified approach will give the industry a better chance to enable self-regulation and minimize negative media reporting.

The privacy issue gives Web marketers a window of opportunity to build deep relationships with consumers. Providing a privacy policy and giving users knowledge of how the information is used will build trust.

Brands that have already established *offline* trust will have an advantage of establishing online trust. Web-based companies can also build new brands and trust if they go above and beyond in addressing their users' trust.

Informed Consent

Since its creation, the Web has had its own culture that has two important characteristics: freedom of speech and choice. As evidence of the controversy around privacy on the Internet, Web users want more choice over what marketing messages they receive on line. With television, magazine, telemarketing, and direct mail, people do not have ultimate control over the marketing messages they receive. In these traditional formats, customers can exert some control and choice. They can change the channel on the television when a commercial is broadcast. People can remove themselves from a direct-mailing list. On the Internet, consumers are seeking a higher degree of control. They want to make the initial choice of whether they receive commercial marketing messages, or at least easily remove themselves from an e-mail list, or simply ignore advertising by not clicking on the online ad. At the same time, many people have elected to join free e-mail or Internet services in exchange for viewing and responding to online advertisements. The online audience will do this if they perceive they are receiving more in return for their effort in participating in online advertising. All of this comes down to the basic request of online users: informed consent.

In an interview with *WebWeek* magazine (June 12, 1997), David Sobel, legal counsel for Electronic Privacy Information Center (EPIC) stated, "Surreptitious collection [of personal information] under any circumstances is reprehensible, and if I had my way, there would be legal restrictions on the ability of sites to do that. But when information is knowingly provided, it's just a question of getting consent of the individual to use it for the purpose it's going to be used for." In its article, "Surfer Beware: Personal Privacy and the Internet," EPIC had these recommendations:

- Web sites should make available a privacy policy that is easy to find. Ideally the policy should be accessible from the homepage by looking for the word "privacy."

- Privacy policies should state clearly how and when personal information is collected.

- Web sites should make it possible for individuals to get access to their own data.

- Cookie transactions should be more transparent. (Users should know when cookies are activated.)

- Web sites should continue to support anonymous access for Internet users.

Many advocates like EPIC would like users to have control over online marketing messages and would like to go as far as letting users actively participate in controlling, accessing, and modifying the type of information that is being collected by Web marketers. Privacy advocates also promote anonymity as the ultimate way to protect privacy, but this may be limiting to most one-to-one Web marketers, even if these marketers never intend to sell their users' information.

Offering Incentives

One common philosophy that is evolving to balance the desires of Web marketers and online users is that there be a fair *value exchange*, a concept promoted by the FireFly (www.firefly.net) online community, between the information that users provide and what is given to users by Web marketers for the information. One way to achieve an optimum value exchange is to offer incentives. FreeRide and HotMail have already established successful advertiser-supported online businesses where they exchange free services in exchange for the user profiles they collect. Incentives can include

Protecting privacy. This can be one of the strongest incentives for online customers who are very conservative or sensitive about their privacy. If you are collecting information to serve your customers better, and have no need to sell their information to third parties, then you can build immediate trust among your customers or users by prominently displaying these types of privacy policies.

Personalized information that is useful. Web sites that have built businesses that primarily focus on delivering customized information can strike a successful balance between privacy and value, as long as the information the user provides does not exceed the perceived value of the information received.

Discounted or free products or services. Software companies have widely used incentives such as free technical support, free upgrades, and discounts on related products or services in exchange for getting customers to fill out product registration forms. This can be an effective tool that provides something that a customer already values: your company and its offerings. In addition to trust, it can build loyalty.

Freebies. People enjoy receiving something for free, as long as it doesn't have too high of an *intangible* cost. In other words, customers will not give away their personal information just to receive something for free. There is always a cost, even if it is not tangible (i.e., money, time), associated with free services and products.

One-to-One Marketing Gurus Promote Privacy Practices

In their second book together, *Enterprise One to One*: *Tools for Competing in the Interactive Age*, Peppers and Rogers make recommendations on how to approach the delicate balance of obtaining customer profile information while protecting the customer's privacy. Here is an excerpt from the book on how to establish a "Privacy Bill of Rights":

"The Interactive Age could easily become the Age of Privacy Invasion. Companies already have problems getting their own customers to send in warranty registration cards for fear that they will be deluged with more mail. How can the 1:1 enterprise ever expect even its best customers to participate willingly in a series of more and more intimate dialogues if it can't assure them that their privacy will be respected? Customers whose privacy is violated—or customers who simply don't feel they have control over their own information—are not likely to become willing participants in any dialogue interactions.

If your firm is going into the business of creating relationships with customers based on individual information, you needed to adopt an explicit privacy policy early on—then publicize it, and use it. The Privacy Bill of Rights should spell out:

- The kind of information generally need from customers.

- Any benefits customers will enjoy from the enterprise's use of this individual information.

- The specific things the enterprise will never do with individual information.

- An individual's options for directing the enterprise to not use or disclose certain kinds of information.

- Any events that might precipitate a notification to the customer by the enterprise.

Privacy Statements and Policies

Implementing privacy practices and formulating policies is still new, but there will come a time when everyone who collects information—directly or indirectly—will have a privacy initiative, especially one-to-one Web marketers. Samples of current online privacy policies are shown in the sections following.

IBM

IBM (www.ibm.com) is a worldwide computer hardware and software company. Here are their privacy policies as shown on their Web site, which are directly available from a link on their Web site:

Information on IBM Homepage Privacy Practices

At IBM, we intend to give you as much control as possible over your personal information. In general, you can surf this site (www.ibm.com) without telling us who you are or revealing any information about yourself. There are times, however, when we may need information from you, such as your name and address. It is our intent to let you know before we collect personal information from you on the Internet.

If you choose to give us personal information via the Internet that we and our business partners may need—to correspond with you, process an order, or provide you with a subscription, for example—you can be assured that IBM will let you know how we will use such information. If you tell us that you do not wish to have this information distributed to others, or if you tell us that you do not wish to receive additional information from us or our business partners, we will respect your wishes.

We are implementing these practices for the IBM Corporate Homepage. We are also instructing our employees around the world to include information on privacy practices on each IBM Web site, tailored to what each site does and reflecting the practices outlined there.

IBM is also supporting the development of some promising tools that will let you manage and control the release of your personal information wherever you go on the Internet. We'll soon be sharing information with you about efforts under way in organizations such as the World Wide Web Consortium and TRUSTe.

If you have any questions about our privacy practices, you can contact us at mailto:askibm@vnet.ibm.com.

An easily accessible and easy-to-understand privacy policy is key to establishing your online users' trust. But don't stop there. You will want to be up front with your Web users as to what you plan to do with the information you are receiving from them.

Privacy Branding

TRUSTe (www.truste.orge) is a nonprofit organization that was founded by the Electronic Frontier Foundation (www.eff.org) and CommerceNet (www.commerce.net) to promote online privacy. TRUSTe created a branding program that provides a privacy labeling system to inform online users of what will be done with the information that is collected by a site, who the information will be shared with, and how the personal information will be used by other parties. TRUSTe created *trustmarks* that enable users to make an informed decision on whether or not they will disclose their personal information to the Web site. As stated on the TRUSTe Web site, trustmarks include:

No Exchange. If a site bears the No Exchange trustmark, it informs users that they will be completely anonymous as they view a site—no personal data is being collected about users or shared with any other party. Specifically, this trustmark signifies that:

—The site is not tracking the user, or retaining any individual data about the user.

—The site is not asking the user for personally identifiable information.

—The site is not providing a form or mailto that would identify the user's e-mail address.

—The site is not monitoring chat or bulletin boards.

The No Exchange trustmark means that your personally identifiable information will not be collected by the site. The one exception is IP addresses, which are automatically collected by Web sites. Under No Exchange, IP addresses may be collected, but never linked to any other information, or used by the site.

1-to-1 Exchange. The 1-to-1 Exchange trustmark means user information will be kept solely within the organization to deal with him or her on a one-to-one basis. User information will not be transferred, shared with, or sold to any third parties. A site qualifies for 1-to-1 Exchange if the site shares information with third parties used in the distribution chain and if there is an agreement in place that prohibits the intermediary from using the information for anything other than to complete the original transaction.

3rd Party Exchange. If a site bears the 3rd Party Exchange trustmark, it signifies to users that a site will exchange or pass information to third parties. It does not mean a site will necessarily sell the information. 3rd Party Exchange simply means that the information is going beyond the site's sphere of influence. It is important for users to know that many 3rd Party Exchange sites may need to pass personally identifiable information to shipping agents, clearinghouses, other businesses, distributors, nonlicensed divisions of a company, credit card companies, and banks in order to complete the distribution chain. As a user, you should click the TRUSTe mark and read the privacy statement so you are aware of what is being done with your information. If you have further questions about the privacy statement, the site coordinator's e-mail address is posted on the privacy statement.

Privacy Standards and Technologies

There are many initiatives and technologies emerging for the protection of privacy and for enabling the collection of user information. To date there are three initiatives that will govern the future of privacy practices and technologies: the Platform for Privacy Preferences Project, the Open Profile Standard, and the Internet Engineering Task Forces' standards for cookie technology.

IETF Standards on Cookies

The Internet Engineering Task Force (www.ietf.org) created a proposal, "RFC 2109 State Management Mechanism," to create industry standards on the use of cookie technology. The proposal was intended to give users more control over which cookies would be accepted. This standard was to be incorporated in the next version of Web browsers such as version 4.0 of Microsoft Internet Explorer and Netscape Navigator. The proposal required browsers to notify users of impending cookies and allow them to accept or reject them—as the default. Users would be able to block all cookies, accept cookies from preferred sites, delete cookies after accepting them, as well as block cookies from third parties (e.g., Web banner advertisements).

The IETF proposal created a stir in the industry and many Web marketers felt that this was the wrong reaction to the cookie controversy. In April 1997 the Association for Online Professionals (www.aop.org) wrote a letter to the IETF urging them to reconsider their proposal because of the

- Potential loss of services from online services that rely on cookies for passwords, preferences, etc.
- Loss of electronic commerce that rely on cookies, including some shopping cart methods.
- Loss of one of the major methods to analyze online advertising effectiveness.

- Large investment of time hundreds of thousands of Web sites will incur in reprogramming.

In mid 1997, Netscape decided not to implement these standards in version 4.0 of the Navigator Web browser and the World Wide Web Consortium has begun to propose amendments to the IETF proposal.

Platform for Privacy Preferences Project (P3P)

The World Wide Web Consortium (www.w3c.org), also known as W3C, is a guiding organization that is led by Tim Berners-Lee—the creator of the Web—and is dedicated to the creation of common protocols as the Web evolves. The W3C has created the Platform for Privacy Preferences Project (P3P) to ensure there are common privacy practices and technology protocols that enable Web marketers to collect user preference and personal information while giving online users choice in the collection process. The P3P project's goals are to establish a vocabulary and architecture for expressing privacy practices and for collecting user profile information. This is known as their *privacy assertion and transportation mechanism*. P3P promotes the idea of *informed consent* in order to establish trust between the user and the Web marketer and the idea that protocols can be at the heart of privacy statements and data collection technologies.

P3P-enabled technologies will provide the user with the choice of whether he or she wants to be involved in data collection or not. Once there is a privacy agreement between the user and the Web site owner, then information can be captured in a secure manner, while informing the user of how the data will be used. P3P also works in conjunction with other initiatives and technologies such as cookies and the Open Profile Standard (OPS) discussed next.

Open Profile Standard (OPS)

The Open Profile Standard (OPS), a standard created by Netscape, FireFly, and VeriSign, proposes a way to exchange user profile information. OPS involves practices to store and release—with the user's permission—user information that is often requested by Web sites. The standard gives users' control over their user profile, including what information is stored and where the information is disclosed. The user profile information is collected and managed in an encrypted and secure way. There are three areas that are addressed with the OPS initiative:

Permissions management. These are constraints that allow or prevent access or modification of profile information.

Standard attributes. Provides for a common information foundation for identification, demographic, numeric, personal, contact, currency, and user agent preference information.

Transaction logging. Logs fulfill user requests and context of online transactions. It will also log the exchange of user information with third parties.

For additional information, visit the World Wide Web Consortium's Web site at www.w3c.org and on FireFly's Web site at people.firefly.com/OPS/QandA.html.

Online Privacy Resources

As the online privacy issue continues to unfold, you may want to monitor these privacy resources on the Web:

Direct Marketing Association	www.the-dma.org
Electronic Frontier Foundation	www.eff.org
Electronic Privacy Information Center	www.epic.org
Federal Trade Commission	www.ftc.gov
TRUSTe	www.truste.org
World Wide Web Consortium	www.w3c.org

Chapter 12, "The One-to-One Web Marketing Future," outlines the future of one-to-one marketing on the Web. Most of the technologies and techniques already covered in this book are still relatively new and there is a bright future for highly targeted and one-to-one communications over the Internet. The future of one-to-one Web marketing will also resonate across traditional marketing methods as well. Marketing in cyberspace is teaching all of us marketers how to take a fresh look at how we market, sell, and service in the real world.

THE ONE-TO-ONE WEB MARKETING FUTURE

"In the real-time communities of cyberspace, we are dwellers on the threshold between the real and virtual, unsure of our footing, inventing ourselves as we go along."

Sherry Turkle, *Life on the Screen: Identity in the Age of the Internet* (1997, Touchstone Books)

Although the always-open-for-business World Wide Web is still a new phenomenon, we are looking ahead to a way to communicate that was never before conceivable. The Web is teaching us new ways to think and apply our marketing methods. We will move from trying to apply physical world (a.k.a. RL—real life) conventions to the Web, to naturally letting the uniqueness of the Web paradigm show us new ways of interacting and marketing.

Marketing is about *markets*—communicating with, selling, and servicing them. We have moved from mass marketing to direct marketing, and now to one-to-one marketing. One-to-one marketing is being facilitated by the decreasing cost of applying technology and intelligent data to marketing, enabling us to develop a targeted message, identify target markets and even individuals, and transmit or put that specific message in front of the right person at the right time. Then we can use technology to measure response from the various target markets and even individuals. This is definitely marketing nirvana! The Internet brings a whole world of numerous target markets to our fingertips. Technology allows us to reach out and touch each person on the Web.

The Web is already teaching us a new way to communicate with our markets—interactively. We are now taking what we are experiencing and learning on the Web to the physical world. Marketers are integrating the physical world to the Web and, more importantly, vice versa. Marketers can now apply one-to-one Web marketing to other communications vehicles such as direct mail where customized catalogs are created using user preferences and purchase histories to create a personalized catalog of products and services that are tailored to that particular customer. This chapter gives a sneak peek into what is possible in the next generation of marketing on the Web, one-to-one Web marketing, and the future of one-to-one communications on and off the Web.

One-to-One Possibilities

In this book, we discuss the principles of relationship, one-to-one, and loyalty marketing and how the many leading-edge technologies on the Web can leverage these ideas. According to Peppers and Rogers, the resident one-to-one marketing gurus, we are in the age of mass customization where we can provide information, products, and services that are tailored to each customer. Here are some real-life examples:

Delany Linen Service. The first sentence of their company description on their Web site reads, "DELANEY LINEN SERVICE is a 54-year-old company with headquarters in Watertown, MA. Delaney is small enough to provide high-quality customized and personalized service, but large enough to meet all of your uniform and work garment needs." They provide a specialized service to allow companies to customize uniforms including company name, employee name, special stitching such as an extra pocket, and special requirements such as unique trim or garment cut (www.alluniforms.com).

Levi Strauss & Company's Personal Pair. This service is provided by Levi's retail stores, where the store customer service representatives take customer measurements in order to create custom jeans for customers. Once the representative measures the customer's waist, inseam, hips, and rise, the rep inputs the information in a retail touchscreen computer to determine which of the over 500 Levi's jean prototypes best fits the customer. The information is then sent to a Levi's factory where the customer's jeans are made in a few weeks (www.levi.com).

Lands' End Specialty Shopper. Lands' End is a successful mail-order clothing catalog. The company offers a free personalized service, called the Specialty Shopper, via phone or e-mail. There are dedicated customer service representatives that help customers with their clothes shopping with assistance such as coordinating outfits or whole wardrobes, offering fabric care tips, helping with gift selections, keeping files on customers' sizes, tastes, past purchases, even addresses and credit card numbers for future reference. Just imagine if Lands' End provided this free service in real-time using chat or a database-driven system on the Web (www.landsend.com)?

MySki. This company creates custom snow skis for anyone from beginner skiers to expert skiers. It also facilitates the process of customizing and ordering skis with its Web site. MySki provides an Online Ski Selector and Customization System where customers can interact and provide their specifications to the company. Customers can also view the ski in 3-D virtual reality (www.myski.com).

Perkins Engines. VarityPerkins in England is a leading manufacturer of engines that produces over 100,000 engines per year. It developed the 1000 Series engine as "an engine with 1 trillion possibilities." The diesel engine was designed to be tailor-made to customer specifications. The engines are designed for the customer using a paperless, fully CAD process (www.varityperkins.co.uk).

Used Sail Database. This company has a database of over 5000 boat sails. They will search their database to find a sail that is the closest to the customer's specification. They will also provide sail cutting and alteration services to create a custom sail (www.usedsale.com).

In a simple sense, this one-to-one service is enabled by technology—databases and specialized manufacturing or delivery systems. However, the magic comes with the imagination of the marketer and customer service experts. We are very excited to see this kind of personalization come to the Web, and to be facilitated by the Web. The rest of this chapter is dedicated to seeing what the future holds for each one-to-one Web marketing technology.

When contemplating your one-to-one strategy, think of these words from David Packard, cofounder of Hewlett-Packard:

> *"The first principle of management is that the driving force for the development of new products is not technology, not money, but the imagination of people."*

The Future of One-to-One Web Site Interactivity

As bandwidth and creativity continue to grow on the Internet, Web site interactivity will become just that: more interactive. Advances in animation, 3-D/virtual reality, audio, video, and databases will allow marketers to present a different interactive Web experience for each individual user. Interactivity will become more purposeful, rather than being flashy. It will go beyond the purpose of attracting users, to engaging users. It will help customers *bond* with the site and the company. With the goal of getting users to visit your site more often and to stay longer, interactivity can be the key.

The Future of One-to-One E-Mail

Once the spam controversy fades into the cyberhorizon, e-mail will become a marketing staple. Today, marketers can send one-to-one e-mail messages that contain HTML, graphics, video, audio, and hyperlinks. If you have a newer version of an e-mail program, then you probably have received e-mail that contains content that looks as if you are looking into your Web browser. With the integration of databases and schedulers, personalized and automated e-mail will be happily received by your users because it provides content and advertising that they prefer to get, because they are getting something of value to them.

John Funk, founder of InfoBeat—the popular e-mail news service that delivers more than 3 million e-mail messages each day (www.infobeat.com)—sees a bright future for e-mail marketing: "E-mail will continue to evolve from being a personal communications tool to a company-to-customer communications tool. It has the ability to enhance and cement the relationship. Databases and data mining will be used to remember each individual user, and predict and recommend products and services that customers will buy. This process will be valued by the customer." Funk also has an important message about spam. "Spam is an uneducated and unthoughtful method to marketing. It may be able to build a customer database, but it cannot build relationships with customers like solicited e-mail can." Funk believes that spam is the equivalent of the snake oil salesman that comes to town, sells products, and makes a quick exit. Spam is not a good practice for one-to-one Web marketers who will need to take a long-term stance that the process forming loyal and profitable relationships requires. Funk has created a service bureau that companies can use to take advantage of their patented e-mail technology and their one-to-one marketing expertise.

The Future of One-to-One Web Site Personalization

In addition to sophisticated Web site personalization, the future of one-to-one Web site personalization will be the integration of offline processes to the Web. There will be more availability of other data to the Web site in real time. There will be an enhanced ability for customers to access their own data and account information in order to modify preferences and track their transaction history. Web sites will also become part of the entire marketing, sales, and service process. Just imagine allowing users to browse through an online product catalog and dial up a service representative in a call center using voice and video over the Web. Web site interaction can also be taken to offline activities, such as identifying an online customer when he or she comes into your retail store or to a local seminar. Imagine being able to instruct your favorite company to create customer electronic and print catalogs that are tailored to your preferences and purchases. A company could use the Web and other data to create one-to-one electronic and physical mailers that contain only information pertinent to each user's need.

The Future of One-to-One Push

Push is a significant force on the Internet. Applications vary from news and information delivery to corporate intranets chock full of employee news and personnel information. The beauty of push will be the convenient ability to push information to users without them firing up their Web browser. Push will incorporate intelligence to push out only new content. Push will push out entertainment, information, advertising, software applications and updates, and more. PointCast started the revolution that will become a regular way to communicate with users. Because of the use of databases, push communications can be targeted. With the tripling of bandwidth from year to year, push will become more prevalent than today. As Paul Boutin said in Webmonkey-Geek Talk (www.hotwired.com/webmonkey/), "Push media isn't really the result of new technical specs or breakthroughs in software. It's the result of rethinking the way we interact with the content our networks can already deliver." That is really how one-to-one Web marketing fits into all of this. Marketers need to rethink how to deliver their messages to their customers one at a time, and if implemented correctly, push can be the way to get that message across.

The Future of One-to-One Community

In their 1997 book, *NetGain* (Harvard Business School Press), John Hagel and Arthur Armstrong described how online communities will redefine markets by becoming the markets. Communities will move from being a novel way to interact among users to becoming a standard feature on many corporations' Web sites as a way to create a dialog with customers. For example, Manufacturing Marketplace (www.manufacturing.net) is a supersite dedicated to engineering, design, purchasing, logistics, and distribution professionals. The site includes an online community with discussion forums, newsgroups, and other community-related content and activities. Here is an excerpt from Hagel and Armstrong's book about the future of virtual communities:

> *"Virtual communities are likely to set in motion a broad range of changes in today's business landscape. By shifting the emphasis from the producer's perspective to the customer's, communities will reshape market and industry structures. By evening out information asymmetries, they will help drive the expansion of markets. By making markets more efficient, they'll disseminate information more widely...By giving rise to a wave of electronic start-ups across a broad spectrum of industries, they will challenge the established position of some of today's largest corporations."*

The Future of One-to-One Web Presentation and Conferencing

The two main advancements that will need to take place in order for Web presentations and conferencing to be commonplace are improvements in Internet transmission bandwidth and improvements in video and audio technologies. These advancements will make Web conferencing closer to real-life meetings without delay and poor communications or resolution. Today corporations with high-speed networks are taking advantage of high-quality videoconferencing. There will be the emergence of virtual seminars and trade shows with real-time presentations that allow audience participation including chat, voice, and whiteboard capabilities. Of course, there will still be the need for face-to-face meetings despite the impressive future possibilities of Web conferencing.

The Future of One-to-One Advertising and Promotion

Increased interactivity, convenient transactions, and audience audits will mark the future of online advertising and promotion. Bandwidth and technology enhancements will enable advertisers to create interactive brand games such as online scratch-n-win and multiplayer contests; target consumers by their street address; and incorporate response and transaction within the online ad itself. Future ads will look like television ads, sound like radio ads, and behave like direct mail, but with a one-to-one orientation. Ads will not be thought of as annoying by the online audience because they will be targeted to their needs and preferences—ads will be convenient and informative. All of the mystery surrounding audience, impressions, and click-through measurement will be solved by advertising management software and by such companies as the Audit Bureau of Circulation (www.accessabc.com), which will verify Web site demographics and traffic.

The Future of One-to-One Web Site Tracking and Analysis

Web site tracking and traffic analysis will become more useful in the future. There is a lot of Web server data being generated by logging tools, but what does it mean? The future of tracking and traffic analysis will integrate user data and log data. Since the majority of sites in the future will be database driven, log analysis and reporting tools will have to support databases in addition to Web server activity. This will help move from *inferring* to *knowing*. To refit a golden rule for when we cross the street to apply it to Web marketing: Listen, look, and learn. We will *listen* to our customers with user-profile building and interactive communications. Then we will *look* and observe what our customers are doing on our Web site. The combination of listen and look is the best way to *learn* more about your customers. What users tell us about themselves alone is insufficient. What we observe in our site traffic logs and reports alone is insufficient. The combination is the most powerful way to turn data into information, and to turn information into knowledge.

The Future of One-to-One Integration

Databases will become the norm rather than the exception on the Web. Clearly, if the primary reason for your existence is electronic commerce, then databases are of critical importance. Web-to-database integration will help you personalize content, but the true power of integration lies in enabling more sophisticated processes such as commerce, account management, and customer support, including access to a plethora of product and service information and online self-help applications. FedEx (www.fedex.com) and Amazon.com (www.amazon.com) are just two of the pioneers that take Web-database integration to the outer limits. To see one example of a company leveraging databases on the Web to serve a few different customer types (e.g., direct customers, partners, and resellers), visit Cisco Systems' site at www.cisco.com.

Leading Edge One-to-One

One-to-one marketing on the Web is not simply a possibility, it is a reality. Throughout this book you have seen many examples of how one-to-one marketing and communications is occurring. Just for fun, we have put together a few examples of the one-to-one computing future on the Internet using a combination of online and offline vehicles.

Convergence. In a keynote speech at Internet World Summer 1997, Eric Schmidt, CEO of Novell, predicted networks would be designed for mobility, servers would be self-configuring, and all telephones will have IP addresses. We are seeing the convergence of voice, data, video, and wireless communications on the Internet and the creation of personal devices that give users access to the Internet via phones, personal digital assistants (PDAs), set-top boxes, cable boxes, Web television, Internet call center integration, and more. Nortel has created a Java phone that allows customers to make phone calls and access the Internet (www.nortel.com).

Digital signatures. Digital signatures are an *electronic simulation* of a handwritten signature. It is not a handwritten signature scanned into a computer, but a digital identification that is attached to messages being sent over the Internet. It allows one person to send a highly secure message to a recipient who will be assured that the message is not a forgery. Digital signatures are made when a message is encrypted incorporating a private and unique digital key (www.w3.org/Security/DSig/Overview.html).

Home automation and personal robots. Just like Star Trek—infrared sensors and personal computers that operate thermostats and home appliances. People can input their preferences such as home temperature, the time when the coffeemaker starts brewing the morning coffee, and playing favorite music in the CD player. Sensors can activate systems when the homeowner comes into his or her living room to turn on lights at the preferred brightness. It won't be too far into the future when many of us can have our own personal robot scurrying around the house or yard vacuuming the house or mowing the lawn.

Internet call centers. Fast becoming a reality, customers who are Web shopping can interact with customer service representatives. Sometimes users need more personal assistance with their online purchases than the Web site can provide. Depending on the sophistication of the product or service, the user may want to contact or be contacted by a real live human, without having to call an 800 number. People are using the Web instead of going to a retail store or calling an order number, so they do not want to have to call people to purchase items on the Web. Here is just a sample of companies providing these solutions: AT&T (www.att.com/easycommerce/wss/), eFusion (www.efusion.com), Lucent (www.lucent.com/BusinessWorks/callcenter/brochures/icc_page.html), Nortel (www.nortel.com), Venturian (www.home.venturian.com), and WebLine Communications (www.webline.com).

Local markets. One of the hot growth areas for online advertising is the local market. National, regional, and local advertisers can target messages as specifically as a particular postal or zip code. The popular directory CitySearch (www.citysearch.com) allows users to select particular businesses and retailers in their neighborhood to send e-mail promotions.

Micropayments. There is a lot of activity in the area of micropayments. Micropayments allow users to pay for many items on line by use and in very small increments (i.e., cents). The Music Boulevard Web site (www.musicboulevard.com) allows customers to pay for one song at a time with its e_mod singles service. Users can download a song and pay as little as 99 cents. Micropayments will allow people to make one-to-one online transactions.

NetHead Red. Digital Equipment Corporation (www.digital.com) created a persona to showcase its DECface software technology. The smart kiosk technology first appeared in the Harvard Square cybercafé, CyberSmith (www.cybersmith.com), as NetHead Red. The smart kiosk can interact with users and passersby by tracking people's movements. NetHead Red follows people with eye and head movement and initiates conversation. NetHead Red is a real-time, customizable, synthetic, talking head that syncronizes facial expressions and lip movements to computer-generated speech. NetHead Red also exhibits emotion with humanlike expressions. The technology is what Digital calls the combination of speech recognition, machine *vision*, and *anywhere* wireless communications.

Personal Area Network (PAN). IBM is working on a Personal Area Network technology that allows two people to exchange information simply by exchanging hands. Each person has a personally identified PAN card, containing a transmitter and receiver, and their handshake completes the circuit. The information is then transferred to each person's computer. Because the human body has a natural ability to conduct electrical current, PAN can use the body to transmit the information. IBM is exploring other applications, including the ability for people to interact with household appliances and other digital products using their PAN cards. Household appliances such as stereos and toaster ovens can respond to personal preferences stored in the PAN card (www.ibm.com).

Shopping agents. Using user profiles and intelligent agents (a.k.a bots), there is a growing service on the Internet of shopping agents that will scour Web sites to find products and services on behalf of users. Some of the early entrants include BargainFinder from Anderson Consulting (www.ac.com), Jango from Netbot (www.jango.com), RoboShopper from RoboShopper International (www.roboshopper.com), and Shopping Explorer from Dunstan Thomas (www.shoppingexplorer.com).

Smart cards. Imagine carrying one smart card for all of those cards bulking up your wallet—ATM card, credit cards, phone cards, library card, driver's license, and so forth. It might seem scary, but it could also be extremely convenient to carry your personal information on a single card.

Wearable personal computers. The Massachusetts Institute of Technology's Media Lab is creating wearable computers. Imagine reading your e-mail while you are strolling down the street or in the cab on your way to the airport. M.I.T. has been doing research on creating wearable computers and integrating computing within clothing. Wearable computers contain batteries, digital cellular modem and Internet access, and the Twiddler, which is a one-handed keyboard and mouse. *Wearables* can store information such as phone numbers and notes and allow real-time messaging (media.mit.edu, wearables.www.media.mit.edu/projects/wearables/).

The Internet has been an exciting phenomenon to watch and experience so far, and it has an exciting future. We hope that you have found our book to be a useful one-to-one Web marketing tool. Please come visit our Web site, One-to-One Web Marketing Online, at www.1to1web.com to see the Web marketing discipline evolve. We wish you success in your cybermarketing efforts. Good luck!

INDEX

Children's online privacy, 346-347
Churn, 66
Cinema U, 35, 36
CIOs. *See* Chief Information Officers
CitySearch, 69
Classes, 263-264
Classification and Regression Trees (CART), 322
Clickthroughs, 242, 250
Client/partner education. *See* One-to-one community
Clusters, 281
    identification. *See* Customers; Individuals
C|Net, 68, 127, 193, 253, 263
CNN News, 103, 125, 127, 128, 133
Coalition Against Unsolicited Commercial E-Mail, 48, 55
Collaborative filtering, 14, 99
Comma Separated Value (CSV), 325, 327
Commerce, 315-316
    sites, 253
Commerce-based Web server, 333
CommerceNet, 353
Commercial e-mail. *See* Unsolicited commercial e-mail
Commercial online services, 154
Commercial orientation, 169, 175-182
Communications. *See* Content/communications; Salesforce communications conflict, elimination, 306
Community. *See* Bulletin board; Corporate communities; One-to-one web; Personalized community applications. *See* Community/products
    benefits. *See* One-to-one community
    business model. *See* One-to-one community; Virtual community

business model
    competition, 167
    content, 167-168
    control, 168
    controversies, 166-168
    definition, 160-163
    fantasy, 160, 163
    future, 183-187
    impact. *See* Internet
    implementation ideas, 182-183
    interaction, needs, 160
    interest, 160-161
    Marketing, 137
    members, 167-168
    relationship, 160, 161-163
    reputation, 166-167
    resources, 183
    sites, 257
    starting, 164
    transaction, 160, 163
Community/products, applications, 168-182
    focus, 168-171
Compassware, InfoMagnet, 140, 143
Competing publishers/vendors, access, 169, 175
Competitive rules, 8
CompuServe, 154, 273
Computer identification, cookie usage, 285-287
Computerized databases, 345
Conferencing. *See* Chat conferencing; Internet-based conferencing; One-to-one community; One-to-one web; Organizations; Training; World Wide Web
    benefits. *See* One-to-one web
    future. *See* One-to-one web
    technology. *See* One-to-one web
Consensual marketing, 4-5
Consumer
    confidence

recommendations, 348-351
solutions, 343-356
online privacy, 345-346
Consumer Internet Privacy Protection
Act of 1997, 343
Content. *See* Member-generated
content
creation, 313
management, 313-314
provider, 253
Content/communications, integration
capacity, 168, 171-173
Contests, 261-262, 263-264
Convergence, 363
Cookies, 108, 236-237, 252, 270, 340,
342-343. *See also* Bad cookie
cutter software, 236
file, 343
IETF standards, 354-355
limitations, 286
usage. *See* Computer identification
advantages, 285
Corporate communities, 159-160
Cost per thousand (CPM), 88, 230
CPM. *See* Cost per thousand
Credit card payments, processing,
330-333
Cross-platform solution, 45
Cross-sell related products, 305
Cross-selling, 85
Cross-selling/upselling. *See* Personalized
cross-selling/upselling
CSV. *See* Comma Separated Value
CU-*See*Me 3.0, 214
Customer Driven Strategy, 306
Customer-driven competition, 87
Customers, 196. *See also* Below-Zero cus-
tomers; Most Valuable Customers;
Second-Tier Customers
acquisition/retention, 7
agent, 166
applications, 148-149

cluster identification, RFM analysis
usage, 307-308
communication, 306
convenience, 8-9
databases, 108
development, 305
dialog, 8
feedback, 108-109
identification, 305
incentive, 8-9
loyalty, 85-86, 226
profitability, 86
referrals, 86
second chances, 86
recognition, 305
relationship, formation, 49-50
resource, 121
service, 39-41, 316-317. *See also*
Online customer service
personalization, 306
share, 7
support. *See* Online
tracking, 87
usage, 305
videoconferencing, 218
visits/purchases, increasing, 50-52
Customerization, ability, 165
Customer-to-Advertiser dialog, 226-227
Cyber Dialogue, 238
Cyberatlas, 124
Cybercitizen Report (1997), 31-32, 84
CyberGold, 264
CyberPromotions, 53

D
Data collection. *See* Online
Data mining, 14. *See also* One-to-one
web
definition, 319-322
products, 322-323
software tools, 322
techniques, 322

Electronic trash, 74
Elliptic Curve Cryptosystem (ECC), 329
E-mail, 124-125, 258, 324. *See also*
   Bounced back e-mails; Direct e-mail;
   HTML-based e-mails; HTML-
   enabled e-mail; One-to-one e-mail;
   Unsolicited commercial e-mail;
   Unsolicited marketing e-mail
   advertising
      benefits/costs, 77-78
      products/services, 78
      space purchasing, 77-78
   applications. *See* One-to-one e-mail
   future. *See* One-to-one e-mail
      lists. *See* Non-targeted e-mail
      lists
   marketers, 57, 76, 77
   marketing
      conducting, 56-60
      issues, 54-55
      relevancy, 57
   messages, writing, 58-60
   news service
      advertising space purchasing,
        77-78
      benefits/costs, 79
      products/services, 79-80
   newsletter service
      advertising space purchasing,
        77-78
      benefits/costs, 79
      products/services, 78
   provider, 57
   push, 74
   reach, 53
   reading, 59
   recommendations, 96
   related promotions, 77
   services, 56, 58. *See also* Free
      e-mail services
      management. *See* Personalized
      e-mail service
   writing. *See* Direct e-mail

Empathy, impact, 336
Embedded hyperlinks, 64
Enliven, 246
   Client, 45
Enterprise One to One, 8-9
Enterprise-wide systems, 318
EPIC. *See* Electronic Privacy
   Information Center
error_log, 270
ESPN, 127
Events/activities, 263
Excite, 83, 87, 253
Experience-based marketing, 6
Expert systems, 99
Explanatory presentation, 192
Extended Common Log File, 289
Extensible Markup Language (XML),
   314
Extranet, 129, 183
E-zines, 244

F

Fast interactivity, 22
Federal Trade Commission (FTC), 341,
   344-347
   Act, 345, 347
   guidelines, 346
Feedback. *See* Customers
   mechanisms, 8
Fields. *See* Address field; Date field;
   Method field; Size field; Status field;
   Time field
File size, 287
FireFly, 177, 181, 238, 337, 350
FirstFloor Smart Delivery, 129-130
Flame message, 224
Flash, 19
Flashing copy, 22
Format, 313
Free products/services, 350
Freebies, 350-351

videoconferencing, 211-217
   audio/video, 213
   brands, interaction, 213
   collaboration, 214
   hardware products, 215
   products, evaluation, 213-214
   setup, 213
   software products, 214-215
   technology overview, 212-213
   Years, 117
Internet Phone, 211
   Team Station, 215
Internet Protocol (IP), 123
   address, 226, 270-273, 285, 353
Internet Service Providers (ISPs), 53, 54,
   64, 123, 208, 252, 273, 277, 289
Internet-based collaborative techniques,
   192
Internet-based conferencing, 190
Internet-based customer service, 39-41
Internet-wide promotions, 263-265
Intersititals, 250-251. *See also* Animated
   interstitials
IntraExpress. *See* Diffusion
   business challenges, 146-148
Intranet, 182-183
   delivery, 129, 140-149
IP. *See* Internet Protocol
I/PRO, 181, 255, 293
   NetLine, 292-293
iQVC Goldrush, 261-262
ISDN search, 41
I-Server. *See* PointCast
ISPs. *See* Internet Service Providers
iVALS. *See* Internet
iVillage, 62, 64, 127, 175-177

J

Jack of All Trades, 42
Java, 19, 23, 45, 122, 128
   applets, 33, 37, 45, 163, 202

comparison. *See* Channel
   Definition Format
JavaScript, 122, 128
Job-tracking software, 21
JPEG, 278
Junkmail, 48
Junkmail.org, 54-55
Juno, 77
Jupiter Communications, 36, 45-46, 159,
   225, 227, 232, 251, 348

K

Knowledge Ability Ltd., 34
Knowledge-based marketing, 6
Known model, comparison. *See* Inferred
   model
Kodak Picture Network, 39, 40, 41

L

Lands' End Specialty Shopper, 358
Law of repeat purchases. *See* Repeat
   purchases
LCC. *See* School of Literature,
   Communication, and Culture
Leading edge. *See* One-to-one
   marketing
Leading-edge one-to-one, 363-365
Leads
   capturing/tracking, 295-298
   management. *See* Sales
Learning Relationship, 8, 9
   establishment, 120-121
Levi Strauss & Company's Personal Pair,
   358
Lifestyle-oriented interests, 239
Lifestyles, 335
Lifetime Value (LTV), 91
LikeMinds, 10
LiveLAN. *See* PictureTel
Local markets, 364

Prodigy, 154, 273

Productivity, 41

Products
applications. *See* Community/
products; Push
research, 306

Profile information, integration. *See*
Tracking/profile information

Profile-building process, 102

Profiling/personalization, 237-238

Profitability. *See* Customers

Profit-per-customer effect, 9

Progressive Networks, 181

Project tracking, 183

Promotion, 38-39. *See also* E-mail;
Internet-wide promotions; One-to-
one web
benefits. *See* One-to-one web
future. *See* One-to-one web
hurdles. *See* One-to-one web
networks/services. *See* Online

ProShare, 215, 218

Prospects, 195-196

Pull-down, 245

Purple Moon, 24-25

Push. *See* Dominance; E-mail
advertising, 257-258
benefits. *See* One-to-one push
building. *See* Applications
controversies. *See* One-to-one push
definition. *See* One-to-one push
delivery models, types, 128
evolution. *See* One-to-one push
first push, 125
future, 149-150
involvement. *See* One-to-one push
mechanism, 49
providing, 52-53
new push, 125-127
original push, 124-125
products, applications, 128-149
usage. *See* Healthcare providers;

House of Blues; Managed care
processing; Marketers

Q

QED, 185

QNews, 51

QoS. *See* Quality of Service

QTVR, 44

Quack, 153-154

QUALCOMM, 132

Quality of Service (QoS), 212

Quantum, 53

QuickCache, 131

QuickCam, 204, 213

Quicken, 28
Financial Network, 253

Quote.com, 51, 244, 253

R

RDBMS. *See* Relational Database

RDM. *See* Relational Database

Real-time voting, 220

Reality. *See* Perception/reality

Real-time processing, 324

RealVideo, 207

Receive-only mailing lists, 67-68

Recency, 307, 309

Recency, Frequency, Monetary (RFM)
analysis, 305, 307-308
usage. *See* Customers

Recommender, 296, 297

Recordability, 227

Referer log, 277
referer_log, 270

Referrals. *See* Customers

Registration forms. *See* Online

Relational database, design, 310-311

Relational Database
Management System (RDBMS),
311
Model (RDM), 310

Relationship marketing, 6-7

Relationship-building capabilities, 112

Relationship-building platform. *See* World Wide Web

Repeat purchases, law, 7, 90-91

Research Triangle Institute (RTI), 32, 33

Resource Reservation Protocol (RSVP), 210

Resource sites. *See* Targeted consumer commerce/resource sites

Retail course, 35-38

Return on investment (ROI), 38, 45, 164, 225, 227

Revnet, 74

RFM. *See* Customers; Recency, Frequency, Monetary

Riddler, 26

Roadblocks, 251

ROI. *See* Return-on-investment

RSA, 328

RSVP. *See* Resource Reservation Protocol

RTI. *See* Research Triangle Institute

Rules-based systems, 99

S

SABRE, 70, 71

Sales
automation system, 325
lead management, 324-325
leads, 228

Salesforce communications, 183

School of Literature, Communication, and Culture (LCC), 185

SciQuest, 155, 156, 159, 175
pre-launch survey, 156-158

Scout, 69, 70

Search engines, 244

Second-Tier Valuable Customers (SVCs), 91

Secure Electronic Transactions (SET), 329, 332

Secure Sockets Layer (SSL), 328, 332

Security, 316. *See also* Internet

*Seek*er, 233

Seismic Entertainment, 173

Self-service delivery, 128-132

Self-service library, 21

Session IDs, 286-287

SET. *See* Secure Electronic Transactions

Seussville, 26

ShareCentral, 24, 25

Shockwave, 19, 23, 43, 44

Shopping agents, 365

Short-term memory, 219

ShowStation IP. *See* PolyCom

SIC code, 252

Side Doors links, 244

Silicon Valley Internet Partners, 149

Simple banners, 242-243

Sites. *See* Targeted sites
data enhancement. *See* World Wide Web
guestbook usage process, 293-295
personalization. *See* One-to-one web
applications. *See* One-to-one web
benefits. *See* One-to-one web
future. *See* One-to-one web
products. *See* One-to-one web
resources. *See* One-to-one web
services. *See* One-to-one web
technology overview. *See* One-to-one web
tracking. *See* One-to-one web; Web site tracking

Size field, 276-277

Smart cards, 365

Sociable (user), 233

Socialite, 233

Source notification, 57

Spam, 48, 74, 340
    controversy, 53-55, 359
    marketing issues, 54-55
    Media Tracker, 55
SPAM Attack Pro, 48
Spangler and Associates, 43
SparkNet Corporation, 69
Spinning logos, 22
Sponsorships, 251-252
Sport Utility Vehicle (SUV), 243, 244
Sprynet, 160
SQL. *See* Structural Query Language
SSL. *See* Secure Sockets Layer
Standard attributes, 355
StarBurst Multicast, 140
Starpoint, 238
Status field, 275-276
Streaming audio, 19
Streaming video, 19
    products, 206-208
    usage. *See* World Wide Web
Structural Query Language (SQL), 311
Subject lines, writing, 57-58
Subscription-based sites, 252
Success codes, 275
Surfer, 233
SUV. *See* Sport Utility Vehicle
SVIP. *See* Silicon Valley Internet
    Partners
Sybase, 113, 303
Systems/processing. *See* One-to-one web

T
3-D VRML browser, 163
3rd party exchange, 354
Tagging, 286-287
Talk City, 36-38, 166, 173
Target advertising, ad types, 252
Target information, accuracy, 231-232
Target marketing, 5

Targeted audience, 165
Targeted advertising vehicle, 122
Targeted banners, 243-244
Targeted consumer commerce/resource
    sites, 159
Targeted consumer/vendor malls, 155-
    156
Targeted marketing, 234-235
Targeted sites, 243-244
Targeting, 235-239
Tater Man!, 25
Team Station. *See* Intel
Telephony. *See* Internet
The Gap, 29, 39
The Palace Avatar Costume Ball, 262
The Palace Inc., 177-178
    commercial servers, 177-178
The Well, 152, 171
Three Letter Acronyms (TLAs), 328
Thrilogy Profiler Companion Site
    (NBC), 42, 43
TIBCO, 134
    TIB/Rendevous, 140, 149
TIB/Rendevous. *See* TIBCO
Tickers, 246
Ticketmaster Online, 30
Time field, 273-274
Tip Wizard, 107
TipWorld, 52
TLAs. *See* Three Letter Acronyms
TMO Plus, 92
Tourism industry, web camera usage,
    203-204
Tracking. *See* Individuals; Interaction
    tracking; Project tracking
    applications, 280-284
    benefits/costs. *See* World Wide
    Web
    future, 298-299
Tracking/profile information, integra-
    tion, 110-111

VPDN. *See* Virtual Private Data
    Network
VRML. *See* Virtual Reality Modeling
    Language

W

W3C. *See* World Wide Web
WAIS. *See* Wide Area Information
    Server
Wayfarer, INCISA, 140-142
Wearable personal computers, 365
Weather Channel, 262
Web. *See* World Wide Web
Web Theater, 207
Web-based chat systems, technology
    overview, 163-164
Web-based discussion group, 171
Webcasting, 119
    news/weather, 121
    options, 118
WebChat Broadcasting System, 183
WebCrawler, 87, 169, 253
WebFlyer.com, 263-264
Webisodes, 23, 42
Webmonkey Newsletter, 79
Webmonkey-Geek Talk, 150, 361
WebTalk, 211
Web-to-database integration, 302-303
    benefits, 303-311
    future, 333-336
Webtop, 128
WebTrends, 289
Well. *See* The Well
Whole Earth Networks, 152
Whole Web Site, 240-241
Wide Area Information Server (WAIS),
    339
Windows 3.1, 213
Windows 95, 64, 213, 214, 289
Windows NT, 64, 131, 214
Wired News Delivery, 79

Wizard, 233
Worker, 233
World Wide Web
    advertising. *See* One-to-one web
      forms. *See* Alternative web
        advertising forms
      types. *See* Next-generation web
        advertising types
    analysis, benefits/costs, 279-284
    audience, benefits, 339-340
    browser, 4
    camera
      examples, 204-205
      products, 204
      usage, 203-205. *See also* Tourism
        industry
      usage, technology overview, 203
    community. *See* One-to-one web
    conferencing, 23-24, 362. *See also*
      One-to-one web
    technology, selection, 197-219
    Consortium (W3C), 122, 230, 352,
      355, 356
    direct marketing, application, 281
      284
      examples, 281-282
    experience. *See* Personalized web
    guides, 11
    inquiries, capturing, 325
    interactivity. *See* One-to-one web
      definition, 18-19
    log files, 326-327
    marketers, 18, 20
    marketers, one-to-one web site
      personalization benefits, 85-92
      benefits, 338-339
      competitive advantage, 86-88
      loyalty, 85-86
      marketing costs, 88-91
      products/services,
        adaptation/improvement, 92
      relationships, 91-92
    marketing. *See* One-to-one web

future. *See* One-to-one web
history, 3-5
matrix. *See* One-to-one web
odyssey, 1-3
pages. *See* HTML-based Web pages
presentation. *See* One-to-one web
   examples, 202-203
processes types, integration,
   311-318
   customization, 314
   products/services, 317
promotion. *See* One-to-one web
relationship-building platform,
   10-11
security, 327-333
server. *See* Commerce-based Web
   server
   connection. *See* Datacenter
site, 193, 261-263. *See also*
   Aggregated web sites
   advertising vehicle, 240-241
site content, 109-110
site data enhancement, guestbook
   registration usage, 293-298
site leverage, 147-148
site personalization, 100-101.
   See also One-to-one web
   benefits. *See* One-to-one web;
     World Wide Web
   cost, 99-100
   possibilities, 101-107
   technology approaches, 99
site tracking, 267-299
sites/services, sampling. *See*
   Personalized web sites/services
streaming video
   examples, 208-210
   technology overview, 205-208
   usage, 205-210
systems types, integration, 311-318
   customization, 314
   products/services, 317

tracking
   benefits/costs, 279-284
traffic analysis program,
   products/services, 287-293
video creation, 207-208

X
XML. *See* Extensible Markup Language

Y
Yahoo!, 84, 87, 131, 133, 169, 253, 256,
   277
Yoyodyne, 265

Z
Zapa Digital, 246-247